Book of

DOCTRINE AND COVENANTS

CAREFULLY SELECTED FROM THE REVELATIONS OF GOD,
AND GIVEN IN THE ORDER OF THEIR DATES

THIS ENLARGED AND IMPROVED EDITION CONTAINS A
HISTORICAL PREFACE FOR EACH REVELATION
OR SECTION; MOST OF THE PARAGRAPHS
ARE SUBDIVIDED

REORGANIZED CHURCH OF JESUS CHRIST
OF LATTER DAY SAINTS

HERALD PUBLISHING HOUSE

INDEPENDENCE, MISSOURI

1976

BOOK OF DOCTRINE AND COVENANTS

Copyright, © 1970

THE BOARD OF PUBLICATION OF THE
REORGANIZED CHURCH OF JESUS CHRIST
OF LATTER DAY SAINTS

INDEPENDENCE, MISSOURI

ENLARGED AND IMPROVED EDITION
WITH NEW FORMAT AUTHORIZED
BY 1970 WORLD CONFERENCE

Third Printing 1976

Library of Congress Card No. 78-134922
ISBN 0-8309-0035-7

PRINTED IN THE UNITED STATES OF AMERICA

CONTENTS

CONTENTS

CONTENTS 5

6 CONTENTS

CONTENTS

INTRODUCTION TO 1970 EDITION

The first attempt to publish the early revelations in book form was begun in November 1831. Before the work could be completed, a mob destroyed the press on July 20, 1833, and pages of the book as it had been reproduced in print up to that point were scattered through the streets. A high council held in Kirtland, September 24, 1834, authorized a second attempt. The committee selected at that time was instructed to "arrange the items of the doctrine of Jesus Christ for the government of the church." The committee consisted of Elders Joseph Smith, Jr., Oliver Cowdery, Sidney Rigdon, and Frederick G. Williams.

The quorums of the church met at Kirtland in general assembly, August 17, 1835, to take under consideration the labors of this committee. The minutes of the organization meeting and of the subsequent assembly at which the first edition of the Book of Doctrine and Covenants was presented and adopted were published in the first edition as Section 103. More recently they have appeared as Section 108A and read as follows:

1 a. "The assembly being duly organized, and after transacting certain business of the church, proceeded to appoint a committee to arrange the items of doctrine of Jesus Christ, for the government of his Church of the Latter Day Saints, which church was organized and commenced its rise on the 6th day of April, 1830.

b. "These items are to be taken from the Bible, Book of Mormon, and the revelations which have been given to said church up to this date, or shall be until such arrangement is made.

2 "Elder Samuel H. Smith, for the assembly, moved that presiding elders, Joseph Smith, Jr., Oliver Cowdery, Sidney Rigdon, and Frederick G. Williams compose said committee. The nomination was seconded by Elder Hyrum Smith, whereupon it received the unanimous vote of the assembly.

"(Signed)   "OLIVER COWDERY
"ORSON HYDE
"Clerks"

3 a. Wherefore Presidents O. Cowdery and S. Rigdon, proceeded and organized the high council of the church at Kirtland, and Presidents W. W. Phelps and J. Whitmer proceeded and organized the high council of the church in Missouri.

b. Bishop Newel K. Whitney proceeded and organized his counselors of the church in Kirtland, and acting Bishop John Corrill, organized the counselors of the church in Missouri:

c. and also Presidents Leonard Rich, Levi W. Hancock, Sylvester Smith and Lyman Sherman, organized the council of the seventy; and also Elder John Gould, acting president, organized the traveling elders;

d. and also Ira Ames, acting president, organized the priests, and also Erastus Babbit, acting president, organized the teachers, and also William Burgess, acting president, organized the deacons,

e. and also Thomas Gates, assisted by John Young, William Cowdery, Andrew H. Aldrich, Job S. Lewis, and Oliver Higley, as presidents of the day, organized the whole assembly.

f. Elder Levi W. Hancock appointed chorister: a hymn was then sung and the services of the day opened by the prayer of President O. Cowdery, and the solemnities of eternity rested upon the audience.

g. Another hymn was sung: after transacting some business for the church the audience adjourned for one hour.

4 a. Afternoon.—After a hymn was sung, President Cowdery arose and introduced the "Book of Doctrine and Covenants of the Church of the Latter Day Saints," in behalf of the committee:

b. he was followed by President Rigdon, who explained the manner by which they intended to obtain the voice of the assembly for or against said book: the other two committee,* named above, were absent.

c. According to said arrangement, W. W. Phelps bore record that the book presented to the assembly was true. President John Whitmer also arose and testifed that it was true.

d. Elder John Smith, taking the lead of the high council in Kirtland, bore record that the revelations in said book were true, and that the lectures were judiciously arranged and compiled, and were profitable for doctrine;

---

* This evidently should read, "the other two committee members."

e. whereupon the high council of Kirtland accepted them and acknowledged them as the doctrine and covenants of their faith, by a unanimous vote.

f. Elder Levi Jackman, taking the lead of the high council of the church in Missouri, bore testimony that the revelations in said book were true, and the said high council of Missouri accepted and acknowledged them as the doctrine and covenants of their faith, by a unanimous vote.

5 a. President W. W. Phelps then read the written testimony of the Twelve, as follows: "The testimony of the witnesses to the book of the Lord's commandments, which he gave to his church through Joseph Smith, Jr., who was appointed by the voice of the church for this purpose:

b. "We therefore feel willing to bear testimony to all the world of mankind, to every creature upon the face of all the earth, and upon the islands of the sea, that the Lord has borne record to our souls, through the Holy Ghost shed forth upon us, that these commandments were given by inspiration of God, and are profitable for all men, and are verily true.

c. "We give this testimony unto the world, the Lord being our helper: and it is through the grace of God, the Father, and his Son Jesus Christ, that we are permitted to have this privilege of bearing this testimony unto the world, in the which we rejoice exceedingly, praying the Lord always that the children of men may be profited thereby."

d. Elder Leonard Rich bore record of the truth of the book and the council of the Seventy accepted and acknowledged it as the doctrine and covenants of their faith, by a unanimous vote.

6 Bishop N. K. Whitney bore record of the truth of the book, and with his counselors accepted and acknowledged it as the doctrine and covenants of their faith, by a unanimous vote.

7 Acting bishop, John Corrill, bore record of the truth of the book, and with his counselors accepted and acknowledged it as the doctrine and covenants of their faith, by a unanimous vote.

8 Acting president, John Gould, gave his testimony in favor of the book, and with the traveling elders, accepted

and acknowledged it as the doctrine and covenants of their faith, by a unanimous vote.

9 Ira Ames, acting president of the priests, gave his testimony in favor of the book, and with the priests, accepted and acknowledged it as the doctrine and covenants of their faith, by a unanimous vote.

10 Erastus Babbit, acting president of the teachers, gave his testimony in favor of the book, and they accepted and acknowledged it as the doctrine and covenants of their faith, by a unanimous vote.

11 William Burgess, acting president of the deacons, bore record of the truth of the book, and they accepted and acknowledged it as the doctrine and covenants of their faith, by a unanimous vote.

12 The venerable president, Thomas Gates, then bore record of the truth of the book, and with his five silver-headed assistants, and the whole congregation, accepted and acknowledged it as the doctrine and covenants of their faith, by a unanimous vote. The several authorities, and the general assembly, by a unanimous vote, accepted of the labors of the committee.

13 President W. W. Phelps then read an article on Marriage, which was accepted and adopted, and ordered to be printed in said book, by a unanimous vote.

14 President O. Cowdery then read an article on "Governments and laws in general," which was accepted and adopted, and ordered to be printed in said book, by a unanimous vote.

15 A hymn was then sung. President S. Rigdon returned thanks, after which the assembly was blessed by the Presidency, with uplifted hands, and dismissed.

THOMAS BURDICK
WARREN PARRISH
SYLVESTER SMITH
Clerks

Additional sections were published in 1844 and in later editions of the book. Some of these were included without prior conference or quorum approval and have remained in the later editions on the basis of custom but with otherwise uncertain authority. This present edition is so arranged that the items of uncertain authority are included in a historical appendix and prefaced with introductions explaining the circumstances of publication and the reasons for placement in the appendix.

Those sections which make up the body of the book include only those which were approved by the 1835 General Assembly or by a General or World Conference of the church. The approval of the format of this edition by the 1970 World Conference specifically authorized the retention of Sections 22, 36, 100, 102, 105, and 106 which had appeared in earlier editions without Conference approval.

As a record of the revelations of God and statements of basic doctrine based upon them, we present to the Saints and to the world the Book of Doctrine and Covenants. May the Holy Spirit enlighten all who study its content.

THE FIRST PRESIDENCY

W. Wallace Smith
Maurice L. Draper
Duane E. Couey

THE

COVENANTS AND COMMANDMENTS

OF THE LORD

SECTION 1

Revelation given through Joseph Smith, Jr., at a special conference held at Hiram, Portage County, Ohio, November 1, 1831. It was to serve as a preface to the "Book of Commandments." W. W. Phelps and Company began the printing of the "Book of Commandments" at Independence, Missouri, but the plant was destroyed by a mob in July 1833 before the book could be completed. The last section to be set up ended with the words, "blood of Ephraim" (D. and C. 64:7b).

When the first edition of the Doctrine and Covenants was published in 1835, it included the sections (chapters) set in type for the "Book of Commandments" and also instructions received prior to July 1833 but not included in the "Book of Commandments." To this was added further instruction received and a statement of principles approved prior to the date of publication. The preface was continued as Section 1.

If the preface had been included in the order it was received, it would have appeared immediately prior to Section 67 in recent editions.

A revelation received November 3, 1831, known as the Appendix, does not appear in the "Book of Commandments," as was originally intended, but will be found as Section 100 of the 1835 edition of the Doctrine and Covenants and as Section 108 in all subsequent editions.

1 a. Hearken, O ye people of my church, saith the voice of him who dwells on high, and whose eyes are upon all men; yea, verily I say, Hearken ye people from afar, and ye that are upon the islands of the sea, listen together;

b. for verily the voice of the Lord is unto all men, and there is none to escape, and there is no eye that shall not see, neither ear that shall not hear, neither heart that shall not be penetrated;

c. and the rebellious shall be pierced with much sorrow, for their iniquities shall be spoken upon the housetops, and their secret acts shall be revealed;

d. and the voice of warning shall be unto all people, by the mouths of my disciples, whom I have chosen in these last days, and they shall go forth and none shall stay them, for I the Lord have commanded them.

2 a. Behold, this is mine authority, and the authority of my servants, and my preface unto the book of my commandments, which I have given them to publish unto you, O inhabitants of the earth;

b. wherefore fear and tremble, O ye people, for what I the Lord have decreed, in them, shall be fulfilled.

c. And verily, I say unto you, that they who go forth, bearing these tidings unto the inhabitants of the earth, to them is power given to seal, both on earth and in heaven, the unbelieving and rebellious;

d. yea, verily, to seal them up unto the day when the wrath of God shall be poured out upon the wicked without measure;

e. unto the day when the Lord shall come to recompense unto every man according to his work, and measure to every man according to the measure which he has measured to his fellow-man.

3 a. Wherefore the voice of the Lord is unto the ends of the earth, that all that will hear may hear;

b. prepare ye, prepare ye for that which is to come, for the Lord is nigh; and the anger of the Lord is kindled, and his sword is bathed in heaven, and it shall fall upon the inhabitants of the earth; and the arm of the Lord shall be revealed;

c. and the day cometh that they who will not hear the voice of the Lord, neither the voice of his servants, neither give heed to the words of the prophets and apostles, shall be cut off from among the people;

d. for they have strayed from mine ordinances, and have broken mine everlasting covenant; they seek not the Lord to establish his righteousness,

e. but every man walketh in his own way, and after the image of his own god, whose image is in the likeness of the world, and whose substance is that of an idol, which waxeth old and shall perish in Babylon, even Babylon the great, which shall fall.

4 a. Wherefore I the Lord, knowing the calamity which should come upon the inhabitants of the earth, called upon my servant Joseph Smith, Jr., and spake unto him from heaven, and gave him commandments, and also gave commandments to others, that they should proclaim these things unto the world;

b. and all this that it might be fulfilled, which was written by the prophets;

c. the weak things of the world shall come forth and break down the mighty and strong ones, that man should not counsel his fellow-man, neither trust in the arm of flesh, but that every man might speak in the name of God the Lord, even the Savior of the world;

d. that faith also might increase in the earth; that mine everlasting covenant might be established;

e. that the fullness of my gospel might be proclaimed by the weak and the simple, unto the ends of the world, and before kings and rulers.

5 a. Behold, I am God, and have spoken it; these commandments are of me, and were given unto my servants in their weakness, after the manner of their language, that they might come to understanding;

b. and inasmuch as they erred it might be made known; and inasmuch as they sought wisdom they might be instructed;

c. and inasmuch as they sinned they might be chastened, that they might repent; and inasmuch as they were humble, they might be made strong, and blessed from on high, and receive knowledge from time to time;

d. and after having received the record of the Nephites, yea, even my servant Joseph Smith, Jr., might have power to translate, through the mercy of God, by the power of God, the Book of Mormon;

e. and also those to whom these commandments were given might have power to lay the foundation of this church, and to bring it forth out of obscurity, and out of darkness, the only true and living church upon the face of the whole earth, with which I the Lord am well pleased, speaking unto the church collectively and not individually;

f. for I the Lord can not look upon sin with the least degree of allowance; nevertheless, he that repents and does the commandments of the Lord shall be forgiven;

g. and he that repents not, from him shall be taken even the light which he has received, for my Spirit shall not always strive with man, saith the Lord of Hosts.

6 a. And again, verily I say unto you, O inhabitants of the earth, I, the Lord, am willing to make these things known unto all flesh, for I am no respecter of persons,

b. and will that all men shall know that the day speedily cometh—the hour is not yet, but is nigh at hand—when peace shall be taken from the earth, and the Devil shall have power over his own dominion;

c. and also the Lord shall have power over his saints, and shall reign in their midst, and shall come down in judgment upon *Idumea, or the world.

7 Search these commandments, for they are true and faithful, and the prophecies and promises which are in them shall all be fulfilled.

8 a. What I, the Lord, have spoken I have spoken, and I excuse not myself;

b. and though the heavens and the earth pass away, my word shall not pass away, but shall all be fulfilled, whether by mine own voice, or by the voice of my servants, it is the same;

c. for behold, and lo, the Lord is God, and the Spirit beareth record, and the record is true, and the truth abideth for ever and ever. Amen.

*Idumea: Edom (ancient).

SECTION 2

By July 1828 a total of 116 pages of the Book of Mormon manuscript had been translated. Martin Harris served as Joseph's scribe at this time and wrote most of the translation. To quiet the ridicule of some of his relatives, Martin borrowed the manuscript, promising to preserve it with the utmost care, but the foolscap sheets were stolen from him and never recovered. Under these circumstances the following instruction and rebuke were given to Joseph. The revelation was received at Harmony, Pennsylvania, in July 1828.

1 a. The works, and the designs, and the purposes of God, can not be frustrated, neither can they come to naught, for God doth not walk in crooked paths;

b. neither doth he turn to the right hand nor to the left;

c. neither doth he vary from that which he hath said; therefore his paths are straight and his course is one eternal round.

2 a. Remember, remember, that it is not the work of God that is frustrated, but the work of men;

b. for although a man may have many revelations, and have power to do many mighty works, yet, if he boast in his own strength, and sets at naught the counsels of God, and follows after the dictates of his own will and carnal desires, he must fall and incur the vengeance of a just God upon him.

3 a. Behold, you have been intrusted with these things, but how strict were your commandments;

b. and remember, also, the promises which were made to you, if you did not transgress them; and, behold, how oft you have transgressed the commandments and the laws of God, and have gone on in the persuasions of men:

c. for, behold, you should not have feared man more than God, although men set at naught the counsels of God, and despise his words, yet you should have been faithful and he would have extended his arm, and supported you against all the fiery darts of the adversary; and he would have been with you in every time of trouble.

4 a. Behold, thou art Joseph, and thou wast chosen to do the work of the Lord, but because of transgression, if thou art not aware thou wilt fall, but remember God is merciful;

b. therefore, repent of that which thou hast done, which is contrary to the commandment which I gave you, and thou art still chosen, and art again called to the work;

c. except thou doest this, thou shalt be delivered up and become as other men, and have no more gift.

5 a. And when thou deliveredst up that which God had given thee sight and power to translate thou deliveredst up that which was sacred into the hands of a wicked man who has set at naught the counsels of God, and has broken the most sacred promises, which were made before God, and has depended upon his own judgment, and boasted in his own wisdom;

b. and this is the reason that thou hast lost thy privileges for a season, for thou hast suffered the counsel of thy director to be trampled upon from the beginning.

6 a. Nevertheless, my work shall go forth, for, inasmuch as the knowledge of a Savior has come unto the world, through the testimony of the Jews, even so shall the knowledge of a Savior come unto my people, and to the Nephites, and the Jacobites, and the Josephites, and the Zoramites, through the testimony of their fathers;

b. and this testimony shall come to the knowledge of the Lamanites, and the Lemuelites, and the Ishmaelites, who dwindled in unbelief because of the iniquity of their fathers, whom the Lord has suffered to destroy their brethren the Nephites, because of their iniquities and their abominations;

c. and for this very purpose are these plates preserved which contain these records, that the promises of the Lord might be fulfilled, which he made to his people;

d. and that the Lamanites might come to the knowledge of their fathers, and that they might know the promises of the Lord,

e. and that they may believe the gospel and rely upon the merits of Jesus Christ, and be glorified through faith in his name, and that through their repentance they might be saved. Amen.

SECTION 3

*After the loss of that portion of the Book of Mormon
manuscript which had been translated before July 1828, the
mind of Joseph was "darkened" (D. and C. 3:1b). After
humbling himself, Joseph was again enlightened, and was
permitted to resume his work. Instruction received in this
connection is recorded in the following revelation, which was
received while Joseph was still at Harmony, Pennsylvania,
in July or August 1828.*

1 a. Now, behold, I say unto you, that because you delivered up those writings which you had power given unto you
to translate, by the means of the Urim and Thummim, into
the hands of a wicked man, you have lost them;

b. and you also lost your gift at the same time, and your
mind became darkened;

c. nevertheless, it is now restored unto you again, therefore see that you are faithful and continue on unto the finish-
ing of the remainder of the work of translation as you have
begun.

d. Do not run faster, or labor more than you have strength
and means provided to enable you to translate;

e. but be diligent unto the end; pray always, that you may
come off conqueror; yea, that you may conquer Satan, and
that you may escape the hands of the servants of Satan, that
do uphold his work.

f. Behold, they have sought to destroy you; yea, even the
man in whom you have trusted, has sought to destroy you.

g. And for this cause I said, that he is a wicked man, for
he has sought to take away the things wherewith you have
been intrusted;

h. and he has also sought to destroy your gift, and because
you have delivered the writings into his hands, behold, wicked
men have taken them from you; therefore, you have delivered
them up; yea, that which was sacred unto wickedness.

i. And, behold, Satan has put it into their hearts to alter
the words which you have caused to be written, or which
you have translated, which have gone out of your hands;

j. and, behold, I say unto you, that because they have altered the words, they read contrary from that which you translated and caused to be written;

k. and on this wise the Devil has sought to lay a cunning plan, that he may destroy this work; for he has put it into their hearts to do this, that by lying they may say they have caught you in the words which you have pretended to translate.

2 a. Verily I say unto you, that I will not suffer that Satan shall accomplish his evil design in this thing, for, behold, he has put it into their hearts to get thee to tempt the Lord thy God, in asking to translate it over again;

b. and then, behold, they say and think in their hearts, We will see if God has given him power to translate, if so, he will also give him power again; and if God giveth him power again, or if he translate again, or in other words, if he bringeth forth the same words, behold, we have the same with us, and we have altered them;

c. therefore, they will not agree, and we will say that he has lied in his words, and that he has no gift, and that he has no power;

d. therefore, we will destroy him, and also the work, and we will do this that we may not be ashamed in the end, and that we may get glory of the world.

3 a. Verily, verily I say unto you, that Satan has great hold upon their hearts; he stirreth them up to iniquity against that which is good, and their hearts are corrupt, and full of wickedness and abominations, and they love darkness rather than light, because their deeds are evil; therefore they will not ask of me.

b. Satan stirreth them up, that he may lead their souls to destruction.

c. And thus he has laid a cunning plan, thinking to destroy the work of God, but I will require this at their hands, and it shall turn to their shame and condemnation in the day of judgment;

d. yea, he stirreth up their hearts to anger against this work; yea, he saith unto them, Deceive and lie in wait to catch, that ye may destroy; behold, this is no harm;

e. and thus he flattereth them, and telleth them that it is no sin to lie, that they may catch a man in a lie, that they may destroy him; and thus he flattereth them, and leadeth them along until he draggeth their souls down to hell;

f. and thus he causeth them to catch themselves in their own snare; and thus he goeth up and down, to and fro in the earth, seeking to destroy the souls of men.

4 Verily, verily I say unto you, Woe be unto him that lieth to deceive, because he supposes that another lieth to deceive, for such are not exempt from the justice of God.

5 Now, behold, they have altered those words, because Satan saith unto them, He hath deceived you; and thus he flattereth them away to do iniquity, to get thee to tempt the Lord thy God.

6 a. Behold, I say unto you, that you shall not translate again those words which have gone forth out of your hands; for, behold, they shall not accomplish their evil designs in lying against those words.

b. For, behold, if you should bring forth the same words they will say that you have lied; that you have pretended to translate, but that you have contradicted yourself;

c. and, behold, they will publish this, and Satan will harden the hearts of the people to stir them up to anger against you, that they will not believe my words.

d. Thus Satan thinketh to overpower your testimony in this generation, that the work may not come forth in this generation;

e. but, behold, here is wisdom, and because I show unto you wisdom, and give you commandments concerning these things, what you shall do, show it not unto the world until you have accomplished the work of translation.

7 a. Marvel not that I said unto you, Here is wisdom, show it not unto the world; for I said, Show it not unto the world, that you may be preserved.

b. Behold, I do not say that you shall not show it unto the righteous; but as you can not always judge the righteous, or as you can not always tell the wicked from the righteous;

c. therefore, I say unto you, Hold your peace until I shall see fit to make all things known unto the world concerning the matter.

8 a. And now, verily I say unto you, that an account of those things that you have written, which have gone out of your hands, are engraven upon the plates of Nephi;

b. yea, and you remember, it was said in those writings, that a more particular account was given of these things upon the plates of Nephi.

9 a. And now, because the account which is engraven upon the plates of Nephi, is more particular concerning the things which in my wisdom I would bring to the knowledge of the people in this account,

b. therefore, you shall translate the engravings which are on the plates of Nephi, down even till you come to the reign of King Benjamin, or until you come to that which you have translated, which you have retained;

c. and, behold, you shall publish it as the record of Nephi, and thus I will confound those who have altered my words.

d. I will not suffer that they shall destroy my work; yea, I will show unto them that my wisdom is greater than the cunning of the Devil.

10 a. Behold, they have only got a part, or an abridgment of the account of Nephi.

b. Behold, there are many things engraven on the plates of Nephi, which do throw greater views upon my gospel; therefore, it is wisdom in me, that you should translate this first part of the engravings of Nephi, and send forth in this work.

c. And, behold, all the remainder of this work, does contain all those parts of my gospel which my holy prophets, yea, and also my disciples, desired in their prayers, should come forth unto this people.

d. And I said unto them, that it should be granted unto them according to their faith in their prayers;

e. yea, and this was their faith, that my gospel which I gave unto them, that they might preach in their days, might come unto their brethren, the Lamanites, and also, all that had become Lamanites, because of their dissensions.

11 a. Now this is not all, their faith in their prayers was, that this gospel should be made known also, if it were possible that other nations should possess this land;

b. and thus they did leave a blessing upon this land in their prayers, that whosoever should believe in this gospel, in this land, might have eternal life;

c. yea, that it might be free unto all of whatsoever nation, kindred, tongue, or people, they may be.

12 And now, behold, according to their faith in their prayers, will I bring this part of my gospel to the knowledge of my people. Behold, I do not bring it to destroy that which they have received, but to build it up.

13 a. And for this cause have I said, If this generation harden not their hearts, I will establish my church among them.

b. Now I do not say this to destroy my church, but I say this to build up my church; therefore, whosoever belongeth to my church need not fear, for such shall inherit the kingdom of heaven;

c. but it is they who do not fear me, neither keep my commandments, but build up churches unto themselves, to get gain; yea, and all those that do wickedly, and build up the kingdom of the Devil;

d. yea, verily, verily I say unto you, that it is they that I will disturb, and cause to tremble and shake to the center.

14 a. Behold, I am Jesus Christ, the Son of God. I came unto my own, and my own received me not.

b. I am the light which shineth in darkness, and the darkness comprehendeth it not.

c. I am he who said, Other sheep have I which are not of this fold, unto my disciples, and many there were that understood me not.

15 a. And I will show unto this people, that I had other sheep, and that they were a branch of the house of Jacob; and I will bring to light their marvelous works, which they did in my name;

b. yea, and I will also bring to light my gospel, which was ministered unto them, and, behold, they shall not deny that which you have received, but they shall build it up, and shall bring to light the true points of my doctrine; yea, and the only doctrine which is in me;

c. and this I do, that I may establish my gospel, that there may not be so much contention;

d. yea, Satan doth stir up the hearts of the people to contention, concerning the points of my doctrine; and in these things they do err, for they do wrest the Scriptures, and do not understand them;

e. therefore, I will unfold unto them this great mystery; for, behold, I will gather them as a hen gathereth her chickens under her wings, if they will not harden their hearts; yea, if they will come, they may, and partake of the waters of life freely.

16 a. Behold, this is my doctrine: Whosoever repenteth and cometh unto me, the same is my church;

b. whosoever declareth more or less than this, the same is not of me, but is against me; therefore, he is not of my church.

17 And now, behold, whosoever is of my church, and endureth of my church to the end, him will I establish upon my Rock, and the gates of hell shall not prevail against him.

18 And now, remember the words of him who is the life and light of the world, your Redeemer, your Lord, and your God. Amen.

SECTION 4

Revelation given to Joseph Smith, Sr., through his son, the prophet, at Harmony, Pennsylvania, February 1829.

1 a. Now, behold, a marvelous work is about to come forth among the children of men,

b. therefore, O ye that embark in the service of God, see that ye serve him with all your heart, might, mind, and strength, that ye may stand blameless before God at the last day;

c. therefore, if ye have desires to serve God, ye are called to the work, for, behold, the field is white already to harvest,

d. and lo, he that thrusteth in his sickle with his might, the same layeth up in store that he perish not, but bringeth salvation to his soul;

e. and faith, hope, charity, and love, with an eye single to the glory of God, qualifies him for the work.

2 a. Remember, faith, virtue, knowledge, temperance, patience, brotherly kindness, godliness, charity, humility, diligence.

b. Ask and ye shall receive, knock and it shall be opened unto you. Amen.

SECTION 5

Revelation given to Joseph Smith and Martin Harris in Harmony, Pennsylvania, March 1829. It was called forth by Martin's insistent desire to know whether Joseph had the records of the Nephites in his possession.

1 a. Behold, I say unto you, that as my servant Martin Harris has desired a witness at my hand, that you, my servant Joseph Smith, Jr., have got the plates of which you have testified and borne record that you have received of me;

b. and now, behold, this shall you say unto him: He who spake unto you said unto you, I, the Lord, am God, and have given these things unto you, my servant Joseph Smith, Jr., and have commanded you that you should stand as a witness of these things,

c. and I have caused you that you should enter into a covenant with me, that you should not show them except to those persons to whom I command you; and you have no power over them except I grant it unto you.

d. And you have a gift to translate the plates, and this is the first gift that I bestowed upon you, and I have commanded that you should pretend to no other gift until my purpose is fulfilled in this; for I will grant unto you no other gift until it is finished.

2 a. Verily, I say unto you, that woe shall come unto the inhabitants of the earth if they will not hearken unto my words;

b. for hereafter you shall be ordained and go forth and deliver my words unto the children of men.

c. Behold, if they will not believe my words, they would not believe you, my servant Joseph, if it were possible that you could show them all these things which I have committed unto you.

d. Oh, this unbelieving and stiff-necked generation, mine anger is kindled against them!

3 a. Behold, verily, I say unto you, I have reserved those things which I have intrusted unto you, my servant Joseph, for a wise purpose in me, and it shall be made known unto future generations; but this generation shall have my word through you;

b. and in addition to your testimony, the testimony of three of my servants, whom I shall call and ordain, unto whom I will show these things;

c. and they shall go forth with my words that are given through you; yea, they shall know of a surety that these things are true; for from heaven will I declare it unto them;

d. I will give them power that they may behold and view these things as they are; and to none else will I grant this power, to receive this same testimony, among this generation, in this, the beginning of the rising up, and the coming forth of my church out of the wilderness; clear as the moon and fair as the sun, and terrible as an army with banners.

e. And the testimony of three witnesses will I send forth of my word; and, behold, whosoever believeth on my words, them will I visit with the manifestation of my Spirit, and they shall be born of me, even of water and of the Spirit.

f. And you must wait yet a little while, for you are not yet ordained; and their testimony shall also go forth unto the condemnation of this generation, if they harden their hearts against them;

g. for a desolating scourge shall go forth among the inhabitants of the earth, and shall continue to be poured out, from time to time, if they repent not, until the earth is empty, and the inhabitants thereof are consumed away, and utterly destroyed by the brightness of my coming.

h. Behold, I tell you these things even as I also told the people of the destruction of Jerusalem, and my word shall be verified at this time as it hath hitherto been verified.

4 a. And now I command you, my servant Joseph, to repent and walk more uprightly before me, and yield to the persuasions of men no more;

b. and that you be firm in keeping the commandments wherewith I have commanded you, and if you do this, behold, I grant unto you eternal life, even if you should be slain.

5 a. And now again I speak unto you, my servant Joseph, concerning the man that desires the witness:

b. Behold, I say unto him, he exalts himself and does not humble himself sufficiently before me; but if he will bow down before me, and humble himself in mighty prayer and faith, in the sincerity of his heart, then will I grant unto him a view of the things which he desires to see.

c. And then he shall say unto the people of this generation, Behold, I have seen the things which the Lord has shown unto Joseph Smith, Jr., and I know of a surety that they are true, for I have seen them; for they have been shown unto me by the power of God and not of man.

d. And I, the Lord, command him, my servant Martin Harris, that he shall say no more unto them concerning these things, except he shall say, I have seen them, and they have been shown unto me by the power of God, and these are the words which he shall say:

e. but if he deny this he will break the covenant which he has before covenanted with me, and behold he is condemned.

f. And now, except he humble himself and acknowledge unto me the things that he has done which are wrong, and covenant with me that he will keep my commandments, and exercise faith in me, behold, I say unto him, he shall have no such views;

g. for I will grant unto him no views of the things of which I have spoken.

h. And if this be the case, I command you, my servant Joseph, that you shall say unto him, that he shall do no more, nor trouble me any more concerning this matter.

6 a. And if this be the case, behold, I say unto thee, Joseph, When thou hast translated a few more pages thou shalt stop for a season, even until I command thee again; then thou mayest translate again.

b. And except thou do this, behold, thou shalt have no more gift, and I will take away the things which I have intrusted with thee.

c. And now, because I foresee the lying in wait to destroy thee; yea, I foresee that if my servant Martin Harris humbleth not himself, and receive a witness from my hand, that he will fall into transgression; and there are many that lie in wait to destroy thee from off the face of the earth;

d. and for this cause, that thy days may be prolonged, I have given unto thee these commandments; yea, for this cause

I have said, Stop and stand still until I command thee, and I will provide means whereby thou mayest accomplish the thing which I have commanded thee;

e. and if thou art faithful in keeping my commandments, thou shalt be lifted up at the last day. Amen.

SECTION 6

Oliver Cowdery met Joseph Smith on April 5, 1829. Two days later he began to write for Joseph as the prophet dictated the translation of the Book of Mormon. The following inspired instruction was received at Harmony, Pennsylvania, during the latter part of the month. It was addressed to Oliver Cowdery.

1 a. A great and marvelous work is about to come forth unto the children of men:

b. behold, I am God, and give heed unto my word, which is quick and powerful, sharper than a two-edged sword, to the dividing asunder of both joints and marrow:

c. therefore, give heed unto my words.

2 a. Behold, the field is white already to harvest, therefore, whoso desireth to reap, let him thrust in his sickle with his might, and reap while the day lasts, that he may treasure up for his soul everlasting salvation in the kingdom of God;

b. yea, whosoever will thrust in his sickle and reap, the same is called of God;

c. therefore, if you will ask of me you shall receive, if you will knock it shall be opened unto you.

3 a. Now, as you have asked, behold, I say unto you, Keep my commandments, and seek to bring forth and establish the cause of Zion:

b. seek not for riches but for wisdom; and, behold, the mysteries of God shall be unfolded unto you, and then shall you be made rich.

c. Behold, he that hath eternal life is rich.

4 a. Verily, verily I say unto you, Even as you desire of me, so shall it be unto you; and if you desire, you shall be the means of doing much good in this generation.

b. Say nothing but repentance unto this generation: keep my commandments, and assist to bring forth my work according to my commandments, and you shall be blessed.

5 a. Behold, thou hast a gift, and blessed art thou because of thy gift.

b. Remember it is sacred and cometh from above: and if thou wilt inquire, thou shalt know mysteries which are great and marvelous;

c. therefore, thou shalt exercise thy gift, that thou mayest find out mysteries, that thou mayest bring many to the knowledge of the truth; yea, convince them of the error of their ways.

d. Make not thy gift known unto any, save it be those who are of thy faith. Trifle not with sacred things.

e. If thou wilt do good, yea, and hold out faithful to the end, thou shalt be saved in the kingdom of God, which is the greatest of all the gifts of God; for there is no gift greater than the gift of salvation.

6 a. Verily, verily I say unto thee, Blessed art thou for what thou hast done, for thou hast inquired of me, and, behold, as often as thou hast inquired, thou hast received instruction of my Spirit.

b. If it had not been so, thou wouldst not have come to the place where thou art at this time.

7 a. Behold, thou knowest that thou hast inquired of me, and I did enlighten thy mind; and now I tell thee these things, that thou mayest know that thou hast been enlightened by the spirit of truth;

b. yea, I tell thee, that thou mayest know that there is none else save God, that knowest thy thoughts and the intents of thy heart.

c. I tell thee these things as a witness unto thee, that the words or the work which thou hast been writing is true.

8 a. Therefore be diligent, stand by my servant Joseph faithfully in whatsoever difficult circumstances he may be, for the word's sake.

b. Admonish him in his faults and also receive admonition of him.

c. Be patient; be sober; be temperate: have patience, faith, hope, and charity.

9 a. Behold, thou art Oliver, and I have spoken unto thee because of thy desires; therefore, treasure up these words in thy heart.

b. Be faithful and diligent in keeping the commandments of God, and I will encircle thee in the arms of my love.

10 a. Behold, I am Jesus Christ, the Son of God.

b. I am the same that came unto my own and my own received me not.

c. I am the light which shineth in darkness, and the darkness comprehendeth it not.

11 a. Verily, verily I say unto you, If you desire a further witness, cast your mind upon the night that you cried unto me in your heart, that you might know concerning the truth of these things; did I not speak peace to your mind concerning the matter?

b. What greater witness can you have than from God?

c. And now, behold, you have received a witness, for if I have told you things which no man knoweth, have you not received a witness?

d. And, behold, I grant unto you a gift, if you desire of me, to translate even as my servant Joseph.

12 a. Verily, verily I say unto you, that there are records which contain much of my gospel, which have been kept back because of the wickedness of the people;

b. and now I command you, that if you have good desires, a desire to lay up treasures for yourself in heaven, then shall you assist in bringing to light, with your gift, those parts of my Scriptures which have been hidden because of iniquity.

13 a. And now, behold, I give unto you, and also unto my servant Joseph, the keys of this gift, which shall bring to light this ministry;

b. and in the mouth of two or three witnesses, shall every word be established.

14 a. Verily, verily I say unto you, If they reject my words, and this part of my gospel and ministry, blessed are ye, for they can do no more unto you than unto me;

b. and if they do unto you, even as they have done unto me, blessed are ye, for you shall dwell with me in glory:

c. but if they reject not my words, which shall be established by the testimony which shall be given, blessed are they; and then shall ye have joy in the fruit of your labors.

15 a. Verily, verily I say unto you, as I said unto my disciples,

b. Where two or three are gathered together in my name, as touching one thing, behold, there will I be in the midst of them; even so am I in the midst of you.

c. Fear not to do good, my sons, for whatsoever ye sow, that shall ye also reap:

d. therefore, if ye sow good, ye shall also reap good for your reward:

16 a. Therefore fear not, little flock, do good, let earth and hell combine against you, for if ye are built upon my Rock, they can not prevail.

b. Behold, I do not condemn you, go your ways and sin no more: perform with soberness the work which I have commanded you; look unto me in every thought, doubt not, fear not:

c. behold the wounds which pierced my side, and also the prints of the nails in my hands and feet; be faithful; keep my commandments, and ye shall inherit the kingdom of heaven. Amen.

SECTION 7

Revelation given to Joseph Smith, Jr., and Oliver Cowdery in Harmony, Pennsylvania, April 1829, in response to their prayers concerning the meaning of John 21:20-24. The 1835 edition of the Doctrine and Covenants states that this was "translated from parchment, written and hid up by himself [John]."

1 a. And the Lord said unto me, John, my beloved, what desirest thou? For if ye shall ask what you will, it shall be granted unto you.

b. And I said unto him, Lord, give unto me power over death, that I may live and bring souls unto thee.

c. And the Lord said unto me, Verily, verily I say unto thee, because thou desirest this thou shalt tarry until I come in my glory, and shalt prophesy before nations, kindreds, tongues, and people.

2 a. And for this cause the Lord said unto Peter, If I will that he tarry till I come, what is that to thee? For he desiredst of me that he might bring souls unto me; but thou desiredst that thou might speedily come unto me in my kingdom.

b. I say unto thee, Peter, this was a good desire, but my beloved has desired that he might do more, or a greater work yet among men, than what he has before done; yea, he has undertaken a greater work;

c. therefore, I will make him as flaming fire, and a ministering angel; he shall minister for those who shall be heirs of salvation who dwell on the earth;

d. and I will make thee to minister for him and for thy brother James; and unto you three I give this power and the keys of this ministry until I come.

3 Verily I say unto you, Ye shall both have according to your desires, for ye both joy in that which ye have desired.

SECTION 8

Revelation given through Joseph Smith, Jr., to Oliver Cowdery, April 1829, at Harmony, Pennsylvania. It was occasioned by Oliver's questions and concerns as he entered into more intimate association with Joseph during this first month of their acquaintance.

1 a. Oliver Cowdery, verily, verily I say unto you, that assuredly as the Lord liveth, who is your God and your Redeemer,

b. even so sure shall you receive a knowledge of whatsoever things you shall ask in faith, with an honest heart, believing that you shall receive a knowledge concerning the engravings of old records, which are ancient, which contain those parts of my scripture of which have been spoken, by the manifestation of my Spirit;

c. yea, behold, I will tell you in your mind and in your heart by the Holy Ghost, which shall come upon you, and which shall dwell in your heart.

2 a. Now, behold, this is the spirit of revelation; behold, this is the Spirit by which Moses brought the children of Israel through the Red Sea on dry ground;

b. therefore this is thy gift; apply unto it and blessed art thou, for it shall deliver you out of the hands of your enemies, when, if it were not so, they would slay you, and bring your soul to destruction.

3 a. Oh, remember these words, and keep my commandments! Remember this is your gift.

b. Now this is not all your gift, for you have another gift, which is the gift of Aaron; behold, it has told you many things; behold, there is no other power save the power of God that can cause this gift of Aaron to be with you;

c. therefore doubt not, for it is the gift of God, and you shall hold it in your hands, and do marvelous works; and no power shall be able to take it away out of your hands, for it is the work of God.

d. And, therefore, whatsoever you shall ask me to tell you by that means, that will I grant unto you, and you shall have knowledge concerning it; remember, that without faith you can do nothing.

e. Therefore, ask in faith.

f. Trifle not with these things; do not ask for that which you ought not; ask that you may know the mysteries of God, and that you may translate and receive knowledge from all those ancient records which have been hid up, that are sacred, and according to your faith shall it be done unto you.

g. Behold, it is I that have spoken it; and I am the same who spake unto you from the beginning. Amen.

SECTION 9

*Revelation given through Joseph Smith, Jr., to Oliver
Cowdery in Harmony, Pennsylvania, during April 1829. It
followed and explained Oliver's failure as a translator and
encouraged him to continue as Joseph's scribe, which he did.*

1 a. Behold, I say unto you, my son, that because you did
not translate according to that which you desired of me, and
did commence again to write for my servant Joseph Smith,
Jr., even so I would that you should continue until you have
finished this record, which I have intrusted unto him;

b. and then, behold, other records have I, that I will give
unto you power that you may assist to translate.

2 a. Be patient, my son, for it is wisdom in me, and it is
not expedient that you should translate at this present time.

b. Behold, the work which you are called to do is to write
for my servant Joseph;

c. and, behold, it is because that you did not continue as
you commenced, when you began to translate, that I have
taken away this privilege from you.

d. Do not murmur, my son, for it is wisdom in me that
I have dealt with you after this manner.

3 a. Behold, you have not understood; you have supposed
that I would give it unto you, when you took no thought,
save it was to ask me;

b. but, behold, I say unto you, that you must study it
out in your mind;

c. then you must ask me if it be right, and if it is right,
I will cause that your bosom shall burn within you; therefore, you shall feel that it is right;

d. but if it be not right, you shall have no such feelings,
but you shall have a stupor of thought, that shall cause you
to forget the thing which is wrong;

e. therefore, you can not write that which is sacred, save it
be given you from me.

4 a. Now, if you had known this, you could have translated; nevertheless, it is not expedient that you should trans-

late now. Behold, it was expedient when you commenced, but you feared, and the time is past, and it is not expedient now;

b. for, do you not behold that I have given unto my servant Joseph sufficient strength, whereby it is made up, and neither of you have I condemned?

5 a. Do this thing which I have commanded you, and you shall prosper. Be faithful, and yield to no temptation.

b. Stand fast in the work wherewith I have called you, and a hair of your head shall not be lost, and you shall be lifted up at the last day. Amen.

SECTION 10

Revelation given through Joseph Smith, Jr., to his brother, Hyrum Smith, May 1829, at Harmony, Pennsylvania. The first four paragraphs contain the same assurances and counsel as had been given to Oliver Cowdery during the preceding months (D. and C. 6).

1. a. A great and marvelous work is about to come forth among the children of men.

b. Behold, I am God, and give heed to my word, which is quick and powerful, sharper than a two-edged sword, to the dividing asunder of both joints and marrow;

c. therefore, give heed unto my word.

2 a. Behold, the field is white already to harvest, therefore, whoso desireth to reap, let him thrust in his sickle with his might, and reap while the day lasts, that he may treasure up for his soul everlasting salvation in the kingdom of God;

b. yea, whosoever will thrust in his sickle and reap, the same is called of God;

c. therefore, if you will ask of me, you shall receive; if you will knock, it shall be opened unto you.

3 a. Now as you have asked, behold, I say unto you, Keep my commandments, and seek to bring forth and establish the cause of Zion.

b. Seek not for riches, but for wisdom, and, behold, the mysteries of God shall be unfolded unto you, and then shall you be made rich;

c. behold, he that hath eternal life is rich.

4 a. Verily, verily I say unto you, Even as you desire of me, so shall it be done unto you; and, if you desire you shall be the means of doing much good in this generation.

b. Say nothing but repentance unto this generation.

c. Keep my commandments, and assist to bring forth my work according to my commandments, and you shall be blessed.

5 a. Behold, thou hast a gift, or thou shalt have a gift if thou wilt desire of me in faith, with an honest heart, believing in the power of Jesus Christ, or in my power which speaketh unto thee;

b. for, behold, it is I that speak; behold, I am the light which shineth in darkness, and by my power I give these words unto thee.

6 And now, verily, verily I say unto thee, Put thy trust in that Spirit which leadeth to do good; yea, to do justly, to walk humbly, to judge righteously; and this is my Spirit.

7 a. Verily, verily I say unto you, I will impart unto you of my Spirit, which shall enlighten your mind, which shall fill your soul with joy,

b. and then shall ye know, or by this shall you know, all things whatsoever you desire of me, which is pertaining unto things of righteousness, in faith believing in me that you shall receive.

8 a. Behold, I command you, that you need not suppose that you are called to preach until you are called:

b. wait a little longer, until you shall have my word, my rock, my church, and my gospel, that you may know of a surety my doctrine;

c. and then, behold, according to your desires, yea, even according to your faith, shall it be done unto you.

9 a. Keep my commandments; hold your peace; appeal unto my Spirit;

b. yea, cleave unto me with all your heart, that you may assist in bringing to light those things of which have been spoken; yea, the translation of my work; be patient until you shall accomplish it.

10 a. Behold, this is your work, to keep my commandments; yea, with all your might, mind, and strength; seek not to declare my word, but first seek to obtain my word, and then shall your tongue be loosed;

b. then, if you desire, you shall have my Spirit, and my word; yea, the power of God unto the convincing of men;

c. but now hold your peace; study my word which hath gone forth among the children of men, and also study my word which shall come forth among the children of men, or that which is now translating;

d. yea, until you have obtained all which I shall grant unto the children of men in this generation; and then shall all things be added thereunto.

11 a. Behold, thou art Hyrum, my son; seek the kingdom of God, and all things shall be added according to that which is just.

b. Build upon my rock, which is my gospel; deny not the spirit of revelation, nor the spirit of prophecy, for woe unto him that denieth these things;

c. therefore, treasure up in your hearts until the time which is in my wisdom that you shall go forth: behold, I speak unto all who have good desires, and have thrust in their sickles to reap.

12 a. Behold, I am Jesus Christ, the Son of God. I am the life and the light of the world. I am the same who came unto my own, and my own received me not;

b. but verily, verily I say unto you, that as many as receive me, them will I give power to become the sons of God, even to them that believe on my name. Amen.

SECTION 11

Revelation given through Joseph Smith, Jr., the prophet, in response to the earnest prayers of Joseph Knight, Sr. On several occasions Mr. Knight brought provisions to Joseph and Oliver so they could continue their work of translation without interruption. This revelation was given in May 1829, at Harmony, Pennsylvania. Note the similarity between the opening affirmations and commandments of this revelation and those given to Oliver Cowdery (D. and C. 6), Hyrum Smith (D. and C. 10), and David Whitmer (D. and C. 12).

1 a. A great and marvelous work is about to come forth among the children of men.

b. Behold, I am God, and give heed to my word, which is quick and powerful, sharper than a two-edged sword, to the dividing asunder of both joints and marrow;

c. therefore, give heed unto my word.

2 a. Behold, the field is white already to harvest; therefore, whoso desireth to reap, let him thrust in his sickle with his might, and reap while the day lasts, that he may treasure up for his soul everlasting salvation in the kingdom of God;

b. yea, whosoever will thrust in his sickle and reap, the same is called of God;

c. therefore, if you will ask of me you shall receive, if you will knock it shall be opened unto you.

3 a. Now, as you have asked, behold, I say unto you,

b. Keep my commandments, and seek to bring forth and establish the cause of Zion.

4 a. Behold, I speak unto you, and also to all those who have desires to bring forth and establish this work;

b. and no one can assist in this work, except he shall be humble and full of love, having faith, hope, and charity, being temperate in all things whatsoever shall be intrusted to his care.

5 a. Behold, I am the light and the life of the world, that speak these words;

b. therefore, give heed with your might, and then you are called. Amen.

SECTION 12

At the invitation of the Whitmer family, Joseph Smith and Oliver Cowdery went from Harmony, Pennsylvania, to Fayette, Seneca County, New York, where they stayed in the Whitmer home until the translation of the Book of Mormon was completed. The following revelation, addressed to David Whitmer, was received in June 1829, while the prophet was still in Fayette.

1 a. A great and marvelous work is about to come forth unto the children of men.

b. Behold, I am God, and give heed to my word, which is quick and powerful, sharper than a two-edged sword, to the dividing asunder of both joints and marrow;

c. therefore, give heed unto my word.

2 a. Behold, the field is white already to harvest, therefore, whoso desireth to reap, let him thrust in his sickle with his might, and reap while the day lasts, that he may treasure up for his soul everlasting salvation in the kingdom of God;

b. yea, whosoever will thrust in his sickle and reap, the same is called of God; therefore, if you will ask of me you shall receive, if you will knock it shall be opened unto you.

3 a. Seek to bring forth and establish my Zion.

b. Keep my commandments in all things; and if you keep my commandments and endure to the end, you shall have eternal life; which gift is the greatest of all the gifts of God.

4 a. And it shall come to pass, that if you shall ask the Father in my name, in faith believing, you shall receive the Holy Ghost, which giveth utterance, that you may stand as a witness of the things of which you shall both hear and see;

b. and also, that you may declare repentance unto this generation.

5 a. Behold, I am Jesus Christ the Son of the living God, who created the heavens and the earth; a light which can not be hid in darkness;

b. wherefore, I must bring forth the fullness of my gospel from the Gentiles unto the house of Israel.

c. And, behold, thou art David, and thou art called to assist; which thing if thou doest, and art faithful, thou shalt be blessed both spiritually and temporally, and great shall be thy reward. Amen.

SECTION 13

Revelation given through Joseph Smith, Jr., the prophet, to John Whitmer, June 1829, at the home of Peter Whitmer, Sr., John's father, at Fayette, Seneca County, New York. John Whitmer became one of the eight witnesses whose testimony is published with all editions of the Book of Mormon.

1 a. Hearken, my servant John, and listen to the words of Jesus Christ, your Lord and your Redeemer;

b. for, behold, I speak unto you with sharpness and with power, for mine arm is over all the earth, and I will tell you that which no man knows save me and you alone;

c. for many times you have desired of me to know that which would be of the most worth unto you.

2 Behold, blessed are you for this thing, and for speaking my words, which I have given you, according to my commandments.

3 And now, behold, I say unto you, that the thing which will be of the most worth unto you, will be to declare repentance unto this people, that you may bring souls unto me, that you may rest with them in the kingdom of my Father. Amen.

SECTION 14

Revelation given through Joseph Smith, Jr., to Peter Whitmer, Jr. It is identical with the message to John, Peter's brother, and was received at the same time and place, June 1829, at Fayette, Seneca County, New York.

1 a. Hearken, my servant Peter, and listen to the words of Jesus Christ, your Lord and your Redeemer;

b. for, behold, I speak unto you with sharpness and with power, for mine arm is over all the earth, and I will tell you that which no man knows save me and you alone;

c. for many times you have desired of me to know that which would be of the most worth unto you.

2 Behold, blessed are you for this thing, and for speaking my words, which I have given you, according to my commandments.

3 And now, behold, I say unto you, that the thing which will be of the most worth unto you, will be to declare repentance unto this people, that you may bring souls unto me, that you may rest with them in the kingdom of my Father. Amen.

SECTION 15

In June, 1829, Martin Harris visited Fayette, New York, to inquire concerning the progress being made in the translation of the Book of Mormon. During this visit he joined Oliver Cowdery and David Whitmer in asking that they might be chosen as the three special witnesses to the divinity of the Book of Mormon, mentioned in the prophecies of Nephi and Moroni (II Nephi 11:133; Ether 2:2-3).

The following revelation was received in answer to Joseph's prayer on behalf of his three associates. A few days later the promise it contained was fulfilled, and Oliver Cowdery, David Whitmer, and Martin Harris became the three special witnesses to the fact that Joseph truly had the Book of Mormon plates and that these plates had been translated "by the gift and power of God." Their testimony was maintained to the end of their lives and has been included in every edition of the Book of Mormon.

1 a. Behold, I say unto you, that you must rely upon my word,

b. which if you do, with full purpose of heart, you shall have a view of the plates, and also the breastplate, the sword of Laban, the Urim and Thummim, which were given to the Brother of Jared upon the mount, when he talked with the Lord face to face, and the miraculous directors which were given to Lehi while in the wilderness, on the borders of the Red Sea;

c. and it is by your faith that you shall obtain a view of them, even by that faith which was had by the prophets of old.

2 a. And after that you have obtained faith, and have seen them with your eyes, you shall testify of them, by the power of God;

b. and this you shall do that my servant Joseph Smith, Jr., may not be destroyed, that I may bring about my righteous purposes unto the children of men, in this work.

c. And ye shall testify that ye have seen them, even as my servant Joseph Smith, Jr., has seen them, for it is by my power that he has seen them, and it is because he had faith;

d. and he has translated the book, even that part which I have commanded him, and as your Lord and your God liveth, it is true.

3 a. Wherefore you have received the same power, and the same faith, and the same gift like unto him;

b. and if you do these last commandments of mine, which I have given you, the gates of hell shall not prevail against you; for my grace is sufficient for you; and you shall be lifted up at the last day.

c. And I, Jesus Christ, your Lord and your God, have spoken it unto you, that I might bring about my righteous purposes unto the children of men. Amen.

SECTION 16

Although Martin Harris is not mentioned in this revelation given in June 1829, at Fayette, he joined Oliver Cowdery and David Whitmer in selecting the first apostles in the Quorum of Twelve in the Restoration. The selection was made at Kirtland, February 14, 1835. Those chosen were ordained under the hands of Oliver, David, and Martin (the Three Witnesses), each praying separately.

1 a. Now, behold, because of the thing which you, my servant Oliver Cowdery, have desired to know of me, I give unto you these words:

b. Behold, I have manifested unto you, by my Spirit in many instances, that the things which you have written are true; wherefore you know that they are true;

c. and if you know that they are true, behold, I give unto you a commandment, that you rely upon the things which are written; for in them are all things written concerning the foundation of my church, my gospel, and my Rock;

d. wherefore, if you shall build up my church upon the foundation of my gospel and my Rock, the gates of hell shall not prevail against you.

2 a. Behold, the world is ripening in iniquity, and it must needs be that the children of men are stirred up unto repentance, both the Gentiles, and also the house of Israel;

b. wherefore, as thou hast been baptized by the hand of my servant, Joseph Smith, Jr., according to that which I have commanded him, he hath fulfilled the thing which I commanded him.

c. And now marvel not that I have called him unto mine own purpose, which purpose is known in me;

d. wherefore, if he shall be diligent in keeping my commandments, he shall be blessed unto eternal life, and his name is Joseph.

3 a. And now, Oliver Cowdery, I speak unto you, and also unto David Whitmer, by the way of commandment;

b. for, behold, I command all men everywhere to repent, and I speak unto you, even as unto Paul mine apostle, for you are called even with that same calling with which he was called.

c. Remember the worth of souls is great in the sight of God; for, behold, the Lord your Redeemer suffered death in the flesh; wherefore he suffered the pain of all men, that all men might repent and come unto him.

d. And he hath risen again from the dead, that he might bring all men unto him on conditions of repentance.

e. And how great is his joy in the soul that repenteth. Wherefore you are called to cry repentance unto this people.

f. And if it so be that you should labor all your days, in crying repentance unto this people, and bring save it be one soul unto me, how great shall be your joy with him in the kingdom of my Father!

4 a. And now, if your joy will be great with one soul that you have brought unto me into the kingdom of my Father, how great will be your joy, if you should bring many souls unto me!

b. Behold, you have my gospel before you, and my Rock, and my salvation.

c. Ask the Father in my name, in faith believing that you shall receive, and you shall have the Holy Ghost which manifesteth all things, which is expedient unto the children of men.

d. And if you have not faith, hope, and charity, you can do nothing. Contend against no church, save it be the church of the Devil.

e. Take upon you the name of Christ, and speak the truth in soberness; and as many as repent, and are baptized in my name, which is Jesus Christ, and endure to the end, the same shall be saved.

f. Behold, Jesus Christ is the name which is given of the Father, and there is none other name given whereby man can be saved;

g. wherefore, all men must take upon them the name which is given of the Father, for in that name shall they be called at the last day; wherefore, if they know not the name by which they are called, they can not have place in the kingdom of my Father.

5 a. And now, behold, there are others who are called to declare my gospel, both unto Gentile and unto Jew; yea, even twelve; and the twelve shall be my disciples, and they shall take upon them my name;

b. and the twelve are they who shall desire to take upon

them my name, with full purpose of heart; and if they desire to take upon them my name, with full purpose of heart, they are called to go into all the world to preach my gospel unto every creature;

c. and they are they who are ordained of me to baptize in my name, according to that which is written; and you have that which is written before you; wherefore you must perform it according to the words which are written.

d. And now I speak unto the twelve: Behold, my grace is sufficient for you; you must walk uprightly before me and sin not.

e. And, behold, you are they who are ordained of me to ordain priests and teachers to declare my gospel, according to the power of the Holy Ghost which is in you, and according to the callings and gifts of God unto men; and I, Jesus Christ, your Lord and your God, have spoken it.

f. These words are not of men, nor of man, but of me; wherefore, you shall testify they are of me, and not of man; for it is my voice which speaketh them unto you; for they are given by my Spirit unto you;

g. and by my power you can read them one to another, and save it were by my power, you could not have them; wherefore you can testify that you have heard my voice, and know my words.

6 a. And now, behold, I give unto you, Oliver Cowdery, and also unto David Whitmer, that you shall search out the twelve who shall have the desires of which I have spoken; and by their desires and their works, you shall know them;

b. and when you have found them you shall show these things unto them.

c. And you shall fall down and worship the Father in my name; and you must preach unto the world, saying,

d. You must repent and be baptized in the name of Jesus Christ; for all men must repent and be baptized, and not only men, but women; and children who have arrived to the years of accountability.

7 a. And now, after that you have received this, you must keep my commandments in all things;

b. and by your hands I will work a marvelous work among the children of men, unto the convincing of many of

their sins, that they may come unto repentance, and that they
may come unto the kingdom of my Father;

c. wherefore, the blessings which I give unto you are
above all things.

d. And after that you have received this, if you keep not
my commandments, you can not be saved in the kingdom
of my Father.

e. Behold, I, Jesus Christ, your Lord and your God, and
your Redeemer, by the power of my Spirit, have spoken it.
Amen.

SECTION 17

*This section is a compilation of instructions received from
time to time in connection with the organization of the
church. The "Book of Commandments" describes the section as "the Articles and Covenants of the Church of Christ,
given in Fayette, New York, June, 1830," but that part
of the instruction which set the date for the organization
of the church was given prior to April 6, 1830.*

Joseph wrote in "Times and Seasons" (3:928):

> *"In this manner did the Lord continue to give us instruc-
> tions from time to time concerning the duties which
> now devolved upon us, and among many other things
> of the kind, we obtained of him the following, by the
> spirit of prophecy and revelation, which not only gave
> us much information, but also pointed out to us the
> precise day upon which according to his will and com-
> mandment, we should proceed to organize his church
> once again, here upon the earth."*

*All editions of the Doctrine and Covenants include para-
graphs 16 and 17 of this section, which did not appear in
the "Book of Commandments." This further instruction was
probably received after July 20, 1833, and selected for inclusion with related material in this section on the same principle as other material received at different times.*

1 a. The rise of the church of Christ in these last days, being one thousand eight hundred and thirty years since the coming of our Lord and Savior Jesus Christ in the flesh, it being regularly organized and established agreeably to the laws of our country, by the will and commandments of God in the fourth month, and on the sixth day of the month which is called April;

b. which commandments were given to Joseph Smith, Jr., who was called of God and ordained an apostle of Jesus Christ, to be the first elder of this church; and to Oliver Cowdery, who was also called of God an apostle of Jesus Christ, to be the second elder of this church, and ordained under his hand:

c. and this according to the grace of our Lord and Savior Jesus Christ, to whom be all glory both now and for ever. Amen.

2 a. After it was truly manifested unto this first elder that he had received a remission of his sins, he was entangled again in the vanities of the world;

b. but after repenting, and humbling himself, sincerely, through faith, God ministered unto him by an holy angel whose countenance was as lightning, and whose garments were pure and white above all other whiteness,

c. and gave unto him commandments which inspired him, and gave him power from on high, by the means which were before prepared, to translate the Book of Mormon,

d. which contains a record of a fallen people, and the fullness of the gospel of Jesus Christ to the Gentiles, and to the Jews also, which was given by inspiration,

e. and is confirmed to others by the ministering of angels, and is declared unto the world by them, proving to the world that the Holy Scriptures are true,

f. and that God does inspire men and call them to his holy work in this age and generation, as well as in generations of old,

g. thereby showing that he is the same God yesterday, today, and for ever. Amen.

3 a. Therefore, having so great witnesses, by them shall the world be judged, even as many as shall hereafter come to a knowledge of this work;

b. and those who receive it in faith and work righteousness, shall receive a crown of eternal life;

c. but those who harden their hearts in unbelief and reject it, it shall turn to their own condemnation, for the Lord God has spoken it;

d. and we, the elders of the church, have heard and bear witness to the words of the glorious Majesty on high, to whom be glory for ever and ever. Amen.

4 a. By these things we know that there is a God in heaven who is infinite and eternal, from everlasting to everlasting the same unchangeable God, the framer of heaven and earth and all things which are in them, and that he created man male and female;

b. after his own image and in his own likeness created he them, and gave unto them commandments that they should love and serve him the only living and true God, and that he should be the only being whom they should worship.

c. But by the transgression of these holy laws, man became sensual and devilish, and became fallen man.

5 a. Wherefore the almighty God gave his only begotten Son, as it is written in those scriptures which have been given of him:

b. he suffered temptations but gave no heed unto them;

c. he was crucified, died, and rose again the third day;

d. and ascended into heaven to sit down on the right hand of the Father, to reign with almighty power according to the will of the Father, that as many as would believe and be baptized, in his holy name, and endure in faith to the end, should be saved:

e. not only those who believed after he came in the meridian of time in the flesh, but all those from the beginning, even as many as were before he came,

f. who believed in the words of the holy prophets, who spake as they were inspired by the gift of the Holy Ghost,

g. who truly testified of him in all things, should have eternal life, as well as those who should come after, who should believe in the gifts and callings of God by the Holy Ghost,

h. which beareth record of the Father, and of the Son, which Father, Son, and Holy Ghost are one God, infinite and eternal, without end. Amen.

6 a. And we know that all men must repent and believe
on the name of Jesus Christ and worship the Father in his
name, and endure in faith on his name to the end, or they
can not be saved in the kingdom of God.

b. And we know that justification through the grace of
our Lord and Savior Jesus Christ, is just and true;

c. and we know, also, that sanctification through the
grace of our Lord and Savior Jesus Christ, is just and true,
to all those who love and serve God with all their mights,
minds, and strength;

d. but there is a possibility that man may fall from grace
and depart from the living God.

e. Therefore let the church take heed and pray always,
lest they fall into temptations; yea, and even let those who
are sanctified, take heed also.

f. And we know that these things are true and according
to the revelations of John, neither adding to, nor diminish-
ing from the prophecy of his book, the Holy Scriptures, or
the revelations of God which shall come hereafter by the gift
and power of the Holy Ghost, the voice of God, or the
ministering of angels:

g. and the Lord God has spoken it; and honor, power,
and glory, be rendered to his holy name, both now and ever.
Amen.

7 a. *And again by way of commandment to the church
concerning the manner of baptism:*

b. All those who humble themselves before God and desire
to be baptized, and come forth with broken hearts and contrite spirits, and witness before the church that they have
truly repented of all their sins,

c. and are willing to take upon them the name of Jesus
Christ, having a determination to serve him to the end,

d. and truly manifest by their works that they have received of the Spirit of Christ unto the remission of their sins,
shall be received by baptism into his church.

8 a. *The duty of the elders, priests, teachers, deacons, and
members of the church of Christ:*

b. An apostle is an elder, and it is his calling to baptize,
and to ordain other elders, priests, teachers, and deacons,
and to administer bread and wine—the emblems of the flesh
and blood of Christ—

c. and to confirm those who are baptized into the church, by the laying on of hands for the baptism of fire and the Holy Ghost, according to the Scriptures;

d. and to teach, expound, exhort, baptize, and watch over the church;

e. and to confirm the church by the laying on of the hands, and the giving of the Holy Ghost,

f. and to take the lead of all meetings.

9 The elders are to conduct the meetings as they are led by the Holy Ghost, according to the commandments and revelations of God.

10 a. The priest's duty is to preach, teach, expound, exhort, and baptize, and administer the sacrament,

b. and visit the house of each member, and exhort them to pray vocally and in secret, and attend to all family duties:

c. and he may also ordain other priests, teachers, and deacons;

d. and he is to take the lead of meetings when there is no elder present, but when there is an elder present he is only to preach, teach, expound, exhort, and baptize, and visit the house of each member, exhorting them to pray vocally and in secret, and attend to all family duties.

e. In all these duties the priest is to assist the elder if occasion requires.

11 a. The teacher's duty is to watch over the church always, and be with, and strengthen them, and see that there is no iniquity in the church, neither hardness with each other; neither lying, back-biting, nor evil speaking;

b. and see that the church meet together often, and also see that all the members do their duty,

c. and he is to take the lead of meetings in the absence of the elder or priest,

d. and is to be assisted always, in all his duties in the church, by the deacons, if occasion requires;

e. but neither teachers nor deacons have authority to baptize, administer the sacrament, or lay on hands;

f. they are, however, to warn, expound, exhort, and teach, and invite all to come unto Christ.

12 a. Every elder, priest, teacher, or deacon, is to be ordained according to the gifts and callings of God unto him;

b. and he is to be ordained by the power of the Holy Ghost which is in the one who ordains him.

13 The several elders composing this church of Christ are to meet in conference once in three months, or from time to time, as said conferences shall direct or appoint; and said conferences are to do whatever church business is necessary to be done at the time.

14 The elders are to receive their licenses from other elders, by vote of the church to which they belong, or from the conferences.

15 Each priest, teacher, or deacon, who is ordained by a priest, may take a certificate from him at the time, which certificate, when presented to an elder, shall entitle him to a license, which shall authorize him to perform the duties of his calling; or he may receive it from a conference.

16 a. No person is to be ordained to any office in this church, where there is a regularly organized branch of the same, without the vote of that church;

b. but the presiding elders, traveling bishops, high councilors, high priests, and elders, may have the privilege of ordaining, where there is no branch of the church, that a vote may be called.

17 Every president of the high priesthood (or presiding elder), bishop, high councilor, and high priest, is to be ordained by the direction of a high council, or General Conference.

18 a. *The duty of the members after they are received by baptism:*

b. The elders or priests are to have a sufficient time to expound all things concerning the church of Christ to their understanding, previous to their partaking of the sacrament, and being confirmed by the laying on of the hands of the elders; so that all things may be done in order.

c. And the members shall manifest before the church, and also before the elders, by a godly walk and conversation that they are worthy of it, that there may be works and faith agreeable to the Holy Scriptures, walking in holiness before the Lord.

19 Every member of the church of Christ having children, is to bring them unto the elders before the church, who are to lay their hands upon them in the name of Jesus Christ, and bless them in his name.

20 No one can be received into the church of Christ unless he has arrived unto the years of accountability before God, and is capable of repentance.

21 a. Baptism is to be administered in the following manner unto all those who repent:

b. The person who is called of God and has authority from Jesus Christ to baptize, shall go down into the water with the person who has presented him or herself for baptism, and shall say, calling him or her by name:

c. Having been commissioned of Jesus Christ, I baptize you in the name of the Father, and of the Son, and of the Holy Ghost, Amen.

d. Then shall he immerse him or her in the water, and come forth again out of the water.

22 a. It is expedient that the church meet together often to partake of bread and wine in remembrance of the Lord Jesus;

b. and the elder or priest shall administer it; and after this manner shall he administer it:

c. He shall kneel with the church and call upon the Father in solemn prayer, saying,

d. O God, the eternal Father, we ask thee in the name of thy Son Jesus Christ, to bless and sanctify this bread to the souls of all those who partake of it, that they may eat in remembrance of the body of thy Son, and witness unto thee, O God, the eternal Father, that they are willing to take upon them the name of thy Son, and always remember him and keep his commandments which he has given them, that they may always have his Spirit to be with them. Amen.

23 a. The manner of administering the wine: He shall take the cup also, and say:

b. O God, the eternal Father, we ask thee in the name of thy Son Jesus Christ, to bless and sanctify this wine to the souls of all those who drink of it, that they may do it in remembrance of the blood of thy Son which was shed for them, that they may witness unto thee, O God, the eternal Father, that they do always remember him, that they may have his Spirit to be with them. Amen.

24 a. Any member of the church of Christ transgressing, or being overtaken in a fault, shall be dealt with as the Scriptures direct.

25 a. It shall be the duty of the several churches composing the church of Christ to send one or more of their teachers to attend the several conferences, held by the elders of the church, with a list of the names of the several members uniting themselves with the church since the last conference,

b. or send by the hand of some priest, so that a regular list of all the names of the whole church may be kept in a book, by one of the elders, whoever the other elders shall appoint from time to time,

c. and also if any have been expelled from the church, so that their names may be blotted out of the General Church record of names.

26 All members removing from the church where they reside, if going to a church where they are not known, may take a letter certifying that they are regular members and in good standing, which certificate may be signed by any elder or priest, if the member receiving the letter is personally acquainted with the elder or priest, or it may be signed by the teachers or deacons of the church.

SECTION 18

Revelation given through Joseph Smith, Jr., to Martin Harris, March 1830, at Manchester, New York.

1 a. I am Alpha and Omega, Christ the Lord; yea, even I am He, the beginning and the end, the Redeemer of the world:

b. I having accomplished and finished the will of him whose I am, even the Father, concerning me; having done this, that I might subdue all things unto myself;

c. retaining all power, even to the destroying of Satan and his works at the end of the world, and the last great day of judgment, which I shall pass upon the inhabitants thereof, judging every man according to his works, and the deeds which he has done.

d. And surely every man must repent or suffer, for I God am endless; wherefore, I revoke not the judgments which I shall pass, but woes shall go forth, weeping, wailing, and gnashing of teeth;

e. yea, to those who are found on my left hand; nevertheless, it is not written that there shall be no end to this torment; but it is written endless torment.

2 a. Again, it is written eternal damnation; wherefore it is more express than other scriptures, that it might work upon the hearts of the children of men, altogether for my name's glory;

b. wherefore, I will explain unto you this mystery, for it is meet unto you to know even as mine apostles.

c. I speak unto you that are chosen in this thing, even as one, that you may enter into my rest; for, behold, the mystery of godliness, how great is it?

d. For, behold, I am endless, and the punishment which is given from my hand is endless punishment, for Endless is my name; wherefore—

e. Eternal punishment is God's punishment.
Endless punishment is God's punishment.

f. Wherefore, I command you to repent, and keep the commandments which you have received by the hand of my servant Joseph Smith, Jr., in my name;

g. and it is by my almighty power that you have received them; therefore I command you to repent—repent, lest I smite you by the rod of my mouth, and by my wrath, and by my anger, and your sufferings be sore—how sore you know not! how exquisite you know not! yea, how hard to bear you know not!

h. For, behold, I, God, have suffered these things for all, that they might not suffer, if they would repent; but if they would not repent, they must suffer even as I;

i. which suffering caused myself, even God, the greatest of all, to tremble because of pain, and to bleed at every pore, and to suffer both body and spirit, and would that I might not drink the bitter cup, and shrink;

j. nevertheless, glory be to the Father, and I partook and finished my preparations unto the children of men;

k. wherefore, I command you again to repent, lest I humble you by my almighty power, and that you confess your sins, lest you suffer these punishments of which I have spoken, of which in the smallest, yea, even in the least degree, you have tasted at the time I withdrew my Spirit.

l. And I command you that you preach naught but repentance, and show not these things unto the world until it is wisdom in me;

m. for they can not bear meat now, but milk they must receive; wherefore, they must not know these things, lest they perish.

n. Learn of me, and listen to my words; walk in the meekness of my Spirit and you shall have peace in me.

o. I am Jesus Christ; I came by the will of the Father, and I do his will.

3 a. And again, I command thee that thou shalt not covet thy neighbor's wife; nor seek thy neighbor's life.

b. And again, I command thee that thou shalt not covet thine own property, but impart it freely to the printing of the Book of Mormon, which contains the truth and the word of God.

c. which is my word to the Gentiles, that soon it may go to the Jew, of whom the Lamanites are a remnant, that they may believe the gospel, and look not for a Messiah to come who has already come.

4 a. And again, I command thee that thou shalt pray vocally as well as in thy heart; yea, before the world as well as in secret; in public as well as in private.

b. And thou shalt declare glad tidings; yea, publish it upon the mountains, and upon every high place, and among every people that thou shalt be permitted to see.

c. And thou shalt do it with all humility, trusting in me, reviling not against revilers.

d. And of tenets thou shalt not talk, but thou shalt declare repentance and faith on the Savior, and remission of sins by baptism and by fire; yea, even the Holy Ghost.

5 a. Behold, this is a great, and the last commandment which I shall give unto you concerning this matter; for this shall suffice for thy daily walk even unto the end of thy life.

b. And misery thou shalt receive, if thou wilt slight these counsels; yea, even the destruction of thyself and property.

c. Impart a portion of thy property; yea, even part of thy lands, and all save the support of thy family.

d. Pay the debt thou hast contracted with the printer. Release thyself from bondage.

e. Leave thy house and home, except when thou shalt desire to see thy family; and speak freely to all;

f. yea, preach, exhort, declare the truth, even with a loud voice; with a sound of rejoicing, cry Hosanna! hosanna! Blessed be the name of the Lord God!

6 a. Pray always and I will pour out my Spirit upon you, and great shall be your blessing; yea, even more than if you should obtain treasures of earth and corruptibleness to the extent thereof.

b. Behold, canst thou read this without rejoicing and lifting up thy heart for gladness? or canst thou run about longer as a blind guide? or canst thou be humble and meek and conduct thyself wisely before me?

c. yea, come unto me thy Savior. Amen.

SECTION 19

Revelation given through Joseph Smith, Jr., the prophet, on the day the church was organized, April 6, 1830, at Fayette, Seneca County, New York, before or, possibly, during the organization meeting, and is addressed to both Joseph and the church. It refers to the organization in the past tense and gives instruction concerning the ordination of Joseph Smith and Oliver Cowdery as though this were yet to be consummated. The ordinations did take place at the organization meeting, after the other brethren participating had indicated their willingness to accept Joseph and Oliver as their teachers and leaders.

1 a. Behold, there shall be a record kept among you, and in it thou shalt be called a seer, a translator, a prophet, an apostle of Jesus Christ, an elder of the church through the will of God the Father, and the grace of your Lord Jesus Christ;

b. being inspired of the Holy Ghost to lay the foundation thereof, and to build it up unto the most holy faith;

c. which church was organized and established, in the year of your Lord eighteen hundred and thirty, in the fourth month, and on the sixth day of the month, which is called April.

2 a. Wherefore, meaning the church, thou shalt give heed unto all his words, and commandments, which he shall give unto you, as he receiveth them, walking in all holiness before me;

b. for his word ye shall receive, as if from mine own mouth, in all patience and faith; for by doing these things, the gates of hell shall not prevail against you;

c. yea, and the Lord God will disperse the powers of darkness from before you, and cause the heavens to shake for your good, and his name's glory.

d. For thus saith the Lord God, him have I inspired to move the cause of Zion in mighty power for good; and his diligence I know, and his prayers I have heard:

e. yea, his weeping for Zion I have seen, and I will cause that he shall mourn for her no longer, for his days of rejoicing are come unto the remission of his sins, and the manifestations of my blessings upon his works.

3 a. For, behold, I will bless all those who labor in my vineyard, with a mighty blessing, and they shall believe on his words, which are given him through me, by the Comforter, which manifesteth that Jesus was crucified by sinful men for the sins of the world; yea, for the remission of sins unto the contrite heart.

b. Wherefore, it behooveth me, that he should be ordained by you, Oliver Cowdery, mine apostle; this being an ordinance unto you, that you are an elder under his hand, he being the first unto you, that you might be an elder unto this church of Christ, bearing my name;

c. and the first preacher of this church, unto the church, and before the world; yea, before the Gentiles; yea, and thus saith the Lord God, lo, lo! to the Jews, also. Amen.

SECTION 20

Revelation given through Joseph Smith, Jr., prophet and seer to the church, April 1830, at Manchester, New York. This instruction came in answer to Joseph Smith's inquiry concerning the status of those who desired to unite with the church and who had already been baptized.

1 a. Behold, I say unto you, that all old covenants have I caused to be done away in this thing, and this is a new and everlasting covenant; even that which was from the beginning.

b. Wherefore, although a man should be baptized an hundred times, it availeth him nothing; for you can not enter in at the strait gate by the Law of Moses, neither by your dead works;

c. for it is because of your dead works, that I have caused this last covenant, and this church to be built up unto me; even as in days of old.

d. Wherefore, enter ye in at the gate, as I have commanded, and seek not to counsel your God. Amen.

SECTION 21

This section is a composite of five revelations given through Joseph Smith, Jr., at Manchester, New York, April 1830, and addressed to Oliver Cowdery, Hyrum Smith, Samuel H. Smith, Joseph Smith, Sr., and Joseph Knight, Sr. They were given in answer to the prayers of these brethren concerning their relation to the work of the church. Each paragraph in Doctrine and Covenants 21 was printed as a separate chapter in the "Book of Commandments," but the chapters were combined in the 1835 (first) edition of the Doctrine and Covenants and have been published in this form ever since. They were received on the day the church was organized.

1 a. Behold, I speak unto you, Oliver, a few words. Behold, thou art blessed, and art under no condemnation. But beware of pride, lest thou shouldst enter into temptation.

b. Make known thy calling unto the church, and also before the world; and thy heart shall be opened to preach the truth from henceforth and for ever. Amen.

2 a. Behold, I speak unto you, Hyrum, a few words, for thou also art under no condemnation, and thy heart is opened, and thy tongue loosed; and thy calling is to exhortation, and to strengthen the church continually.

b. Wherefore thy duty is unto the church for ever; and this because of thy family. Amen.

3 Behold, I speak a few words unto you, Samuel, for thou also art under no condemnation, and thy calling is to exhortation, and to strengthen the church. And thou art not as yet called to preach before the world. Amen.

4 Behold, I speak a few words unto you, Joseph; for thou also art under no condemnation, and thy calling also is to exhortation, and to strengthen the church. And this is thy duty from henceforth and for ever. Amen.

5 a. Behold, I manifest unto you, Joseph Knight, by these words, that you must take up your cross, in the which you must pray vocally before the world, as well as in secret, and in your family, and among your friends, and in all places.

b. And, behold, it is your duty to unite with the true church, and give your language to exhortation continually, that you may receive the reward of the laborer. Amen.

SECTION 22

Revelation given to Joseph Smith, Jr., at Colesville, New York, in June 1830, but was not included in the 1835 edition of the Doctrine and Covenants. It was first printed in "Times and Seasons" (4:71) and has been included in the Doctrine and Covenants since the Cincinnati edition of 1864. It was specifically approved by the 1970 World Conference. It is also printed in the forepart of the Inspired Version (pp. 7-9).

1 The words of God which he spake unto Moses, at a time when Moses was caught up into an exceeding high

mountain, and he saw God face to face, and he talked with him, and the glory of God was upon Moses; therefore Moses could endure his presence.

2 And God spake unto Moses, saying, Behold, I am the Lord God Almighty, and Endless is my name, for I am without beginning of days or end of years; and is not this endless?

3 a. And behold, thou art my son, wherefore look, and I will show thee the workmanship of mine hands, but not all;

b. for my works are without end, and also my words, for they never cease;

c. wherefore, no man can behold all my works except he behold all my glory;

d. and no man can behold all my glory, and afterwards remain in the flesh, on the earth.

4 a. And I have a work for thee, Moses, my son; and thou art in the similitude of mine Only Begotten; and my Only Begotten is and shall be the Savior, for he is full of grace and truth;

b. but there is no God beside me; and all things are present with me, for I know them all.

5 And now, behold, this one thing I show unto thee, Moses, my son; for thou art in the world, and now I show it unto thee.

6 a. And it came to pass, that Moses looked and beheld the world upon which he was created.

b. And as Moses beheld the world, and the ends thereof, and all the children of men, which are and which were created; of the same he greatly marveled, and wondered.

c. And the presence of God withdrew from Moses, that his glory was not upon Moses; and Moses was left unto himself; and as he was left unto himself, he fell unto the earth.

7 a. And it came to pass, that it was for the space of many hours before Moses did again receive his natural strength like unto man; and he said unto himself,

b. Now, for this cause, I know that man is nothing, which thing I never had supposed; but now mine eyes have beheld God; but not mine natural but my spiritual eyes, for mine natural eyes could not have beheld, for I should have withered and died in his presence;

c. but his glory was upon me, and I beheld his face, for I was transfigured before him.

8 a. And now it came to pass, that when Moses had said these words, behold, Satan came tempting him, saying, Moses, son of man, worship me.

b. And it came to pass that Moses looked upon Satan, and said, Who art thou, for behold I am a son of God, in the similitude of his Only Begotten; and where is thy glory, that I should worship thee?

c. For, behold, I could not look upon God except his glory should come upon me, and I were transfigured before him. But I can look upon thee in the natural man. Is it not so surely?

9 a. Blessed be the name of my God, for his Spirit hath not altogether withdrawn from me; or else where is thy glory, for it is darkness unto me, and I can judge between thee and God;

b. for God said unto me, Worship God, for him only shalt thou serve.

c. Get thee hence, Satan, deceive me not; for God said unto me, Thou art after the similitude of mine Only Begotten.

10 And he also gave unto me commandment, when he called unto me out of the burning bush, saying, Call upon God in the name of mine Only Begotten, and worship me.

11 And again, Moses said, I will not cease to call upon God. I have other things to inquire of him; for his glory has been upon me, and it is glory unto me; wherefore, I can judge between him and thee. Depart hence, Satan.

12 And now, when Moses had said these words, Satan cried with a loud voice, and went upon the earth, and commanded, saying, I am the Only Begotten, worship me.

13 And it came to pass, that Moses began to fear exceedingly; and as he began to fear, he saw the bitterness of hell; nevertheless, calling upon God he received strength, and

he commanded, saying, Depart hence, Satan; for this one God only will I worship, which is the God of glory.

14 And now, Satan began to tremble, and the earth shook, and Moses received strength and called upon God in the name of the Only Begotten, saying to Satan, Depart hence.

15 And it came to pass, that Satan cried with a loud voice, with weeping, and wailing, and gnashing of teeth, and departed hence; yea, from the presence of Moses, that he beheld him not.

16 And now, of this thing Moses bore record; but because of wickedness, it is not had among the children of men.

17 a. And it came to pass, that when Satan had departed from the presence of Moses, that Moses lifted up his eyes unto heaven, being filled with the Holy Ghost, which beareth record of the Father and the Son;

b. and calling upon the name of God, he beheld again his glory; for it rested upon him, and he heard a voice, saying,

c. Blessed art thou, Moses, for I, the Almighty, have chosen thee, and thou shalt be made stronger than many waters; for they shall obey thy command even as if thou wert God.

18 And lo, I am with thee, even unto the end of thy days, for thou shalt deliver my people from bondage; even Israel my chosen.

19 a. And it came to pass, as the voice was still speaking, he cast his eyes and beheld the earth; yea, even all the face of it; and there was not a particle of it which he did not behold, discerning it by the Spirit of God.

b. And he beheld also the inhabitants thereof, and there was not a soul which he beheld not, and he discerned them by the Spirit of God, and their numbers were great, even as numberless as the sand upon the seashore.

c. And he beheld many lands, and each land was called earth; and there were inhabitants on the face thereof.

20 And it came to pass, that Moses called upon God, saying, Tell me, I pray thee, why these things are so, and by what thou madest them? And behold the glory of God

was upon Moses, so that Moses stood in the presence of God, and he talked with him face to face.

21 a. And the Lord God said unto Moses, For mine own purpose have I made these things. Here is wisdom, and it remaineth in me.

b. And by the word of my power have I created them, which is mine Only Begotten Son, who is full of grace and truth.

c. And worlds without number have I created, and I also created them for mine own purpose; and by the Son I created them, which is mine Only Begotten. And the first man of all men have I called Adam, which is many.

d. But only an account of this earth, and the inhabitants thereof, give I unto you; for behold there are many worlds which have passed away by the word of my power;

e. and there are many also which now stand, and numberless are they unto man; but all things are numbered unto me; for they are mine, and I know them.

22 a. And it came to pass, that Moses spake unto the Lord, saying,

b. Be merciful unto thy servant, O God, and tell me concerning this earth, and the inhabitants thereof; and also the heavens, and then thy servant will be content.

23 a. And the Lord God spake unto Moses, saying, The heavens, they are many and they can not be numbered unto man, but they are numbered unto me, for they are mine; and as one earth shall pass away, and the heavens thereof, even so shall another come;

b. and there is no end to my works, neither to my words; for this is my work and my glory, to bring to pass the immortality, and eternal life of man.

24 a. And now, Moses, my son, I will speak unto you concerning this earth upon which you stand; and you shall write the things which I shall speak.

b. And in a day when the children of men shall esteem my words as naught, and take many of them from the book which you shall write, behold I will raise up another like unto you, and they shall be had again among the children of men, among even as many as shall believe.

25 These words were spoken unto Moses in the mount, the name of which shall not be known among the children of men. And now they are spoken unto you. Amen.

SECTION 23

Revelation given through Joseph Smith, Jr., July 1830, at Harmony, Pennsylvania. It is addressed to Joseph and Oliver, who were in need of reassurance because of the persecution to which they had been subjected after the publication of the Book of Mormon and the organization of the church.

1 a. Behold, thou wast called and chosen to write the Book of Mormon, and to my ministry;

b. and I have lifted thee up out of thy afflictions, and have counseled thee, that thou hast been delivered from all thine enemies, and thou hast been delivered from the powers of Satan, and from darkness!

c. Nevertheless, thou art not excusable in thy transgressions; nevertheless go thy way and sin no more.

2 a. Magnify thine office; and after thou hast sowed thy fields and secured them, go speedily unto the church which is in Colesville, Fayette, and Manchester, and they shall support thee; and I will bless them both spiritually and temporally;

b. but if they receive thee not, I will send upon them a cursing instead of a blessing.

3 a. And thou shalt continue in calling upon God in my name, and writing the things which shall be given thee by the Comforter, and expounding all scriptures unto the church, and it shall be given thee, in the very moment, what thou shalt speak and write;

b. and they shall hear it, or I will send unto them a cursing instead of a blessing.

4 a. For thou shalt devote all thy service in Zion. And in this thou shalt have strength.

b. Be patient in afflictions, for thou shalt have many; but endure them, for lo, I am with you, even unto the end of thy days.

c. And in temporal labors thou shalt not have strength, for this is not thy calling.

d. Attend to thy calling and thou shalt have wherewith to magnify thine office, and to expound all Scriptures.

e. And continue in laying on of the hands, and confirming the churches.

5 a. And thy brother Oliver shall continue in bearing my name before the world, and also to the church. And he shall not suppose that he can say enough in my cause; and lo, I am with him to the end.

b. In me he shall have glory, and not of himself, whether in weakness or in strength, whether in bonds or free.

c. And at all times and in all places, he shall open his mouth and declare my gospel as with the voice of a trump, both day and night. And I will give unto him strength such as is not known among men.

6 a. Require not miracles, except I shall command you; except casting out devils; healing the sick; and against poisonous serpents; and against deadly poisons; and these things ye shall not do, except it be required of you by them who desire it, that the Scriptures might be fulfilled, for ye shall do according to that which is written.

b. And in whatsoever place ye shall enter, and they receive you not, in my name, ye shall leave a cursing instead of a blessing, by casting off the dust of your feet against them as a testimony, and cleansing your feet by the wayside.

7 a. And it shall come to pass, that whosoever shall lay their hands upon you by violence, ye shall command to be smitten in my name, and behold I will smite them according to your words, in mine own due time.

b. And whosoever shall go to law with thee shall be cursed by the law.

c. And thou shalt take no purse, nor scrip, neither staves, neither two coats, for the church shall give unto thee in the very hour what thou needest for food, and for raiment, and for shoes, and for money, and for scrip; for thou art called to prune my vineyard with a mighty pruning, yea, even for the last time.

d. Yea, and also, all those whom thou hast ordained. And they shall do even according to this pattern. Amen.

SECTION 24

Revelation addressed to Emma Smith, wife of the prophet. It was given through Joseph Smith at Harmony, Pennsylvania, in July 1830. The selection of hymns that Emma was directed to make was completed and published in 1835. This hymnbook was used at the dedication of the Kirtland Temple.

1 a. Hearken unto the voice of the Lord your God, while I speak unto thee, Emma Smith, my daughter, for verily I say unto thee, All those who receive my gospel are sons and daughters in my kingdom.

b. A revelation I give unto thee concerning my will, and if thou art faithful and walk in the paths of virtue before me, I will preserve thy life, and thou shalt receive an inheritance in Zion.

c. Behold, thy sins are forgiven thee, and thou art an elect lady, whom I have called.

d. Murmur not because of the things which thou hast not seen, for they are withheld from thee, and from the world, which is wisdom in me in a time to come.

2 a. And the office of thy calling shall be for a comfort unto my servant Joseph Smith, Jr., thy husband, in his afflictions, with consoling words, in the spirit of meekness.

b. And thou shalt go with him at the time of his going, and be unto him for a scribe, while there is no one to be a scribe for him, that I may send my servant Oliver Cowdery whithersoever I will.

c. And thou shalt be ordained under his hand to expound Scriptures, and to exhort the church, according as it shall be given thee by my Spirit; for he shall lay his hands upon thee, and thou shalt receive the Holy Ghost, and thy time shall be given to writing, and to learning much.

d. And thou needest not fear, for thy husband shall support thee in the church; for unto them is his calling, that all things might be revealed unto them, whatsoever I will, according to their faith.

3 a. And verily I say unto thee, that thou shalt lay aside the things of this world, and seek for the things of a better.

b. And it shall be given thee, also, to make a selection of sacred hymns, as it shall be given thee, which is pleasing unto me, to be had in my church; for my soul delighteth in the song of the heart; yea, the song of the righteous is a prayer unto me.

c. And it shall be answered with a blessing upon their heads. Wherefore, lift up thy heart and rejoice, and cleave unto the covenants which thou hast made.

4 a. Continue in the spirit of meekness, and beware of pride. Let thy soul delight in thy husband, and the glory which shall come upon him.

b. Keep my commandments continually, and a crown of righteousness thou shalt receive. And except thou do this, where I am thou canst not come.

c. And verily, verily I say unto you, that this is my voice unto all. Amen.

SECTION 25

Revelation given through Joseph Smith at Harmony, Pennsylvania, in July 1830, to Joseph Smith, Jr., Oliver Cowdery, and John Whitmer. It is specifically important because of its affirmation of the principle of "common consent" in the government of the church.

1 a. Behold, I say unto you, that you shall let your time be devoted to the studying of the Scriptures, and to preaching, and to confirming the church at Colesville; and to performing your labors on the land, such as is required, until after you shall go to the west, to hold the next conference; and then it shall be made known what you shall do.

b. And all things shall be done by common consent in the church, by much prayer and faith; for all things you shall receive by faith. Amen.

SECTION 26

The first paragraph of this revelation was given to Joseph Smith, Jr., early in August 1830 at Harmony, Pennsylvania, and was written down at that time. It was given through the personal ministry of a "heavenly messenger" as Joseph was seeking wine for the Sacrament which he and his wife and John Whitmer (Joseph's secretary at the time) wished to share with Newel Knight and his wife. Mrs. Smith and Mrs. Knight had just been confirmed. The "Book of Commandments" gives the date of this revelation as September 4, 1830. This was probably when the later paragraphs of the revelation were received.

1 a. Listen to the voice of Jesus Christ, your Lord, your God, and your Redeemer, whose word is quick and powerful.

b. For, behold, I say unto you, that it mattereth not what ye shall eat, or what ye shall drink, when ye partake of the sacrament, if it so be that ye do it with an eye single to my glory;

c. remembering unto the Father my body which was laid down for you, and my blood which was shed for the remission of your sins;

d. wherefore a commandment I give unto you, that you shall not purchase wine, neither strong drink of your enemies; wherefore ye shall partake of none, except it is made new among you; yea, in this my Father's kingdom which shall be built up on the earth.

2 a. Behold, this is wisdom in me; wherefore marvel not, for the hour cometh that I will drink of the fruit of the vine with you on the earth, and with Moroni, whom I have sent unto you to reveal the Book of Mormon, containing the fullness of my everlasting gospel;

b. to whom I have committed the keys of the record of the stick of Ephraim; and also with Elias, to whom I have committed the keys of bringing to pass the restoration of all things, or the restorer of all things spoken by the mouth of all the holy prophets since the world began, concerning the last days;

c. and also John the son of Zacharias, which Zacharias he (Elias) visited and gave promise that he should have a son, and his name should be John, and he should be filled with the spirit of Elias;

d. which John I have sent unto you, my servants, Joseph Smith, Jr., and Oliver Cowdery, to ordain you unto this first priesthood which you have received, that you might be called and ordained even as Aaron;

e. and also Elijah, unto whom I have committed the keys of the power of turning the hearts of the fathers to the children and the hearts of the children to the fathers, that the whole earth may not be smitten with a curse;

f. and also with Joseph, and Jacob, and Isaac, and Abraham, your fathers; by whom the promises remain; and also with Michael, or Adam, the father of all, the prince of all, the ancient of days.

3 a. And also with Peter, and James, and John, whom I have sent unto you, by whom I have ordained you and confirmed you to be apostles and especial witnesses of my name, and bear the keys of your ministry;

b. and of the same things which I revealed unto them; unto whom I have committed the keys of my kingdom, and a dispensation of the gospel for the last times;

c. and for the fullness of times, in the which I will gather together in one all things, both which are in heaven and which are on earth; and also with all those whom my Father hath given me out of the world;

d. wherefore lift up your hearts and rejoice, and gird up your loins, and take upon you my whole armor, that ye may be able to withstand the evil day, having done all ye may be able to stand.

e. Stand, therefore, having your loins girt about with truth, having on the breastplate of righteousness, and your feet shod with the preparation of the gospel of peace, which I have sent mine angels to commit unto you, taking the shield of faith wherewith ye shall be able to quench all the fiery darts of the wicked;

f. and take the helmet of salvation, and the sword of my Spirit, which I will pour out upon you, and my word which

I reveal unto you, and be agreed as touching all things
whatsoever ye ask of me,

g. and be faithful until I come, and ye shall be caught
up, that where I am ye shall be also. Amen.

SECTION 27

*Revelation given to Oliver Cowdery through Joseph
Smith, Jr., in September 1830 at Fayette, New York.*

*Hiram Page had come into possession of a stone by use
of which he had obtained certain "revelations" concerning
the building of Zion, church organization, and similar matters. Oliver Cowdery and the Whitmer family, to whom
Hiram was related, tended to accept his claims. The instruction now received appoints Oliver to an important mission and then sets forth the associated principles of prophetic
guidance and common consent according to the church covenants and the prayer of faith. It should be noted that Oliver,
who had shared responsibility for the difficulties which had
arisen, is now commanded to take responsibility for their
settlement.*

1 Behold, I say unto thee, Oliver, that it shall be given
unto thee that thou shalt be heard by the church in all things
whatsoever thou shalt teach them by the Comforter, concerning the revelations and commandments which I have given.

2 a. But, behold, verily, verily I say unto thee, No one
shall be appointed to receive commandments and revelations in this church excepting my servant Joseph Smith, Jr.,
for he receiveth them even as Moses;

b. and thou shalt be obedient unto the things which I
shall give unto him, even as Aaron, to declare faithfully
the commandments and revelations, with power and authority
unto the church.

c. And if thou art led at any time by the Comforter to
speak or teach, or at all times by the way of commandment unto the church, thou mayest do it.

d. But thou shalt not write by way of commandment, but by wisdom; and thou shalt not command him who is at thy head, and at the head of the church, for I have given him the keys of the mysteries and the revelations, which are sealed, until I shall appoint unto them another in his stead.

3 a. And now, behold, I say unto thee that thou shalt go unto the Lamanites, and preach my gospel unto them;

b. and inasmuch as they receive thy teachings, thou shalt cause my church to be established among them, and thou shalt have revelations, but write them not by way of commandment.

c. And now, behold, I say unto thee, that it is not revealed, and no man knoweth where the city shall be built, but it shall be given hereafter.

d. Behold, I say unto thee that it shall be on the borders by the Lamanites.

4 a. Thou shalt not leave this place until after the conference, and my servant Joseph shall be appointed to preside over the conference by the voice of it, and what he saith to thee thou shalt tell.

b. And again, thou shalt take thy brother Hiram Page between him and thee alone, and tell him that those things which he hath written from that stone are not of me, and that Satan deceiveth him; for, behold, these things have not been appointed unto him;

c. neither shall anything be appointed unto any of this church contrary to the church covenants, for all things must be done in order and by common consent in the church, by the prayer of faith.

5 a. And thou shalt assist to settle all these things, according to the covenants of the church, before thou shalt take thy journey among the Lamanites.

b. And it shall be given thee from the time thou shalt go, until the time thou shalt return, what thou shalt do.

c. And thou must open thy mouth at all times, declaring my gospel with the sound of rejoicing. Amen.

SECTION 28

*Revelation given through Joseph Smith, prophet and seer
to the church, in August 1830. This revelation was given at
Fayette, New York, in the presence of six elders, prior to
the second conference of the church which was held at that
place on September 1, 1830.*

1 a. Listen to the voice of Jesus Christ, your Redeemer,
the great I AM, whose arm of mercy hath atoned for your
sins, who will gather his people even as a hen gathereth her
chickens under her wings, even as many as will hearken to
my voice, and humble themselves before me, and call upon
me in mighty prayer.

b. Behold, verily, verily I say unto you, that at this time
your sins are forgiven you, therefore ye receive these things;
but remember to sin no more, lest perils shall come upon you.

2 a. Verily I say unto you, that ye are chosen out of
the world to declare my gospel with the sound of rejoicing, as with the voice of a trump;

b. lift up your hearts and be glad, for I am in your
midst, and am your advocate with the Father; and it is his
good will to give you the kingdom;

c. and as it is written, Whatsoever ye shall ask in faith,
being united in prayer according to my command, ye shall
receive; and ye are called to bring to pass the gathering of
mine elect, for mine elect hear my voice and harden not
their hearts;

d. wherefore the decree hath gone forth from the Father
that they shall be gathered in unto one place, upon the face
of this land, to prepare their hearts, and be prepared in
all things, against the day when tribulation and desolation
are sent forth upon the wicked;

e. for the hour is nigh, and the day soon at hand, when
the earth is ripe; and all the proud, and they that do wickedly, shall be as stubble, and I will burn them up, saith the
Lord of Hosts, that wickedness shall not be upon the earth;

f. for the hour is nigh, and that which was spoken by
mine apostles must be fulfilled; for as they spoke, so shall
it come to pass;

g. for I will reveal myself from heaven with power and great glory, with all the hosts thereof, and dwell in righteousness with men on earth a thousand years, and the wicked shall not stand.

3 a. And again, verily, verily I say unto you, and it hath gone forth in a firm decree, by the will of the Father,

b. that mine apostles, the twelve which were with me in my ministry at Jerusalem, shall stand at my right hand, at the day of my coming, in a pillar of fire, being clothed with robes of righteousness, with crowns upon their heads, in glory even as I am, to judge the whole house of Israel, even as many as have loved me and kept my commandments, and none else;

c. for a trump shall sound, both long and loud, even as upon Mount Sinai, and all the earth shall quake, and they shall come forth, yea, even the dead which died in me, to receive a crown of righteousness, and to be clothed upon, even as I am, to be with me, that we may be one.

4 a. But, behold, I say unto you, that before this great day shall come, the sun shall be darkened, and the moon shall be turned into blood, and the stars shall fall from heaven;

b. and there shall be greater signs in heaven above, and in the earth beneath; and there shall be weeping and wailing among the hosts of men; and there shall be a great hailstorm sent forth to destroy the crops of the earth;

c. and it shall come to pass, because of the wickedness of the world, that I will take vengeance upon the wicked, for they will not repent; for the cup of mine indignation is full; for, behold, my blood shall not cleanse them if they hear me not.

5 a. Wherefore, I, the Lord God, will send forth flies upon the face of the earth, which shall take hold of the inhabitants thereof, and shall eat their flesh, and shall cause maggots to come in upon them,

b. and their tongues shall be stayed that they shall not utter against me, and their flesh shall fall from off their bones, and their eyes from their sockets;

c. and it shall come to pass that the beasts of the forest and the fowls of the air shall devour them up; and the great

and abominable church, which is the whore of all the earth,
shall be cast down by devouring fire, according as it is
spoken by the mouth of Ezekiel the prophet, which spoke
of these things, which have not come to pass, but surely
must, as I live, for abomination shall not reign.

6 a. And again, verily, verily I say unto you, that when
the thousand years are ended, and men again begin to deny
their God, then will I spare the earth but for a little season;
    b. and the end shall come, and the heaven and the earth
shall be consumed, and pass away, and there shall be a
new heaven and a new earth;
    c. for all old things shall pass away, and all things shall
become new, even the heaven and the earth, and all the
fullness thereof, both men and beasts, the fowls of the air,
and the fishes of the sea;
    d. and not one hair, neither mote, shall be lost, for it is
the workmanship of mine hand.

7 a. But, behold, verily I say unto you, Before the earth
shall pass away, Michael, mine archangel, shall sound his
trump, and then shall all the dead awake, for their graves
shall be opened, and they shall come forth; yea, even all;
    b. and the righteous shall be gathered on my right hand
unto eternal life; and the wicked on my left hand will I be
ashamed to own before the Father;
    c. wherefore I will say unto them, Depart from me ye
cursed into everlasting fire, prepared for the Devil and his
angels.

8 a. And now, behold, I say unto you, Never at any time,
have I declared from my own mouth that they should return, for where I am they can not come, for they have
no power;
    b. but remember that all my judgments are not given unto
men; and as the words have gone forth out of my mouth,
even so shall they be fulfilled;
    c. that the first shall be last, and the last shall be first
in all things, whatsoever I have created by the word of
my power, which is the power of my Spirit; for by the
power of my Spirit, created I them;
    d. yea, all things both spiritual and temporal: firstly

spiritual, secondly temporal, which is the beginning of my
work; and again, firstly temporal, and secondly spiritual,
which is the last of my work;

e. speaking unto you that you may naturally understand,
but unto myself my works have no end, neither beginning;
but it is given unto you that ye may understand, because
ye have asked it of me and are agreed.

9 a. Wherefore, verily I say unto you, that all things unto
me are spiritual, and not at any time have I given unto you
a law which was temporal, neither any man, nor the children of men; neither Adam your father, whom I created;

b. behold, I gave unto him that he should be an agent
unto himself; and I gave unto him commandment, but no
temporal commandment gave I unto him;

c. for my commandments are spiritual; they are not
natural, nor temporal, neither carnal nor sensual.

10 a. And it came to pass, that Adam being tempted of
the Devil, for, behold, the Devil was before Adam, for he
rebelled against me, saying,

b. Give me thine honor, which is my power; and also a
third part of the hosts of heaven turned he away from me
because of their agency;

c. and they were thrust down, and thus became the Devil
and his angels; and, behold, there is a place prepared for
them from the beginning, which place is hell;

d. and it must needs be that the Devil should tempt the
children of men, or they could not be agents unto themselves,
for if they never should have bitter, they could not know
the sweet.

11 a. Wherefore, it came to pass, that the Devil tempted
Adam and he partook the forbidden fruit, and transgressed
the commandment, wherein he became subject to the will
of the Devil, because he yielded unto temptation;

b. wherefore, I the Lord God caused that he should be
cast out from the garden of Eden. from my presence, because of his transgression:

c. wherein he became spiritually dead, which is the first
death, even that same death, which is the last death, which
is spiritual, which shall be pronounced upon the wicked
when I shall say, Depart ye cursed.

12 a. But, behold, I say unto you, that I, the Lord God, gave unto Adam and unto his seed, that they should not die as to the temporal death, until I, the Lord God, should send forth angels to declare unto them repentance and redemption through faith on the name of mine only begotten Son;

b. and thus did I, the Lord God, appoint unto man the days of his probation;

c. that by his natural death, he might be raised in immortality unto eternal life, even as many as would believe, and they that believed not, unto eternal damnation;

d. for they can not be redeemed from their spiritual fall, because they repent not, for they will love darkness rather than light, and their deeds are evil, and they receive their wages of whom they list to obey.

13 a. But, behold, I say unto you, that little children are redeemed from the foundation of the world, through mine Only Begotten; wherefore they can not sin, for power is not given unto Satan to tempt little children, until they begin to become accountable before me;

b. for it is given unto them even as I will, according to mine own pleasure, that great things may be required at the hand of their fathers.

14 a. And again I say unto you, that whoso having knowledge, have I not commanded to repent?

b. and he that hath no understanding, it remaineth in me to do according as it is written.

c. And now, I declare no more unto you at this time. Amen.

SECTION 29

Revelation given to David Whitmer, Peter Whitmer, Jr., and John Whitmer through Joseph Smith, Jr., September 1830 at Fayette, New York. It was received at the close of the second conference of the church. The Hiram Page "peepstone" difficulty (see Section 27) was in the background of the message to David Whitmer.

1 a. Behold, I say unto you, David, that you have feared man and have not relied on me for strength, as you ought;

b. but your mind has been on the things of the earth more than on the things of me, your Maker, and the ministry whereunto you have been called; and you have not given heed unto my Spirit, and to those who were set over you, but have been persuaded by those whom I have not commanded;

c. wherefore, you are left to inquire for yourself, at my hand, and ponder upon the things which you have received.

d. And your home shall be at your father's house, until I give unto you further commandments.

e. And you shall attend to the ministry in the church, and before the world, and in the regions round about. Amen.

2 a. Behold, I say unto you, Peter, that you shall take your journey with your brother, Oliver, for the time has come, that it is expedient in me, that you shall open your mouth to declare my gospel;

b. therefore, fear not but give heed unto the words and advice of your brother, which he shall give you.

c. And be you afflicted in all his afflictions, ever lifting up your heart unto me in prayer, and faith, for his and your deliverance; for I have given unto him power to build up my church among the Lamanites;

d. and none have I appointed to be his counselor, over him, in the church, concerning church matters, except it is his brother Joseph Smith, Jr.

e. Wherefore, give heed unto these things, and be diligent in keeping my commandments, and you shall be blessed unto eternal life. Amen.

3 a. Behold, I say unto you, my servant John, that thou shalt commence from this time forth to proclaim my gospel, as with the voice of a trump.

b. And your labor shall be at your brother Philip Burroughs', and in that region round about; yea, wherever you can be heard, until I command you to go from hence.

c. And your whole labor shall be in Zion, with all your soul, from henceforth; yea, you shall ever open your mouth in my cause, not fearing what man can do, for I am with you. Amen.

SECTION 30

Revelation given through Joseph Smith, Jr., at Fayette, New York, September 1830 at the close of the second conference of the church. It is addressed to Thomas B. Marsh, who had recently been baptized. Thomas is here designated as physician to the church. Later he became the first president of the Council of Twelve.

1 a. Thomas, my son, blessed are you because of your faith in my work.

b. Behold, you have had many afflictions because of your family: nevertheless I will bless you, and your family: yea, your little ones, and the day cometh that they will believe and know the truth and be one with you in my church.

2 a. Lift up your heart and rejoice, for the hour of your mission is come; and your tongue shall be loosed, and you shall declare glad tidings of great joy unto this generation.

b. You shall declare the things which have been revealed to my servant Joseph Smith, Jr.

c. You shall begin to preach from this time forth; yea, to reap in the field which is white already to be burned;

d. therefore, thrust in your sickle with all your soul; and your sins are forgiven you; and you shall be laden with sheaves upon your back, for the laborer is worthy of his hire. Wherefore your family shall live.

3 a. Behold, verily I say unto you, Go from them only for a little time, and declare my word, and I will prepare a place for them; yea, I will open the hearts of the people and they will receive you.

b. And I will establish a church by your hand; and you shall strengthen them and prepare them against the time when they shall be gathered.

c. Be patient in afflictions, revile not against those that revile. Govern your house in meekness, and be steadfast.

4 a. Behold, I say unto you, that you shall be a physician unto the church, but not unto the world, for they will not receive you.

b. Go your way whithersoever I will, and it shall be given you by the Comforter what you shall do, and whither you shall go.

c. Pray always, lest you enter into temptation, and lose your reward. Be faithful unto the end, and lo, I am with you.

d. These words are not of man nor of men, but of me, even Jesus Christ, your Redeemer, by the will of the Father. Amen.

SECTION 31

Revelation to Parley P. Pratt and Ziba Peterson, given through Joseph Smith, Jr., prophet and seer to the church, October 1830 at Fayette, New York. The appointment of Oliver Cowdery and Peter Whitmer to take the message of the Restoration to the Lamanites aroused considerable interest and enthusiasm among the ministry. This mission to the West was most important. Men were anxious to go.

1 a. And now concerning my servant Parley P. Pratt, behold, I say unto him, that as I live I will that he shall declare my gospel and learn of me, and be meek and lowly of heart;

b. and that which I have appointed unto him, is that he shall go with my servants Oliver Cowdery and Peter Whitmer, Jr., into the wilderness, among the Lamanites;

c. and Ziba Peterson, also, shall go with them, and I myself will go with them and be in their midst; and I am their Advocate with the Father, and nothing shall prevail.

d. And they shall give heed to that which is written and pretend to no other revelation, and they shall pray always that I may unfold them to their understanding;

e. and they shall give heed unto these words and trifle not, and I will bless them. Amen.

SECTION 32

Revelation given to Ezra Thayre and Northrop Sweet through the prophet, Joseph Smith, Jr., October 1830 at Fayette, New York.

1 a. Behold, I say unto you, my servants Ezra and Northrop,

b. Open ye your ears and hearken to the voice of the Lord your God, whose word is quick and powerful, sharper than a two-edged sword, to the dividing asunder of the joints and marrow, soul and spirit; and is a discerner of the thoughts and intents of the heart.

c. For verily, verily I say unto you, that ye are called to lift up your voices as with the sound of a trump, to declare my gospel unto a crooked and a perverse generation:

d. for, behold, the field is white already to harvest; and it is the eleventh hour, and for the last time that I shall call laborers into my vineyard.

e. And my vineyard has become corrupted every whit; and there is none which doeth good save it be a few; and they err in many instances, because of priestcrafts, all having corrupt minds.

2 a. And verily, verily I say unto you, that this church have I established and called forth out of the wilderness;

b. and even so will I gather mine elect from the four quarters of the earth, even as many as will believe in me, and hearken unto my voice;

c. yea, verily, verily I say unto you, that the field is white already to harvest; wherefore, thrust in your sickle, and reap with all your might, mind, and strength.

d. Open your mouths and they shall be filled; and you shall become as Nephi of old, who journeyed from Jerusalem in the wilderness;

e. yea, open your mouths and spare not, and you shall be laden with sheaves upon your backs, for lo, I am with you;

f. yea, open your mouths and they shall be filled, saying, Repent, repent and prepare ye the way of the Lord, and make his paths straight; for the kingdom of heaven is at hand;

g. yea, repent and be baptized every one of you, for the remission of your sins; yea, be baptized even by water, and then cometh the baptism of fire and the Holy Ghost.

3 a. Behold, verily, verily I say unto you, This is my gospel, and remember that they shall have faith in me, or they can in nowise be saved; and upon this Rock I will build my church;

b. yea, upon this Rock ye are built, and if ye continue, the gates of hell shall not prevail against you; and ye shall remember the church articles and covenants to keep them;

c. and whoso having faith you shall confirm in my church, by the laying on of the hands, and I will bestow the gift of the Holy Ghost upon them.

d. And the Book of Mormon, and the Holy Scriptures, are given of me for your instruction; and the power of my Spirit quickeneth all things;

e. wherefore, be faithful, praying always, having your lamps trimmed and burning, and oil with you, that you may be ready at the coming of the Bridegroom; for, behold, verily, verily I say unto you, that I come quickly; even so. Amen.

SECTION 33

Revelation given through Joseph Smith, Jr., to Orson Pratt November 1830 at Fayette, New York. Orson had recently been baptized by his brother, Parley P. Pratt. Later both he and Parley became members of the Council of Twelve.

1 a. My son Orson, hearken and hear and behold what I, the Lord God, shall say unto you, even Jesus Christ your Redeemer, the light and the life of the world; a light which shineth in darkness and the darkness comprehendeth it not;

b. who so loved the world that he gave his own life, that as many as would believe might become the sons of God;

c. wherefore you are my son, and blessed are you because you have believed, and more blessed are you because you are called of me to preach my gospel;

d. to lift up your voice as with the sound of a trump, both long and loud, and cry repentance unto a crooked and perverse generation; preparing the way of the Lord for his second coming; for, behold, verily, verily I say unto you,

e. The time is soon at hand, that I shall come in a cloud with power and great glory, and it shall be a great day at the time of my coming, for all nations shall tremble.

2 a. But before that great day shall come, the sun shall be darkened, and the moon be turned into blood, and the stars shall refuse their shining, and some shall fall, and great destructions await the wicked; wherefore lift up your voice and spare not, for the Lord God hath spoken.

b. Therefore prophesy and it shall be given by the power of the Holy Ghost; and if you are faithful, behold, I am with you until I come; and verily, verily I say unto you, I come quickly.

c. I am your Lord and your Redeemer. Even so. Amen.

SECTION 34

Revelation addressed to Sidney Rigdon, given through Joseph Smith, Jr. It was received at Fayette, New York, in December 1830. Sidney Rigdon, Edward Partridge, and others had been converted at Mentor and Kirtland, Ohio, by the missionaries going west, and these two had come to visit Joseph in order to learn more about the church. It will be noted that Sidney was immediately called into close association with Joseph. The prophet had commenced the revision of the Bible in June 1830, and this close association with Sidney was undoubtedly of great value to him.

1 a. Listen to the voice of the Lord your God, even Alpha and Omega, the beginning and the end, whose course is one eternal round, the same to-day as yesterday and for ever.

b. I am Jesus Christ, the Son of God, who was crucified for the sins of the world, even as many as will believe on my name, that they may become the sons of God, even one in me as I am in the Father, as the Father is one in me, that we may be one.

2 a. Behold, verily, verily I say unto my servant Sidney, I

have looked upon thee and thy works. I have heard thy prayers and prepared thee for a greater work.

b. Thou art blessed, for thou shalt do great things. Behold, thou wast sent forth even as John, to prepare the way before me, and before Elijah which should come, and thou knew it not.

c. Thou didst baptize by water unto repentance, but they received not the Holy Ghost; but now I give unto thee a commandment, that thou shalt baptize by water, and they shall receive the Holy Ghost by the laying on of the hands, even as the apostles of old.

3 a. And it shall come to pass, that there shall be a great work in the land, even among the Gentiles, for their folly and their abominations shall be made manifest, in the eyes of all people;

b. for I am God, and mine arm is not shortened, and I will show miracles, signs and wonders, unto all those who believe on my name.

c. And whoso shall ask it in my name, in faith, they shall cast out devils; they shall heal the sick; they shall cause the blind to receive their sight, and the deaf to hear, and the dumb to speak, and the lame to walk:

d. and the time speedily cometh that great things are to be shown forth unto the children of men; but without faith shall not anything be shown forth except desolations upon Babylon, the same which has made all nations drink of the wine of the wrath of her fornication.

e. And there are none that doeth good except those who are ready to receive the fullness of my gospel, which I have sent forth unto this generation.

4 a. Wherefore, I have called upon the weak things of the world, those who are unlearned and despised, to thresh the nations by the power of my Spirit;

b. and their arm shall be my arm, and I will be their shield and their buckler, and I will gird up their loins, and they shall fight manfully for me;

c. and their enemies shall be under their feet; and I will let fall the sword in their behalf; and by the fire of mine indignation will I preserve them.

d. And the poor and the meek shall have the gospel

preached unto them, and they shall be looking forth for the time of my coming, for it is nigh at hand;

e. and they shall learn the parable of the fig tree; for even now already summer is nigh, and I have sent forth the fullness of my gospel by the hand of my servant Joseph;

f. and in weakness have I blessed him, and I have given unto him the keys of the mystery of those things which have been sealed, even things which were from the foundation of the world, and the things which shall come from this time until the time of my coming, if he abide in me, and if not, another will I plant in his stead.

5 a. Wherefore watch over him that his faith fail not, and it shall be given by the Comforter, the Holy Ghost, that knoweth all things; and a commandment I give unto thee, that thou shalt write for him;

b. and the Scriptures shall be given even as they are in mine own bosom, to the salvation of mine own elect; for they will hear my voice, and shall see me, and shall not be asleep, and shall abide the day of my coming, for they shall be purified even as I am pure.

c. And now I say unto you, Tarry with him and he shall journey with you; forsake him not and surely these things shall be fulfilled.

d. And inasmuch as ye do not write, behold, it shall be given unto him to prophesy; and thou shalt preach my gospel; and call on the holy prophets to prove his words, as they shall be given him.

6 a. Keep all the commandments and covenants by which ye are bound, and I will cause the heavens to shake for your good, and Satan shall tremble, and Zion shall rejoice upon the hills, and flourish; and Israel shall be saved in mine own due time.

b. And by the keys which I have given shall they be led, and no more be confounded at all.

c. Lift up your hearts and be glad; your redemption draweth nigh.

d. Fear not, little flock, the kingdom is yours until I come. Behold, I come quickly. Even so. Amen.

SECTION 35

Revelation given to Edward Partridge through Joseph Smith, Jr., in December 1830 at Fayette, New York. Edward Partridge had accompanied Sidney Rigdon from Ohio. Three months later he became the first bishop of the church (D. and C. 41:3).

1 a. Thus saith the Lord God, the Mighty One of Israel, Behold, I say unto you, my servant Edward, that you are blessed, and your sins are forgiven you, and you are called to preach my gospel as with the voice of a trump;

b. and I will lay my hand upon you by the hand of my servant Sidney Rigdon, and you shall receive my Spirit, the Holy Ghost, even the Comforter, which shall teach you the peaceable things of the kingdom;

c. and you shall declare it with a loud voice, saying, Hosanna, blessed be the name of the most high God.

2 a. And now this calling and commandment give I unto you concerning all men, that as many as shall come before my servants Sidney Rigdon and Joseph Smith, Jr., embracing this calling and commandment, shall be ordained and sent forth to preach the everlasting gospel among the nations, crying repentance, saying,

b. Save yourselves from this untoward generation, and come forth out of the fire, hating even the garments spotted with the flesh.

3 a. And this commandment shall be given unto the elders of my church, that every man which will embrace it with singleness of heart, may be ordained and sent forth, even as I have spoken.

b. I am Jesus Christ, the Son of God; wherefore gird up your loins and I will suddenly come to my temple. Even so. Amen.

SECTION 36

*In June 1830 Joseph Smith began an inspired correction
of the Holy Scriptures, the necessity for which had been
pointed out in the revelation of June 1830 (D. and C. 22:24).
While engaged in this work in December 1830, Joseph received the following revelation which is an extract from the
prophecy of Enoch. This revelation now forms Genesis
7:1-78 of the Inspired Version of the Holy Scriptures. It was
given at Fayette, New York. The 1835 edition did not
include this section. It has appeared as Section 36 since
1864 and was specifically approved at the 1970 World Conference for retention in its present place.*

1 a. And it came to pass that Enoch continued his speech,
saying, Behold, our father Adam taught these things, and
many have believed and become the sons of God, and many
have believed not and perished in their sins, and are looking
forth with fear in torment, for the fiery indignation of the
wrath of God to be poured out upon them.

b. And from that time forth Enoch began to prophesy,
saying unto the people that, as I was journeying, and stood
upon the place Manhujah, I cried unto the Lord, and there
came a voice out of heaven, saying, Turn ye and get ye
upon the Mount Simeon.

c. And it came to pass that I turned and went upon the
mount, and, as I stood upon the mount, I beheld the heavens
open, and I was clothed upon with glory, and I saw the Lord;

d. he stood before my face, and he talked with me, even
as a man talks one with another, face to face; and he said
unto me, Look, and I will show unto you the world for the
space of many generations.

e. And it came to pass that I beheld the valley Shum,
and lo! a great people which dwelt in tents, which were the
people of Shum.

f. And again the Lord said unto me, Look, and I looked
toward the north, and I beheld the people of Cainan, which
dwelt in tents.

g. And the Lord said unto me, Prophesy, and I prophesied,
saying, Behold the people of Cainan, which are numerous,

shall go forth in battle array against the people of Shum, and shall slay them, that they shall utterly be destroyed;

h. and the people of Cainan shall divide themselves in the land, and the land shall be barren and unfruitful and none other people shall dwell there but the people of Cainan; for, behold, the Lord shall curse the land with much heat, and the barrenness thereof shall go forth for ever.

i. And there was blackness come unto all the children of Cainan, that they were despised among all people.

j. And it came to pass that the Lord said unto me, Look, and I looked and beheld the land of Sharon, and the land of Enoch, and the land of Omner, and the land of Heni, and the land of Shem, and the land of Haner, and the land of Hanannihah, and all the inhabitants thereof.

k. And the Lord said unto me, Go to this people and say unto them, Repent, lest I come out and smite them with a curse, and they die.

l. And he gave unto me a commandment that I should baptize in the name of the Father and the Son, which is full of grace and truth, and the Holy Spirit, which bears record of the Father and the Son.

2 a. And it came to pass that Enoch continued to call upon all the people, save it were the people of Cainan, to repent.

b. And so great was the faith of Enoch that he led the people of God, and their enemies came to battle against them, and he spake the word of the Lord, and the earth trembled, and the mountains fled, even according to his command;

c. and the rivers of water were turned out of their course, and the roar of the lions was heard out of the wilderness, and all nations feared greatly, so powerful was the word of Enoch, and so great was the power of language which God had given him.

d. There also came up a land out of the depth of the sea; and so great was the fear of the enemies of the people of God, that they fled and stood afar off, and went upon the land which came up out of the depths of the sea.

e. And the giants of the land, also, stood afar off; and there went forth a curse upon all the people which fought against God.

f. And from that time forth there were wars and bloodsheds among them; but the Lord came and dwelt with his people, and they dwelt in righteousness.

g. The fear of the Lord was upon all nations, so great was the glory of the Lord which was upon his people. And the Lord blessed the land, and they were blessed upon the mountains, and upon the high places, and did flourish.

h. And the Lord called his people Zion, because they were of one heart and one mind, and dwelt in righteousness;

i. and there was no poor among them; and Enoch continued his preaching in righteousness unto the people of God.

3 a. And it came to pass in his days that he built a city that was called the city of holiness, even ZION.

b. And it came to pass that Enoch talked with the Lord, and he said unto the Lord, Surely Zion shall dwell in safety for ever.

c. But the Lord said unto Enoch, Zion have I blessed, but the residue of the people have I cursed.

d. And it came to pass that the Lord showed unto Enoch all the inhabitants of the earth, and he beheld, and lo! Zion, in process of time, was taken up into heaven.

4 And the Lord said unto Enoch, Behold my abode for ever; and Enoch also beheld the residue of the people which were the sons of Adam, and they were a mixture of all the seed of Adam, save it were the seed of Cain, for the seed of Cain were black, and had not place among them.

5 a. And after that Zion was taken up into heaven, Enoch beheld, and lo! all the nations of the earth were before him.

b. And there came generation upon generation, and Enoch was high and lifted up, even in the bosom of the Father and the Son of man; and, behold, the power of Satan was upon all the face of the earth.

c. And he saw angels descending out of heaven, and he heard a loud voice, saying, Woe, woe be unto the inhabitants of the earth!

d. And he beheld Satan, and he had a great chain in his hand, and it veiled the whole face of the earth with darkness, and he looked up and laughed, and his angels rejoiced.

6 a. And Enoch beheld angels descending out of heaven, bearing testimony of the Father and Son; and the Holy Spirit fell on many, and they were caught up by the powers of heaven into Zion.

b. And it came to pass that the God of heaven looked upon the residue of the people, and he wept, and Enoch bore record of it, saying, How is it the heavens weep and shed forth their tears as the rain upon the mountains?

c. And Enoch said unto the Lord, How is it that you can weep, seeing you are holy, and from all eternity to all eternity?

d. And were it possible that man could number the particles of the earth, and millions of earths like this, it would not be a beginning to the number of your creations;

e. and your curtains are stretched out still, and yet you are there, and your bosom is there; and also you are just; you are merciful and kind for ever.

f. You have taken Zion to your own bosom from all your creations, from all eternity to all eternity, and naught but peace, justice, and truth is the habitation of your throne; and mercy shall go before your face, and have no end. How is it that you can weep?

7 a. The Lord said unto Enoch, Behold these your brethren; they are the workmanship of my own hands, and I gave unto them their knowledge, in the day I created them;

b. and in the garden of Eden gave I unto man his agency; and unto your brethren have I said, and also gave commandments, that they should love one another, and that they should choose me, their Father;

c. but, behold, they are without affection, and they hate their own blood, and the fire of my indignation is kindled against them, and in my hot displeasure will I send in the floods upon them, for my fierce anger is kindled against them.

d. Behold, I am God; Man of Holiness is my name; Man of Counsel is my name; and Endless and Eternal is my name, also.

e. Wherefore, I can stretch forth my hands and hold all the creations which I have made, and my eye can pierce them, also; and among all the workmanship of my hand there has not been so great wickedness as among your brethren; but, behold, their sins shall be upon the heads of their fathers.

f. Satan shall be their father, and misery shall be their doom; and the whole heavens shall weep over them, even all the workmanship of my hands.

g. Wherefore, should not the heavens weep, seeing these shall suffer?

h. But, behold, these which your eyes are upon, shall perish in the floods; and, behold, I will shut them up: a prison have I prepared for them.

i. And that which I have chosen has plead before my face. Wherefore he suffers for their sins, inasmuch as they will repent in the day that my chosen shall return unto me; and until that day they shall be in torment.

j. Wherefore, for this shall the heavens weep; yea, and all the workmanship of my hands.

8 a. And it came to pass that the Lord spake unto Enoch, and told Enoch all the doings of the children of men.

b. Wherefore Enoch knew and looked upon their wickedness and their misery, and wept and stretched forth his arms, and his heart swelled wide as eternity, and his bowels yearned, and all eternity shook.

c. And Enoch saw Noah, also, and his family, that the posterity of all the sons of Noah should be saved with a temporal salvation.

d. Wherefore he saw that Noah built an ark, and the Lord smiled upon it, and held it in his own hand; but upon the residue of the wicked came floods and swallowed them up.

e. And as Enoch saw thus, he had bitterness of soul, and wept over his brethren, and said unto the heavens, I will refuse to be comforted; but the Lord said unto Enoch, Lift up your heart and be glad, and look.

9 a. And it came to pass that Enoch looked, and, from Noah, he beheld all the families of the earth; and he cried unto the Lord, saying, When shall the day of the Lord come?

b. When shall the blood of the righteous be shed, that all they that mourn may be sanctified, and have eternal life?

c. And the Lord said, It shall be in the meridian of time, in the days of wickedness and vengeance.

d. And, behold, Enoch saw the day of the coming of the Son of Man, even in the flesh; and his soul rejoiced, saying,

The righteous is lifted up, and the Lamb is slain from the foundation of the world; and, through faith, I am in the bosom of the Father; and, behold, Zion is with me!

10 a. And it came to pass, that Enoch looked upon the earth, and he heard a voice from the bowels thereof, saying, Woe, woe is me the mother of men! I am pained: I am weary because of the wickedness of my children!

b. When shall I rest, and be cleansed from the filthiness which has gone forth out of me? When will my Creator sanctify me, that I may rest, and righteousness, for a season, abide upon my face?

c. And when Enoch heard the earth mourn, he wept, and cried unto the Lord, saying, O Lord, will you not have compassion upon the earth? Will you not bless the children of Noah?

d. And it came to pass that Enoch continued his cry unto the Lord, saying, I ask you, O Lord, in the name of your Only Begotten, even Jesus Christ, that you will have mercy upon Noah and his seed, that the earth might never more be covered by the floods?

e. And the Lord could not withhold; and he covenanted with Enoch, and swore unto him with an oath, that he would stay the floods; that he would call upon the children of Noah:

f. and he sent forth an unalterable decree, that a remnant of his seed should always be found among all nations, while the earth should stand;

g. and the Lord said, Blessed is he through whose seed Messiah shall come: for he says, I am Messiah, the King of Zion; the Rock of heaven, which is broad as eternity.

h. Whoso comes in at the gate and climbs up by me shall never fall: wherefore, blessed are they of whom I have spoken, for they shall come forth with songs of everlasting joy.

11 a. And it came to pass, that Enoch cried unto the Lord, saying, When the Son of Man comes in the flesh, shall the earth rest? I pray you show me these things.

b. And the Lord said unto Enoch, Look, and he looked and beheld the Son of Man lifted upon the cross, after the manner of men; and he heard a loud voice; and the heavens were veiled; and all the creations of God mourned; and the earth groaned; and the rocks were rent;

c. and the saints arose and were crowned at the right hand of the Son of Man, with crowns of glory; and as many of the spirits as were in prison, came forth and stood on the right hand of God; and the remainder were reserved in chains of darkness until the judgment of the great day.

d. And again, Enoch wept and cried unto the Lord, saying, When shall the earth rest?

12 a. And Enoch beheld the Son of Man ascend up unto the Father; and he called unto the Lord, saying, Will you not come again upon the earth, for inasmuch as you are God, and I know you, and you have sworn unto me, and commanded me that I should ask in the name of your Only Begotten,

b. you have made me, and given unto me a right to your throne, and not of myself, but through your own grace; wherefore, I ask you if you will not come again on the earth?

c. And the Lord said unto Enoch, As I live, even so will I come in the last days—in the days of wickedness and vengeance, to fulfill the oath which I made unto you, concerning the children of Noah:

d. and the day shall come that the earth shall rest, but before that day, shall the heavens be darkened, and a veil of darkness shall cover the earth;

e. and the heavens shall shake, and also the earth; and great tribulations shall be among the children of men, but my people will I preserve; and righteousness will I send down out of heaven; and truth will I send forth out of the earth, to bear testimony of my Only Begotten;

f. his resurrection from the dead; yea, and also the resurrection of all men; and righteousness and truth will I cause to sweep the earth as with a flood, to gather out my own elect from the four quarters of the earth unto a place which I shall prepare;

g. a holy city, that my people may gird up their loins, and be looking forth for the time of my coming; for there shall be my tabernacle, and it shall be called Zion, a New Jerusalem.

13 a. And the Lord said unto Enoch, Then shall you and

all your city meet them there, and we will receive them into our bosom, and they shall see us, and we will fall upon their necks, and they shall fall upon our necks, and we will kiss each other,

b. and there shall be my abode, and it shall be Zion which shall come forth out of all the creations which I have made; and for the space of a thousand years shall the earth rest.

14 a. And it came to pass that Enoch saw the days of the coming of the Son of Man, in the last days, to dwell on the earth in righteousness, for the space of a thousand years.

b. But before that day he saw great tribulations among the wicked; and he also saw the sea, that it was troubled, and men's hearts failing them, looking forth with fear for the judgments of the Almighty God, which should come upon the wicked.

c. And the Lord showed Enoch all things, even unto the end of the world; and he saw the day of the righteous, the hour of their redemption, and received a fullness of joy:

d. and all the days of Zion in the days of Enoch, were three hundred and sixty-five years:

e. and Enoch and all his people walked with God, and he dwelt in the midst of Zion: and it came to pass that Zion was not, for God received it up into his own bosom; and from thence went forth the saying, Zion is fled.

SECTION 37

Revelation given through Joseph Smith, Jr., to Joseph and Sidney Rigdon in December 1830. It led to a temporary suspension of their work on the Inspired Version, and called for the removal of the body of the Saints to Ohio. There was already a strong nucleus in the Kirtland area.

1 a. Behold, I say unto you, that it is not expedient in me that ye should translate any more until ye shall go to the Ohio; and this because of the enemy and for your sakes.

b. And again, I say unto you, that ye shall not go until ye have preached my gospel in those parts, and have strengthened up the church whithersoever it is found, and more especially in Colesville; for, behold, they pray unto me in much faith.

2 a. And again a commandment I give unto the church, that it is expedient in me that they should assemble together at the Ohio, against the time that my servant Oliver Cowdery shall return unto them.

b. Behold, here is wisdom, and let every man choose for himself until I come. Even so. Amen.

SECTION 38

Revelation given to Joseph Smith, Jr., at Fayette, New York, in the opening days of 1831. It gives basic instruction concerning the work of the priesthood, the principle of stewardship, and the care of the poor. It was in preparation for the gathering to Ohio for which the Saints were already making preparation.

1 a. Thus saith the Lord your God, even Jesus Christ, the great I AM, Alpha and Omega, the beginning and the end, the same which looked upon the wide expanse of eternity, and all the seraphic hosts of heaven, before the world was made;

b. the same which knoweth all things, for all things are present before mine eyes: I am the same which spake and the world was made, and all things came by me: I am the same which have taken the Zion of Enoch into mine own bosom;

c. and verily I say, even as many as have believed on my name, for I am Christ, and in mine own name, by virtue of the blood which I have spilt, have I plead before the Father for them:

d. but, behold, the residue of the wicked have I kept in chains of darkness until the judgment of the great day, which shall come at the end of the earth;

e. and even so will I cause the wicked to be kept, that will not hear my voice but harden their hearts, and woe, woe, woe is their doom.

2 a. But, behold, verily, verily I say unto you, that mine eyes are upon you:

b. I am in your midst and ye can not see me, but the day soon cometh that ye shall see me and know that I am; for the veil of darkness shall soon be rent, and he that is not purified shall not abide the day: wherefore, gird up your loins and be prepared.

c. Behold, the kingdom is yours and the enemy shall not overcome.

3 a. Verily I say unto you, Ye are clean but not all; and there is none else with whom I am well pleased, for all flesh is corruptible before me,

b. and the powers of darkness prevail upon the earth, among the children of men, in the presence of all the hosts of heaven, which causeth silence to reign, and all eternity is pained,

c. and the angels are waiting the great command to reap down the earth, to gather the tares that they may be burned; and, behold, the enemy is combined.

4 a. And now I show unto you a mystery, a thing which is had in secret chambers, to bring to pass even your destruction, in process of time, and ye knew it not, but now I tell it unto you,

b. and ye are blessed, not because of your iniquity, neither your hearts of unbelief, for verily some of you are guilty before me; but I will be merciful unto your weakness.

c. Therefore, be ye strong from henceforth; fear not for the kingdom is yours: and for your salvation I give unto you a commandment, for I have heard your prayers, and the poor have complained before me, and the rich have I made, and all flesh is mine, and I am no respecter of persons.

d. And I have made the earth rich, and, behold, it is my footstool: wherefore, again I will stand upon it; and I hold forth and deign to give unto you greater riches, even a land of promise;

e. a land flowing with milk and honey, upon which there shall be no curse when the Lord cometh; and I will give it unto you for the land of your inheritance, if you seek it with all your hearts:

f. and this shall be my covenant with you, Ye shall have it for the land of your inheritance, and for the inheritance of your children for ever, while the earth shall stand; and ye shall possess it again in eternity, no more to pass away.

5 a. But verily I say unto you, that, in time, ye shall have no king nor ruler, for I will be your king and watch over you.

b. Wherefore, hear my voice and follow me, and you shall be a free people, and ye shall have no laws but my laws, when I come, for I am your lawgiver, and what can stay my hand?

c. But verily I say unto you, Teach one another according to the office wherewith I have appointed you, and let every man esteem his brother as himself, and practice virtue and holiness before me.

d. And again I say unto you, Let every man esteem his brother as himself: for what man among you having twelve sons, and is no respecter to them, and they serve him obediently, and he saith unto the one, Be thou clothed in robes and sit thou here; and to the other, Be thou clothed in rags and sit thou there, and looketh upon his sons and saith, I am just.

6 a. Behold, this I have given unto you a parable, and it is even as I am: I say unto you, Be one; and if ye are not one, ye are not mine.

b. And again I say unto you, that the enemy in the secret chambers seeketh your lives.

c. Ye hear of wars in far countries, and you say that there will soon be great wars in far countries, but ye know not the hearts of men in your own land.

d. I tell you these things because of your prayers; wherefore, treasure up wisdom in your bosoms, lest the wickedness of men reveal these things unto you, by their wickedness, in a manner that shall speak in your ears, with a voice louder than that which shall shake the earth: but if ye are prepared, ye shall not fear.

7 a. And that ye might escape the power of the enemy, and be gathered unto me a righteous people, without spot and blameless:

b. wherefore, for this cause I gave unto you the commandment, that you should go to the Ohio; and there I will give unto you my law;

c. and there you shall be endowed with power from on

high, and from thence, whosoever I will, shall go forth among all nations, and it shall be told them what they shall do;

d. for I have a great work laid up in store, for Israel shall be saved, and I will lead them whithersoever I will, and no power shall stay my hand.

8 a. And now I give unto the church in these parts, a commandment, that certain men among them shall be appointed, and they shall be appointed by the voice of the church;

b. and they shall look to the poor and the needy, and administer to their relief, that they shall not suffer; and send them forth to the place which I have commanded them;

c. and this shall be their work, to govern the affairs of the property of this church.

d. And they that have farms that can not be sold, let them be left or rented as seemeth them good.

e. See that all things are preserved, and when men are endowed with power from on high, and sent forth, all these things shall be gathered unto the bosom of the church.

9 a. And if ye seek the riches which it is the will of the Father to give unto you, ye shall be the richest of all people; for ye shall have the riches of eternity;

b. and it must needs be that the riches of the earth are mine to give: but beware of pride, lest ye become as the Nephites of old.

c. And again I say unto you, I give unto you a commandment, that every man, both elder, priest, teacher, and also member, go to with his might, with the labor of his hands, to prepare and accomplish the things which I have commanded.

d. And let your preaching be the warning voice, every man to his neighbor, in mildness and in meekness.

e. And go ye out from among the wicked. Save yourselves. Be ye clean that bear the vessels of the Lord. Even so. Amen.

SECTION 39

*Revelation given through Joseph Smith, Jr., January 1831,
at Fayette, New York. This message was addressed to James
Covill, a Baptist minister, who had sought light concerning
his relation to the Restoration movement.*

1 a. Hearken and listen to the voice of him who is from
all eternity to all eternity, the great I AM, even Jesus Christ,
the light and the life of the world; a light which shineth in
darkness, and the darkness comprehendeth it not;

b. the same which came in the meridian of time unto my
own, and my own received me not;

c. but to as many as received me, gave I power to become
my sons, and even so will I give unto as many as will receive me, power to become my sons.

2 a. And verily, verily I say unto thee, He that receiveth
my gospel, receiveth me; and he that receiveth not my gospel, receiveth not me.

b. And this is my gospel: repentance and baptism by
water, and then cometh the baptism of fire and the Holy
Ghost, even the Comforter, which showeth all things, and
teacheth the peaceable things of the kingdom.

3 a. And now, behold, I say unto thee, my servant James,
I have looked upon thy works, and I know thee; and verily
I say unto thee, Thine heart is now right before me at this
time, and, behold, I have bestowed great blessings upon thy
head;

b. nevertheless thou hast seen great sorrow, for thou hast
rejected me many times because of pride, and the cares of
the world;

c. but, behold, the days of thy deliverance are come, if
thou wilt hearken to my voice, which saith unto thee, Arise
and be baptized, and wash away thy sins, calling on my name,
and thou shalt receive my Spirit, and a blessing so great as
thou hast never known.

d. And if thou doest this, I have prepared thee for a
greater work.

e. Thou shalt preach the fullness of my gospel which I
have sent forth in these last days; the covenant which I have

sent forth to recover my people, which are of the house of Israel.

4 a. And it shall come to pass that power shall rest upon thee; thou shalt have great faith and I will be with thee and go before thy face.

b. Thou art called to labor in my vineyard, and to build up my church, and to bring forth Zion, that it may rejoice upon the hills and flourish.

c. Behold, verily, verily I say unto thee, Thou art not called to go into the eastern countries, but thou art called to go to the Ohio.

d. And inasmuch as my people shall assemble themselves to the Ohio, I have kept in store a blessing such as is not known among the children of men, and it shall be poured forth upon their heads. And from thence men shall go forth into all nations.

5 a. Behold, verily, verily I say unto thee, that the people in Ohio call upon me in much faith, thinking I will stay my hand in judgment upon the nations, but I can not deny my word; wherefore lay to with thy might and call faithful laborers into my vineyard, that it may be pruned for the last time.

b. And inasmuch as they do repent and receive the fullness of my gospel, and become sanctified, I will stay mine hand in judgment; wherefore, go forth, crying with a loud voice, saying, The kingdom of heaven is at hand; crying, Hosanna! blessed be the name of the most high God.

c. Go forth baptizing with water, preparing the way before my face, for the time of my coming; for the time is at hand; the day nor the hour no man knoweth; but it surely shall come, and he that receiveth these things receiveth me; and they shall be gathered unto me in time and in eternity.

6 And again, it shall come to pass, that on as many as ye shall baptize with water, ye shall lay your hands, and they shall receive the gift of the Holy Ghost, and shall be looking forth for the signs of my coming, and shall know me. Behold, I come quickly. Even so. Amen.

SECTION 40

Revelation addressed to Joseph Smith, Jr., and Sidney Rigdon. It was received through Joseph at Fayette, New York, January 1831, and is a sequel to the revelation given to James Covill (D. and C. 39).

1 a. Behold, verily I say unto you, that the heart of my servant James Covill was right before me, for he covenanted with me, that he would obey my word.

b. And he received the word with gladness, but straightway Satan tempted him; and the fear of persecution, and the cares of the world, caused him to reject the word; wherefore he broke my covenant,

c. and it remaineth with me to do with him as seemeth me good. Amen.

SECTION 41

Revelation given through Joseph Smith, Jr., February 4, 1831. This was the first revelation received in Kirtland, Ohio, Joseph having arrived shortly before this time. It should be noted that while the revelation is addressed to the whole church, special responsibilities are placed on the elders in connection with the administration of church affairs.

1 a. Hearken and hear, O ye my people, saith the Lord and your God, ye whom I delight to bless with the greatest blessings; ye that hear me: and ye that hear me not will I curse, that have professed my name, with the heaviest of all cursings.

b. Hearken, O ye elders of my church whom I have called: behold, I give unto you a commandment, that ye shall assemble yourselves together to agree upon my word, and by the prayer of your faith ye shall receive my law, that ye may know how to govern my church, and have all things right before me.

2 a. And I will be your Ruler when I come; and, behold, I come quickly; and ye shall see that my law is kept.

b. He that receiveth my law and doeth it, the same is my disciple; and he that saith he receiveth it and doeth it not, the same is not my disciple, and shall be cast out from among you;

c. for it is not meet that the things which belong to the children of the kingdom, should be given to them that are not worthy, or to dogs, or the pearls to be cast before swine.

3 a. And again, it is meet that my servant Joseph Smith, Jr., should have a house built, in which to live and translate.

b. And again, it is meet that my servant Sidney Rigdon should live as seemeth him good, inasmuch as he keepeth my commandments.

c. And again, I have called my servant Edward Partridge, and give a commandment, that he should be appointed by the voice of the church, and ordained a bishop unto the church, to leave his merchandise and spend all his time in the labors of the church; to see to all things as it shall be appointed unto him in my laws in the day that I shall give them.

d. And this because his heart is pure before me, for he is like unto Nathaniel of old, in whom there is no guile.

e. These words are given unto you, and they are pure before me; wherefore, beware how you hold them, for they are to be answered upon your souls in the day of judgment. Even so. Amen.

SECTION 42

Revelation given through Joseph Smith, Jr., and addressed to the elders of the church. It was given February 9, 1831, in the presence of twelve elders who had assembled at Kirtland, Ohio, in harmony with instruction given them in an earlier revelation (D. and C. 41:1b). In the 1835 edition of the Doctrine and Covenants this revelation appears as Section 13, and is headed "Laws of the Church."

1 a. Hearken, O ye elders of my church, who have assembled themselves together, in my name, even Jesus Christ, the

Son of the living God, the Savior of the world, inasmuch as they believe on my name and keep my commandments;

b. again I say unto you, Hearken and hear and obey the law which I shall give unto you; for verily I say,

c. As ye have assembled yourselves together according to the commandment wherewith I commanded you, and are agreed as touching this one thing, and have asked the Father in my name, even so ye shall receive.

2 a. Behold, verily I say unto you, I give unto you this first commandment, that ye shall go forth in my name, every one of you, excepting my servants Joseph Smith, Jr., and Sidney Rigdon.

b. And I give unto them a commandment that they shall go forth for a little season, and it shall be given by the power of my Spirit when they shall return;

c. and ye shall go forth in the power of my Spirit, preaching my gospel, two by two, in my name, lifting up your voices as with the voice of a trump, declaring my word like unto angels of God;

d. and ye shall go forth baptizing with water, saying, Repent ye, repent ye, for the kingdom of heaven is at hand.

3 a. And from this place ye shall go forth into the regions westward;

b. and inasmuch as ye shall find them that will receive you, ye shall build up my church in every region, until the time shall come when it shall be revealed unto you from on high, when the city of the New Jerusalem shall be prepared, that ye may be gathered in one, that ye may be my people, and I will be your God.

c. And again, I say unto you, that my servant Edward Partridge shall stand in the office wherewith I have appointed him. And it shall come to pass that if he transgress, another shall be appointed in his stead. Even so. Amen.

4 Again I say unto you that it shall not be given to anyone to go forth to preach my gospel, or to build up my church, except he be ordained by some one who has authority, and it is known to the church that he has authority, and has been regularly ordained by the heads of the church.

5 a. And again, the elders, priests, and teachers of this church shall teach the principles of my gospel which are in the Bible and the Book of Mormon, in which is the fullness of the gospel;

b. and they shall observe the covenants and church articles to do them, and these shall be their teachings, as they shall be directed by the Spirit; and the Spirit shall be given unto you by the prayer of faith, and if ye receive not the Spirit ye shall not teach.

c. And all this ye shall observe to do as I have commanded concerning your teaching, until the fullness of my Scriptures is given.

d. And as ye shall lift up your voices by the Comforter, ye shall speak and prophesy as seemeth me good; for, behold, the Comforter knoweth all things, and beareth record of the Father and of the Son.

6 And now, behold, I speak unto the church. Thou shalt not kill; and he that kills shall not have forgiveness in this world, nor in the world to come.

7 a. And again, I say, Thou shalt not kill; but he that killeth shall die.

b. Thou shalt not steal; and he that stealeth and will not repent, shall be cast out.

c. Thou shalt not lie; he that lieth and will not repent, shall be cast out.

d. Thou shalt love thy wife with all thy heart, and shall cleave unto her and none else; and he that looketh upon a woman to lust after her, shall deny the faith, and shall not have the Spirit; and if he repents not, he shall be cast out.

e. Thou shalt not commit adultery; and he that committeth adultery and repenteth not, shall be cast out; but he that hath committed adultery and repents with all his heart, and forsaketh it, and doeth it no more, thou shalt forgive; but if he doeth it again, he shall not be forgiven, but shall be cast out.

f. Thou shalt not speak evil of thy neighbor, nor do him any harm.

g. Thou knowest my laws concerning these things are given in my Scriptures; he that sinneth and repenteth not, shall be cast out.

8 a. If thou lovest me, thou shalt serve me and keep all my commandments.

b. And, behold, thou wilt remember the poor, and consecrate of thy properties for their support, that which thou hast to impart unto them, with a covenant and a deed which can not be broken;

c. and inasmuch as ye impart of your substance unto the poor, ye will do it unto me, and it shall be laid before the bishop of my church and his counselors, two of the elders, or high priests, such as he shall or has appointed and set apart for that purpose.

9 a. And it shall come to pass that after they are laid before the bishop of my church, and after that he has received these testimonies concerning the consecration of the properties of my church, that they can not be taken from the church, agreeable to my commandments;

b. every man shall be made accountable unto me a steward over his own property, or that which he has received by consecration, inasmuch as is sufficient for himself and family.

10 a. And again, if there shall be properties in the hands of the church, or any individuals of it, more than is necessary for their support, after this first consecration, which is a residue, to be consecrated unto the bishop, it shall be kept to administer unto those who have not, from time to time, that every man who has need may be amply supplied, and receive according to his wants.

b. Therefore, the residue shall be kept in my storehouse, to administer to the poor and the needy, as shall be appointed by the high council of the church, and the bishop and his council, and for the purpose of purchasing lands for the public benefit of the church, and building houses of worship,

c. and building up of the New Jerusalem which is hereafter to be revealed, that my covenant people may be gathered in one, in that day when I shall come to my temple. And this I do for the salvation of my people.

11 a. And it shall come to pass that he that sinneth and repenteth not, shall be cast out of the church, and shall not

receive again that which he has consecrated unto the poor and the needy of my church, or, in other words, unto me;

b. for inasmuch as ye do it unto the least of these, ye do it unto me; for it shall come to pass that which I spake by the mouths of my prophets shall be fulfilled;

c. for I will consecrate of the riches of those who embrace my gospel, among the Gentiles, unto the poor of my people who are of the house of Israel.

12 a. And again, thou shalt not be proud in thy heart; let all thy garments be plain, and their beauty the beauty of the work of thine own hands, and let all things be done in cleanliness before me.

b. Thou shalt not be idle; for he that is idle shall not eat the bread nor wear the garments of the laborer.

c. And whosoever among you are sick, and have not faith to be healed, but believe, shall be nourished with all tenderness with herbs and mild food, and that not by the hand of an enemy.

d. And the elders of the church, two or more, shall be called, and shall pray for, and lay their hands upon them in my name; and if they die, they shall die unto me, and if they live, they shall live unto me.

e. Thou shalt live together in love, insomuch that thou shalt weep for the loss of them that die, and more especially for those that have not hope of a glorious resurrection.

f. And it shall come to pass that those that die in me shall not taste of death, for it shall be sweet unto them; and they that die not in me, woe unto them, for their death is bitter.

13 a. And again, it shall come to pass, that he that has faith in me to be healed, and is not appointed unto death, shall be healed; he who has faith to see shall see; he who has faith to hear shall hear, the lame who have faith to leap shall leap;

b. and they who have not faith to do these things, but believe in me, have power to become my sons; and inasmuch as they break not my laws, thou shalt bear their infirmities.

14 a. Thou shalt stand in the place of thy stewardship; thou shalt not take thy brother's garment; thou shalt pay for that which thou shalt receive of thy brother;

b. and if thou obtainest more than that which would be

for thy support, thou shalt give it unto my storehouse, that all things may be done according to that which I have said.

15 a. Thou shalt ask, and my Scriptures shall be given as I have appointed, and they shall be preserved in safety; and it is expedient that thou shouldst hold thy peace concerning them, and not teach them until thou hast received them in full.

b. And I give unto you a commandment, that then ye shall teach them unto all men; for they shall be taught unto all nations, kindreds, tongues, and people.

16 a. Thou shalt take the things which thou hast received, which have been given unto thee in my Scriptures for a law, to be my law, to govern my church;

b. and he that doeth according to these things, shall be saved, and he that doeth them not shall be damned, if he continues.

17 a. If thou shalt ask, thou shalt receive revelation upon revelation, knowledge upon knowledge, that thou mayest know the mysteries, and peaceable things; that which bringeth joy, that which bringeth life eternal.

b. Thou shalt ask, and it shall be revealed unto thee in mine own due time, where the New Jerusalem shall be built.

18 a. And, behold, it shall come to pass, that my servants shall be sent forth to the east, and to the west, to the north, and to the south; and even now, let him that goeth to the east, teach them that shall be converted to flee to the west; and this in consequence of that which is coming on the earth, and of secret combinations.

b. Behold, thou shalt observe all these things, and great shall be thy reward; for unto thee it is given to know the mysteries of the kingdom, but unto the world it is not given to know them.

c. Ye shall observe the laws which ye have received, and be faithful.   And ye shall hereafter receive church covenants, such as shall be sufficient to establish you, both here, and in the New Jerusalem.

d. Therefore, he that lacketh wisdom, let him ask of me, and I will give him liberally, and upbraid him not.

e. Lift up your hearts and rejoice, for unto you the king-dom, or in other words, the keys of the church, have been given. Even so. Amen.

19 a. The priests and teachers shall have their steward-ships, even as the members; and the elders, or high priests who are appointed to assist the bishop as counselors, in all things are to have their families supported out of the prop-erty which is consecrated to the bishop,

b. for the good of the poor, and for other purposes, as before mentioned, or they are to receive a just remuneration for all their services; either a stewardship, or otherwise, as may be thought best, or decided by the counselors and bishop.

c. And the bishop also shall receive his support, or a just remuneration for all his services, in the church.

20 a. Behold, verily I say unto you, that whatever persons among you having put away their companions for the cause of fornication, or in other words, if they shall testify before you in all lowliness of heart that this is the case, ye shall not cast them out from among you;

b. but if ye shall find that any persons have left their com-panions for the sake of adultery, and they themselves are the offenders, and their companions are living, they shall be cast out from among you.

c. And again I say unto you, that ye shall be watchful and careful, with all inquiry, that ye receive none such among you if they are married, and if they are not married, they shall repent of all their sins, or ye shall not receive them.

21 a. And again, every person who belongeth to this church of Christ shall observe to keep all the command-ments and covenants of the church.

b. And it shall come to pass, that if any persons among you shall kill, they shall be delivered up and dealt with according to the laws of the land;

c. for remember that he hath no forgiveness; and it shall be proven according to the laws of the land.

22 a. And if any man or woman shall commit adultery, he or she shall be tried before two elders of the church or

more, and every word shall be established against him or her
by two witnesses of the church, and not of the enemy;

b. but if there are more than two witnesses it is better;
but he or she shall be condemned by the mouth of two
witnesses,

c. and the elders shall lay the case before the church, and
the church shall lift up their hands against him or her, that
they may be dealt with according to the law of God.

d. And if it can be, it is necessary that the bishop is
present also.

e. And thus ye shall do in all cases which shall come before you.

f. And if a man or woman shall rob, he or she shall be
delivered up unto the law of the land.

g. And if he or she shall steal, he or she shall be delivered up unto the law of the land.

h. And if he or she shall lie, he or she shall be delivered up unto the law of the land.

i. If he or she do any manner of iniquity, he or she
shall be delivered up unto the law, even that of God.

23 a. And if thy brother or sister offend thee, thou shalt
take him or her between him or her and thee alone; and if he
or she confess, thou shalt be reconciled.

b. And if he or she confess not, thou shalt deliver him or
her up unto the church, not to the members, but to the elders.

c. And it shall be done in a meeting, and that not before
the world.

d. And if thy brother or sister offend many, he or she
shall be chastened before many.

e. And if anyone offend openly, he or she shall be rebuked openly, that he or she may be ashamed.

f. And if he or she confess not, he or she shall be delivered up unto the law of God.

g. If any shall offend in secret, he or she shall be rebuked
in secret, that he or she may have opportunity to confess
in secret to him or her whom he or she has offended, and to
God, that the church may not speak reproachfully of him
or her.

h. And thus shall ye conduct in all things.

SECTION 43

Revelation given through Joseph Smith, Jr., February 1831 at Kirtland, Ohio. It is addressed to the elders of the church, and contains directions sought by Joseph for the guidance of some who had been misled by a Mrs. Hubble, who claimed to have received "revelations" concerning the government of the church. A similar difficulty had arisen in connection with Hiram Page's "peepstone" (see Section 27). The church was not again disturbed over this question until the death of Joseph Smith in 1844.

1 a. O hearken, ye elders of my church, and give ear to the words which I shall speak unto you: for, behold, verily, verily I say unto you, that ye have received a commandment for a law unto my church, through him whom I have appointed unto you, to receive commandments and revelations from my hand.

b. And this ye shall know assuredly, that there is none other appointed unto you to receive commandments and revelations until he be taken, if he abide in me.

2 a. But verily, verily I say unto you, that none else shall be appointed unto this gift except it be through him, for if it be taken from him he shall not have power, except to appoint another in his stead;

b. and this shall be a law unto you, that ye receive not the teachings of any that shall come before you as revelations, or commandments; and this I give unto you, that you may not be deceived, that you may know they are not of me.

c. For verily I say unto you, that he that is ordained of me, shall come in at the gate and be ordained as I have told you before, to teach those revelations which you have received, and shall receive through him whom I have appointed.

3 a. And now, behold, I give unto you a commandment, that when ye are assembled together, ye shall instruct and edify each other, that ye may know how to act and direct my church how to act upon the points of my law and commandments, which I have given;

b. and thus ye shall become instructed in the law of my church, and be sanctified by that which ye have received, and ye shall bind yourselves to act in all holiness before me, that inasmuch as ye do this, glory shall be added to the kingdom which ye have received.

c. Inasmuch as ye do it not, it shall be taken; even that which ye have received.

d. Purge ye out the iniquity which is among you; sanctify yourselves before me, and if ye desire the glories of the kingdom, appoint ye my servant Joseph Smith, Jr., and uphold him before me by the prayer of faith.

e. And again, I say unto you, that if ye desire the mysteries of the kingdom, provide for him food and raiment and whatsoever thing he needeth to accomplish the work, wherewith I have commanded him;

f. and if ye do it not, he shall remain unto them that have received him, that I may reserve unto myself a pure people before me.

4 a. Again I say, hearken ye elders of my church whom I have appointed:

b. ye are not sent forth to be taught, but to teach the children of men the things which I have put into your hands by the power of my Spirit;

c. and ye are to be taught from on high.

d. Sanctify yourselves and ye shall be endowed with power, that ye may give even as I have spoken.

5 a. Hearken ye, for, behold, the great day of the Lord is nigh at hand.

b. For the day cometh that the Lord shall utter his voice out of heaven; the heavens shall shake and the earth shall tremble, and the trump of God shall sound both long and loud, and shall say to the sleeping nations;

c. Ye saints arise and live: Ye sinners stay and sleep until I shall call again: wherefore gird up your loins, lest ye be found among the wicked. Lift up your voices and spare not.

d. Call upon the nations to repent, both old and young, both bond and free; saying,

e. Prepare yourselves for the great day of the Lord: for if I, who am a man, do lift up my voice and call upon you

to repent, and ye hate me, what will ye say when the day
cometh when the thunders shall utter their voices from the
ends of the earth, speaking to the ears of all that live, saying:

f. Repent, and prepare for the great day of the Lord; yea,
and again, when the lightnings shall streak forth from the
east unto the west, and shall utter forth their voices unto all
that live, and make the ears of all tingle, that hear, saying
these words:

g. Repent ye, for the great day of the Lord is come.

6 a. And again, the Lord shall utter his voice out of
heaven, saying: Hearken, O ye nations of the earth, and hear
the words of that God who made you.

b. O, ye nations of the earth, how often would I have
gathered you together as a hen gathereth her chickens under
her wings, but ye would not?

c. How oft have I called upon you by the mouth of my
servants, and by the ministering of angels, and by mine own
voice, and by the voice of thunderings, and by the voice of
lightnings, and by the voice of tempests, and by the voice
of earthquakes, and great hailstorms, and by the voice of
famines and pestilences of every kind, and by the great
sound of a trump, and by the voice of judgment, and by
the voice of mercy all the day long, and by the voice of
glory and honor, and the riches of eternal life, and would
have saved you with an everlasting salvation, but ye would
not?

d. Behold, the day has come, when the cup of the wrath
of mine indignation is full.

7 a. Behold, verily I say unto you, that these are the
words of the Lord your God; wherefore, labor ye, labor
ye in my vineyard for the last time:

b. for the last time call upon the inhabitants of the earth,
for in my own due time will I come upon the earth in
judgment; and my people shall be redeemed and shall reign
with me on earth;

c. for the great millennial, which I have spoken by the
mouth of my servants, shall come; for Satan shall be bound;
and when he is loosed again, he shall only reign for a little
season, and then cometh the end of the earth;

d. and he that liveth in righteousness, shall be changed in the twinkling of an eye;

e. and the earth shall pass away so as by fire;

f. and the wicked shall go away into unquenchable fire;

g. and their end no man knoweth, on earth, nor ever shall know, until they come before me in judgment.

8 a. Hearken ye to these words, behold, I am Jesus Christ, the Savior of the world.

b. Treasure these things up in your hearts, and let the solemnities of eternity rest upon your minds.

c. Be sober. Keep all my commandments. Even so. Amen.

SECTION 44

Revelation given through Joseph Smith, Jr., at Kirtland, Ohio, February 1831. Two urgent problems prompted the prayers which led to this revelation: the need for enough members to enable the Saints to organize for their work and the economic situation in Kirtland. The poor were in great distress.

1 a. Behold, thus saith the Lord unto you, my servants,

b. It is expedient in me that the elders of my church should be called together, from the east, and from the west, and from the north, and from the south, by letter, or some other way.

2 a. And it shall come to pass, that inasmuch as they are faithful, and exercise faith in me, I will pour out my Spirit upon them in the day that they assemble themselves together.

b. And it shall come to pass that they shall go forth into the regions round about, and preach repentance unto the people;

c. and many shall be converted, insomuch that ye shall obtain power to organize yourselves according to the laws of man, that your enemies may not have power over you, that you may be preserved in all things, that you may be enabled to keep my laws, that every band may be broken where-with the enemy seeketh to destroy my people.

3 Behold, I say unto you, that ye must visit the poor and the needy, and administer to their relief, that they may be kept until all things may be done according to my law, which ye have received. Amen.

SECTION 45

Revelation given through Joseph Smith, Jr., March 7, 1831, at Kirtland, Ohio. In connection with this manifestation Joseph wrote: "To the joy of the Saints who had to struggle against everything that prejudice and wickedness could invent, I received the following:"

1 a. Hearken, O ye people of my church, to whom the kingdom has been given, hearken ye, and give ear to him who laid the foundation of the earth, who made the heavens and all the hosts thereof, and by whom all things were made which live and move and have a being.

b. And again I say, Hearken unto my voice, lest death shall overtake you; in an hour when ye think not, the summer shall be past, and the harvest ended, and your souls not saved.

c. Listen to him who is the Advocate with the Father, who is pleading your cause before him, saying,

d. Father, behold the sufferings and death of him who did no sin, in whom thou wast well pleased; behold the blood of thy Son which was shed, the blood of him whom thou gavest that thyself might be glorified;

e. wherefore, Father, spare these my brethren that believe on my name, that they may come unto me and have everlasting life.

2 a. Hearken, O ye people of my church, and ye elders, listen together, and hear my voice, while it is called today, and harden not your hearts;

b. for verily I say unto you that I am Alpha and Omega, the beginning and the end, the light and the life of the world; a light that shineth in darkness, and the darkness comprehendeth it not.

c. I came unto my own, and my own received me not; but unto as many as received me gave I power to do many miracles and to become the sons of God, and even unto them that believed on my name gave I power to obtain eternal life.

d. And even so I have sent mine everlasting covenant into the world, to be a light to the world, and to be a standard for my people and for the Gentiles to seek to it, and to be a messenger before my face to prepare the way before me.

e. Wherefore come ye unto it; and with him that cometh I will reason as with men in days of old, and I will show unto you my strong reasoning;

f. wherefore hearken ye together, and let me show it unto you, even my wisdom, the wisdom of him who ye say is the God of Enoch and his brethren, who were separated from the earth, and were received unto myself;

g. a city reserved until a day of righteousness shall come:

h. a day which was sought for by all holy men, and they found it not, because of wickedness and abominations, and confessed that they were strangers and pilgrims on the earth, but obtained a promise that they should find it, and see it in their flesh.

i. Wherefore hearken, and I will reason with you, and I will speak unto you and prophesy, as unto men in days of old;

j. and I will show it plainly, as I showed it unto my disciples, as I stood before them in the flesh, and spake unto them, saying,

k. As ye have asked of me concerning the signs of my coming, in the day when I shall come in my glory in the clouds of heaven, to fulfill the promises that I have made unto your fathers;

l. for as ye have looked upon the long absence of your spirits from your bodies to be a bondage, I will show unto you how the day of redemption shall come, and also the restoration of the scattered Israel.

3 a. And now ye behold this temple which is in Jerusalem, which ye call the house of God, and your enemies say that this house shall never fall.

b. But verily I say unto you that desolation shall come upon this generation as a thief in the night, and this people shall be destroyed and scattered among all nations.

c. And this temple which ye now see shall be thrown down, that there shall not be left one stone upon another.

d. And it shall come to pass that this generation of Jews shall not pass away until every desolation which I have told you concerning them shall come to pass.

e. Ye say that ye know that the end of the world cometh; ye say, also, that ye know that the heavens and the earth shall pass away; and in this ye say truly, for so it is; but these things which I have told you shall not pass away until all shall be fulfilled.

f. And this I have told you concerning Jerusalem; and when that day shall come, shall a remnant be scattered among all nations, but they shall be gathered again; but they shall remain until the times of the Gentiles be fulfilled.

4 a. And in that day shall be heard of wars and rumors of wars, and the whole earth shall be in commotion, and men's hearts shall fail them, and they shall say that Christ delayeth his coming until the end of the earth.

b. And the love of men shall wax cold, and iniquity shall abound; and when the time of the Gentiles is come in, a light shall break forth among them that sit in darkness, and it shall be the fullness of my gospel;

c. but they receive it not, for they perceive not the light, and they turn their hearts from me because of the precepts of men;

d. and in that generation shall the times of the Gentiles be fulfilled; and there shall be men standing in that generation that shall not pass, until they shall see an overflowing scourge, for a desolating sickness shall come over the land;

e. but my disciples shall stand in holy places, and shall not be moved; but among the wicked, men shall lift up their voices and curse God, and die.

f. And there shall be earthquakes, also, in divers places and many desolations; yet men will harden their hearts against me, and they will take up the sword one against another, and they will kill one another.

5 a. And now, when I the Lord had spoken these words unto my disciples, they were troubled;

b. and I said unto them, Be not troubled, for when all these things shall come to pass, ye may know that the promises which have been made unto you shall be fulfilled;

c. and when the light shall begin to break forth, it shall be with them like unto a parable which I shall show you;

d. ye look and behold the fig trees, and ye see them with your eyes, and ye say, when they begin to shoot forth and their leaves are yet tender, that summer is now nigh at hand;

e. even so it shall be in that day, when they shall see all these things, then shall they know that the hour is nigh.

6 a. And it shall come to pass that he that feareth me shall be looking forth for the great day of the Lord to come, even for the signs of the coming of the Son of Man;

b. and they shall see signs and wonders, for they shall be shown forth in the heavens above, and in the earth beneath;

c. and they shall behold blood and fire, and vapors of smoke; and before the day of the Lord shall come, the sun shall be darkened, and the moon be turned into blood, and stars fall from heaven;

d. and the remnant shall be gathered unto this place; and then they shall look for me, and behold I will come;

e. and they shall see me in the clouds of heaven, clothed with power and great glory, with all the holy angels; and he that watches not for me shall be cut off.

7 a. But before the arm of the Lord shall fall, an angel shall sound his trump, and the saints that have slept, shall come forth to meet me in the cloud;

b. wherefore if ye have slept in peace, blessed are you, for as you now behold me and know that I am, even so shall ye come unto me and your souls shall live, and your redemption shall be perfected, and the saints shall come forth from the four quarters of the earth.

8 a. Then shall the arm of the Lord fall upon the nations, and then shall the Lord set his foot upon this mount, and it shall cleave in twain, and the earth shall tremble and reel to and fro;

b. and the heavens also shall shake, and the Lord shall utter his voice and all the ends of the earth shall hear it, and the nations of the earth shall mourn,

c. and they that have laughed shall see their folly, and calamity shall cover the mocker, and the scorner shall be consumed, and they that have watched for iniquity, shall be hewn down and cast into the fire.

9 a. And then shall the Jews look upon me and say, What are these wounds in thy hands, and in thy feet?

b. Then shall they know that I am the Lord; for I will say unto them, These wounds are the wounds with which I was wounded in the house of my friends.

c. I am he who was lifted up. I am Jesus that was crucified. I am the Son of God.

d. And then shall they weep because of their iniquities; then shall they lament because they persecuted their King.

10 a. And then shall the heathen nations be redeemed, and they that knew no law shall have part in the first resurrection; and it shall be tolerable for them; and Satan shall be bound that he shall have no place in the hearts of the children of men.

b. And at that day when I shall come in my glory, shall the parable be fulfilled which I spake concerning the ten virgins; for they that are wise and have received the truth, and have taken the Holy Spirit for their guide, and have not been deceived, verily I say unto you,

c. They shall not be hewn down and cast into the fire, but shall abide the day, and the earth shall be given unto them for an inheritance;

d. and they shall multiply and wax strong, and their children shall grow up without sin unto salvation, for the Lord shall be in their midst, and his glory shall be upon them, and he will be their King and their lawgiver.

11 a. And now, behold, I say unto you, It shall not be given unto you to know any further concerning this chapter, until the New Testament be translated, and in it all these things shall be made known;

b. wherefore I give unto you that you may now translate it, that ye may be prepared for the things to come; for verily I say unto you, that great things await you;

c. ye hear of wars in foreign lands, but, behold, I say unto you, They are nigh, even at your doors, and not many years hence ye shall hear of wars in your own lands.

12 a. Wherefore, I the Lord have said, Gather ye out

from the eastern lands, assemble ye yourselves together ye elders of my church;

b. go ye forth unto the western countries, call upon the inhabitants to repent, and inasmuch as they do repent, build up churches unto me;

c. and with one heart and with one mind, gather up your riches that ye may purchase an inheritance which shall hereafter be appointed unto you, and it shall be called the New Jerusalem, a land of peace, a city of refuge, a place of safety for the saints of the most high God;

d. and the glory of the Lord shall be there, and the terror of the Lord also shall be there, insomuch that the wicked will not come unto it; and it shall be called Zion.

13 a. And it shall come to pass, among the wicked, that every man that will not take his sword against his neighbor, must needs flee unto Zion for safety.

b. And there shall be gathered unto it out of every nation under heaven; and it shall be the only people that shall not be at war one with another.

c. And it shall be said among the wicked, Let us not go up to battle against Zion, for the inhabitants of Zion are terrible, wherefore we can not stand.

14 And it shall come to pass that the righteous shall be gathered out from among all nations, and shall come to Zion singing, with songs of everlasting joy.

15 a. And now I say unto you, Keep these things from going abroad unto the world, until it is expedient in me, that ye may accomplish this work in the eyes of the people and in the eyes of your enemies, that they may not know your works until ye have accomplished the thing which I have commanded you;

b. that when they shall know it, that they may consider these things, for when the Lord shall appear he shall be terrible unto them, that fear may seize upon them, and they shall stand afar off and tremble;

c. and all nations shall be afraid because of the terror of the Lord, and the power of his might. Even so. Amen.

SECTION 46

Revelation addressed to the church, given through Joseph Smith, Jr., March 8, 1831, at Kirtland, Ohio. This instruction was very important in setting the patterns of public worship in the church, especially in regard to the Sacrament services and the exercise of the spiritual gifts. It was greatly needed, since converts came into the church from so many diverse denominational backgrounds.

1 a. Hearken, O ye people of my church, for verily I say unto you, that these things were spoken unto you for your profit and learning;

b. but notwithstanding those things which are written, it always has been given to the elders of my church, from the beginning, and ever shall be, to conduct all meetings as they are directed and guided by the Holy Spirit;

c. nevertheless, ye are commanded never to cast anyone out from your public meetings, which are held before the world.

d. Ye are also commanded not to cast anyone, who belongeth to the church, out of your sacrament meetings; nevertheless, if any have trespassed, let him not partake until he makes reconciliation.

2 And again I say unto you, Ye shall not cast anyone out of your sacrament meetings, who is earnestly seeking the kingdom; I speak this concerning those who are not of the church.

3 a. And again I say unto you, concerning your confirmation meetings, that if there be any that is not of the church, that is earnestly seeking after the kingdom, ye shall not cast them out;

b. but ye are commanded in all things to ask of God, who giveth liberally, and that which the Spirit testifies unto you, even so I would that you should do in all holiness of heart,

c. walking uprightly before me, considering the end of your salvation, doing all things with prayer and thanksgiving, that ye may not be seduced by evil spirits, or doctrines of devils, or the commandments of men, for some are of men, and others of devils.

4 a. Wherefore, beware, lest ye are deceived, and that ye may not be deceived, seek ye earnestly the best gifts, always remembering for what they are given;

b. for verily I say unto you, They are given for the benefit of those who love me and keep all my commandments, and him that seeketh so to do, that all may be benefited, that seeketh or that asketh of me, that asketh and not for a sign that he may consume it upon his lusts.

5 a. And again, verily I say unto you, I would that ye should always remember, and always retain in your minds what those gifts are, that are given unto the church, for all have not every gift given unto them;

b. for there are many gifts, and to every man is given a gift by the Spirit of God:

c. to some it is given one, and to some is given another, that all may be profited thereby;

d. to some it is given by the Holy Ghost to know that Jesus Christ is the Son of God, and that he was crucified for the sins of the world;

e. to others it is given to believe on their words, that they also might have eternal life, if they continue faithful.

6 a. And again, to some it is given by the Holy Ghost to know the differences of administration, as it will be pleasing unto the same Lord, according as the Lord will, suiting his mercies according to the conditions of the children of men.

b. And again, it is given by the Holy Ghost to some to know the diversities of operations, whether it be of God, that the manifestations of the Spirit may be given to every man to profit withal.

7 a. And again, verily I say unto you, To some it is given, by the Spirit of God, the word of wisdom;

b. to another it is given the word of knowledge, that all may be taught to be wise and to have knowledge.

c. And again, to some it is given to have faith to be healed, and to others it is given to have faith to heal.

d. And again, to some it is given the workings of miracles;

and to others it is given to prophesy, and to others the discerning of spirits.

e. And again, it is given to some to speak with tongues, and to another it is given the interpretation of tongues:

f. and all these gifts come from God, for the benefit of the children of God.

g. And unto the bishop of the church, and unto such as God shall appoint and ordain to watch over the church, and to be elders unto the church, are to have it given unto them to discern all those gifts, lest there be any among you professing and yet be not of God.

8 a. And it shall come to pass that he that asketh in spirit shall receive in spirit; that unto some it may be given to have all those gifts, that there may be a head, in order that every member may be profited thereby:

b. he that asketh in the spirit, asketh according to the will of God, wherefore it is done even as he asketh.

9 a. And again I say unto you, All things must be done in the name of Christ, whatsoever you do in the spirit;

b. and ye must give thanks unto God in the spirit for whatever blessing ye are blessed with; and ye must practice virtue and holiness before me continually. Even so. Amen.

SECTION 47

Revelation given through Joseph Smith, Jr., March 8, 1831, at Kirtland, Ohio, and addressed to John Whitmer. Oliver Cowdery's departure upon the mission to the West had left Joseph without a scribe who could keep an unofficial record of the church's history. John Whitmer, who was now called to this responsibility, wrote only eighty-five pages. These included many of the revelations given prior to 1838.

1 a. Behold, it is expedient in me that my servant John should write and keep a regular history, and assist you, my servant Joseph, in transcribing all things which shall be given you, until he is called to further duties.

b. Again, verily I say unto you, that he can also lift up his voice in meetings, whenever it shall be expedient.

2 a. And again, I say unto you, that it shall be appointed unto him to keep the church record and history continually, for Oliver Cowdery I have appointed to another office.

b. Wherefore, it shall be given him, inasmuch as he is faithful, by the Comforter, to write these things. Even so. Amen.

SECTION 48

Revelation given through Joseph Smith, Jr., March 8, 1831, at Kirtland, Ohio. This is addressed to the Saints in Kirtland who needed guidance concerning the manner of locating members of the church arriving from the East (D. and C. 45:12). They were uncertain about the advisability of purchasing land in view of the projected move farther west, and about the Zionic principles on which lands should be allocated.

1 a. It is necessary that ye should remain, for the present time, in your places of abode, as it shall be suitable to your circumstances;

b. and inasmuch as ye have lands, ye shall impart to the eastern brethren;

c. and inasmuch as ye have not lands, let them buy for the present time in those regions round about as seemeth them good, for it must needs be that they have places to live for the present time.

2 a. It must needs be, that ye save all the money that ye can, and that ye obtain all that ye can in righteousness, that in time ye may be enabled to purchase lands for an inheritance, even the city.

b. The place is not yet to be revealed, but after your brethren come from the east, there are to be certain men appointed, and to them it shall be given to know the place, or to them it shall be revealed;

c. and they shall be appointed to purchase the lands, and to make a commencement, to lay the foundation of the city;

d. and then ye shall begin to be gathered with your families, every man according to his family, according to his circumstances, and as is appointed to him by the presidency and the bishop of the church, according to the laws and commandments, which ye have received, and which ye shall hereafter receive. Even so. Amen.

SECTION 49

Revelation given through Joseph Smith, Jr., March 1831, at Kirtland, Ohio, addressed to Sidney Rigdon, Parley P. Pratt, and Lemon Copley. These elders were sent on a mission to the Shakers. Copley had been a member of the Society of Shakers but had recently joined the church. The revelation sets forth the major teachings of the Restoration wherein they differ from those of the Shakers.

1 a. Hearken unto my word, my servants Sidney, and Parley, and Lemon, for, behold, verily I say unto you, that I give unto you a commandment, that you shall go and preach my gospel, which ye have received, even as ye have received it, unto the Shakers.

b. Behold, I say unto you, that they desire to know the truth in part, but not all, for they are not right before me, and must needs repent;

c. wherefore I send you, my servants Sidney and Parley, to preach the gospel unto them; and my servant Lemon shall be ordained unto this work, that he may reason with them,

d. not according to that which he has received of them, but according to that which shall be taught him by you, my servants, and by so doing I will bless him, otherwise he shall not prosper:

e. thus saith the Lord, for I am God and have sent mine only Begotten Son into the world, for the redemption of the world, and have decreed that he that receiveth him shall be saved, and he that receiveth him not shall be damned.

2 a. And they have done unto the Son of Man even as they listed; and he has taken his power on the right hand of his glory, and now reigneth in the heavens, and will reign till he descends on the earth to put all enemies under his feet; which time is nigh at hand:

b. I, the Lord God, have spoken it; but the hour and the day no man knoweth, neither the angels in heaven, nor shall they know until he comes;

c. wherefore I will that all men shall repent, for all are under sin, except them which I have reserved unto myself, holy men that ye know not of;

d. wherefore I say unto you, that I have sent unto you mine everlasting covenant, even that which was from the beginning, and that which I have promised I have so fulfilled, and the nations of the earth shall bow to it;

e. and, if not of themselves, they shall come down, for that which is now exalted of itself, shall be laid low of power;

f. wherefore I give unto you a commandment that ye go among this people and say unto them, like unto mine apostle of old, whose name was Peter:

g. Believe on the name of the Lord Jesus, who was on the earth, and is to come, the beginning and the end; repent and be baptized in the name of Jesus Christ, according to the holy commandment, for the remission of sins;

h. and whoso doeth this, shall receive the gift of the Holy Ghost, by the laying on of the hands of the elders of this church.

3 a. And again, I say unto you, that whoso forbiddeth to marry, is not ordained of God, for marriage is ordained of God unto man;

b. wherefore it is lawful that he should have one wife, and they twain shall be one flesh, and all this that the earth might answer the end of its creation;

c. and that it might be filled with the measure of man, according to his creation before the world was made.

d. And whoso forbiddeth to abstain from meats, that man should not eat the same, is not ordained of God;

e. for, behold, the beasts of the field, and the fowls of the air, and that which cometh of the earth, is ordained for the use of man, for food, and for raiment, and that he might have in abundance, but it is not given that one man should possess that which is above another;

f. wherefore the world lieth in sin; and woe be unto man that sheddeth blood or that wasteth flesh and hath no need.

4 a. And again, verily I say unto you, that the Son of Man cometh not in the form of a woman, neither of a man traveling on the earth;

b. wherefore be not deceived, but continue in steadfastness, looking forth for the heavens to be shaken; and the earth to tremble, and to reel to and fro as a drunken man;

c. and for the valleys to be exalted; and for the mountains to be made low; and for the rough places to become smooth; and all this when the angel shall sound his trumpet.

5 a. But before the great day of the Lord shall come, Jacob shall flourish in the wilderness; and the Lamanites shall blossom as the rose.

b. Zion shall flourish upon the hills, and rejoice upon the mountains, and shall be assembled together unto the place which I have appointed.

c. Behold, I say unto you, Go forth as I have commanded you; repent of all your sins; ask and ye shall receive; knock and it shall be opened unto you:

d. behold, I will go before you, and be your rearward; and I will be in your midst, and you shall not be confounded; behold, I am Jesus Christ, and I come quickly. Even so. Amen.

SECTION 50

Revelation given to the elders of the church through Joseph Smith, Jr., May 1831, at Kirtland, Ohio. Some of the elders who returned from their missions in order to share in the June conference (D. and C. 44) reported that they had been embarrassed by strange and unedifying spiritual manifestations which were experienced among the congregations of the Saints. Joseph sought the Lord for guidance, and the following revelation was given him.

1 a. Hearken, O ye elders of my church, and give ear to the voice of the living God; and attend to the words of wisdom which shall be given unto you, according as ye have asked and are agreed as touching the church, and the spirits which have gone abroad in the earth.

b. Behold, verily I say unto you, that there are many spirits which are false spirits, which have gone forth in the earth, deceiving the world: and also Satan hath sought to deceive you, that he might overthrow you.

2 a. Behold, I the Lord have looked upon you, and have seen abominations in the church that professes my name; but blessed are they who are faithful and endure, whether in life or in death, for they shall inherit eternal life.

b. But woe unto them that are deceivers, and hypocrites, for thus saith the Lord, I will bring them to judgment.

3 a. Behold, verily I say unto you, There are hypocrites among you, and have deceived some, which has given the adversary power, but, behold, such shall be reclaimed;

b. but the hypocrites shall be detected and shall be cut off, either in life or in death, even as I will, and woe unto them who are cut off from my church, for the same are overcome of the world;

c. wherefore, let every man beware lest he do that which is not in truth and righteousness before me.

4 a. And now come, saith the Lord, by the Spirit, unto the elders of his church, and let us reason together, that ye

may understand: let us reason even as a man reasoneth one with another face to face:

b. now when a man reasoneth, he is understood of man, because he reasoneth as a man; even so will I, the Lord, reason with you that you may understand: wherefore I, the Lord, asketh you this question, Unto what were ye ordained?

c. To preach my gospel by the Spirit, even the Comforter, which was sent forth to teach the truth: and then received ye spirits which ye could not understand, and received them to be of God, and in this are ye justified?

d. Behold, ye shall answer this question yourselves, nevertheless I will be merciful unto you; he that is weak among you hereafter shall be made strong.

5 a. Verily I say unto you, He that is ordained of me and sent forth to preach the word of truth by the Comforter, in the spirit of truth, doth he preach it by the spirit of truth, or some other way? and if it be by some other way, it be not of God.

b. And again, he that receiveth the word of truth, doth he receive it by the spirit of truth, or some other way? if it be some other way, it be not of God:

c. therefore, why is it that ye can not understand and know that he that receiveth the word by the spirit of truth, receiveth it as it is preached by the spirit of truth?

6 a. Wherefore, he that preacheth and he that receiveth, understandeth one another, and both are edified and rejoice together;

b. and that which doth not edify, is not of God, and is darkness: that which is of God is light, and he that receiveth light and continueth in God, receiveth more light, and that light groweth brighter and brighter, until the perfect day.

c. And again, verily I say unto you, and I say it that you may know the truth, that you may chase darkness from among you, for he that is ordained of God and sent forth, the same is appointed to be the greatest, notwithstanding he is least, and the servant of all:

d. wherefore, he is possessor of all things, for all things

are subject unto him, both in heaven and on the earth, the life, and the light, the spirit, and the power, sent forth by the will of the Father, through Jesus Christ, his Son;

e. but no man is possessor of all things, except he be purified and cleansed from all sin; and if ye are purified and cleansed from all sin, ye shall ask whatsoever you will in the name of Jesus, and it shall be done:

f. but know this, it shall be given you what you shall ask, and as ye are appointed to the head, the spirits shall be subject unto you.

7 a. Wherefore, it shall come to pass, that if you behold a spirit manifested that you can not understand, and you receive not that spirit, ye shall ask of the Father, in the name of Jesus, and if he give not unto you that spirit, that you may know that it is not of God;

b. and it shall be given unto you power over that spirit, and you shall proclaim against that spirit with a loud voice, that it is not of God;

c. not with railing accusation, that ye be not overcome; neither with boasting, nor rejoicing, lest you be seized therewith:

d. he that receiveth of God, let him account it of God, and let him rejoice that he is accounted of God worthy to receive, and by giving heed and doing these things which ye have received, and which ye shall hereafter receive;

e. and the kingdom is given you of the Father, and power to overcome all things, which is not ordained of him;

f. and, behold, verily I say unto you, Blessed are you who are now hearing these words of mine from the mouth of my servant, for your sins are forgiven you.

8 a. Let my servant Joseph Wakefield, in whom I am well pleased, and my servant Parley P. Pratt, go forth among the churches and strengthen them by the word of exhortation;

b. and also my servant John Corrill, or as many of my servants as are ordained unto this office, and let them labor in the vineyard; and let no man hinder them of doing that which I have appointed unto them:

c. wherefore in this thing my servant Edward Partridge, is not justified, nevertheless let him repent and he shall be forgiven.

d. Behold, ye are little children, and ye can not bear all things now; ye must grow in grace and in the knowledge of the truth.

e. Fear not, little children, for you are mine, and I have overcome the world, and you are of them that my Father hath given me; and none of them that my Father hath given me shall be lost;

f. and the Father and I are one; I am in the Father and the Father in me; and inasmuch as ye have received me, ye are in me, and I in you; wherefore I am in your midst;

g. and I am the good Shepherd (and the stone of Israel: he that buildeth upon this rock shall never fall), and the day cometh that you shall hear my voice and see me, and know that I am. Watch, therefore, that ye may be ready. Even so. Amen.

SECTION 51

Revelation given through Joseph Smith, Jr., to Edward Partridge at Kirtland, Ohio, May 1831. This revelation has the same background as Doctrine and Covenants 48, both being concerned with locating the Saints from the East in harmony with Zionic principles. Edward Partridge was the only bishop in the church at this time.

1 a. Hearken unto me, saith the Lord your God, and I will speak unto my servant Edward Partridge, and give unto him directions; for it must needs be that he receive directions how to organize this people; for it must needs be that they are organized according to my laws; if otherwise, they will be cut off;

b. wherefore let my servant Edward Partridge, and those whom he has chosen, in whom I am well pleased, appoint unto this people their portion, every man equal according to their families, according to their circumstances, and their wants and needs;

c. and let my servant Edward Partridge, when he shall appoint a man his portion, give unto him a writing that shall secure unto him his portion, that he shall hold it, even this right and this inheritance in the church, until he transgresses and is not accounted worthy by the voice of the church, according to the laws and covenants of the church, to belong to the church;

d. and if he shall transgress, and is not accounted worthy to belong in the church, he shall not have power to claim that portion which he has consecrated unto the bishop for the poor and the needy of my church;

e. therefore he shall not retain the gift, but shall only have claim on that portion that is deeded unto him. And thus all things shall be made sure according to the laws of the land.

2 a. And let that which belongs to this people be appointed unto this people; and the money which is left unto this people, let there be an agent appointed unto this people to take the money, to provide food and raiment, according to the wants of this people.

b. And let every man deal honestly, and be alike among this people, and receive alike, that ye may be one, even as I have commanded you.

3 a. And let that which belongeth to this people not be taken and given unto that of another church;

b. wherefore, if another church would receive money of this church, let them pay unto this church again, according as they shall agree;

c. and this shall be done through the bishop or the agent, which shall be appointed by the voice of the church.

4 a. And again, let the bishop appoint a storehouse unto this church, and let all things, both in money and in meat, which is more than is needful for the want of this people, be kept in the hands of the bishop.

b. And let him also reserve unto himself, for his own wants, and for the wants of his family, as he shall be employed in doing this business.

c. And thus I grant unto this people a privilege of organizing themselves according to my laws; and I consecrate unto them this land for a little season, until I, the Lord, shall provide for them otherwise, and command them to go hence; and the hour and the day is not given unto them;

d. wherefore let them act upon this land as for years, and this shall turn unto them for their good.

5 a. Behold, this shall be an example unto my servant Edward Partridge, in other places, in all churches.

b. And whoso is found a faithful, a just, and a wise steward, shall enter into the joy of his Lord, and shall inherit eternal life.

c. Verily, I say unto you, I am Jesus Christ, who cometh quickly, in an hour you think not. Even so. Amen.

SECTION 52

Revelation given through Joseph Smith, Jr., early in June 1831 at Kirtland, Ohio. This revelation is addressed to the elders of the church. It was received the day following a conference at which the first high priests in the Restoration were ordained. Missouri is designated as the land of the inheritance of the Saints. The specific location of the point of gathering is not stated, but it must have been sufficiently understood for the elders to meet there after traveling and preaching along many different routes.

1 a. Behold, thus saith the Lord unto the elders whom he hath called and chosen, in these last days, by the voice of his Spirit, saying,

b. I, the Lord, will make known unto you what I will that ye shall do from this time until the next Conference, which shall be held in Missouri, upon the land which I will consecrate unto my people, which are a remnant of Jacob, and those who are heirs according to the covenant.

2 a. Wherefore, verily I say unto you, Let my servants Joseph Smith, Jr., and Sidney Rigdon, take their journey as soon as preparations can be made to leave their homes, and journey to the land of Missouri.

b. And inasmuch as they are faithful unto me, it shall be made known unto them what they shall do; and it shall also, inasmuch as they are faithful, be made known unto them the land of your inheritance.

c. And inasmuch as they are not faithful, they shall be cut off, even as I will, as seemeth me good.

3 a. And again, verily I say unto you, Let my servant Lyman Wight, and my servant John Corrill, take their journey speedily; and also my servant John Murdock, and my servant Hyrum Smith, take their journey unto the same place, by the way of Detroit.

b. And let them journey from thence, preaching the word by the way, saying none other things than that which the prophets and apostles have written, and that which is taught them by the Comforter, through the prayer of faith.

c. Let them go two by two, and thus let them preach by the way in every congregation, baptizing by water, and the laying on of the hands by the water's side;

d. for thus saith the Lord, I will cut my work short in righteousness, for the days cometh that I will send forth judgment unto victory. And let my servant Lyman Wight beware, for Satan desireth to sift him as chaff.

4 a. And, behold, he that is faithful shall be made ruler over many things.

b. And again, I will give unto you a pattern in all things, that ye may not be deceived; for Satan is abroad in the land, and he goeth forth deceiving the nations;

c. wherefore he that prayeth whose spirit is contrite, the same is accepted of me, if he obey mine ordinances.

d. He that speaketh, whose spirit is contrite, whose language is meek, and edifieth, the same is of God, if he obey mine ordinances.

e. And again, he that trembleth under my power shall be made strong, and shall bring forth fruits of praise, and wisdom, according to the revelations and truths which I have given you.

5 a. And again, he that is overcome and bringeth not forth fruits, even according to this pattern, is not of me; wherefore by this pattern ye shall know the spirits in all cases, under the whole heavens.

b. And the days have come, according to men's faith it shall be done unto them. Behold, this commandment is given unto all the elders whom I have chosen.

c. And again, verily I say unto you, Let my servant Thomas B. Marsh, and my servant Ezra Thayre, take their journey also, preaching the word by the way, unto this same land.

d. And again, let my servant Isaac Morley, and my servant Ezra Booth, take their journey, also preaching the word by the way, unto the same land.

6 a. And again, let my servants Edward Partridge and Martin Harris take their journey with my servants Sidney Rigdon and Joseph Smith, Jr.

b. Let my servants David Whitmer and Harvey Whitlock also take their journey, and preach by the way, unto the same land. Let my servants Parley P. Pratt and Orson Pratt take their journey, and preach by the way, even unto this same land.

c. And let my servants Solomon Hancock and Simeon Carter also take their journey unto this same land, and preach by the way. Let my servants Edson Fuller and Jacob Scott also take their journey.

d. Let my servants Levi Hancock and Zebedee Coltrin also take their journey. Let my servants Reynolds Cahoon and Samuel H. Smith also take their journey. Let my servants Wheeler Baldwin and William Carter also take their journey.

7 a. And let my servants Newel Knight and Selah J. Griffin both be ordained and also take their journey: yea, verily I say, Let all these take their journey unto one place, in their several courses, and one man shall not build upon another's foundation, neither journey in another's track.

b. He that is faithful, the same shall be kept and blessed with much fruit.

8 a. And again, I say unto you, Let my servants Joseph Wakefield and Solomon Humphrey take their journey into the eastern lands.

b. Let them labor with their families, declaring none other things than the prophets and apostles, that which they have seen, and heard, and most assuredly believe, that the prophecies may be fulfilled.

c. In consequence of transgression, let that which was bestowed upon Heman Bassett, be taken from him, and placed upon the head of Simonds Rider.

9 a. And again, verily I say unto you, Let Jared Carter

be ordained a priest, and also George James be ordained a priest. Let the residue of the elders watch over the churches, and declare the word in the regions among them.

b. And let them labor with their own hands, that there be no idolatry nor wickedness practiced.

c. And remember in all things, the poor and the needy, the sick and the afflicted, for he that doeth not these things, the same is not my disciple.

d. And again, let my servants Joseph Smith, Jr., and Sidney Rigdon, and Edward Partridge, take with them a recommend from the church.

e. And let there be one obtained for my servant Oliver Cowdery also; and thus, even as I have said, if ye are faithful, ye shall assemble yourselves together to rejoice upon the land of Missouri, which is the land of your inheritance, which is now the land of your enemies.

f. But, behold, I the Lord, will hasten the city in its time, and will crown the faithful with joy and with rejoicing. Behold, I am Jesus Christ the Son of God, and I will lift them up at the last day. Even so. Amen.

SECTION 53

Revelation given to Sidney Gilbert through Joseph Smith, Jr., June 1831, at Kirtland, Ohio. Sidney went to Missouri and served ably and faithfully until his death in June 1834.

1 Behold, I say unto you, my servant Sidney Gilbert, that I have heard your prayers, and you have called upon me, that it should be made known unto you, of the Lord your God, concerning your calling and election in this church, which I, the Lord, have raised up in these last days.

2 a. Behold, I, the Lord, who was crucified for the sins of the world, giveth unto you a commandment, that you shall forsake the world.

b. Take upon you mine ordinances, even that of an elder, to preach faith and repentance, and remission of sins, according to my word, and the reception of the Holy Spirit by the laying on of hands.

c. And also to be an agent unto this church in the place which shall be appointed by the bishop, according to commandments which shall be given hereafter.

3 a. And again, verily I say unto you, You shall take your journey with my servants Joseph Smith, Jr., and Sidney Rigdon.

b. Behold, these are the first ordinances which you shall receive; and the residue shall be made known in a time to come, according to your labor in my vineyard.

c. And again, I would that ye should learn that it is he only who is saved, that endureth unto the end. Even so. Amen.

SECTION 54

Revelation given through Joseph Smith, Jr., at Kirtland, Ohio, in June 1831. It is addressed to Newel Knight, who was president of the Colesville, New York, branch of the church whose members had recently settled at Thompson, Ohio, in the vicinity of Kirtland. Some of the brethren previously settled at Thompson had broken an agreement to share their land with the Colesville Saints, and this caused resentment and confusion. The revelation enabled Elder Knight to unite the faithful and to lead them to Missouri in a body. They arrived in what is now Kansas City late in July 1831.

1 a. Behold, thus saith the Lord, even Alpha and Omega, the beginning and the end, even he who was crucified for the sins of the world.

b. Behold, verily, verily I say unto you, my servant Newel Knight, You shall stand fast in the office wherewith I have appointed you; and if your brethren desire to escape their enemies let them repent of all their sins, and become truly humble before me and contrite;

c. and as the covenant which they made unto me has been broken, even so it has become void and of none effect;

d. and woe to him by whom this offense cometh, for it had been better for him that he had been drowned in the depth of the sea;

e. but blessed are they who have kept the covenant, and observed the commandment, for they shall obtain mercy.

2 a. Wherefore, go to now and flee the land, lest your enemies come upon you; and take your journey, and appoint whom you will to be your leader, and to pay moneys for you.

b. And thus you shall take your journey into the regions westward, and unto the land of Missouri, unto the borders of the Lamanites.

c. And after you have done journeying, behold, I say unto you, Seek ye a living like unto men, until I prepare a place for you.

3 And again, be patient in tribulation until I come; and behold, I come quickly, and my reward is with me, and they who have sought me early, shall find rest to their souls. Even so. Amen.

SECTION 55

Revelation given through Joseph Smith, Jr., at Kirtland, Ohio, in June 1831. While Joseph and those who were to accompany him were preparing for their journey to Missouri, William W. Phelps and his family arrived at Kirtland. William desired to know the will of God concerning his work and was instructed to join the church and accompany Joseph and his party to Missouri. He made a major literary and musical contribution to the church during the next few years.

1 a. Behold, thus saith the Lord unto you, my servant William; yea, even the Lord of the whole earth,

b. You are called and chosen, and after you have been baptized by water, which if you do with an eye single to my glory, you shall have a remission of your sins, and a reception of the Holy Spirit, by the laying on of hands.

c. And then you shall be ordained by the hand of my servant Joseph Smith, Jr., to be an elder unto this church, to preach repentance and remission of sins by way of baptism in the name of Jesus Christ, the Son of the living God;

d. and on whomsoever you shall lay your hands, if they are contrite before me, you shall have power to give the Holy Spirit.

2 a. And again, you shall be ordained to assist my servant Oliver Cowdery to do the work of printing, and of selecting, and writing books for schools, in this church, that little children also may receive instruction before me as is pleasing unto me.

b. And again, verily I say unto you, For this cause you shall take your journey with my servants Joseph Smith, Jr., and Sidney Rigdon, that you may be planted in the land of your inheritance, to do this work.

3 And again let my servant Joseph Coe also take his journey with them. The residue shall be made known hereafter; even as I will. Amen.

SECTION 56

Revelation given through the prophet Joseph Smith, Jr., at Kirtland, Ohio, June 1831. Lemon Copley and Ezra Thayre had entered into a stewardship covenant with the Saints at Thompson, but later refused to carry out its provisions. In view of this, Ezra Thayre's commission to travel with Thomas B. Marsh to Missouri was revoked. Of more permanent interest is the fundamental statement on stewardship which the situation called forth (vs. 5).

1 a. Hearken, O ye people who profess my name, saith the Lord your God, for, behold, mine anger is kindled against the rebellious, and they shall know mine arm and mine indignation in the day of visitation and of wrath upon the nations.

b. And he that will not take up his cross and follow me, and keep my commandments, the same shall not be saved.

2 a. Behold, I the Lord commandeth, and he that will not obey shall be cut off in mine own due time; and after that I have commanded and the commandment is broken,

wherefore I the Lord command and revoke, as it seemeth me good, and all this to be answered upon the heads of the rebellious, saith the Lord;

b. wherefore I revoke the commandment which was given unto my servants Thomas B. Marsh and Ezra Thayre, and give a new commandment unto my servant Thomas, that he shall take up his journey speedily to the land of Missouri; and my servant Selah J. Griffin shall also go with him:

c. for, behold, I revoke the commandment which was given unto my servants Selah J. Griffin and Newel Knight, in consequence of the stiff-neckedness of my people which are in Thompson; and their rebellions;

d. wherefore let my servant Newel Knight remain with them, and as many as will go, may go, that are contrite before me, and be led by him to the land which I have appointed.

3 a. And again, verily I say unto you, that my servant Ezra Thayre must repent of his pride, and of his selfishness, and obey the former commandment which I have given him concerning the place upon which he lives;

b. and if he will do this, as there shall be no divisions made upon the land, he shall be appointed still to go to the land of Missouri;

c. otherwise he shall receive the money which he has paid, and shall leave the place, and shall be cut off out of my church, saith the Lord of hosts;

d. and though the heaven and the earth pass away, these words shall not pass away, but shall be fulfilled.

4 a. And if my servant Joseph Smith, Jr., must needs pay the money, behold, I, the Lord, will pay it unto him again in the land of Missouri, that those of whom he shall receive may be rewarded again, according to that which they do.

b. For according to that which they do, they shall receive; even in lands for their inheritance.

c. Behold, thus saith the Lord unto my people, You have many things to do, and to repent of; for, behold, your sins have come up unto me, and are not pardoned, because you seek to counsel in your own ways.

d. And your hearts are not satisfied. And ye obey not the truth, but have pleasure in unrighteousness.

5 a. Woe unto you rich men, that will not give your substance to the poor, for your riches will canker your souls; and this shall be your lamentation in the days of visitation, and of judgment, and of indignation:

b. The harvest is past, the summer is ended, and my soul is not saved!

c. Woe unto you poor men, whose hearts are not broken, whose spirits are not contrite, and whose bellies are not satisfied, and whose hands are not stayed from laying hold upon other men's goods, whose eyes are full of greediness, who will not labor with their own hands!

6 a. But blessed are the poor, who are pure in heart, whose hearts are broken, and whose spirits are contrite, for they shall see the kingdom of God coming in power and great glory unto their deliverance; for the fatness of the earth shall be theirs;

b. for, behold, the Lord shall come, and his recompense shall be with him, and he shall reward every man, and the poor shall rejoice; and their generations shall inherit the earth from generation to generation, for ever and ever.

c. And now I make an end of speaking unto you. Even so. Amen.

SECTION 57

Revelation addressed to the elders who had come to Independence, Missouri, in fulfillment of the instructions given them in Kirtland. It was given through Joseph Smith, Jr., in July 1831. In it the Center Place and "the spot for the temple" are designated, and the instructions previously given to Edward Partridge, Sidney Gilbert, W. W. Phelps, and Oliver Cowdery are confirmed.

1 a. Hearken, O ye elders of my church saith the Lord your God, who have assembled yourselves together, according to my commandments, in this land which is the land of Missouri, which is the land which I have appointed and consecrated for the gathering of the Saints:

b. wherefore this is the land of promise, and the place for the city of Zion.

c. And thus saith the Lord your God, If you will receive wisdom here is wisdom.

d. Behold, the place which is now called Independence, is the Center Place, and the spot for the temple is lying westward upon a lot which is not far from the courthouse;

e. wherefore it is wisdom that the land should be purchased by the Saints; and also every tract lying westward, even unto the line running directly between Jew and Gentile.

f. And also every tract bordering by the prairies, inasmuch as my disciples are enabled to buy lands.

g. Behold, this is wisdom, that they may obtain it for an everlasting inheritance.

2 And let my servant Sidney Gilbert, stand in the office which I have appointed him, to receive moneys, to be an agent unto the church, to buy land in all the regions round about, inasmuch as can be in righteousness, and as wisdom shall direct.

3 And let my servant Edward Partridge, stand in the office which I have appointed him, to divide the Saints their inheritance, even as I have commanded; and also those whom he has appointed to assist him.

4 a. And again, verily I say unto you, Let my servant Sidney Gilbert plant himself in this place, and establish a store, that he may sell goods without fraud, that he may obtain money to buy lands for the good of the Saints, and that he may obtain whatsoever things the disciples may need to plant them in their inheritance.

b. And also let my servant Sidney Gilbert obtain a license (behold, here is wisdom, and whoso readeth let him understand), that he may send goods also unto the people, even by whom he will as clerks, employed in his service, and thus provide for my saints, that my gospel may be preached unto those who sit in darkness and in the region and shadow of death.

5 a. And again, verily I say unto you, Let my servant William W. Phelps be planted in this place, and be established as a printer unto the church; and lo, if the world receiveth his writings (behold, here is wisdom), let him obtain

whatsoever he can obtain in righteousness, for the good of the Saints.

b. And let my servant Oliver Cowdery assist him, even as I have commanded, in whatsoever place I shall appoint unto him, to copy, and to correct, and select, that all things may be right before me, as it shall be proved by the Spirit through him.

c. And thus let those of whom I have spoken, be planted in the land of Zion, as speedily as can be, with their families, to do those things even as I have spoken.

6 a. And now concerning the gathering, let the bishop and the agent make preparations for those families which have been commanded to come to this land, as soon as possible, and plant them in their inheritance.

b. And unto the residue of both elders and members, further directions shall be given hereafter. Even so. Amen.

SECTION 58

Revelation given through Joseph Smith, Jr., prophet and seer to the church, August 1, 1831, in Jackson County, Missouri. Groups of Saints were arriving in Jackson County. The Colesville Saints from the Thompson Branch arrived under the leadership of Newel Knight. On the first Sunday after the arrival of the prophet and party, W. W. Phelps preached to a mixed audience of white pioneers, Negroes, and Indians. On this day two were baptized. The Saints were eager for the dedication of the land and to learn of God's will concerning their work. This revelation is addressed to the elders of the church in Missouri, the "Land of Promise," the place for the "City of Zion."

1 a. Hearken, O ye elders of my church, and give ear to my word, and learn of me what I will concerning you, and also concerning this land unto which I have sent you;

b. for verily I say unto you, Blessed is he that keepeth my commandments, whether in life or in death; and he that is faithful in tribulation, the reward of the same is greater in the kingdom of heaven.

2 a. Ye can not behold with your natural eyes, for the present time, the design of your God concerning those things which shall come hereafter, and the glory which shall follow, after much tribulation.

b. For after much tribulation come the blessings. Wherefore the day cometh that ye shall be crowned with much glory; the hour is not yet, but is nigh at hand.

3 a. Remember this which I tell you before, that you may lay it to heart, and receive that which shall follow.

b. Behold, verily I say unto you, For this cause I have sent you that you might be obedient, and that your hearts might be prepared to bear testimony of the things which are to come;

c. and also that you might be honored of laying the foundation, and of bearing record of the land upon which the Zion of God shall stand; and also that a feast of fat things might be prepared for the poor;

d. yea, a feast of fat things, of wine on the lees well refined, that the earth may know that the mouths of the prophets shall not fail; yea, a supper of the house of the Lord, well prepared, unto which all nations shall be invited.

e. Firstly, the rich and the learned, the wise and the noble; and after that cometh the day of my power;

f. then shall the poor, the lame, and the blind, and the deaf, come in unto the marriage of the Lamb, and partake of the supper of the Lord, prepared for the great day to come. Behold, I, the Lord, have spoken it.

4 a. And that the testimony might go forth from Zion; yea, from the mouth of the city of the heritage of God; yea, for this cause I have sent you hither, and have selected my servant Edward Partridge, and have appointed unto him his mission in this land;

b. but if he repent not of his sins, which are unbelief and blindness of heart, let him take heed lest he fall.

c. Behold, his mission is given unto him, and it shall not be given again.

d. And whoso standeth in this mission is appointed to be a judge in Israel, like as it was in ancient days, to divide the lands of the heritage of God unto his children, and to judge his people by the testimony of the just, and by the assistance of his counselors, according to the laws of the kingdom which are given by the prophets of God;

e. for verily I say unto you, My law shall be kept on this land.

5 a. Let no man think that he is ruler, but let God rule him that judgeth, according to the counsel of his own will; or, in other words, him that counseleth or sitteth upon the judgment seat.

b. Let no man break the laws of the land, for he that keepeth the laws of God hath no need to break the laws of the land; wherefore be subject to the powers that be, until He reigns whose right it is to reign, and subdues all enemies under his feet.

c. Behold, the laws which ye have received from my hand are the laws of the church, and in this light ye shall hold them forth. Behold, here is wisdom.

6 a. And now, as I spake concerning my servant Edward Partridge, this land is the land of his residence, and those whom he has appointed for his counselors, and also the land of the residence of him whom I have appointed to keep my storehouse;

b. wherefore let them bring their families to this land, as they shall counsel between themselves and me;

c. for, behold, it is not meet that I should command in all things, for he that is compelled in all things, the same is a slothful and not a wise servant; wherefore he receiveth no reward.

d. Verily I say, Men should be anxiously engaged in a good cause, and do many things of their own free will, and bring to pass much righteousness; for the power is in them, wherein they are agents unto themselves.

e. And inasmuch as men do good, they shall in nowise lose their reward.

f. But he that doeth not anything until he is commanded, and receiveth a commandment with doubtful heart, and keepeth it with slothfulness, the same is damned.

g. Who am I that made man, saith the Lord, that will hold him guiltless that obeys not my commandments?

h. Who am I, saith the Lord, that have promised and have not fulfilled?

i. I command and a man obeys not, I revoke and they receive not the blessing; then they say in their hearts, This is not the work of the Lord, for his promises are not fulfilled. But woe unto such, for their reward lurketh beneath, and not from above.

7 a. And now I give unto you further directions concerning this land.

b. It is wisdom in me that my servant Martin Harris should be an example unto the church, in laying his moneys before the bishop of the church.

c. And also, this is a law unto every man that cometh unto this land, to receive an inheritance, and he shall do with his moneys according as the law directs.

d. And it is wisdom, also, that there should be lands purchased in Independence, for the place of the storehouse, and also for the house of the printing.

8 a. And other directions, concerning my servant Martin Harris, shall be given him of the Spirit, that he may receive his inheritance as seemeth him good.

b. And let him repent of his sins, for he seeketh the praise of the world.

9 a. And also let my servant William W. Phelps stand in the office which I have appointed him, and receive his inheritance in the land.

b. And, also, he hath need to repent, for I, the Lord, am not well pleased with him, for he seeketh to excel, and he is not sufficiently meek before me.

c. Behold, he who has repented of his sins, the same is forgiven, and I, the Lord, remembereth them no more.

d. By this ye may know if a man repenteth of his sins. Behold, he will confess them and forsake them.

e. And now, verily I say, concerning the residue of the elders of my church, The time has not yet come, for many years, for them to receive their inheritance in this land, except they desire it through the prayer of faith, only as it shall be appointed unto them of the Lord.

f. For, behold, they shall push the people together from the ends of the earth; wherefore assemble yourselves together, and they who are not appointed to stay in this land, let them preach the gospel in the regions round about; and after that, let them return to their homes.

g. Let them preach by the way, and bear testimony of the truth in all places, and call upon the rich, the high, and the low, and the poor, to repent; and let them build up churches, inasmuch as the inhabitants of the earth will repent.

10 And let there be an agent appointed by the voice of the church, unto the church in Ohio, to receive moneys to purchase lands in Zion.

11 a. And I give unto my servant Sidney Rigdon a commandment that he shall write a description of the land of Zion, and a statement of the will of God, as it shall be made known by the Spirit, unto him;

b. and an epistle and subscription, to be presented unto all the churches, to obtain moneys, to be put into the hands of the bishop, to purchase lands for an inheritance for the children of God, of himself or the agent, as seemeth him good, or as he shall direct.

c. For, behold, verily I say unto you, The Lord willeth that the disciples, and the children of men, should open their hearts even to purchase this whole region of country, as soon as time will permit.

d. Behold, here is wisdom; let them do this lest they receive none inheritance, save it be by the shedding of blood.

12 a. And again, inasmuch as there is land obtained, let there be workmen sent forth, of all kinds, unto this land, to labor for the saints of God. Let all these things be done in order.

b. And let the privileges of the lands be made known, from time to time, by the bishop, or the agent of the church; and let the work of the gathering be not in haste, nor by flight, but let it be done as it shall be counseled by the elders of the church at the conferences, according to the knowledge which they receive from time to time.

13 a. And let my servant Sidney Rigdon consecrate and dedicate this land, and the spot of the temple, unto the Lord.

b. And let a conference meeting be called, and after that let my servants Sidney Rigdon and Joseph Smith, Jr., return, and also Oliver Cowdery with them, to accomplish the residue of the work which I have appointed unto them in their own land, and the residue as shall be ruled by the conferences.

14 a. And let no man return from this land, except he bear record, by the way, of that which he knows and most assuredly believes.

b. Let that which has been bestowed upon Ziba Peterson be taken from him, and let him stand as a member in the church, and labor with his own hands, with the brethren, until he is sufficiently chastened for all his sins, for he confesseth them not, and he thinketh to hide them.

15 a. Let the residue of the elders of this church, who are coming to this land, some of whom are exceedingly blessed, even above measure, also hold a conference upon this land.

b. And let my servant Edward Partridge direct the conference which shall be held by them.

c. And let them also return, preaching the gospel by the way, bearing record of the things which are revealed unto them;

d. for, verily, the sound must go forth from this place into all the world; and unto the uttermost parts of the earth, the gospel must be preached unto every creature, with signs following them that believe. And behold, the Son of Man cometh. Amen.

SECTION 59

Revelation given through Joseph Smith, Jr., prophet and seer to the church, August 7, 1831, in Missouri. Events were happening very rapidly during the week of August 1 to August 7. Monday, August 2, Joseph assisted the Colesville Saints to lay the first log for a house as the foundation for Zion. It was consecrated and dedicated by Elder Rigdon for the gathering of the Saints. August 3, the spot for the Temple, a little west of the center of Independence, was dedicated. August 4, the first conference in the land of Zion

was held in the home of Joshua Lewis in Kaw township.
August 7 was the funeral of Polly Knight, mother of Newel
Knight. This was the first death in the church in the land
of Zion. These important events constitute the background
for this revelation.

1 a. Behold, blessed, saith the Lord, are they who have come up unto this land with an eye single to my glory, according to my commandments; for they that live shall inherit the earth, and they that die shall rest from all their labors, and their works shall follow them, and they shall receive a crown in the mansions of my Father, which I have prepared for them;

b. yea, blessed are they whose feet stand upon the land of Zion, who have obeyed my gospel, for they shall receive for their reward the good things of the earth;

c. and it shall bring forth in its strength; and they shall also be crowned with blessings from above; yea, and with commandments not a few, and with revelations in their time; they that are faithful and diligent before me.

2 a. Wherefore I give unto them a commandment, saying thus: Thou shalt love the Lord thy God, with all thy heart, with all thy might, mind, and strength; and in the name of Jesus Christ thou shalt serve him.

b. Thou shalt love thy neighbor as thyself.

c. Thou shalt not steal; neither commit adultery, nor kill, nor do anything like unto it.

d. Thou shalt thank the Lord thy God in all things.

e. Thou shalt offer a sacrifice unto the Lord thy God in righteousness; even that of a broken heart and a contrite spirit.

f. And that thou mayest more fully keep thyself unspotted from the world, thou shalt go to the house of prayer and offer up thy sacraments upon my holy day; for verily this is a day appointed unto thee to rest from thy labors, and to pay thy devotions unto the Most High;

g. nevertheless thy vows shall be offered up in righteousness on all days, and at all times;

h. but remember that on this, the Lord's day, thou shalt offer thine oblations, and thy sacraments, unto the Most High, confessing thy sins unto thy brethren, and before the Lord.

3 a. And on this day thou shalt do none other thing, only let thy food be prepared with singleness of heart, that thy fasting may be perfect; or in other words, that thy joy may be full.

b. Verily this is fasting and prayer; or, in other words, rejoicing and prayer.

4 a. And inasmuch as ye do these things, with thanksgiving, with cheerful hearts, and countenances; not with much laughter, for this is sin, but with a glad heart and a cheerful countenance;

b. verily I say, that inasmuch as ye do this the fullness of the earth is yours: the beasts of the fields, and the fowls of the air, and that which climbeth upon the trees, and walketh upon the earth;

c. yea, and the herb, and the good things which come of the earth, whether for food or for raiment, or for houses or for barns, or for orchards, or for gardens, or for vineyards;

d. yea, all things which come of the earth, in the season thereof, are made for the benefit and the use of man, both to please the eye, and to gladden the heart; yea, for food and for raiment, for taste and for smell, to strengthen the body, and to enliven the soul.

5 a. And it pleaseth God that he hath given all these things unto man; for unto this end were they made, to be used with judgment, not to excess, neither by extortion:

b. and in nothing doth man offend God, or against none is his wrath kindled, save those who confess not his hand in all things, and obey not his commandments.

c. Behold, this is according to the law and the prophets: wherefore trouble me no more concerning this matter, but learn that he who doeth the works of righteousness, shall receive his reward, even peace in this world, and eternal life in the world to come.

d. I, the Lord, have spoken it and the Spirit beareth record. Amen.

SECTION 60

This is the last of four revelations given through Joseph Smith, Jr., during the first visit of the leading elders of the church to the land of Zion. It was received August 8, 1831. During their stay in Independence the Center Place and "the spot for the temple" had been pointed out, and some sound basic instruction had been given. Now the work in Kirtland demanded Joseph's attention, and he and some of his immediate associates prepared to return. This message is addressed to those who were returning, and to the elders who were known to be on their way but who had not yet reached Independence.

1 a. Behold, thus saith the Lord unto the elders of his church, who are to return speedily to the land from whence they came.

b. Behold, it pleaseth me, that you have come up hither; but with some I am not well pleased, for they will not open their mouths, but hide the talent which I have given unto them, because of the fear of man. Woe unto such, for mine anger is kindled against them.

2 a. And it shall come to pass, if they are not more faithful unto me, it shall be taken away, even that which they have, for I, the Lord, ruleth in the heavens above, and among the armies of the earth;

b. and in the day when I shall make up my jewels, all men shall know what it is that bespeaketh the power of God.

c. But verily I will speak unto you concerning your journey unto the land from whence you came.

d. Let there be a craft made, or bought, as seemeth you good, it mattereth not unto me, and take your journey speedily for the place which is called Saint Louis.

e. And from thence let my servants Sidney Rigdon, and Joseph Smith, Jr., and Oliver Cowdery, take their journey for Cincinnati: and in this place let them lift up their voice, and declare my word with loud voices, without wrath or doubting, lifting up holy hands upon them.

f. For I am able to make you holy, and your sins are forgiven you.

3 a. And let the residue take their journey from Saint Louis, two by two, and preach the word, not in haste, among the congregations of the wicked, until they return to the churches from whence they came.

b. And all this for the good of the churches; for this intent have I sent them.

c. And let my servant Edward Partridge impart of the money which I have given him, a portion unto mine elders, who are commanded to return; and he that is able, let him return it by way of the agent, and he that is not, of him it is not required.

d. And now I speak of the residue who are to come unto this land. Behold, they have been sent to preach my gospel among the congregations of the wicked; wherefore, I give unto them a commandment thus:

e. Thou shalt not idle away thy time; neither shalt thou bury thy talent that it may not be known.

4 a. And after thou hast come up unto the land of Zion, and hast proclaimed my word, thou shalt speedily return, proclaiming my word among the congregations of the wicked.

b. Not in haste, neither in wrath nor with strife; and shake off the dust of thy feet against those who receive thee not, not in their presence, lest thou provoke them, but in secret, and wash thy feet as a testimony against them in the day of judgment.

c. Behold, this is sufficient for you, and the will of him who hath sent you.

d. And by the mouth of my servant Joseph Smith, Jr., it shall be made known concerning Sidney Rigdon and Oliver Cowdery, the residue hereafter. Even so. Amen.

SECTION 61

Revelation given to eleven elders camped at McIlwain's Bend on the Missouri River, August 12, 1831. It was received by Joseph Smith, Jr., after prayer concerning a vision received by W. W. Phelps in which was depicted the danger of travel by water.

1 a. Behold, and hearken unto the voice of him who has all power, who is from everlasting to everlasting, even Alpha and Omega, the beginning and the end.

b. Behold, verily thus saith the Lord unto you, O ye elders of my church, who are assembled upon this spot, whose sins are now forgiven you, for I the Lord forgiveth sins, and am merciful unto those who confess their sins with humble hearts;

c. but verily I say unto you, that it is not needful for this whole company of mine elders, to be moving swiftly upon the waters, whilst the inhabitants on either side are perishing in unbelief;

d. nevertheless, I suffered it that ye might bear record; behold, there are many dangers upon the waters and more especially hereafter, for I the Lord have decreed, in mine anger, many destructions upon the waters;

e. yea, and especially upon these waters; nevertheless, all flesh is in mine hand, and he that is faithful among you, shall not perish by the waters.

2 a. Wherefore it is expedient that my servant Sidney Gilbert, and my servant William W. Phelps, be in haste upon their errand and mission;

b. nevertheless I would not suffer that ye should part until you are chastened for all your sins, that you might be one; that you might not perish in wickedness;

c. but now verily I say, It behooveth me that ye should part; wherefore let my servants Sidney Gilbert and William W. Phelps, take their former company, and let them take their journey in haste that they may fill their mission, and through faith they shall overcome; and inasmuch as they are faithful, they shall be preserved, and I, the Lord, will be with them.

d. And let the residue take that which is needful for clothing. Let my servant Sidney Gilbert take that which is not needful with him, as you shall agree.

e. And now, behold, for your good, I gave unto you a commandment concerning these things; and I, the Lord, will reason with you as with men in days of old.

3 a. Behold, I, the Lord, in the beginning, blessed the waters, but in the last days by the mouth of my servant John, I cursed the waters;

b. wherefore, the days will come that no flesh shall be safe upon the waters, and it shall be said in days to come, that none is able to go up to the land of Zion, upon the waters, but he that is upright in heart.

c. And, as I, the Lord, in the beginning cursed the land, even so in the last days have I blessed it, in its time, for the use of my saints, that they may partake the fatness thereof.

d. And now I give unto you a commandment, and what I say unto one I say unto all, that you shall forewarn your brethren concerning these waters, that they come not in journeying upon them, lest their faith fail, and they are caught in her snares;

e. I, the Lord, have decreed, and the destroyer rideth upon the face thereof, and I revoke not the decree; I, the Lord, was angry with you yesterday, but today mine anger is turned away.

f. Wherefore let those concerning whom I have spoken, that should take their journey in haste—again I say unto you, Let them take their journey in haste, and it mattereth not unto me, after a little, if it so be that they fill their mission, whether they go by water or by land; let this be as it is made known unto them according to their judgments hereafter.

4 a. And now, concerning my servants Sidney Rigdon, and Joseph Smith, Jr., and Oliver Cowdery, let them come not again upon the waters, save it be upon the canal, while journeying unto their homes, or, in other words, they shall not come upon the waters to journey, save upon the canal.

b. Behold, I, the Lord, have appointed a way for the

journeying of my saints, and, behold, this is the way; that after they leave the canal, they shall journey by land, inasmuch as they are commanded to journey and go up unto the land of Zion; and they shall do like unto the children of Israel, pitching their tents by the way.

5 a. And, behold, this commandment you shall give unto all your brethren; nevertheless unto whom it is given power to command the waters, unto him it is given by the Spirit to know all his ways;

b. wherefore let him do as the Spirit of the living God commandeth him, whether upon the land or upon the waters, as it remaineth with me to do hereafter; and unto you it is given the course for the Saints, or the way for the Saints of the camp of the Lord, to journey.

c. And again, verily I say unto you, My servants Sidney Rigdon, and Joseph Smith, Jr., and Oliver Cowdery, shall not open their mouths in the congregations of the wicked, until they arrive at Cincinnati;

d. and in that place they shall lift up their voices unto God against that people; yea, unto him whose anger is kindled against their wickedness; a people who are well-nigh ripened for destruction;

e. and from thence let them journey for the congregations of their brethren, for their labors, even now, are wanted more abundantly among them, than among the congregations of the wicked.

6 a. And now concerning the residue, let them journey and declare the word among the congregations of the wicked, inasmuch as it is given, and inasmuch as they do this they shall rid their garments, and they shall be spotless before me;

b. and let them journey together, or two by two, as seemeth them good, only let my servant Reynolds Cahoon, and my servant Samuel H. Smith, with whom I am well pleased, be not separated until they return to their homes, and this for a wise purpose in me.

c. And now verily I say unto you, and what I say unto one I say unto all, Be of good cheer, little children, for I am in your midst, and I have not forsaken you, and inasmuch as you have humbled yourselves before me, the blessings of the kingdom are yours.

d. Gird up your loins and be watchful, and be sober, looking forth for the coming of the Son of Man, for he cometh in an hour you think not.

e. Pray always that you enter not into temptation, that you may abide the day of his coming, whether in life or in death. Even so. Amen.

SECTION 62

Revelation given through Joseph Smith, Jr., on the bank of the Missouri River, August 13, 1831. The prophet and his party on their way from Independence to Kirtland met several elders who were going to the land of Zion. This revelation is addressed to these elders.

1 a. Behold, and hearken, O ye elders of my church, saith the Lord your God; even Jesus Christ, your Advocate; who knoweth the weakness of man and how to succor them who are tempted; and verily mine eyes are upon those who have not as yet gone up unto the land of Zion; wherefore your mission is not yet full;

b. nevertheless ye are blessed, for the testimony which ye have borne is recorded in heaven for the angels to look upon, and they rejoice over you, and your sins are forgiven you.

2 a. And now continue your journey. Assemble yourselves upon the land of Zion, and hold a meeting and rejoice together, and offer a sacrament unto the Most High;

b. and then you may return to bear record; yea, even all together, or two by two, as seemeth you good; it mattereth not unto me, only be faithful, and declare glad tidings unto the inhabitants of the earth, or among the congregations of the wicked.

c. Behold, I, the Lord, have brought you together that the promise might be fulfilled, that the faithful among you should be preserved and rejoice together in the land of Missouri. I, the Lord, promised the faithful and can not lie.

3 a. I, the Lord, am willing, if any among you desireth to ride upon horses, or upon mules, or in chariots, he shall receive this blessing, if he receive it from the hand of the Lord, with a thankful heart in all things.

b. These things remain with you to do according to judgment and the directions of the Spirit. Behold, the kingdom is yours. And, behold, and lo, I am with the faithful always. Even so. Amen.

SECTION 63

Joseph Smith, Sidney Rigdon, and Oliver Cowdery arrived in Kirtland, August 27, 1831, from their first visit to the land of Zion. Joseph wrote in his history,

> *"In these infant days of the church, there was great anxiety to obtain the word of the Lord upon every subject that in any way concerned our salvation; and as the "land of Zion" was the most temporal object in view, I inquired of the Lord for further information upon the gathering of the Saints, and the purchase of the land and other matters."*

It was in answer to this petition that Joseph Smith received the following revelation.

1 a. Hearken, O ye people, and open your hearts, and give ear from afar; and listen, you that call yourselves the people of the Lord, and hear the word of the Lord, and his will concerning you;

b. yea, verily, I say, Hear the word of him whose anger is kindled against the wicked and rebellious;

c. who willeth to take even them whom he will take, and preserveth in life them whom he will preserve; who buildeth up at his own will and pleasure; and destroyeth when he pleases, and is able to cast the soul down to hell.

2 a. Behold, I, the Lord, utter my voice, and it shall be obeyed.

b. Wherefore, verily I say, Let the wicked take heed, and let the rebellious fear and tremble; and let the unbelieving hold their lips, for the day of wrath shall come upon them as a whirlwind, and all flesh shall know that I am God.

c. And he that seeketh signs shall see signs, but not unto salvation.

3 a. Verily, I say unto you, There are those among you who seek signs, and there have been such even from the beginning; but, behold, faith cometh not by signs, but signs follow those that believe.

b. Yea, signs come by faith, not by the will of men, nor as they please, but by the will of God.

c. Yea, signs come by faith, unto mighty works, for without faith no man pleaseth God: and with whom God is angry he is not well pleased: wherefore, unto such he showeth no signs, only in wrath unto their condemnation.

4 a. Wherefore, I, the Lord, am not pleased with those among you, who have sought after signs and wonders for faith, and not for the good of men unto my glory; nevertheless, I gave commandments and many have turned away from my commandments and have not kept them.

b. There were among you adulterers and adulteresses; some of whom have turned away from you, and others remain with you, that hereafter shall be revealed.

c. Let such beware and repent speedily, lest judgment shall come upon them as a snare, and their folly shall be made manifest, and their works shall follow them in the eyes of the people.

5 a. And verily I say unto you, as I have said before, He that looketh on a woman to lust after her, or if any shall commit adultery in their hearts, they shall not have the Spirit, but shall deny the faith and shall fear:

b. wherefore, I, the Lord, have said that the fearful, and the unbelieving, and all liars, and whosoever loveth and maketh a lie, and the whoremonger, and the sorcerer, shall have their part in that lake which burneth with fire and brimstone, which is the second death.

c. Verily I say, that they shall not have part in the first resurrection.

6 a. And now, behold, I, the Lord, saith unto you, that ye are not justified because these things are among you;

b. nevertheless he that endureth in faith and doeth my will, the same shall overcome, and shall receive an inheritance upon the earth, when the day of transfiguration shall come; when the earth shall be transfigured, even according to the pattern which was shown unto mine apostles upon the mount; of which account the fullness ye have not yet received.

7 a. And now, verily I say unto you, that as I said that I would make known my will unto you, behold, I will make it known unto you, not by the way of commandment, for there are many who observe not to keep my commandments;

b. but unto him that keepeth my commandments, I will give the mysteries of my kingdom, and the same shall be in him a well of living water, springing up unto everlasting life.

8 a. And now, behold, this is the will of the Lord your God concerning his Saints, that they should assemble themselves together unto the land of Zion, not in haste, lest there should be confusion, which bringeth pestilence.

b. Behold, the land of Zion, I, the Lord, holdeth it in mine own hands; nevertheless, I, the Lord, rendereth unto Caesar the things which are Caesar's:

c. wherefore, I, the Lord, willeth, that you should purchase the lands, that you may have advantage of the world, that you may have claim on the world, that they may not be stirred up unto anger;

d. for Satan putteth it into their hearts to anger against you, and to the shedding of blood; wherefore the land of Zion shall not be obtained but by purchase, or by blood, otherwise there is none inheritance for you.

e. And if by purchase, behold, you are blessed; and if by blood, as you are forbidden to shed blood, lo, your enemies are upon you, and ye shall be scourged from city to city, and from synagogue to synagogue, and but few shall stand to receive an inheritance.

9 a. I, the Lord, am angry with the wicked; I am holding my Spirit from the inhabitants of the earth.

b. I have sworn in my wrath and decreed wars upon the face of the earth, and the wicked shall slay the wicked, and fear shall come upon every man, and the saints also shall hardly escape;

c. nevertheless, I, the Lord, am with them, and will come down in heaven from the presence of my Father, and consume the wicked with unquenchable fire.

d. And, behold, this is not yet, but by and by; wherefore seeing that I, the Lord, have decreed all these things upon the face of the earth, I will that my saints should be assembled upon the land of Zion;

e. and that every man should take righteousness in his hands, and faithfulness upon his loins, and lift a warning voice unto the inhabitants of the earth; and declare both by word and by flight, that desolation shall come upon the wicked.

f. Wherefore let my disciples in Kirtland arrange their temporal concerns, which dwell upon this farm.

10 a. Let my servant Titus Billings, who has the care thereof, dispose of the land, that he may be prepared in the coming spring, to take his journey up unto the land of Zion, with those that dwell upon the face thereof, excepting those whom I shall reserve unto myself, that shall not go until I shall command them.

b. And let all the moneys which can be spared, it mattereth not unto me whether it be little or much, be sent up unto the land of Zion, unto them whom I have appointed to receive.

11 Behold, I, the Lord, will give unto my servant Joseph Smith, Jr., power that he shall be enabled to discern by the Spirit those who shall go up unto the land of Zion, and those of my disciples who shall tarry.

12 a. Let my servant Newel K. Whitney retain his store, or, in other words, the store yet for a little season. Nevertheless let him impart all the money which he can impart, to be sent up unto the land of Zion.

b. Behold, these things are in his own hands, let him do according to wisdom.

c. Verily I say, Let him be ordained as an agent unto the disciples that shall tarry, and let him be ordained unto this power; and now speedily visit the churches, expounding these things unto them, with my servant Oliver Cowdery.

d. Behold, this is my will, obtaining moneys even as I have directed.

13 a. He that is faithful and endureth shall overcome the world.

b. He that sendeth up treasures unto the land of Zion, shall receive an inheritance in this world, and his works shall follow him; and also a reward in the world to come:

c. yea, and blessed are the dead that die in the Lord from henceforth, when the Lord shall come, and old things shall pass away, and all things become new,

d. they shall rise from the dead and shall not die after, and shall receive an inheritance before the Lord, in the holy city, and he that liveth when the Lord shall come, and has kept the faith, blessed is he; nevertheless it is appointed to him to die at the age of man;

e. wherefore children shall grow up until they become old, old men shall die; but they shall not sleep in the dust, but they shall be changed in the twinkling of an eye;

f. wherefore, for this cause preached the apostles unto the world the resurrection of the dead:

g. these things are the things that ye must look for, and speaking after the manner of the Lord, they are now nigh at hand; and in a time to come, even in the day of the coming of the Son of Man, and until that hour, there will be foolish virgins among the wise, and at that hour cometh an entire separation of the righteous and the wicked;

h. and in that day will I send mine angels, to pluck out the wicked, and cast them into unquenchable fire.

14 And now, behold, verily I say unto you, I, the Lord, am not pleased with my ꞊ervant Sidney Rigdon, he exalted himself in his heart, and received not counsel, but grieved the Spirit; wherefore his writing is not acceptable unto the Lord, and he shall make another, and if the Lord receive it not, behold, he standeth no longer in the office which I have appointed him.

15 a. And again, verily I say unto you, Those who desire in their hearts, in meekness, to warn sinners to repentance, let them be ordained unto this power; for this is a day of warning, and not a day of many words.

b. For I, the Lord, am not to be mocked in the last days. Behold, I am from above, and my power lieth beneath.

c. I am over all, and in all, and through all, and searcheth all things; and the day cometh that all things shall be subject unto me. Behold, I am Alpha and Omega, even Jesus Christ.

d. Wherefore let all men beware how they take my name in their lips; for, behold, verily I say, that many there be who are under this condemnation; who use the name of the Lord, and use it in vain, having not authority.

e. Wherefore, let the church repent of their sins, and I, the Lord, will own them; otherwise they shall be cut off.

16 a. Remember that that which cometh from above is sacred, and must be spoken with care, and by constraint of the Spirit, and in this there is no condemnation; and ye receive the Spirit through prayer; wherefore, without this there remaineth condemnation.

b. Let my servants Joseph Smith, Jr., and Sidney Rigdon, seek them a home as they are taught through prayer, by the Spirit.

c. These things remain to overcome, through patience, that such may receive a more exceeding and eternal weight of glory; otherwise, a greater condemnation. Amen.

SECTION 64

Revelation given through Joseph Smith, Jr., September 11, 1831, at Kirtland, Ohio. Joseph was preparing to go to Hiram, more than thirty miles southeast of Kirtland, to continue his work on the Inspired Version of the Scriptures. Meanwhile some of the brethren were busy preparing for their journey to Independence. This revelation is directed primarily to the elders who were leaving for Zion.

This was the last revelation printed in the Book of Commandments, the type having been set as far as "blood of Ephraim" (7b) when the mob at Independence, Missouri, destroyed the press.

1 a. Behold, thus saith the Lord your God unto you, O ye elders of my church, Hearken ye, and hear, and receive my will concerning you; for verily I say unto you, I will that

ye should overcome the world; wherefore I will have compassion upon you.

b. There are those among you who have sinned; but verily I say, For this once, for mine own glory, and for the salvation of souls, I have forgiven you your sins.

2 a. I will be merciful unto you, for I have given unto you the kingdom; and the keys of the mysteries of the kingdom, shall not be taken from my servant Joseph Smith, Jr., through the means I have appointed, while he liveth, inasmuch as he obeyeth mine ordinances.

b. There are those who have sought occasion against him without cause; nevertheless he has sinned, but verily I say unto you, I, the Lord, forgiveth sins unto those who confess their sins before me, and ask forgiveness, who have not sinned unto death.

c. My disciples, in days of old, sought occasion against one another, and forgave not one another in their hearts, and for this evil they were afflicted, and sorely chastened;

d. wherefore I say unto you, that ye ought to forgive one another, for he that forgiveth not his brother his trespasses, standeth condemned before the Lord, for there remaineth in him the greater sin.

e. I, the Lord, will forgive whom I will forgive, but of you it is required to forgive all men; and ye ought to say in your hearts, Let God judge between me and thee, and reward thee according to thy deeds.

f. And he that repenteth not of his sins, and confesseth them not, then ye shall bring him before the church, and do with him as the Scriptures saith unto you, either by commandment, or by revelation.

g. And this ye shall do that God might be glorified, not because ye forgive not, having not compassion, but that ye may be justified in the eyes of the law, that ye may not offend him who is your Lawgiver.

3 a. Verily I say, For this cause ye shall do these things.

b. Behold, I, the Lord, was angry with him who was my servant Ezra Booth; and also my servant Isaac Morley; for they kept not the law, neither the commandments; they sought evil in their hearts, and I the Lord, withheld my Spirit.

c. They condemned for evil that thing in which there was

no evil; nevertheless, I have forgiven my servant Isaac Morley.

d. And also my servant Edward Partridge, behold, he hath sinned, and Satan seeketh to destroy his soul; but when these things are made known unto them, they repent of the evil, and they shall be forgiven.

4 a. And now, verily I say, that it is expedient in me that my servant Sidney Gilbert, after a few weeks, should return upon his business, and to his agency in the land of Zion; and that which he hath seen and heard may be made known unto my disciples, that they perish not. And for this cause have I spoken these things.

b. And again, I say unto you, that my servant Isaac Morley may not be tempted above that which he is able to bear, and counsel wrongfully to your hurt, I gave commandment that this farm should be sold.

c. I do not will that my servant Frederick G. Williams should sell his farm, for I, the Lord, will to retain a strong hold in the land of Kirtland, for the space of five years, in the which I will not overthrow the wicked, that thereby I may save some;

d. and after that day, I, the Lord, will not hold any guilty that shall go, with an open heart, up to the land of Zion; for I, the Lord, require the hearts of the children of men.

5 a. Behold, now it is called to-day (until the coming of the Son of Man), and verily it is a day of sacrifice, and a day for the tithing of my people; for he that is tithed shall not be burned (at his coming); for after to-day cometh the burning: this is speaking after the manner of the Lord;

b. for verily I say, Tomorrow all the proud and they that do wickedly shall be as stubble; and I will burn them up, for I am the Lord of hosts; and I will not spare any that remaineth in Babylon. Wherefore, if ye believe me, ye will labor while it is called to-day.

c. And it is not meet that my servants Newel K. Whitney and Sidney Gilbert should sell their store, and their possessions here, for this is not wisdom until the residue of the church, which remaineth in this place, shall go up unto the land of Zion.

6 a. Behold, it is said in my laws, or forbidden, to get in debt to thine enemies; but, behold, it is not said at any time, that the Lord should not take when he please, and pay as seemeth him good:

b. wherefore, as ye are agents, and ye are on the Lord's errand; and whatever ye do according to the will of the Lord, is the Lord's business, and he hath set you to provide for his Saints in these last days, that they may obtain an inheritance in the land of Zion, and, behold, I, the Lord, declare unto you, and my words are sure and shall not fail, that they shall obtain it;

c. but all things must come to pass in their time; wherefore be not weary in well-doing, for ye are laying the foundation of a great work. And out of small things proceedeth that which is great.

7 a. Behold, the Lord requireth the heart and a willing mind; and the willing and obedient shall eat the good of the land of Zion in these last days;

b. and the rebellious shall be cut off out of the land of Zion, and shall be sent away, and shall not inherit the land; for, verily, I say that the rebellious are not of the blood of Ephraim, wherefore they shall be plucked out.

c. Behold, I, the Lord, have made my church in these last days, like unto a judge sitting on a hill, or in a high place, to judge the nations; for it shall come to pass, that the inhabitants of Zion shall judge all things pertaining to Zion;

d. and liars, and hypocrites shall be proved by them, and they who are not apostles and prophets shall be known.

8 a. And even the bishop, who is a judge, and his counselors, if they are not faithful in their stewardships, shall be condemned, and others shall be planted in their stead; for, behold, I say unto you that Zion shall flourish, and the glory of the Lord shall be upon her, and she shall be an ensign unto the people, and there shall come unto her out of every nation under heaven.

b. And the day shall come, when the nations of the earth shall tremble because of her, and shall fear because of her terrible ones. The Lord hath spoken it. Amen.

SECTION 65

Joseph Smith, Jr., and Sidney Rigdon lived in the home of John Johnson at Hiram, Ohio, during September and October 1831 while they continued work on the Holy Scriptures. Here Joseph received the following revelation on prayer.

1 a. Hearken, and lo, a voice as of one sent down from on high, who is mighty and powerful, whose going forth is unto the ends of the earth; yea, whose voice is unto men, Prepare ye the way of the Lord, make his paths straight.

b. The keys of the kingdom of God are committed unto man on the earth, and from thence shall the gospel roll forth unto the ends of the earth, as the stone which is cut out of the mountain without hands shall roll forth, until it has filled the whole earth;

c. yea, a voice crying, Prepare ye the way of the Lord, prepare ye the supper of the Lamb, make ready for the Bridegroom;

d. pray unto the Lord; call upon his holy name; make known his wonderful works among the people, call upon the Lord, that his kingdom may go forth upon the earth;

e. that the inhabitants thereof may receive it, and be prepared for the days to come, in the which the Son of Man shall come down in heaven, clothed in the brightness of his glory, to meet the kingdom of God which is set up on the earth;

f. wherefore, may the kingdom of God go forth, that the kingdom of heaven may come, that thou, O God, may be glorified in heaven, so on earth, that thy enemies may be subdued; for thine is the honor, power, and glory, for ever and ever. Amen.

SECTION 66

Revelation given through Joseph Smith, Jr., at Orange, Ohio, October 1831. William E. McLellin had recently joined the church. He asked for instruction concerning his work, and this revelation was given in answer to Joseph's prayer on his behalf. In 1835 Elder McLellin became one of the charter members of the Council of Twelve.

1 a. Behold, thus saith the Lord, unto my servant, William E. McLellin, Blessed are you, inasmuch as you have turned away from your iniquities, and have received my truths, saith the Lord your Redeemer, the Savior of the world, even of as many as believe on my name.

b. Verily I say unto you, Blessed are you for receiving mine everlasting covenant, even the fullness of my gospel, sent forth unto the children of men, that they might have life, and be made partakers of the glories, which are to be revealed in the last days, as it was written by the prophets and apostles in days of old.

2 a. Verily I say unto you, my servant William, that you are clean, but not all; repent therefore of those things which are not pleasing in my sight, saith the Lord, for the Lord will show them unto you.

b. And now verily I, the Lord, will show unto you what I will concerning you, or what is my will concerning you; behold, verily I say unto you, that it is my will that you should proclaim my gospel from land to land, and from city to city; yea, in those regions round about where it has not been proclaimed.

3 a. Tarry not many days in this place; go not up unto the land of Zion, as yet; but inasmuch as you can send, send; otherwise think not of thy property.

b. Go unto the eastern lands; bear testimony in every place, unto every people, and in their synagogues; reasoning with the people.

4 Let my servant Samuel H. Smith go with you, and forsake him not, and give him thine instructions; and he that is

faithful shall be made strong in every place, and I, the Lord, will go with you.

5 a. Lay your hands upon the sick and they shall recover. Return not till I, the Lord, shall send you.

b. Be patient in affliction.

c. Ask and ye shall receive. Knock and it shall be opened unto you. Seek not to be cumbered.

d. Forsake all unrighteousness.

e. Commit not adultery, a temptation with which thou hast been troubled.

f. Keep these sayings for they are true and faithful, and thou shalt magnify thine office, and push many people to Zion, with songs of everlasting joy upon their heads.

g. Continue in these things, even unto the end, and you shall have a crown of eternal life at the right hand of my Father, who is full of grace and truth.

h. Verily thus saith the Lord your God, your Redeemer, even Jesus Christ. Amen.

SECTION 67

Revelation addressed to the elders of the church, given through Joseph Smith, Jr., at a special conference held at Hiram, Ohio, November 1831. There had been some criticism among the elders regarding the language of the revelations. William E. McLellin accepted the challenge of this revelation but was unable to produce any improvement.

1 a. Behold, and hearken, O ye elders of my church, who have assembled yourselves together, whose prayers I have heard, and whose hearts I know, and whose desires have come up before me.

b. Behold, and lo, mine eyes are upon you; and the heavens and the earth are in mine hands, and the riches of eternity are mine to give.

c. Ye endeavored to believe that ye should receive the blessing which was offered unto you, but, behold, verily, I say unto you, There were fears in your hearts; and verily this is the reason that ye did not receive.

2 a. And now, I, the Lord, give unto you a testimony of the truth of these commandments which are lying before you; your eyes have been upon my servant Joseph Smith, Jr., and his language you have known; and his imperfections you have known; and you have sought in your hearts knowledge, that you might express beyond his language:

b. this you also know: now seek ye out of the Book of Commandments, even the least that is among them, and appoint him that is the most wise among you;

c. or if there be any among you, that shall make one like unto it, then ye are justified in saying that ye do not know that they are true; but if ye can not make one like unto it, ye are under condemnation if ye do not bear record that they are true;

d. for ye know that there is no unrighteousness in them; and that which is righteous cometh down from above, from the Father of lights.

3 a. And again, verily I say unto you, that it is your privilege, and a promise I give unto you that have been ordained unto this ministry, that inasmuch as you strip yourselves from jealousies and fears, and humble yourselves before me, for ye are not sufficiently humble, the veil shall be rent, and you shall see me and know that I am;

b. not with the carnal, neither natural mind, but with the spiritual; for no man has seen God at any time in the flesh, except quickened by the Spirit of God;

c. neither can any natural man abide the presence of God; neither after the carnal mind; ye are not able to abide the presence of God now, neither the ministering of angels; wherefore continue in patience until ye are perfected.

4 Let not your minds turn back, and when ye are worthy, in mine own due time, ye shall see and know that which was conferred upon you by the hands of my servant Joseph Smith, Jr. Amen.

SECTION 68

Revelation given through Joseph Smith, Jr., November 1831 at a special conference held at Hiram, Ohio. Joseph wrote, "The mind and will of the Lord was made known by the voice of the Spirit to a conference concerning certain elders, and also certain items as made known in addition to the covenants and commandments." The instructions concerning church government found in this revelation should be read in connection with the "Articles and Covenants" which now constitute Section 17.

The message is specifically addressed to Orson Hyde, Luke Johnson, Lyman Johnson, and William E. McLellin, although its contents are of continuing importance to the entire church.

1 a. My servant, Orson Hyde, was called by his ordinance to proclaim the everlasting gospel by the Spirit of the living God, from people to people and from land to land, in the congregations of the wicked, in their synagogues, reasoning with and expounding all Scriptures unto them.

b. And, behold and lo, this is an ensample unto all those who were ordained unto this priesthood, whose mission is appointed unto them to go forth; and this is the ensample unto them, that they shall speak as they are moved upon by the Holy Ghost;

c. and whatsoever they shall speak when moved upon by the Holy Ghost shall be Scripture; shall be the will of the Lord; shall be the mind of the Lord; shall be the word of the Lord; shall be the voice of the Lord, and the power of God unto salvation:

d. behold, this is the promise of the Lord unto you, O ye my servants: wherefore, be of good cheer, and do not fear, for I, the Lord, am with you and will stand by you; and ye shall bear record of me, even Jesus Christ, that I am the Son of the living God, that I was, that I am, and that I am to come.

e. This is the word of the Lord unto you my servant, Orson Hyde, and also unto my servant, Luke Johnson, and unto my servant, Lyman Johnson, and unto my servant, William E. McLellin; and unto all the faithful elders of my church.

f. Go ye into all the world; preach the gospel to every creature, acting in the authority which I have given you, baptizing in the name of the Father, and of the Son, and of the Holy Ghost;

g. and he that believeth, and is baptized, shall be saved, and he that believeth not shall be damned; and he that believeth shall be blessed with signs following, even as it is written;

h. and unto you it shall be given to know the signs of the times, and the signs of the coming of the Son of Man; and of as many as the Father shall bear record, to you shall be given power to seal them up unto eternal life. Amen.

2 a. And now concerning the items in addition to the covenants and commandments, they are these:

b. There remaineth hereafter in the due time of the Lord, other bishops to be set apart unto the church to minister even according to the first;

c. wherefore they shall be high priests who are worthy, and they shall be appointed by the First Presidency of the Melchisedec priesthood, except they be literal descendants of Aaron, and if they be literal descendants of Aaron, they have a legal right to the bishopric, if they are the firstborn among the sons of Aaron; for the firstborn holds the right of the presidency over this priesthood, and the keys or authority of the same.

d. No man has a legal right to this office, to hold the keys of this priesthood, except he be a literal descendant and the firstborn of Aaron; but as a high priest of the Melchisedec priesthood has authority to officiate in all the lesser offices, he may officiate in the office of bishop when no literal descendant of Aaron can be found;

e. provided, he is called and set apart, and ordained unto this power under the hands of the First Presidency of the Melchisedec priesthood.

f. And a literal descendant of Aaron, also must be designated by this presidency, and found worthy, and anointed, and ordained under the hands of this presidency, otherwise they are not legally authorized to officiate in their priesthood;

g. but by virtue of the decree concerning their right of the

priesthood descending from father to son, they may claim
their anointing, if at any time they can prove their lineage,
or do ascertain it by revelation from the Lord under the
hands of the above-named presidency.

3 a. And again, no bishop, or high priest, who shall be
set apart for this ministry, shall be tried or condemned for
any crime, save it be before the First Presidency of the church;
    b. and inasmuch as he is found guilty before this presi-
dency, by testimony that can not be impeached, he shall
be condemned, and if he repents he shall be forgiven, according to the covenants and commandments of the church.

4 a. And again, inasmuch as parents have children in
Zion, or in any of her stakes which are organized, that teach
them not to understand the doctrine of repentance; faith in
Christ the Son of the living God; and of baptism and the
gift of the Holy Ghost by the laying on of the hands when
eight years old, the sin be upon the head of the parents;
    b. for this shall be a law unto the inhabitants of Zion,
or in any of her stakes which are organized; and their children
shall be baptized for the remission of their sins when eight
years old, and receive the laying on of the hands:
    c. and they shall also teach their children to pray, and to
walk uprightly before the Lord.
    d. And the inhabitants of Zion shall also observe the sab-
bath day to keep it holy.
    e. And the inhabitants of Zion, also, shall remember their
labors, inasmuch as they are appointed to labor, in all faithfulness; for the idler shall be had in remembrance before
the Lord.
    f. Now I, the Lord, am not well pleased with the inhabit-
ants of Zion, for there are idlers among them: and their
children are also growing up in wickedness; they also seek
not earnestly the riches of eternity, but their eyes are full
of greediness.
    g. These things ought not to be, and must be done away
from among them; wherefore let my servant Oliver Cowdery
carry these sayings unto the land of Zion.
    h. And a commandment I give unto them, that he that
observeth not his prayers before the Lord in the season there-

of, let him be had in remembrance before the judge of my people.

i. These sayings are true and faithful; wherefore transgress them not, neither take therefrom. Behold, I am Alpha and Omega, and I come quickly. Amen.

SECTION 69

Revelation given through Joseph Smith, Jr., November 1831 at Hiram, Ohio. The compilation of the revelations to comprise the "Book of Commandments" was authorized at one of the four special conferences held in Hiram during the first half of November 1831. It was decided that Oliver Cowdery and John Whitmer should carry the revelations to Independence, Missouri, where they would be printed by W. W. Phelps and Company. This instruction was sought and received in connection with the mission of these brethren.

1 a. Hearken unto me, saith the Lord your God, for my servant Oliver Cowdery's sake: it is not wisdom in me that he should be intrusted with the commandments and the moneys which he shall carry unto the land of Zion, except one go with him who will be true and faithful; wherefore I, the Lord, will that my servant John Whitmer should go with my servant Oliver Cowdery;

b. and also that he shall continue in writing and making a history of all the important things which he shall observe and know concerning my church; and also that he receive counsel and assistance from my servant Oliver Cowdery, and others.

2 a. And also my servants who are abroad in the earth should send forth the accounts of their stewardships to the land of Zion, for the land of Zion shall be a seat and a place to receive and do all these things;

b. nevertheless, let my servant John Whitmer travel many times from place to place, and from church to church, that he may the more easily obtain knowledge—preaching and expounding, writing, copying, selecting, and obtaining all things which shall be for the good of the church, and for the rising generations, that shall grow up on the land of Zion, to possess it from generation to generation, for ever and ever. Amen.

SECTION 70

Revelation given through Joseph Smith, Jr., November 12, 1831, at Hiram, Ohio. The editing and publishing of the revelations occupied much of the time of the elders who were commissioned to do this. In this revelation six of these elders were designated as "stewards over the revelations and commandments," and their remuneration was set forth as part of the basic stewardship law.

1 a. Behold and hearken, O ye inhabitants of Zion, and all ye people of my church, who are far off, and hear the word of the Lord, which I give unto my servant Joseph Smith, Jr., and also unto my servant Martin Harris, and also unto my servant Oliver Cowdery, and also unto my servant John Whitmer, and also unto my servant Sidney Rigdon, and also unto my servant William W. Phelps, by the way of commandment unto them, for I give unto them a commandment;

b. wherefore hearken and hear, for thus saith the Lord unto them, I, the Lord, have appointed them, and ordained them to be stewards over the revelations and commandments which I have given unto them, and which I shall hereafter give unto them;

c. and an account of this stewardship will I require of them in the day of judgment; wherefore I have appointed unto them, and this is their business in the church of God, to manage them and the concerns thereof; yea, the benefits thereof.

2 a. Wherefore a commandment I give unto them, that they shall not give these things unto the church, neither unto the world;

b. nevertheless, inasmuch as they receive more than is needful for their necessities and their wants, it shall be given into my storehouse, and the benefits shall be consecrated unto the inhabitants of Zion and unto their generations, inasmuch as they become heirs according to the laws of the kingdom.

3 a. Behold, this is what the Lord requires of every man in his stewardship, even as I, the Lord, have appointed, or shall hereafter appoint unto any man.

b. And behold, none are exempt from this law who belong to the church of the living God; yea, neither the bishop, neither the agent, who keepeth the Lord's storehouse; neither he who is appointed in a stewardship over temporal things;

c. he who is appointed to administer spiritual things, the same is worthy of his hire, even as those who are appointed to a stewardship, to administer in temporal things; yea, even more abundantly, which abundance is multiplied unto them through the manifestations of the Spirit;

d. nevertheless, in your temporal things you shall be equal, and this not grudgingly, otherwise the abundance of the manifestations of the Spirit shall be withheld.

4 a. Now this commandment I give unto my servants, for their benefit while they remain, for a manifestation of my blessings upon their heads, and for a reward of their diligence, and for their security for food and for raiment, for an inheritance;

b. for houses and for lands, in whatsoever circumstances I, the Lord, shall place them; and whithersoever I, the Lord, shall send them, for they have been faithful over many things, and have done well inasmuch as they have not sinned.

c. Behold, I, the Lord, am merciful, and will bless them, and they shall enter into the joy of these things. Even so. Amen.

SECTION 71

*Revelation given through Joseph Smith, Jr., at Hiram,
Ohio, late in November or on the first of December, 1831.
Ezra Booth had apostatized and was attacking the church in
print. In harmony with the instructions received, Joseph
and Sidney returned to Kirtland and from this base preached
in Shalersville, Ravenna, and other places where the people
had become disturbed. Joseph later wrote that he and
Sidney "did much towards allaying the excited feelings"
which had developed.*

1 Behold, thus saith the Lord unto you, my servants,
Joseph Smith, Jr., and Sidney Rigdon, that the time has
verily come that it is necessary and expedient in me that
you should open your mouths in proclaiming my gospel, the
things of the kingdom, expounding the mysteries thereof out
of the Scriptures, according to that portion of the spirit and
power, which shall be given unto you, even as I will.

2 a. Verily I say unto you, Proclaim unto the world in the
regions round about, and in the church also, for the space of
a season, even until it shall be made known unto you.

b. Verily this is a mission for a season which I give unto
you; wherefore labor ye in my vineyard.

c. Call upon the inhabitants of the earth, and bear record,
and prepare the way for the commandments and revelations
which are to come.

d. Now, behold, this is wisdom; whoso readeth let him
understand and receive also; for unto him that receiveth it
shall be given more abundantly, even power;

e. wherefore, confound your enemies; call upon them to
meet you, both in public and in private; and inasmuch as
ye are faithful, their shame shall be made manifest.

f. Wherefore let them bring forth their strong reasons
against the Lord.

g. Verily thus saith the Lord unto you, There is no weapon
that is formed against you shall prosper; and if any man lift
his voice against you, he shall be confounded in mine own
due time; wherefore, keep these commandments: they are
true and faithful. Even so. Amen.

SECTION 72

Late in 1831 the high priests in Kirtland agreed that since Bishop Partridge was in Missouri, and so unable to give close attention to temporal affairs in Kirtland, a second bishop was needed for Kirtland. In the following revelation, given through Joseph Smith, Jr., they are commended for their care, and further instruction concerning stewardship is given. The revelation was received December 4, 1831, at Kirtland, Ohio.

1 a. Hearken, and listen to the voice of the Lord, O ye who have assembled yourselves together, who are the high priests of my church, to whom the kingdom and power have been given.

b. For verily thus saith the Lord, It is expedient in me for a bishop to be appointed unto you, or of you unto the church, in this part of the Lord's vineyard;

c. and verily in this thing ye have done wisely, for it is required of the Lord, at the hand of every steward, to render an account of his stewardship, both in time and in eternity.

d. For he who is faithful and wise in time is accounted worthy to inherit the mansions prepared for them of my Father.

e. Verily I say unto you, The elders of the church in this part of my vineyard shall render an account of their stewardship unto the bishop which shall be appointed of me, in this part of my vineyard.

f. These things shall be had on record, to be handed over unto the bishop in Zion; and the duty of the bishop shall be made known by the commandments which have been given, and the voice of the conference.

2 And now, verily I say unto you, My servant Newel K. Whitney is the man who shall be appointed and ordained unto this power; this is the will of the Lord your God, your Redeemer. Even so. Amen.

3 a. The word of the Lord, in addition to the law which has been given, making known the duty of the bishop which has been ordained unto the church in this part of the vineyard, which is verily this:

b. to keep the Lord's storehouse; to receive the funds of the church in this part of the vineyard; to take an account of the elders, as before has been commanded; and to administer to their wants, who shall pay for that which they receive, inasmuch as they have wherewith to pay, that this also may be consecrated to the good of the church, to the poor and needy;

c. and he who hath not wherewith to pay, an account shall be taken and handed over to the bishop of Zion, who shall pay the debt out of that which the Lord shall put into his hands;

d. and the labors of the faithful who labor in spiritual things, in administering the gospel and the things of the kingdom unto the church, and unto the world, shall answer the debt unto the bishop in Zion;

e. thus it cometh out of the church, for according to the law every man that cometh up to Zion must lay all things before the bishop in Zion.

4 a. And now, verily I say unto you, That as every elder in this part of the vineyard must give an account of his stewardship unto the bishop in this part of the vineyard, a certificate from the judge or bishop in this part of the vineyard, unto the bishop in Zion, rendereth every man acceptable, and answereth all things, for an inheritance, and to be received as a wise steward and as a faithful laborer; otherwise he shall not be accepted of the bishop in Zion.

b. And now, verily I say unto you, Let every elder who shall give an account unto the bishop of the church, in this part of the vineyard, be recommended by the church, or churches, in which he labors, that he may render himself and his accounts approved in all things.

c. And again, let my servants who are appointed as stewards over the literary concerns of my church have claim for assistance upon the bishop, or bishops, in all things, that the revelations may be published, and go forth unto the ends of the earth,

d. that they also may obtain funds which shall benefit the church in all things, that they also may render themselves approved in all things, and be accounted as wise stewards.

e. And now, behold, this shall be an ensample for all the extensive branches of my church, in whatsoever land they

shall be established.   And now I make an end of my sayings.
Amen.

5 a. A few words in addition to the laws of the kingdom,
respecting the members of the church; they that are appointed by the Holy Spirit to go up unto Zion, and they who
are privileged to go up unto Zion.

b. Let them carry up unto the bishop a certificate from
three elders of the church, or a certificate from the bishop,
otherwise he who shall go up unto the land of Zion shall not
be accounted as a wise steward.   This is also an ensample.
Amen.

SECTION 73

*Joseph and Sidney continued preaching and counseling
with the elders of the Kirtland region until January 10,
1832, when Joseph received the following revelation.*

1 For verily thus saith the Lord, It is expedient in me
that they should continue preaching the gospel, and in exhortation to the churches, in the regions round about, until
Conference; and then, behold, it shall be made known unto
them, by the voice of the Conference, their several missions.

2 a. Now, verily I say unto you, my servants Joseph Smith,
Jr., and Sidney Rigdon, saith the Lord, It is expedient to
translate again, and, inasmuch as it is practicable, to preach
in the regions round about until Conference, and after that
it is expedient to continue the work of translation until it
be finished.

b. And let this be a pattern unto the elders until further
knowledge, even as it is written.   Now, I give no more unto
you at this time.   Gird up your loins and be sober.   Even
so. Amen.

SECTION 74

*After Joseph Smith, Jr., resumed the inspired revision of
the Scriptures, he "received the following explanation of the
First Epistle to the Corinthians, chapter 7, verse 14."*

1 For the unbelieving husband is sanctified by the wife,
and the unbelieving wife is sanctified by the husband, else
were your children unclean; but now are they holy.

2 a. Now in the days of the apostles the law of circumcision was had among all the Jews who believed not the
gospel of Jesus Christ.

b. And it came to pass that there arose a great contention
among the people concerning the law of circumcision, for
the unbelieving husband was desirous that his children should
be circumcised and become subject to the Law of Moses,
which law was fulfilled.

3. a. And it came to pass that the children being brought
up in subjection to the Law of Moses, and giving heed to
the traditions of their fathers, believed not the gospel of
Christ, wherein they became unholy;

b. wherefore for this cause the apostle wrote unto the
church, giving unto them a commandment, not of the Lord,
but of himself, that a believer should not be united to an
unbeliever, except the Law of Moses should be done away
among them, that their children might remain without
circumcision;

c. and that the tradition might be done away, which saith
that little children are unholy, for it was had among the Jews;

d. but little children are holy, being sanctified through
the atonement of Jesus Christ; and this is what the Scriptures
mean.

SECTION 75

A conference was held at Amherst, Lorain County, Ohio,
January 25, 1832. Some of the elders asked Joseph to
"inquire of the Lord that they might know his will, or learn
what would be most pleasing to him for them to do, in
order to bring men to a sense of their condition." Joseph
made inquiry of the Lord and received the following mes-
sage. The conference is also noteworthy because here Joseph
Smith was ordained President of the High Priesthood.

1 a. Verily, verily I say unto you, I who speak even by the
voice of my Spirit; even Alpha and Omega, your Lord and
your God; hearken, O ye who have given your names to go
forth to proclaim my gospel, and to prune my vineyard.

b. Behold, I say unto you, that it is my will that you
should go forth and not tarry, neither be idle, but labor with
your mights, lifting up your voices as with the sound of a
trump, proclaiming the truth according to the revelations
and commandments which I have given you,

c. and thus if ye are faithful ye shall be laden with many
sheaves, and crowned with honor, and glory, and immortality,
and eternal life.

2 a. Therefore, verily I say unto my servant William E.
McLellin, I revoke the commission which I gave unto him,
to go unto the eastern countries, and I give unto him a new
commission and a new commandment, in the which I, the
Lord, chasteneth him for the murmurings of his heart; and
he sinned,

b. nevertheless I forgive him, and say unto him again, Go
ye into the south countries; and let my servant Luke Johnson
go with him and proclaim the things which I have commanded them,

c. calling on the name of the Lord for the Comforter,
which shall teach them all things that are expedient for them,
praying always that they faint not; and inasmuch as they do
this, I will be with them even unto the end. Behold, this
is the will of the Lord your God concerning you. Even so.
Amen.

3 a. And again, verily thus saith the Lord, Let my servant Orson Hyde and my servant Samuel H. Smith take their journey into the eastern countries, and proclaim the things which I have commanded them: and inasmuch as they are faithful, lo, I will be with them even unto the end.

b. And again, verily I say unto my servant Lyman Johnson, and unto my servant Orson Pratt, They shall also take their journey into the eastern countries; and behold and lo, I am with them also even unto the end.

c. And, again, I say unto my servant Asa Dodds, and unto my servant Calves Wilson, that they also shall take their journey unto the western countries, and proclaim my gospel even as I have commanded them.

d. And he who is faithful shall overcome all things, and shall be lifted up at the last day.

e. And again, I say unto my servant Major N. Ashley and my servant Burr Riggs, Let them take their journey also unto the south country; yea, let all those take their journey as I have commanded them, going from house to house, and from village to village, and from city to city;

f. and in whatsoever house ye enter, and they receive you, leave your blessings upon that house; and in whatsoever house ye enter, and they receive you not, ye shall depart speedily from that house, and shake off the dust of your feet as a testimony against them;

g. and you shall be filled with joy and gladness and know this, that in the day of judgment you shall be judges of that house, and condemn them; and it shall be more tolerable for the heathen in the day of judgment, than for that house;

h. therefore gird up your loins and be faithful and ye shall overcome all things and be lifted up at the last day. Even so. Amen.

4 a. And, again, thus saith the Lord unto you, O ye elders of my church, who have given your names that you might know his will concerning you:

b. Behold, I say unto you, that it is the duty of the church to assist in supporting the families of those and also to support the families of those who are called and must needs be sent unto the world to proclaim the gospel unto the world;

c. wherefore, I, the Lord, give unto you this commandment, that ye obtain places for your families, inasmuch as your brethren are willing to open their hearts; and let all such as can, obtain places for their families, and support of the church for them, not fail to go into the world;

d. whether to the east, or to the west, or to the north, or to the south; let them ask and they shall receive, knock and it shall be opened unto them, and made known from on high, even by the Comforter, whither they shall go.

5 a. And again, verily I say unto you, that every man who is obliged to provide for his own family, let him provide and he shall in no wise lose his crown; and let him labor in the church.

b. Let every man be diligent in all things. And the idler shall not have place in the church, except he repents and mends his ways.

c. Wherefore, let my servant Simeon Carter, and my servant Emer Harris be united in the ministry. And also my servant Ezra Thayre and my servant Thomas B. Marsh. Also my servant Hyrum Smith and my servant Reynolds Cahoon; and also my servant Daniel Stanton and my servant Seymour Brunson;

d. and also my servant Sylvester Smith and my servant Gideon Carter; and also my servant Ruggles Eames and my servant Stephen Burnett; and also my servant Micah B. Welton and also my servant Eden Smith. Even so. Amen.

SECTION 76

On their return from the Amherst (Ohio) conference to Hiram, Ohio (D. and C. 75), Joseph Smith resumed translation of the Scriptures with Sidney Rigdon as his scribe. On February 16, 1832, while they were thus engaged, they came to John 5:29. While meditating on the rendition they were given by the spirit of revelation, they shared a vision which they reported in the words of this section.

1 a. Hear, O ye heavens, and give ear, O earth, and rejoice ye inhabitants thereof, for the Lord is God, and beside him there is no Savior;

b. great is his wisdom; marvelous are his ways; and the extent of his doings, none can find out;

c. his purposes fail not, neither are there any who can stay his hand; from eternity to eternity he is the same, and his years never fail.

2 a. For thus saith the Lord, I, the Lord, am merciful and gracious unto those who fear me, and delight to honor those who serve me in righteousness and in truth unto the end;

b. great shall be their reward, and eternal shall be their glory; and to them will I reveal all mysteries; yea, all the hidden mysteries of my kingdom from days of old; and for ages to come will I make known unto them the good pleasure of my will concerning all things pertaining to my kingdom;

c. yea, even the wonders of eternity shall they know, and things to come will I show them, even the things of many generations; their wisdom shall be great, and their understanding reach to heaven; and before them the wisdom of the wise shall perish, and the understanding of the prudent shall come to naught;

d. for by my Spirit will I enlighten them, and by my power will I make known unto them the secrets of my will; yea, even those things which eye has not seen, nor ear heard, nor yet entered into the heart of man.

3 a. We, Joseph Smith, Jr., and Sidney Rigdon, being in the Spirit on the sixteenth of February, in the year of our Lord one thousand eight hundred and thirty-two, by the power of the Spirit our eyes were opened, and our understandings were enlightened, so as to see and understand the things of God;

b. even those things which were from the beginning before the world was, which were ordained of the Father, through his only begotten Son, who was in the bosom of the Father, even from the beginning, of whom we bear record, and the record which we bear is the fullness of the gospel of Jesus Christ, who is the Son, whom we saw and with whom we conversed in the heavenly vision;

c. for while we were doing the work of translation, which the Lord had appointed unto us, we came to the twenty-ninth verse of the fifth chapter of John, which was given unto us as follows:

d. speaking of the resurrection of the dead, concerning those who shall hear the voice of the Son of Man, and shall come forth; they who have done good in the resurrection of the just, and they who have done evil in the resurrection of the unjust.

e. Now this caused us to marvel, for it was given unto us of the Spirit, and while we meditated upon these things, the Lord touched the eyes of our understandings, and they were opened, and the glory of the Lord shone round about;

f. and we beheld the glory of the Son, on the right hand of the Father, and received of his fullness; and saw the holy angels, and they who are sanctified before his throne, worshiping God and the Lamb, who worship him for ever and ever.

g. And, now, after the many testimonies which have been given of him, this is the testimony, last of all, which we give of him, that he lives; for we saw him, even on the right hand of God;

h. and we heard the voice bearing record that he is the Only Begotten of the Father; that by him, and through him, and of him, the worlds are and were created; and the inhabitants thereof are begotten sons and daughters unto God.

i. And this we saw also, and bear record, that an angel of God, who was in authority in the presence of God, who rebelled against the only begotten Son; whom the Father loved, and who was in the bosom of the Father;

j. and was thrust down from the presence of God and the Son, and was called Perdition; for the heavens wept over him; he was Lucifer, a son of the morning. And we beheld, and lo, he is fallen! is fallen! even a son of the morning.

k. And while we were yet in the Spirit, the Lord commanded us that we should write the vision; for we beheld Satan, that old serpent, even the Devil, who rebelled against God, and sought to take the kingdom of our God and his Christ;

l. wherefore he maketh war with the saints of God, and encompasses them round about.

m. And we saw a vision of the sufferings of those with whom he made war and overcame, for thus came the voice of the Lord unto us.

4 a. Thus saith the Lord, concerning all those who know my power, and have been made partakers thereof, and suffered themselves, through the power of the Devil, to be overcome, and to deny the truth, and defy my power;

b. they are they who are the sons of perdition, of whom I say it had been better for them never to have been born;

c. for they are vessels of wrath, doomed to suffer the wrath of God, with the Devil and his angels, in eternity, concerning whom I have said there is no forgiveness in this world nor in the world to come;

d. having denied the Holy Spirit, after having received it, and having denied the only begotten Son of the Father; having crucified him unto themselves, and put him to an open shame:

e. these are they who shall go away into the lake of fire and brimstone, with the Devil and his angels, and the only ones on whom the second death shall have any power; yea, verily, the only ones who shall not be redeemed in the due time of the Lord, after the sufferings of his wrath;

f. for all the rest shall be brought forth by the resurrection of the dead, through the triumph and the glory of the Lamb, who was slain, who was in the bosom of the Father before the worlds were made.

g. And this is the gospel, the glad tidings which the voice out of the heavens bore record unto us, that he came into the world, even Jesus to be crucified for the world, and to bear the sins of the world, and to sanctify the world, and to cleanse it from all unrighteousness;

h. that through him all might be saved, whom the Father had put into his power, and made by him; who glorifies the Father, and saves all the works of his hands, except those sons of perdition, who deny the Son after the Father has revealed him;

i. wherefore he saves all except them; they shall go away into everlasting punishment, which is endless punishment, which is eternal punishment, to reign with the Devil and his angels in eternity, where their worm dieth not and the fire is not quenched, which is their torment, and the end thereof, neither the place thereof, nor their torment, no man knows;

j. neither was it revealed, neither is, neither will be revealed unto man, except to them who are made partakers thereof:

k. nevertheless, I, the Lord, show it by vision unto many; but straightway shut it up again; wherefore the end, the width, the height, the depth, and the misery thereof, they understand not, neither any man except them who are ordained unto this condemnation.

l. And we heard the voice saying, Write the vision, for lo, this is the end of the vision of the sufferings of the ungodly!

5 a. And again, we bear record for we saw and heard, and this is the testimony of the gospel of Christ, concerning them who come forth in the resurrection of the just:

b. They are they who received the testimony of Jesus, and believed on his name, and were baptized after the manner of his burial, being buried in the water in his name, and this according to the commandment which he has given, that by keeping the commandments, they might be washed and cleansed from all their sins,

c. and receive the Holy Spirit by the laying on of the hands of him who is ordained and sealed unto this power;

d. and who overcome by faith, and are sealed by that Holy Spirit of promise, which the Father sheds forth upon all those who are just and true;

e. they are they who are the church of the Firstborn;

f. they are they into whose hands the Father has given all things:

g. they are they who are priests and kings, who have received of his fullness, and of his glory, and are priests of the Most High after the order of Melchisedec, which was after the order of Enoch, which was after the order of the only begotten Son:

h. wherefore, as it is written, they are gods, even the sons of God; wherefore all things are theirs, whether life or death, or things present, or things to come, all are theirs, and they are Christ's, and Christ is God's; and they shall overcome all things;

i. wherefore let no man glory in man, but rather let him glory in God, who shall subdue all enemies under his feet;

j. these shall dwell in the presence of God and his Christ for ever and ever:

k. these are they whom he shall bring with him, when he shall come in the clouds of heaven, to reign on the earth over his people;

l. these are they who shall have part in the first resurrection;

m. these are they who shall come forth in the resurrection of the just;

n. these are they who are come unto Mount Zion, and unto the city of the living God, the heavenly place, the holiest of all;

o. these are they who have come to an innumerable company of angels; to the general assembly and church of Enoch, and of the Firstborn;

p. these are they whose names are written in heaven, where God and Christ are the judge of all;

q. these are they who are just men made perfect through Jesus the mediator of the new covenant, who wrought out this perfect atonement through the shedding of his own blood;

r. these are they whose bodies are celestial, whose glory is that of the sun, even the glory of God the highest of all; whose glory the sun of the firmament is written of as being typical.

6 a. And again, we saw the terrestrial world, and, behold, and lo;

b. these are they who are of the terrestrial, whose glory differs from that of the church of the Firstborn, who have received the fullness of the Father, even as that of the moon differs from the sun of the firmament.

c. Behold, these are they who died without law; and also they who are the spirits of men kept in prison, whom the Son visited, and preached the gospel unto them, that they might be judged according to men in the flesh, who received not the testimony of Jesus in the flesh, but afterwards received it;

d. these are they who are honorable men of the earth, who were blinded by the craftiness of men;

e. these are they who receive of his glory, but not of his fullness;

f. these are they who receive of the presence of the Son, but not of the fullness of the Father; wherefore they are bodies terrestrial, and not bodies celestial, and differ in glory as the moon differs from the sun;

g. these are they who are not valiant in the testimony of Jesus; wherefore they obtained not the crown over the kingdom of our God.

h. And now this is the end of the vision which we saw of the terrestrial, that the Lord commanded us to write while we were yet in the Spirit.

7 a. And again, we saw the glory of the telestial, which glory is that of the lesser, even as the glory of the stars differs from that of the glory of the moon in the firmament;

b. these are they who received not the gospel of Christ, neither the testimony of Jesus;

c. these are they who deny not the Holy Spirit;

d. these are they who are thrust down to hell;

e. these are they who shall not be redeemed from the Devil, until the last resurrection, until the Lord, even Christ the Lamb, shall have finished his work;

f. these are they who receive not of his fullness in the eternal world, but of the Holy Spirit through the ministration of the terrestrial; and the terrestrial through the ministration of the celestial: and also the telestial receive it of the administering of angels, who are appointed to minister for them, or who are appointed to be ministering spirits for them, for they shall be heirs of salvation.

g. And thus we saw in the heavenly vision, the glory of the telestial which surpasses all understanding; and no man knows it except him to whom God has revealed it.

h. And thus we saw the glory of the terrestrial, which excels in all things the glory of the telestial, even in glory, and in power, and in might, and in dominion.

i. And thus we saw the glory of the celestial, which excels in all things; where God, even the Father, reigns upon his throne for ever and ever, before whose throne all things bow in humble reverence and give him glory for ever and ever.

j. They who dwell in his presence are the church of the Firstborn; and they see as they are seen, and know as they are known, having received of his fullness and of his grace; and he makes them equal in power, and in might, and in dominion.

k. And the glory of the celestial is one, even as the glory of the sun is one. And the glory of the terrestrial is one, even as the glory of the moon is one.

l. And the glory of the telestial is one, even as the glory of the stars is one, for as one star differs from another star in glory, even so differs one from another in glory in the telestial world; for these are they who are of Paul, and of Apollos, and of Cephas;

m. these are they who say they are some of one and some

of another, some of Christ, and some of John, and some of Moses, and some of Elias; and some of Esais, and some of Isaiah, and some of Enoch, but received not the gospel, neither the testimony of Jesus, neither the prophets; neither the everlasting covenant;

n. last of all, these all are they who will not be gathered with the saints, to be caught up unto the church of the First-born, and received into the cloud;

o. these are they who are liars, and sorcerers, and adulterers, and whoremongers, and whosoever loves and makes a lie;

p. these are they who suffer the wrath of God on the earth;

q. these are they who suffer the vengeance of eternal fire;

r. these are they who are cast down to hell and suffer the wrath of Almighty God until the fullness of times, when Christ shall have subdued all enemies under his feet, and shall have perfected his work, when he shall deliver up the kingdom and present it unto the Father spotless, saying:

s. I have overcome and have trodden the wine press alone, even the wine press of the fierceness of the wrath of Almighty God; then shall he be crowned with the crown of his glory, to sit on the throne of his power to reign for ever and ever.

t. But, behold, and lo, we saw the glory and the inhabitants of the telestial world, that they were as innumerable as the stars in the firmament of heaven, or as the sand upon the seashore, and heard the voice of the Lord saying:

u. These all shall bow the knee, and every tongue shall confess to him who sits upon the throne for ever and ever;

v. for they shall be judged according to their works; and every man shall receive according to his own works, and his own dominion, in the mansions which are prepared, and they shall be servants of the Most High, but where God and Christ dwell they can not come, worlds without end.

w. This is the end of the vision which we saw, which we were commanded to write while we were yet in the Spirit.

8 a. But great and marvelous are the works of the Lord and the mysteries of his kingdom which he showed unto us, which surpasses all understanding in glory, and in might, and in dominion, which he commanded us we should not write, while we were yet in the Spirit, and are not lawful for man to utter,

b. neither is man capable to make them known, for they

are only to be seen and understood by the power of the Holy Spirit, which God bestows on those who love him and purify themselves before him; to whom he grants this privilege of seeing and knowing for themselves;

c. that through the power and manifestation of the Spirit, while in the flesh, they may be able to bear his presence in the world of glory. And to God and the Lamb be glory, and honor, and dominion for ever and ever. Amen.

SECTION 77

Revelation addressed to the high priests, given through Joseph Smith, Jr., at Hiram, Portage County, Ohio, March 1832. It is concerned with the establishment of a storehouse and the care of the poor, both in the Kirtland area and in Zion.

The unusual names found in this and other revelations were probably used to hide the identity of the men and places mentioned from the enemies of the church. Identifications are suggested as follows:

> "City of Enoch"   .   .   *City of Joseph*
> "Ahashdah"   .   .   *Newel K. Whitney*
> "Gazelam" or "Enoch"   .   *Joseph Smith*
> "Pelagoram"   .   .   *Sidney Rigdon*

1 a. The Lord spake unto Enoch, saying, Hearken unto me saith the Lord your God, who are ordained unto the high priesthood of my church, who have assembled yourselves together,

b. and listen to the counsel of him who has ordained you, from on high, who shall speak in your ears the words of wisdom, that salvation may be unto you in that thing which you have presented before me, saith the Lord God;

c. for verily I say unto you, The time has come, and is now at hand; and, behold, and lo, it must needs be that there be an organization of my people, in regulating and establishing the affairs of the storehouse for the poor of my people, both in this place and in the land of Zion, or in other words, the city of Enoch,

d. for a permanent and everlasting establishment and order unto my church, to advance the cause which ye have espoused, to the salvation of man, and to the glory of your Father who is in heaven, that you may be equal in the bands of heavenly things;

e. yea, and earthly things also, for the obtaining of heavenly things;

f. for if ye are not equal in earthly things, ye can not be equal in obtaining heavenly things;

g. for if you will that I give unto you a place in the celestial world, you must prepare yourselves by doing the things which I have commanded you and required of you.

2 a. And now, verily thus saith the Lord, It is expedient that all things be done unto my glory, that ye should, who are joined together in this order;

b. or in other words, let my servant Ahashdah, and my servant Gazelam, or Enoch, and my servant Pelagoram, sit in council with the Saints which are in Zion;

c. otherwise Satan seeketh to turn their hearts away from the truth, that they become blinded, and understand not the things which are prepared for them;

d. wherefore a commandment I give unto you, to prepare and organize yourselves by a bond or everlasting covenant that can not be broken.

3 a. And he who breaketh it shall lose his office and standing in the church, and shall be delivered over to the buffetings of Satan until the day of redemption.

b. Behold, this is the preparation wherewith I prepare you, and the foundation, and the ensample, which I give unto you, whereby you may accomplish the commandments which are given you,

c. that through my providence, notwithstanding the tribulation which shall descend upon you,

d. that the church may stand independent above all other creatures beneath the celestial world,

e. that you may come up unto the crown prepared for you, and be made rulers over many kingdoms, saith the Lord God, the Holy One of Zion, who hath established the foundations of Adam-ondi-Ahman;

f. who hath appointed Michael, your prince, and established his feet, and set him upon high; and given unto him the keys of salvation under the counsel and direction of the Holy One, who is without beginning of days or end of life.

4 a. Verily, verily I say unto you, Ye are little children, and ye have not as yet understood how great blessings the Father has in his own hands, and prepared for you; and ye can not bear all things now;

b. nevertheless be of good cheer, for I will lead you along; the kingdom is yours and the blessings thereof are yours; and the riches of eternity are yours;

c. and he who receiveth all things, with thankfulness, shall be made glorious, and the things of this earth shall be added unto him, even an hundredfold, yea, more;

d. wherefore do the things which I have commanded you, saith your Redeemer, even the Son Ahman, who prepareth all things before he taketh you; for ye are the church of the Firstborn, and he will take you up in the cloud, and appoint every man his portion.

e. And he that is a faithful and wise steward shall inherit all things. Amen.

SECTION 78

Revelation addressed to Jared Carter given through Joseph Smith, Jr., March 1832, at Hiram, Ohio.

1 a. Verily I say unto you, that it is my will that my servant Jared Carter should go again into the eastern countries, from place to place, and from city to city, in the power of the ordination wherewith he has been ordained,

b. proclaiming glad tidings of great joy, even the everlasting gospel, and I will send upon him the Comforter which shall teach him the truth and the way whither he shall go;

c. and inasmuch as he is faithful I will crown him again with sheaves; wherefore let your heart be glad, my servant Jared Carter, and fear not saith your Lord, even Jesus Christ. Amen.

SECTION 79

*Revelation given through Joseph Smith, Jr., at Hiram,
Ohio, during March 1832. It concerns the missionary labors
of Stephen Burnett and Eden Smith.*

1 a. Verily, thus saith the Lord, unto you, my servant
Stephen Burnett,

b. Go ye, go ye into the world, and preach the gospel to
every creature that cometh under the sound of your voice,
and inasmuch as you desire a companion I will give unto you
my servant Eden Smith;

c. wherefore go ye and preach my gospel, whether to the
north, or to the south; to the east, or to the west, it mattereth not, for ye can not go amiss;

d. therefore declare the things which ye have heard and
verily believe, and know to be true.

e. Behold, this is the will of him who hath called you,
your Redeemer, even Jesus Christ. Amen.

SECTION 80

*Revelation given through Joseph Smith, Jr., in March
1832 at Hiram, Ohio. It is addressed to Frederick G. Williams, who is called to be a high priest and a counselor in
the First Presidency. His ordination took place March 18,
1833.*

1 a. Verily, verily I say unto you, my servant, Frederick
G. Williams,

b. Listen to the voice of him who speaketh, to the word
of the Lord your God, and hearken to the calling wherewith
you are called, even to be a high priest in my church, and
a counselor unto my servant, Joseph Smith, Jr.,

c. unto whom I have given the keys of the kingdom, which
belongeth always unto the Presidency of the high priesthood;

d. therefore, verily I acknowledge him and will bless him,
and also thee, inasmuch as thou art faithful in council, in the
office which I have appointed unto you, in prayer always
vocally, and in thy heart, in public and in private;

e. also in thy ministry in proclaiming the gospel in the land of the living, and among thy brethren;

f. and in doing these things thou wilt do the greatest good unto thy fellow-beings, and will promote the glory of him who is your Lord;

g. wherefore, be faithful, stand in the office which I have appointed unto you, succor the weak, lift up the hands which hang down, and strengthen the feeble knees:

h. and if thou art faithful unto the end thou shalt have a crown of immortality and eternal life in the mansions which I have prepared in the house of my Father.

i. Behold, and lo, these are the words of Alpha and Omega, even Jesus Christ. Amen.

SECTION 81

Joseph Smith left Hiram, Ohio, April 1, 1832, and he and his party reached Independence, Missouri, on April 24. A general council of the church was immediately called to convene April 26, 1832. At this council more inspired instruction was received through Joseph concerning the poor and the enlargement of Zion.

More unusual names are used in this revelation (see D. and C. 77). Their meanings are interpreted as follows:

"Alam and Ahashdah" . . .	*Newel K. Whitney*
"Mahalaleel and Pelagoram" . . .	*Sidney Rigdon*
"Gazelam"	*Joseph Smith*
"Horah and Olihah"	*Oliver Cowdery*
"Shalemanasseh and Mehemson" .	*Martin Harris*
"Land of Shinehah"	*Kirtland*

1 a. Verily I say unto you, my servants, that inasmuch as you have forgiven one another your trespasses, even so I, the Lord, forgive you;

b. nevertheless there are those among you who have sinned exceedingly; yea, even all of you have sinned, but verily I say unto you,

c. Beware from henceforth and refrain from sin lest sore judgments fall upon your heads; for unto whom much is given much is required; and he who sins against the greater light shall receive the greater condemnation.

d. Ye call upon my name for revelations, and I give them unto you; and inasmuch as ye keep not my sayings which I give unto you, ye become transgressors, and justice and judgment is the penalty which is affixed unto my law:

e. therefore, what I say unto one I say unto all, Watch, for the adversary spreadeth his dominions and darkness reigneth; and the anger of God kindleth against the inhabitants of the earth; and none doeth good, for all have gone out of the way.

2 And now, verily I say unto you, I, the Lord, will not lay any sin to your charge; go your ways and sin no more; but unto that soul who sinneth shall the former sins return, saith the Lord your God.

3 a. And again, I say unto you, I give unto you a new commandment, that you may understand my will concerning you, or in other words, I give unto you directions how you may act before me, that it may turn to you for your salvation.

b. I, the Lord, am bound when ye do what I say, but when ye do not what I say, ye have no promise.

4 a. Therefore, verily I say unto you, that it is expedient for my servant Alam and Ahashdah, Mahalaleel and Pelagoram, and my servant Gazelam, and Horah, and Olihah, and Shalemanasseh, and Mehemson, be bound together by a bond and covenant that can not be broken by transgression except judgment shall immediately follow, in your several stewardships,

b. to manage the affairs of the poor, and all things pertaining to the bishopric both in the land of Zion, and in the land of Shinehah, for I have consecrated the land of Shinehah in mine own due time for the benefit of the Saints of the Most High, and for a stake to Zion;

c. for Zion must increase in beauty, and in holiness; her borders must be enlarged; her stakes must be strengthened; yea, verily I say unto you, Zion must arise and put on her beautiful garments;

d. therefore, I give unto you this commandment, that ye bind yourselves by this covenant, and it shall be done according to the laws of the Lord. Behold, here is wisdom, also, in me, for your good.

e. And you are to be equal, or in other words, you are to have equal claims on the properties, for the benefit of managing the concerns of your stewardships, every man according to his wants and his needs, inasmuch as his wants are just;

f. and all this for the benefit of the church of the living God, that every man may improve upon his talent, that every man may gain other talents;

g. yea, even an hundredfold, to be cast into the Lord's storehouse, to become the common property of the whole church, every man seeking the interest of his neighbor, and doing all things with an eye single to the glory of God.

5 a. This order I have appointed to be an everlasting order unto you and unto your successors, inasmuch as you sin not;

b. and the soul that sins against this covenant, and hardeneth his heart against it, shall be dealt with according to the laws of my church, and shall be delivered over to the buffetings of Satan until the day of redemption.

6 a. And now, verily I say unto you, and this is wisdom, Make unto yourselves friends with the mammon of unrighteousness, and they will not destroy you.

b. Leave judgment alone with me, for it is mine and I will repay.

c. Peace be with you; my blessings continue with you, for even yet the kingdom is yours, and shall be for ever if you fall not from your steadfastness. Even so. Amen.

SECTION 82

Revelation given through Joseph Smith, Jr., April 30, 1832, at Independence, Missouri. It was received following council discussion concerning the security of widows and orphans under the stewardship arrangements being worked out.

1 a. Verily thus saith the Lord, in addition to the laws of the church concerning women and children, those who belong to the church, who have lost their husbands or fathers:

b. Women have claim on their husbands for their maintenance until their husbands are taken; and if they are not found transgressors they shall have fellowship in the church;

c. and if they are not faithful, they shall not have fellowship in the church; yet they may remain upon their inheritances according to the laws of the land.

2 a. All children have claim upon their parents for their maintenance until they are of age; and after that, they have claim upon the church; or, in other words, upon the Lord's storehouse, if their parents have not wherewith to give them inheritances.

b. And the storehouse shall be kept by the consecrations of the church, that widows and orphans shall be provided for, as also the poor. Amen.

SECTION 83

Joseph Smith and some of his close associates returned from Independence to Kirtland, and here work on the Scriptures was resumed. During August and September many of the elders who had been on missions in the East also returned to Kirtland. Here, on September 22 and 23, 1832, the following revelation was given through Joseph Smith. It was received in the presence of six elders and is known as "the revelation on priesthood."

In the 1835 edition of the Doctrine and Covenants, this revelation comprised Section 4. It followed the revelations now numbered 17 and 104 and came immediately before those which are now numbered 99, 84, and 85. These six revelations were all concerned with priesthood and church government.

1 a. A revelation of Jesus Christ unto his servant Joseph Smith, Jr., and six elders, as they united their hearts and lifted their voices on high;

b. yea, the word of the Lord concerning his church, established in the last days for the restoration of his people, as he has spoken by the mouth of his prophets, and for the gathering of his Saints to stand upon Mount Zion, which shall be the city New Jerusalem;

c. which city shall be built, beginning at the Temple Lot, which is appointed by the finger of the Lord, in the western boundaries of the State of Missouri, and dedicated by the hand of Joseph Smith, Jr., and others, with whom the Lord was well pleased.

2 a. Verily, this is the word of the Lord, that the city New Jerusalem shall be built by the gathering of the Saints, beginning at this place, even the place of the temple, which temple shall be reared in this generation;

b. for verily, this generation shall not all pass away until an house shall be built unto the Lord, and a cloud shall rest upon it, which cloud shall be even the glory of the Lord, which shall fill the house.

c. And the sons of Moses, according to the holy priesthood, which he received under the hand of his father-in-law, Jethro; and Jethro received it under the hand of Caleb; and Caleb received it under the hand of Elihu;

d. and Elihu under the hand of Jeremy; and Jeremy under the hand of Gad; and Gad under the hand of Esaias; and Esaias received it under the hand of God;

e. Esaias also lived in the days of Abraham and was blessed of him, which Abraham received the priesthood from Melchisedec; who received it through the lineage of his fathers, even till Noah;

f. and from Noah till Enoch, through the lineage of their fathers; and from Enoch to Abel, who was slain by the conspiracy of his brother; who received the priesthood by the commandments of God, by the hand of his father Adam, who was the first man;

g. which priesthood continueth in the church of God in all generations, and is without beginning of days or end of years.

3 a. And the Lord confirmed a priesthood also upon Aaron and his seed throughout all their generations, which priesthood also continueth and abideth for ever, with the priesthood which is after the holiest order of God.

b. And this greater priesthood administereth the gospel and holdeth the key of the mysteries of the kingdom, even the key of the knowledge of God.

c. Therefore, in the ordinances thereof the power of godliness is manifest; and without the ordinances thereof, and the authority of the priesthood, the power of godliness is not manifest unto men in the flesh; for without this, no man can see the face of God, even the Father, and live.

4 a. Now, this Moses plainly taught to the children of Israel in the wilderness, and sought diligently to sanctify his people that they might behold the face of God;

b. but they hardened their hearts, and could not endure his presence, therefore, the Lord, in his wrath (for his anger was kindled against them), swore that they should not enter into his rest, while in the wilderness, which rest is the fullness of his glory.

c. Therefore, he took Moses out of their midst and the holy priesthood also; and the lesser priesthood continued, which priesthood holdeth the key of the ministering of angels and the preparatory gospel, which gospel is the gospel of repentance and of baptism, and the remission of sins, and the law of carnal commandments,

d. which the Lord, in his wrath, caused to continue with the house of Aaron, among the children of Israel until John, whom God raised up, being filled with the Holy Ghost from his mother's womb:

e. for he was baptized while he was yet in his childhood, and was ordained by the angel of God at the time he was eight days old unto this power:

f. to overthrow the kingdom of the Jews, and to make straight the way of the Lord before the face of his people; to prepare them for the coming of the Lord, in whose hand is given all power.

5 a. And again, the office of elder and bishop are necessary appendages belonging unto the high priesthood.

b. And again, the offices of teachers and deacons are necessary appendages belonging to the lesser priesthood, which priesthood was confirmed upon Aaron and his sons.

6 a. Therefore, as I said concerning the sons of Moses— for the sons of Moses and also the sons of Aaron shall offer an acceptable offering and sacrifice in the house of the Lord, which house shall be built unto the Lord in this generation upon the consecrated spot, as I have appointed;

b. and the sons of Moses and of Aaron shall be filled with the glory of the Lord upon Mount Zion in the Lord's house,

whose sons are ye; and also many whom I have called and
sent forth to build up my church;

c. for whoso is faithful unto the obtaining these two
priesthoods of which I have spoken, and the magnifying their
calling, are sanctified by the Spirit unto the renewing of their
bodies:

d. they become the sons of Moses and of Aaron, and the
seed of Abraham, and the church and kingdom and the elect
of God;

e. and also all they who receive this priesthood receiveth
me, saith the Lord, for he that receiveth my servants receiveth
me, and he that receiveth me receiveth my Father, and he that
receiveth my Father receiveth my Father's kingdom.

f. Therefore, all that my Father hath shall be given unto
him; and this is according to the oath and covenant which
belongeth to the priesthood.

g. Therefore, all those who receive the priesthood receive
this oath and covenant of my Father, which he can not break,
neither can it be moved;

h. but whoso breaketh this covenant, after he hath received
it, and altogether turneth therefrom, shall not have forgiveness of sins in this world nor in the world to come.

i. And all those who come not unto this priesthood, which
ye have received, which I now confirm upon you who are
present, this day, by mine own voice out of the heavens, and
even I have given the heavenly hosts and mine angels charge
concerning you.

7 a. And now I give unto you a commandment to beware
concerning yourselves, to give diligent heed to the words
of eternal life; for you shall live by every word that proceedeth forth from the mouth of God.

b. For the word of the Lord is truth, and whatsoever is
truth is light, and whatsoever is light is Spirit, even the
Spirit of Jesus Christ;

c. and the Spirit giveth light to every man that cometh
into the world; and the Spirit enlighteneth every man through
the world, that hearkeneth to the voice of the Spirit;

d. and everyone that hearkeneth to the voice of the Spirit,
cometh unto God, even the Father;

e. and the Father teacheth him of the covenant which he
has renewed and confirmed upon you, which is confirmed

upon you for your sakes, and not for your sakes only, but for the sake of the whole world:

f. and the whole world lieth in sin, and groaneth under darkness and under the bondage of sin:

g. and by this you may know they are under the bondage of sin, because they come not unto me; for whoso cometh not unto me is under the bondage of sin;

h. and whoso receiveth not my voice is not acquainted with my voice, and is not of me;

i. and by this you may know the righteous from the wicked, and that the whole world groaneth under sin and darkness even now.

8 a. And your minds in times past have been darkened because of unbelief, and because you have treated lightly the things you have received, which vanity and unbelief hath brought the whole church under condemnation.

b. And this condemnation resteth upon the children of Zion, even all; and they shall remain under this condemnation until they repent and remember the new covenant, even the Book of Mormon and the former commandments which I have given them, not only to say, but to do according to that which I have written,

c. that they may bring forth fruit meet for their Father's kingdom, otherwise there remaineth a scourge and a judgment to be poured out upon the children of Zion; for, shall the children of the kingdom pollute my holy land? Verily, I say unto you, Nay.

9 a. Verily, verily I say unto you, who now have my words, which is my voice,

b. Blessed are ye inasmuch as you receive these things; for I will forgive you of your sins with this commandment, that you remain steadfast in your minds in solemnity, and the spirit of prayer, in bearing testimony to all the world of those things which are communicated unto you.

10 a. Therefore, go ye into all the world, and whatsoever place ye can not go into, ye shall send, that the testimony may go from you into all the world, unto every creature.

b. And as I said unto mine apostles, even so I say unto you; for you are mine apostles, even God's high priests: ye are they whom my Father hath given me; ye are my friends;

c. therefore, as I said unto mine apostles, I say unto you again, that every soul who believeth on your words, and is baptized by water for the remission of sins, shall receive the Holy Ghost; and these signs shall follow them that believe:

11 a. In my name they shall do many wonderful works;

b. in my name they shall cast out devils:

c. in my name they shall heal the sick:

d. in my name they shall open the eyes of the blind, and unstop the ears of the deaf:

e. and the tongue of the dumb shall speak;

f. and if any man shall administer poison unto them, it shall not hurt them: and the poison of a serpent shall not have power to harm them.

g. But a commandment I give unto them, that they shall not boast themselves of these things, neither speak them before the world: for these things are given unto you for your profit and for salvation.

12 a. Verily, verily, I say unto you, They who believe not on your words, and are not baptized in water, in my name, for the remission of their sins, that they may receive the Holy Ghost, shall be damned, and shall not come into my Father's kingdom, where my Father and I am.

b. And this revelation unto you, and commandment, is in force from this very hour upon all the world, and the gospel is unto all who have not received it.

c. But verily I say unto all those to whom the kingdom has been given, From you it must be preached unto them that they shall repent of their former evil works:

d. for they are to be upbraided for their evil hearts of unbelief: and your brethren in Zion for their rebellion against you at the time I sent you.

13 a. And again I say unto you my friends (for from henceforth I shall call you friends), It is expedient that I give unto you this commandment, that ye become even as my friends in days when I was with them traveling to preach this gospel in my power:

b. for I suffered them not to have purse or scrip, neither two coats; behold, I send you out to prove the world, and the laborer is worthy of his hire.

c. And any man that shall go and preach this gospel of the kingdom, and fail not to continue faithful in all things, shall not be weary in mind, neither darkened, neither in body, limb or joint; and an hair of his head shall not fall to the ground unnoticed. And they shall not go hungry, neither athirst.

14 a. Therefore, take no thought for the morrow, for what ye shall eat, or what ye shall drink, or wherewithal ye shall be clothed;

b. for consider the lilies of the field, how they grow, they toil not, neither do they spin; and the kingdoms of the world, in all their glory, are not arrayed like one of these; for your Father who art in heaven, knoweth that you have need of all these things.

c. Therefore, let the morrow take thought for the things of itself.

d. Neither take ye thought beforehand what ye shall say, but treasure up in your minds continually the words of life, and it shall be given you in the very hour that portion that shall be meted unto every man.

15 a. Therefore, let no man among you (for this commandment is unto all the faithful who are called of God in the church, unto the ministry), from this hour, take purse or scrip, that goeth forth to proclaim this gospel of the kingdom.

b. Behold, I send you out to reprove the world of all their unrighteous deeds, and to teach them of a judgment which is to come.

c. And whoso receiveth you, there will I be also; for I will go before your face: I will be on your right hand and on your left, and my Spirit shall be in your hearts, and my angels round about you, to bear you up.

16 a. Whoso receiveth you receiveth me, and the same will feed you, and clothe you, and give you money.

b. And he who feeds you, or clothes you, or gives you money, shall in no wise lose his reward: and he that doeth not these things is not my disciple: by this you may know my disciples.

c. He that receiveth you not, go away from him alone by

yourselves, and cleanse your feet, even with water, pure water, whether in heat or in cold, and bear testimony of it unto your Father which is in heaven, and return not again unto that man.

d. And into whatsoever village or city ye enter, do likewise. Nevertheless, search diligently and spare not; and woe unto that house, or that village, or city, that rejecteth you, or your words, or testimony concerning me.

e. Woe, I say again, unto that house, or that village, or city, that rejecteth you, or your words, or your testimony of me; for I, the Almighty, have laid my hands upon the nations to scourge them for their wickedness;

f. and plagues shall go forth, and they shall not be taken from the earth until I have completed my work, which shall be cut short in righteousness;

g. until all shall know me, who remain, even from the least unto the greatest, and shall be filled with the knowledge of the Lord, and shall see eye to eye, and shall lift up their voice, and with the voice together sing this new song, saying:

17 a.　The Lord hath brought again Zion:
　　　The Lord hath redeemed his people, Israel,
　　　According to the election of grace,
　　　Which was brought to pass by the faith
　　　And covenant of their fathers.

b.　The Lord hath redeemed his people,
　　　And Satan is bound, and time is no longer:
　　　The Lord hath gathered all things in one:
　　　The Lord hath brought down Zion from above:
　　　The Lord hath brought up Zion from beneath;
　　　The earth hath travailed and brought forth her strength;
　　　And truth is established in her bowels;
　　　And the heavens have smiled upon her,
　　　And she is clothed with the glory of her God:
　　　For he stands in the midst of his people:

c.　Glory, and honor, and power, and might,
　　　Be ascribed to our God, for he is full of mercy,
　　　Justice, grace and truth, and peace,
　　　For ever and ever, Amen.

18 a. And again, verily, verily I say unto you, It is expedient, that every man who goes forth to proclaim mine

everlasting gospel, that inasmuch as they have families, and receive moneys by gift, that they should send it unto them, or make use of it for their benefit, as the Lord shall direct them, for thus it seemeth me good.

b. And let all those who have not families, who receive moneys, send it up unto the bishop in Zion, or unto the bishop in Ohio, that it may be consecrated for the bringing forth of the revelations and the printing thereof, and for establishing Zion.

19 a. And if any man shall give unto any of you a coat, or a suit, take the old and cast it unto the poor, and go your way rejoicing.

b. And if any man among you be strong in the Spirit, let him take with him he that is weak, that he may be edified in all meekness, that he may become strong also.

20 a. Therefore, take with you those who are ordained unto the lesser priesthood, and send them before you to make appointments, and to prepare the way, and to fill appointments that you yourselves are not able to fill.

b. Behold, this is the way that mine apostles, in ancient days, built up my church unto me.

21 a. Therefore, let every man stand in his own office, and labor in his own calling; and let not the head say unto the feet it hath no need of the feet, for without the feet how shall the body be able to stand?

b. Also, the body hath need of every member, that all may be edified together, that the system may be kept perfect.

22 And, behold, the high priests should travel, and also the elders, and also the lesser priests; but the deacons and teachers should be appointed to watch over the church, to be standing ministers unto the church.

23 a. And the bishop, Newel K. Whitney, also, should travel round about and among all the churches, searching after the poor, to administer to their wants by humbling the rich and the proud;

b. he should also employ an agent to take charge and to do his secular business, as he shall direct;

c. nevertheless, let the bishop go unto the city of New York, and also to the city of Albany, and also to the city of Boston, and warn the people of those cities with the sound of the gospel, with a loud voice, of the desolation and utter abolishment which awaits them if they do reject these things;

d. for if they do reject these things, the hour of their judgment is nigh, and their house shall be left unto them desolate.

e. Let him trust in me, and he shall not be confounded, and an hair of his head shall not fall to the ground unnoticed.

24 a. And verily I say unto you, the rest of my servants, Go ye forth as your circumstances shall permit, in your several callings, unto the great and notable cities and villages, reproving the world in righteousness, of all their unrighteous and ungodly deeds, setting forth clearly and understandingly the desolation of abomination in the last days;

b. for with you, saith the Lord Almighty, I will rend their kingdoms; I will not only shake the earth, but the starry heavens shall tremble;

c. for I, the Lord, have put forth my hand to exert the powers of heaven; ye can not see it now, yet a little while and ye shall see it, and know that I am, and that I will come and reign with my people. I am Alpha and Omega, the beginning and the end. Amen.

SECTION 84

An inspired exposition of the parable of the wheat and tares received by Joseph Smith, Jr., December 6, 1832, at Kirtland, Ohio.

1 a. Verily thus saith the Lord unto you, my servants, concerning the parable of the wheat and of the tares:

b. Behold, verily I say that the field was the world, and the apostles were the sowers of the seed;

c. and after they have fallen asleep, the great persecutor of the church, the apostate, the whore, even Babylon, that maketh all nations to drink of her cup, in whose hearts the enemy, even Satan, sitteth to reign;

d. behold, he soweth the tares, wherefore the tares choke the wheat and drive the church into the wilderness.

2 a. But, behold, in the last days, even now, while the Lord is beginning to bring forth the word, and the blade is springing up and is yet tender, behold, verily I say unto you,

b. The angels are crying unto the Lord day and night, who are ready and waiting to be sent forth to reap down the fields; but the Lord saith unto them,

c. Pluck not up the tares while the blade is yet tender (for verily your faith is weak), lest you destroy the wheat also; therefore let the wheat and tares grow together until the harvest is fully ripe;

d. then ye shall first gather out the wheat from among the tares, and after the gathering of the wheat, behold, and lo, the tares are bound in bundles, and the field remaineth to be burned.

3 a. Therefore, thus saith the Lord unto you, with whom the priesthood hath continued through the lineage of your fathers, for ye are lawful heirs, according to the flesh, and have been hid from the world with Christ in God:

b. therefore your life and the priesthood hath remained, and must needs remain, through you and your lineage, until the restoration of all things spoken by the mouths of all the holy prophets since the world began.

4 Therefore, blessed are ye if ye continue in my goodness, a light unto the Gentiles, and through this priesthood, a savor unto my people Israel. The Lord hath said it. Amen.

SECTION 85

Revelation given through Joseph Smith, Jr., at Kirtland, Ohio, December 27, 1832. There had been some friction between leaders in Independence and those in Kirtland. Joseph sent a copy of this revelation with a letter to William W. Phelps, who was in Missouri, and referred to it as the "Olive leaf . . . the Lord's message of peace to us." It has since been known as "The Olive Leaf."

1 a. Verily, thus saith the Lord unto you, who have assembled yourselves together to receive his will concerning you.

b. Behold, this is pleasing unto your Lord, and the angels rejoice over you; the alms of your prayers have come up into the ears of the Lord of Sabaoth, and are recorded in the book of the names of the sanctified, even them of the celestial world.

c. Wherefore I now send upon you another Comforter, even upon you, my friends, that it may abide in your hearts, even the Holy Spirit of promise, which other Comforter is the same that I promised unto my disciples, as is recorded in the testimony of John.

2 a. This Comforter is the promise which I give unto you of eternal life, even the glory of the celestial kingdom; which glory is that of the church of the Firstborn, even of God, the holiest of all, through Jesus Christ, his Son;

b. he that ascended up on high, as also he descended below all things, in that he comprehended all things, that he might be in all and through all things, the light of truth, which truth shineth. This is the light of Christ.

c. As also he is in the sun, and the light of the sun, and the power thereof by which it was made.

d. As also he is in the moon, and is the light of the moon, and the power thereof by which it was made.

e. As also the light of the stars, and the power thereof by which they were made.

f. And the earth also, and the power thereof, even the earth upon which you stand.

3 a. And the light which now shineth, which giveth you light, is through him who enlighteneth your eyes, which is the same light that quickeneth your understandings; which light proceedeth forth from the presence of God, to fill the immensity of space.

b. The light which is in all things; which giveth life to all things; which is the law by which all things are governed; even the power of God who sitteth upon his throne, who is in the bosom of eternity, who is in the midst of all things.

4 a. Now, verily I say unto you, that through the redemption which is made for you, is brought to pass the resurrection from the dead. And the spirit and the body is the soul of man.

b. And the resurrection from the dead is the redemption of the soul; and the redemption of the soul is through him who quickeneth all things, in whose bosom it is decreed, that the poor and the meek of the earth shall inherit it.

c. Therefore, it must needs be sanctified from all unrighteousness, that it may be prepared for the celestial glory; for after it hath filled the measure of its creation, it shall be crowned with glory, even with the presence of God the Father;

d. that bodies who are of the celestial kingdom may possess it for ever and ever; for, for this intent was it made and created; and for this intent are they sanctified.

5 a. And they who are not sanctified through the law which I have given unto you, even the law of Christ, must inherit another kingdom, even that of a terrestrial kingdom, or that of a telestial kingdom.

b. For he who is not able to abide the law of a celestial kingdom, can not abide a celestial glory; and he who can not abide the law of a terrestrial kingdom, can not abide a terrestrial glory; he who can not abide the law of a telestial kingdom, can not abide a telestial glory: therefore, he is not meet for a kingdom of glory.

c. Therefore, he must abide a kingdom which is not a kingdom of glory.

6 a. And again, verily I say unto you, The earth abideth the law of a celestial kingdom, for it filleth the measure of its creation, and transgresseth not the law.

b. Wherefore, it shall be sanctified; yea, notwithstanding it shall die, it shall be quickened again, and shall abide the power by which it is quickened, and the righteous shall inherit it:

c. for, notwithstanding they die, they also shall rise again a spiritual body: they who are of a celestial spirit shall receive the same body, which was a natural body: even ye shall receive your bodies, and your glory shall be that glory by which your bodies are quickened.

d. Ye who are quickened by a portion of the celestial glory, shall then receive of the same, even a fullness;

e. and they who are quickened by a portion of the terrestrial glory, shall then receive of the same, even a fullness:

f. and also they who are quickened by a portion of the telestial glory, shall then receive of the same, even a fullness:

g. and they who remain shall also be quickened; nevertheless, they shall return again to their own place, to enjoy that which they are willing to receive, because they were not willing to enjoy that which they might have received.

7 For what doth it profit a man if a gift is bestowed upon him, and he receive not the gift? Behold, he rejoices not in that which is given unto him, neither rejoices in him who is the giver of the gift.

8 a. And again, verily I say unto you, that which is governed by law, is also preserved by law, and perfected and sanctified by the same.

b. That which breaketh a law, and abideth not by law, but seeketh to become a law unto itself, and willeth to abide in sin, and altogether abideth in sin, can not be sanctified by law, neither by mercy, justice, or judgment; therefore, they must remain filthy still.

9 a. All kingdoms have a law given: and there are many kingdoms; for there is no space in the which there is no kingdom; and there is no kingdom in which there is no space, either a greater or lesser kingdom.

b. And unto every kingdom is given a law; and unto every law there are certain bounds also, and conditions.

10 a. All beings who abide not in those conditions, are not justified; for intelligence cleaveth unto intelligence; wisdom receiveth wisdom; truth embraceth truth; virtue loveth virtue; light cleaveth unto light;

b. mercy hath compassion on mercy, and claimeth her own; justice continueth its course, and claimeth its own; judgment goeth before the face of him who sitteth upon the throne, and governeth and executeth all things:

c. he comprehendeth all things, and all things are before him, and all things are round about him; and he is above all things, and in all things, and is through all things, and is round about all things: and all things are by him, and of him; even God, for ever and ever.

11 a. And again, verily I say unto you, He hath given a law unto all things by which they move in their times, and their seasons; and their courses are fixed; even the courses

of the heavens, and the earth; which comprehend the earth
and all the planets;

b. and they give light to each other in their times, and in
their seasons, in their minutes, in their hours, in their days,
in their weeks, in their months, in their years: all these are
one year with God, but not with man.

12 a. The earth rolls upon her wings; and the sun giveth
his light by day, and the moon giveth her light by night;
and the stars also giveth their light, as they roll upon their
wings, in their glory, in the midst of the power of God.

b. Unto what shall I liken these kingdoms, that ye may
understand?

c. Behold, all these are kingdoms, and any man who hath
seen any or the least of these, hath seen God moving in
his majesty and power.

d. I say unto you, he hath seen him: nevertheless, He who
came unto his own was not comprehended.

e. The light shineth in darkness, and the darkness comprehendeth it not; nevertheless, the day shall come when you
shall comprehend even God; being quickened in him, and
by him.

f. Then shall ye know that ye have seen me, that I am,
and that I am the true light that is in you, and that you
are in me, otherwise ye could not abound.

13 a. Behold, I will liken these kingdoms unto a man having a field, and he sent forth his servants into the field, to
dig in the field;

b. and he said unto the first, Go ye and labor in the field,
and in the first hour I will come unto you, and ye shall behold the joy of my countenance:

c. and he said unto the second, Go ye also into the field,
and in the second hour I will visit you with the joy of my
countenance;

d. and also unto the third, saying, I will visit you; and
unto the fourth, and so on unto the twelfth.

14 a. And the lord of the field went unto the first in the
first hour, and tarried with him all that hour, and he was
made glad with the light of the countenance of his lord;

b. and then he withdrew from the first that he might visit

the second also, and the third, and the fourth, and so on
unto the twelfth;

   c. and thus they all received the light of the countenance of their lord; every man in his hour, and in his time,
and in his season; beginning at the first, and so on unto the
last, and from the last unto the first, and from the first unto
the last;

   d. every man in his own order, until his hour was finished, even according as his lord had commanded him, that
his lord might be glorified in him, and he in him, that they
all might be glorified.

15 Therefore, unto this parable will I liken all these
kingdoms, and the inhabitants thereof; every kingdom in
its hour, and in its time, and in its season; even according to the decree which God hath made.

16 a. And again, verily I say unto you, my friends, I leave
these sayings with you, to ponder in your hearts with this
commandment which I give unto you, that ye shall call upon
me while I am near;

   b. draw near unto me, and I will draw near unto you;

   c. seek me diligently and ye shall find me;

   d. ask and ye shall receive;

   e. knock and it shall be opened unto you;

   f. whatsoever ye ask the Father in my name it shall be
given unto you, that is expedient for you; and if ye ask anything that is not expedient for you, it shall turn unto your
condemnation.

17 Behold, that which you hear is as the voice of one
crying in the wilderness; in the wilderness, because you can
not see him: my voice, because my voice is Spirit; my Spirit
is truth: truth abideth and hath no end; and if it be in you
it shall abound.

18 a. And if your eye be single to my glory, your whole
bodies shall be filled with light, and there shall be no darkness in you, and that body which is filled with light comprehendeth all things.

   b. Therefore, sanctify yourselves that your minds become
single to God, and the days will come that you shall see him:

for he will unveil his face unto you, and it shall be in his own time, and in his own way, and according to his own will.

19 a. Remember the great and last promise which I have made unto you: cast away your idle thoughts and your excess of laughter far from you;

b. tarry ye, tarry ye in this place, and call a solemn assembly, even of those who are the first laborers in this last kingdom; and let those whom they have warned in their traveling, call on the Lord, and ponder the warning in their hearts which they have received, for a little season.

c. Behold, and lo, I will take care of your flocks and will raise up elders and send unto them.

20 a. Behold, I will hasten my work in its time; and I give unto you who are the first laborers in this last kingdom, a commandment, that you assemble yourselves together, and organize yourselves, and prepare yourselves; and sanctify yourselves;

b. yea, purify your hearts, and cleanse your hands and your feet before me, that I may make you clean;

c. that I may testify unto your Father, and your God, and my God, that you are clean from the blood of this wicked generation, that I may fulfill this promise, this great and last promise which I have made unto you, when I will.

21 a. Also, I give unto you a commandment, that ye shall continue in prayer and fasting from this time forth.

b. And I give unto you a commandment, that you shall teach one another the doctrine of the kingdom; teach ye diligently and my grace shall attend you, that you may be instructed more perfectly in theory, in principle, in doctrine, in the law of the gospel, in all things that pertain unto the kingdom of God, that is expedient for you to understand;

c. of things both in heaven, and in earth, and under the earth; things which have been; things which are; things which must shortly come to pass;

d. things which are at home; things which are abroad; the wars and the perplexities of the nations; and the judgments which are on the land;

e. and a knowledge also of countries, and of kingdoms, that ye may be prepared in all things when I shall send you again, to magnify the calling whereunto I have called you, and the mission with which I have commissioned you.

22 a. Behold, I sent you out to testify and warn the people, and it becometh every man who hath been warned, to warn his neighbor; therefore, they are left without excuse, and their sins are upon their own heads.

b. He that seeketh me early shall find me, and shall not be forsaken.

23 a. Therefore, tarry ye, and labor diligently, that you may be perfected in your ministry, to go forth among the Gentiles for the last time, as many as the mouth of the Lord shall name, to bind up the law, and seal up the testimony, and to prepare the saints for the hour of judgment, which is to come;

b. that their souls may escape the wrath of God, the desolation of abomination, which await the wicked, both in this world, and in the world to come.

c. Verily, I say unto you, Let those who are not the first elders, continue in the vineyard, until the mouth of the Lord shall call them, for their time is not yet come; their garments are not clean from the blood of this generation.

24 a. Abide ye in the liberty wherewith ye are made free; entangle not yourselves in sin, but let your hands be clean, until the Lord come,

b. for not many days hence and the earth shall tremble, and reel to and fro as a drunken man, and the sun shall hide his face, and shall refuse to give light, and the moon shall be bathed in blood, and the stars shall become exceeding angry, and shall cast themselves down as a fig that falleth from off a fig tree.

25 a. And after your testimony, cometh wrath and indignation upon the people; for after your testimony cometh the testimony of earthquakes, that shall cause groanings in the midst of her, and men shall fall upon the ground, and shall not be able to stand.

b. And also cometh the testimony of the voice of thunderings, and the voice of lightnings, and the voice of tempests, and the voice of the waves of the sea, heaving themselves beyond their bounds.

c. And all things shall be in commotion; and surely men's hearts shall fail them; for fear shall come upon all people; and angels shall fly through the midst of heaven, crying with a loud voice, sounding the trump of God, saying,

d. Prepare ye, prepare ye, O inhabitants of the earth, for the judgment of our God is come: behold, and lo, the Bridegroom cometh, go ye out to meet him.

26 a. And immediately there shall appear a great sign in heaven, and all people shall see it together.

b. And another angel shall sound his trump, saying, That great church, the mother of abominations, that made all nations drink of the wine of the wrath of her fornication, that persecuteth the saints of God, that shed their blood:

c. she who sitteth upon many waters, and upon the islands of the sea; behold, she is the tares of the earth, she is bound in bundles, her bands are made strong, no man can loose them; therefore, she is ready to be burned.

d. And he shall sound his trump both long and loud, and all nations shall hear it.

27 a. And there shall be silence in heaven for the space of half an hour, and immediately after shall the curtain of heaven be unfolded, as a scroll is unfolded after it is rolled up, and the face of the Lord shall be unveiled;

b. and the saints that are upon the earth, who are alive, shall be quickened, and be caught up to meet him.

c. And they who have slept in their graves, shall come forth; for their graves shall be opened, and they also shall be caught up to meet him in the midst of the pillar of heaven: they are Christ's, the first fruits:

d. they who shall descend with him first, and they who are on the earth, and in their graves, who are first caught up to meet him; and all this by the voice of the sounding of the trump of the angel of God.

28 a. And after this, another angel shall sound, which is the second trump; and then cometh the redemption of those who are Christ's at his coming;

b. who have received their part in that prison which is

prepared for them, that they might receive the gospel, and be judged according to men in the flesh.

29 a. And again, another trump shall sound, which is the third trump: and then cometh the spirits of men who are to be judged, and are found under condemnation:

b. and these are the rest of the dead, and they live not again until the thousand years are ended, neither again, until the end of the earth.

30 And another trump shall sound, which is the fourth trump, saying, These are found among those who are to remain until that great and last day, even the end, who shall remain filthy still.

31 a. And another trump shall sound, which is the fifth trump, which is the fifth angel who committeth the everlasting gospel, flying through the midst of heaven, unto all nations, kindreds, tongues, and people;

b. and this shall be the sound of his trump, saying to all people, both in heaven and in earth, and that are under the earth; for every ear shall hear it, and every knee shall bow, and every tongue shall confess, while they hear the sound of the trump, saying,

c. Fear God, and give glory to him who sitteth upon the throne, for ever and ever: for the hour of his judgment is come.

32 And again, another angel shall sound his trump, which is the sixth angel, saying, She is fallen, who made all nations drink of the wine of the wrath of her fornication: she is fallen! is fallen!

33 a. And again, another angel shall sound his trump, which is the seventh angel, saying: It is finished! it is finished! the Lamb of God hath overcome, and trodden the wine press alone; even the wine press of the fierceness of the wrath of Almighty God;

b. and then shall the angels be crowned with the glory of his might, and the saints shall be filled with his glory, and receive their inheritance and be made equal with him.

34 And then shall the first angel again sound his trump

in the ears of all living, and reveal the secret acts of men,
and the mighty works of God in the first thousandth year.

35 a. And then shall the second angel sound his trump, and
reveal the secret acts of men, and the thoughts and intents
of their hearts, and the mighty works of God in the second
thousandth year:

b. and so on, until the seventh angel shall sound his trump;
and he shall stand forth upon the land and upon the sea, and
swear in the name of him who sitteth upon the throne, that
there shall be time no longer, and Satan shall be bound, that
old serpent, who is called the Devil, and shall not be loosed
for the space of a thousand years.

c. And then he shall be loosed for a little season, that he
may gather together his armies; and Michael, the seventh
angel, even the archangel, shall gather together his armies,
even the hosts of heaven.

d. And the Devil shall gather together his armies, even the
hosts of hell, and shall come up to battle against Michael and
his armies: and then cometh the battle of the great God!

e. And the Devil and his armies shall be cast away into
their own place, that they shall not have power over the
saints any more at all; for Michael shall fight their battles,
and shall overcome him who seeketh the throne of him who
sitteth upon the throne, even the Lamb.

f. This is the glory of God and the sanctified; and they
shall not any more see death.

36 a. Therefore, verily I say unto you, my friends, Call
your solemn assembly, as I have commanded you; and as all
have not faith, seek ye diligently and teach one another
words of wisdom; yea, seek ye out of the best books words
of wisdom; seek learning even by study, and also by faith.

b. Organize yourselves; prepare every needful thing, and
establish a house, even a house of prayer, a house of fasting,
a house of faith, a house of learning, a house of glory, a
house of order, a house of God;

c. that your incomings may be in the name of the Lord;
that your outgoings may be in the name of the Lord; that
all your salutations may be in the name of the Lord, with
uplifted hands unto the Most High.

37 a. Therefore cease from all your light speeches, from

all laughter, from all your lustful desires, from all your pride
and light-mindedness, and from all your wicked doings.

b. Appoint among yourselves a teacher, and let not all be
spokesmen at once, but let one speak at a time, and let all
listen unto his sayings, that when all have spoken, that all
may be edified of all, and that every man may have an equal
privilege.

38 a. See that ye love one another; cease to be covetous;
learn to impart one to another as the gospel requires; cease
to be idle; cease to be unclean; cease to find fault one with
another;

b. cease to sleep longer than is needful; retire to thy bed
early, that ye may not be weary; arise early, that your bodies
and your minds may be invigorated;

c. and above all things, clothe yourselves with the bonds
of charity, as with a mantle, which is the bond of perfectness
and peace; pray always, that you may not faint until I come;
behold, and lo, I will come quickly, and receive you unto
myself. Amen.

39 a. And again, the order of the house prepared for the
presidency of the school of the prophets, established for
their instruction in all things that are expedient for them,
even for all the officers of the church,

b. or, in other words, those who are called to the ministry in the church, beginning at the high priests, even down
to the deacons; and this shall be the order of the house of
the presidency of the school:

c. He that is appointed to be president, or teacher, shall
be found standing in his place, in the house, which shall be
prepared for him; therefore he shall be first in the house of
God, in a place that the congregation in the house may hear
his words carefully and distinctly, not with loud speech.

d. And when he cometh into the house of God (for he
should be first in the house; behold, this is beautiful, that he
may be an example)

40 Let him offer himself in prayer upon his knees before God, in token or remembrance of the everlasting covenant; and when any shall come in after him, let the teacher

arise, and, with uplifted hands to heaven, yea, even directly, salute his brother or brethren with these words:

41 Art thou a brother or brethren, I salute you in the name of the Lord Jesus Christ, in token or remembrance of the everlasting covenant, in which covenant I receive you to fellowship, in a determination that is fixed, immovable, and unchangeable, to be your friend and brother, through the grace of God, in the bonds of love, to walk in all the commandments of God blameless, in thanksgiving, for ever and ever. Amen.

42 And he that is found unworthy of this salutation shall not have place among you; for ye shall not suffer that mine house shall be polluted by them.

43 And he that cometh in and is faithful before me, and is a brother, or if they be brethren, they shall salute the president or teacher, with uplifted hands to heaven, with this same prayer and covenant, or by saying Amen, in token of the same.

44 a. Behold, verily I say unto you, This is a sample unto you for a salutation to one another in the house of God, in the school of the prophets.

b. And ye are called to do this by prayer and thanksgiving, as the Spirit shall give utterance, in all your doings in the house of the Lord, in the school of the prophets, that it may become a sanctuary, a tabernacle, of the Holy Spirit to your edification.

45 And ye shall not receive any among you into this school, save he is clean from the blood of this generation; and he shall be received by the ordinance of the washing of feet, for unto this end was the ordinance of the washing of feet instituted.

46 a. And again, the ordinance of washing feet is to be administered by the president, or presiding elder of the church.

b. It is to be commenced with prayer; and after partaking of bread and wine, he is to gird himself, according to the pattern given in the thirteenth chapter of John's testimony concerning me. Amen.

SECTION 86

This revelation, now known as the Word of Wisdom, was given through Joseph Smith, Jr., to a conference of high priests assembled at Kirtland, Ohio, February 27, 1833. It was described as "A word of wisdom for the benefit of the council of high priests, assembled in Kirtland, and the church; and also, the Saints in Zion. To be sent greeting, not by commandment, or constraint, but by revelation and the word of wisdom; showing forth the order and will of God in the temporal salvation of all Saints in the last days. Given for a principle, with promise; adapted to the capacity of the weak, and the weakest of all Saints, who are or can be called Saints."

1 a. Behold, verily thus saith the Lord unto you, In consequence of evils and designs which do and will exist in the hearts of conspiring men in the last days, I have warned you, and forewarn you, by giving unto you this word of wisdom by revelation,

b. that inasmuch as any man drinketh wine or strong drink among you, behold, it is not good, neither meet in the sight of your Father, only in assembling yourselves together, to offer up your sacraments before him.

c. And behold, this should be wine; yea, pure wine of the grape of the vine, of your own make. And again, strong drinks are not for the belly, but for the washing of your bodies.

d. And again, tobacco is not for the body, neither for the belly, and is not good for man, but is an herb for bruises, and all sick cattle, to be used with judgment and skill.

e. And again, hot drinks are not for the body or belly.

2 a. And again, verily I say unto you, All wholesome herbs God hath ordained for the constitution, nature, and use of man, every herb in the season thereof, and every fruit in the season thereof. All these to be used with prudence and thanksgiving.

b. Yea, flesh also, of beasts and of the fowls of the air, I, the Lord, hath ordained for the use of man, with thanksgiving. Nevertheless, they are to be used sparingly; and it is pleasing unto me that they should not be used only in times of winter, or of cold, or famine.

c. All grain is ordained for the use of man and of beasts, to be the staff of life, not only for man, but for the beasts of the field, and the fowls of heaven, and all wild animals that run or creep on the earth; and these hath God made for the use of man only in times of famine and excess of hunger.

3 a. All grain is good for the food of man, as also the fruit of the vine, that which yieldeth fruit, whether in the ground or above the ground.

b. Nevertheless, wheat for man, and corn for the ox, and oats for the horse, and rye for the fowls, and for swine, and for all beasts of the field, and barley for all useful animals, and for mild drinks, as also other grain.

c. And all Saints who remember to keep and do these sayings, walking in obedience to the commandments, shall receive health in their navel, and marrow to their bones, and shall find wisdom and great treasures of knowledge, even hidden treasures;

d. and shall run and not be weary, and shall walk and not faint; and I, the Lord, give unto them a promise that the destroying angel shall pass by them, as the children of Israel, and not slay them. Amen.

SECTION 87

Revelation received through Joseph Smith, Jr., March 8, 1833, at Kirtland, Ohio. By virtue of this revelation, the First Presidency was fully constituted for the first time in this dispensation. Sidney Rigdon and Frederick G. Williams, who are named here, were ordained under the hands of Joseph Smith, March 18, 1833, to be counselors in the First Presidency and in the Presidency of the High Priesthood.

1 a. Thus saith the Lord, Verily I say unto thee, my son, Thy sins are forgiven thee, according to thy petition, for thy prayers and the prayers of thy brethren have come up into my ears;

b. therefore thou art blessed from henceforth that bear the keys of the kingdom given unto thee; which kingdom is coming forth for the last time.

2 a. Verily I say unto you, The keys of this kingdom shall never be taken from you, while thou art in the world, neither in the world to come; nevertheless, through you shall the oracles be given to another; yea, even unto the church.

b. And all they who receive the oracles of God, let them beware how they hold them, lest they are accounted as a light thing, and are brought under condemnation thereby; and stumble and fall, when the storms descend, and the winds blow, and the rains descend, and beat upon their house.

3 a. And again, verily I say unto thy brethren Sidney Rigdon and Frederick G. Williams, their sins are forgiven them also, and they are accounted as equal with thee in holding the keys of this last kingdom;

b. as also through your administration the keys of the school of the prophets, which I have commanded to be organized, that thereby they may be perfected in their ministry for the salvation of Zion, and of the nations of Israel, and of the Gentiles, as many as will believe,

c. that through your administration, they may receive the word, and through their administration, the word may go forth unto the ends of the earth, unto the Gentiles first, and then, behold, and lo, they shall turn unto the Jews;

d. and then cometh the day when the arm of the Lord shall be revealed in power in convincing the nations, the heathen nations, the house of Joseph, of the gospel of their salvation.

4 For it shall come to pass in that day, that every man shall hear the fullness of the gospel in his own tongue, and in his own language, through those who are ordained unto this power, by the administration of the Comforter, shed forth upon them, for the revelation of Jesus Christ.

5 a. And now, verily I say unto you, I give unto you a commandment, that you continue in the ministry and presidency, and when you have finished the translation of the prophets, you shall from henceforth preside over the affairs of the church and the school;

b. and from time to time, as shall be manifest by the Comforter, receive revelations to unfold the mysteries of the kingdom, and set in order the churches, and study and learn, and become acquainted with all good books, and with languages, tongues, and people.

c. And this shall be your business and mission in all your lives to preside in council and set in order all the affairs of this church and kingdom.

d. Be not ashamed, neither confounded; but be admonished in all your highmindedness and pride, for it bringeth a snare upon your souls.

e. Set in order your houses; keep slothfulness and uncleanliness far from you.

6 a. Now, verily I say unto thee, Let there be a place provided as soon as it is possible, for the family of thy counselor and scribe, even Frederick G. Williams;

b. and let mine aged servant Joseph Smith, Sr., continue with his family upon the place where he now lives, and let it not be sold until the mouth of the Lord shall name.

c. And let thy counselor, even Sidney Rigdon, remain where he now resides, until the mouth of the Lord shall name.

d. And let the bishop search diligently to obtain an agent; and let it be a man who has got riches in store; a man of God and of strong faith; that thereby he may be enabled to discharge every debt; that the storehouse of the Lord may not be brought into disrepute before the eyes of the people.

e. Search diligently, pray always, and be believing, and all things shall work together for your good, if ye walk uprightly, and remember the covenant wherewith ye have covenanted one with another.

f. Let your families be small, especially mine aged servant Joseph Smith, Sr., as pertaining to those who do not belong to your families;

g. that those things that are provided for you, to bring to pass my work, are not taken from you and given to those that are not worthy, and thereby you are hindered in accomplishing those things which I have commanded you.

7 a. And again, verily I say unto you, It is my will that my handmaid, Vienna Jaques, should receive money to bear her expenses, and go up unto the land of Zion; and the residue of the money may be consecrated unto me, and she be rewarded in mine own due time.

b. Verily I say unto you, that it is meet in mine eyes, that she should go up unto the land of Zion, and receive an inheritance from the hand of the bishop, that she may settle down in peace inasmuch as she is faithful, and not be idle in her days from thenceforth.

8 a. And, behold, verily I say unto you, that ye shall write this commandment, and say unto your brethren in Zion, in love greeting, that I have called you also to preside over Zion in mine own due time; therefore let them cease wearying me concerning this matter.

b. Behold, I say unto you, that your brethren in Zion begin to repent, and the angels rejoice over them; nevertheless, I am not well pleased with many things;

c. and I am not well pleased with my servant William E. McLellin, neither with my servant Sidney Gilbert; and the bishop also; and others have many things to repent of;

d. but verily I say unto you, that I, the Lord, will contend with Zion and plead with her strong ones, and chasten her, until she overcomes and is clean before me; for she shall not be removed out of her place. I, the Lord, have spoken it. Amen.

SECTION 88

While working on the revision of the Holy Scriptures, Joseph Smith, Jr., came to the books of the Apocrypha. He inquired of the Lord whether these should be included in the revision and was given the following instruction. The revelation was received March 9, 1833, at Kirtland, Ohio.

1 a. Verily, thus saith the Lord unto you, concerning the Apocrypha,

b. There are many things contained therein that are true, and it is mostly translated correctly; there are many things contained therein that are not true, which are interpolations by the hands of men.

c. Verily I say unto you, that it is not needful that the Apocrypha should be translated.

d. Therefore, whoso readeth it let him understand, for the Spirit manifesteth truth; and whoso is enlightened by the Spirit shall obtain benefit therefrom; and whoso receiveth not by the Spirit, can not be benefited; therefore, it is not needful that it should be translated. Amen.

SECTION 89

Revelation given through Joseph Smith, Jr., March 15, 1833, at Kirtland, Ohio. Shederlaomach (Frederick G. Williams, recently ordained a counselor in the First Presidency) is named for admission into the Order of Enoch.

1 Verily, thus saith the Lord, I give unto the united order, organized agreeable to the commandment previously given, a revelation and commandment concerning my servant Shederlaomach, that ye shall receive him into the order. What I say unto one I say unto all.

2 And again, I say unto you, my servant Shederlaomach, You shall be a lively member in this order; and inasmuch as you are faithful in keeping all former commandments, you shall be blessed for ever. Amen.

SECTION 90

A conference of high priests met in Kirtland, Ohio, May 4, 1833, to consider the building of a schoolhouse for the instruction of the elders in the work of their ministry. This was in harmony with the revelation of December 27, 1832 (D. and C. 85:36). This revelation was received through Joseph Smith two days later, May 6, 1833, at Kirtland, Ohio.

1 a. Verily, thus saith the Lord, It shall come to pass that every soul who forsaketh his sins and cometh unto me, and calleth on my name, and obeyeth my voice, and keepeth my commandments, shall see my face, and know that I am, and that I am the true light that lighteth every man that cometh into the world;

b. and that I am in the Father and the Father in me, and the Father and I are one; the Father because he gave me of his fullness; and the Son because I was in the world and made flesh my tabernacle, and dwelt among the sons of men.

c. I was in the world and received of my Father, and the works of him were plainly manifest; and John saw and bore record of the fullness of my glory; and the fullness of John's record is hereafter to be revealed.

d. And he bore record saying, I saw his glory that he was in the beginning before the world was; therefore, in the beginning the Word was; for he was the Word, even the messenger of salvation, the light and the Redeemer of the world;

e. the Spirit of truth, who came into the world because the world was made by him; and in him was the life of men and the light of men.

f. The worlds were made by him. Men were made by him. All things were made by him, and through him, and of him.

g. And I, John, bear record that I beheld his glory, as the glory of the Only Begotten of the Father, full of grace and truth; even the Spirit of truth which came and dwelt in the flesh, and dwelt among us.

2 a. And I, John, saw that he received not of the fullness at the first, but received grace for grace; and he received not of the fullness at first, but continued from grace to grace, until he received a fullness;

b. and thus he was called the Son of God, because he received not of the fullness at the first.

c. And I, John, bare record, and lo, the heavens were opened and the Holy Ghost descended upon him in the form of a dove, and sat upon him, and there came a voice out of heaven saying, This is my beloved Son.

d. And I, John, bare record that he received a fullness of the glory of the Father; and he received all power, both in heaven and on earth; and the glory of the Father was with him, for he dwelt in him.

3 a. And it shall come to pass, that if you are faithful, you shall receive the fullness of the record of John.

b. I give unto you these sayings that you may understand and know how to worship, and know what you worship, that you may come unto the Father in my name, and in due time receive of his fullness,

c. for if you keep my commandments you shall receive of his fullness and be glorified in me as I am in the Father: therefore, I say unto you, You shall receive grace for grace.

4 a. And now, verily I say unto you, I was in the beginning with the Father, and am the Firstborn; and all those who are begotten through me, are partakers of the glory of the same, and are the church of the Firstborn.

b. Ye were also in the beginning with the Father; that which is Spirit, even the Spirit of truth; and truth is knowledge of things as they are, and as they were, and as they are to come; and whatsoever is more or less than this, is the spirit of that wicked one, who was a liar from the beginning.

c. The Spirit of truth is of God. I am the Spirit of truth.

d. And John bore record of me, saying, He received a fullness of truth; yea, even of all truth, and no man receiveth a fullness unless he keepeth his commandments.

e. He that keepeth his commandments, receiveth truth and light, until he is glorified in truth, and knoweth all things.

5 a. Man was also in the beginning with God. Intelligence, or the light of truth, was not created or made, neither indeed can be.

b. All truth is independent in that sphere in which God has placed it, to act for itself, as all intelligence also, otherwise there is no existence.

c. Behold, here is the agency of man, and here is the condemnation of man, because that which was from the beginning is plainly manifest unto them, and they receive not the light.

d. And every man whose spirit receiveth not the light is under condemnation, for man is spirit.

e. The elements are eternal, and spirit and element, inseparably connected, receiveth a fullness of joy; and when separated, man can not receive a fullness of joy.

f. The elements are the tabernacle of God; yea, man is the tabernacle of God, even temples; and whatsoever temple is defiled, God shall destroy that temple.

6 a. The glory of God is intelligence, or, in other words, light and truth; and light and truth forsaketh that evil one.

b. Every spirit of man was innocent in the beginning, and God having redeemed man from the fall, men became again in their infant state, innocent before God.

c. And that wicked one cometh and taketh away light and truth, through disobedience, from the children of men, and because of the tradition of their fathers.

d. But I have commanded you to bring up your children in light and truth,

e. but verily I say unto you, my servant Frederick G. Williams, You have continued under this condemnation; you have not taught your children light and truth, according to the commandments, and that wicked one hath power, as yet, over you, and this is the cause of your affliction.

f. And now a commandment I give unto you, if you will be delivered: you shall set in order your own house, for there are many things that are not right in your house.

7 Verily I say unto my servant Sidney Rigdon, that in some things he hath not kept the commandments, concerning his children; therefore, firstly set in order thy house.

8 a. Verily I say unto my servant Joseph Smith, Jr., or, in other words, I will call you friends, for you are my friends, and you shall have an inheritance with me.

b. I called you servants for the world's sake, and you are their servants for my sake; and now verily I say unto Joseph Smith, Jr., You have not kept the commandments, and must needs stand rebuked before the Lord.

c. Your family must needs repent and forsake some things, and give more earnest heed unto your sayings, or be removed out of their place.

d. What I say unto one I say unto all: Pray always, lest that wicked one have power in you, and remove you out of your place.

9 My servant Newel K. Whitney, also a bishop of my church, hath need to be chastened, and set in order his family, and see that they are more diligent and concerned at home, and pray always, or they shall be removed out of their place.

10 Now I say unto you, my friends, Let my servant Sidney Rigdon go his journey, and make haste, and also

proclaim the acceptable year of the Lord, and the gospel of
salvation, as I shall give him utterance, and by your prayer
of faith with one consent, I will uphold him.

11 And let my servants Joseph Smith, Jr., and Frederick
G. Williams, make haste also, and it shall be given them even
according to the prayer of faith; and inasmuch as you keep
my sayings, you shall not be confounded in this world, nor
in the world to come.

12 And verily I say unto you, that it is my will that you
should hasten to translate my Scriptures, and to obtain a
knowledge of history, and of countries, and of kingdoms, of
laws of God and man, and all this for the salvation of Zion.
Amen.

SECTION 91

*Instruction given through Joseph Smith, Jr., prophet and
seer to the church, at Kirtland, Ohio, on May 6, 1833, the
same day that the preceding revelation was received.*

1 a. And again, verily I say unto you, my friends, A commandment I give unto you, that ye shall commence a work
of laying out and preparing a beginning and foundation of
the city of the stake of Zion, here in the land of Kirtland,
beginning at my house; and, behold, it must be done according to the pattern which I have given unto you.

b. And let the first lot on the south be consecrated unto
me for the building of an house for the Presidency, for the
work of the Presidency, in obtaining revelations, and for the
work of the ministry of the Presidency, in all things pertaining to the church and kingdom.

2 a. Verily I say unto you, that it shall be built fifty-five
by sixty-five feet in the width thereof, and in the length
thereof, in the inner court; and there shall be a lower court,
and a higher court, according to the pattern which shall be
given unto you hereafter;

b. and it shall be dedicated unto the Lord from the foundation thereof, according to the order of the priesthood, according to the pattern which shall be given unto you here-

after; and it shall be wholly dedicated unto the Lord for the work of the Presidency.

c. And you shall not suffer any unclean thing to come in unto it; and my glory shall be there, and my presence shall be there; but if there shall come into it any unclean thing, my glory shall not be there, and my presence shall not come into it.

3 a. And again, verily I say unto you, The second lot on the south shall be dedicated unto me, for the building of an house unto me, for the work of the printing of the translation of my Scriptures, and all things whatsoever I shall command you;

b. and it shall be fifty-five by sixty-five feet in the width thereof, and the length thereof, in the inner court; and there shall be a lower and a higher court;

c. and this house shall be wholly dedicated unto the Lord from the foundation thereof, for the work of the printing, in all things whatsoever I shall command you, to be holy, undefiled, according to the pattern, in all things, as it shall be given unto you.

4 a. And on the third lot shall my servant Hyrum Smith receive his inheritance.

b. And on the first and second lots, on the north, shall my servants Reynolds Cahoon and Jared Carter receive their inheritance, that they may do the work which I have appointed unto them, to be a committee to build mine houses, according to the commandments which I, the Lord God, have given unto you.

c. These two houses are not to be built until I give unto you a commandment concerning them.

5 And now I give unto you no more at this time. Amen.

SECTION 92

Revelation given through Joseph Smith, Jr., June 1, 1833, at Kirtland, Ohio. It should be studied in connection with sections 85:36, 90, and 91. Following the instruction contained in Doctrine and Covenants 85:36, a schoolhouse building committee had been appointed. It consisted of Hyrum Smith, Jared Carter, and Reynolds Cahoon. This revelation modified the purpose of the committee but retained the same personnel, which now became the building committee for the temple.

1 a. Verily, thus saith the Lord unto you, whom I love; and whom I love I also chasten, that their sins may be forgiven; for with the chastisement I prepare a way for their deliverance, in all things, out of temptation; and I have loved you:

b. Wherefore, ye must needs be chastened and stand rebuked before my face, for ye have sinned against me a very grievous sin, in that ye have not considered the great commandment in all things, that I have given unto you, concerning the building of mine house,

c. for the preparation wherewith I design to prepare mine apostles to prune my vineyard for the last time, that I may bring to pass my strange act, that I may pour out my Spirit upon all flesh.

d. But, behold, verily I say unto you, There are many who have been ordained among you, whom I have called, but few of them are chosen:

e. they who are not chosen have sinned a very grievous sin, in that they are walking in darkness at noonday; and for this cause, I gave unto you a commandment, that you should call your solemn assembly;

f. that your fastings and your mourning might come up into the ears of the Lord of Sabaoth, which is, by interpretation, the Creator of the first day; the beginning and the end.

2 a. Yea, verily I say unto you, I gave unto you a commandment, that you should build an house, in the which house I design to endow those whom I have chosen with power from on high, for this is the promise of the Father unto you;

b. therefore, I commanded you to tarry, even as mine apostles at Jerusalem; nevertheless my servants sinned a very grievous sin; and contentions arose in the school of the prophets, which was very grievous unto me, saith your Lord; therefore I sent them forth to be chastened.

3 a. Verily I say unto you, It is my will that you should build an house; if you keep my commandments, you shall have power to build it; if you keep not my commandments the love of the Father shall not continue with you; therefore you shall walk in darkness.

b. Now here is wisdom and the mind of the Lord: let the house be built, not after the manner of the world, for I give not unto you, that ye shall live after the manner of the world;

c. therefore let it be built after the manner which I shall show unto three of you, whom ye shall appoint and ordain unto this power.

d. And the size thereof shall be fifty and five feet in width, and let it be sixty-five feet in length, in the inner court thereof;

e. and let the lower part of the inner court be dedicated unto me for your sacrament offering, and for your preaching; and your fasting, and your praying, and the offering up your most holy desires unto me, saith your Lord.

f. And let the higher part of the inner court, be dedicated unto me for the school of mine apostles, saith Son Ahman; or, in other words, Alphus; or, in other words, Omegus; even Jesus Christ your Lord. Amen.

SECTION 93

A conference of high priests was held at Kirtland, June 4, 1833, to consider the management of the French farm. The conference could not agree concerning the farm, but did agree to ask for divine guidance. Joseph inquired of the Lord and received the following message. Ahashdah (Newel K. Whitney), who was directed to take charge of the farm, was the bishop in Kirtland. "Zombre" was John Johnson.

1 a. Behold, I say unto you, Here is wisdom whereby ye may know how to act concerning this matter, for it is expedient in me that this stake that I have set for the strength of Zion, should be made strong;

b. therefore, let my servant Ahashdah take charge of the place which is named among you, upon which I design to build mine holy house; and again let it be divided into lots, according to wisdom, for the benefit of those who seek inheritances, as it shall be determined in council among you.

c. Therefore, take heed that ye see to this matter, and that portion that is necessary to benefit mine order, for the purpose of bringing forth my word to the children of men;

d. for, behold, verily I say unto you, This is the most expedient in me, that my word should go forth unto the children of men, for the purpose of subduing the hearts of the children of men, for your good. Even so. Amen.

2 a. And again, verily I say unto you, It is wisdom, and expedient in me, that my servant Zombre, whose offering I have accepted, and whose prayers I have heard, unto whom I give a promise of eternal life, inasmuch as he keepeth my commandments from henceforth; for he is a descendant of Seth, and a partaker of the blessings of the promise made unto his fathers.

b. Verily I say unto you, It is expedient in me that he should become a member of the order, that he may assist in bringing forth my word unto the children of men;

c. therefore ye shall ordain him unto this blessing; and he shall seek diligently to take away incumbrances, that are upon the house named among you, that he may dwell therein. Even so. Amen.

SECTION 94

*Revelation given through Joseph Smith, Jr., at Kirtland,
Ohio, August 2, 1833. This has to do with the work of the
church in Zion. Before the revelation was given the Saints
in Independence had been forced to sign an agreement to
leave Jackson County (July 23, 1833). Word of the agreement did not reach Kirtland until early in September.*

1 a. Verily I say unto you my friends, I speak unto you
with my voice, even the voice of my Spirit, that I may
show unto you my will concerning your brethren in the land
of Zion, many of whom are truly humble, and are seeking
diligently to learn wisdom and to find truth;

b. verily, verily I say unto you, Blessed are all such for
they shall obtain, for I, the Lord, show mercy unto all the
meek, and upon all whomsoever I will, that I may be justified, when I shall bring them unto judgment.

2 a. Behold, I say unto you, concerning the school in
Zion, I, the Lord, am well pleased that there should be a
school in Zion;

b. and also with my servant Parley P. Pratt, for he abideth
in me; and inasmuch as he continueth to abide in me, he
shall continue to preside over the school in the land of Zion,
until I shall give unto him other commandments;

c. and I will bless him with a multiplicity of blessings, in
expounding all Scriptures and mysteries to the edification of
the school, and of the church in Zion;

d. and to the residue of the school, I, the Lord, am willing to show mercy, nevertheless there are those that must
needs be chastened, and their works shall be made known.

e. The ax is laid at the root of the trees, and every tree
that bringeth not forth good fruit, shall be hewn down and
cast into the fire; I, the Lord, have spoken it.

f. Verily I say unto you, All among them who know their
hearts are honest, and are broken, and their spirits contrite,
and are willing to observe their covenants by sacrifice; yea,
every sacrifice which I, the Lord, shall command, they are all
accepted of me,

g. for I, the Lord, will cause them to bring forth as a very fruitful tree which is planted in a goodly land, by a pure stream, that yieldeth much precious fruit.

3 a. Verily I say unto you, that it is my will that an house should be built unto me in the land of Zion, like unto the pattern which I have given you; yea, let it be built speedily by the tithing of my people:

b. behold, this is the tithing and the sacrifice which I, the Lord, require at their hands, that there may be an house built unto me for the salvation of Zion;

c. for a place of thanksgiving, for all Saints, and for a place of instruction for all those who are called to the work of the ministry, in all their several callings, and offices;

d. that they may be perfected in the understanding of their ministry; in theory; in principle and in doctrine; in all things pertaining to the kingdom of God on the earth, the keys of which kingdom have been conferred upon you.

4 a. And inasmuch as my people build an house unto me, in the name of the Lord, and do not suffer any unclean thing to come into it, that it be not defiled, my glory shall rest upon it;

b. yea, and my presence shall be there, for I will come into it, and all the pure in heart that shall come into it, shall see God: but if it be defiled I will not come into it, and my glory shall not be there, for I will not come into unholy temples.

5 a. And now, behold, if Zion do these things, she shall prosper and spread herself and become very glorious, very great, and very terrible;

b. and the nations of the earth shall honor her, and shall say, Surely Zion is the city of our God; and surely Zion can not fall, neither be moved out of her place, for God is there, and the hand of the Lord is there, and he hath sworn by the power of his might to be her salvation, and her high tower;

c. therefore verily thus saith the Lord, Let Zion rejoice, for this is Zion, THE PURE IN HEART; therefore let Zion rejoice, while all the wicked shall mourn;

d. for, behold, and lo, vengeance cometh speedily upon the ungodly, as the whirlwind, and who shall escape it; the

Lord's scourge shall pass over by night and by day; and the report thereof shall vex all people;

e. yet, it shall not be stayed until the Lord come; for the indignation of the Lord is kindled against their abominations, and all their wicked works;

f. nevertheless Zion shall escape if she observe to do all things whatsoever I have commanded her, but if she observe not to do whatsoever I have commanded her, I will visit her according to all her works, with sore affliction, with pestilence, with plague, with sword, with vengeance, with devouring fire;

g. nevertheless, let it be read this once in their ears, that I, the Lord, have accepted of their offering; and if she sin no more, none of these things shall come upon her, and I will bless her with blessings, and multiply a multiplicity of blessings upon her, and upon her generations, for ever and ever, saith the Lord your God. Amen.

SECTION 95

Revelation given through Joseph Smith, Jr., August 6, 1833, at Kirtland, Ohio. No word of the culmination of the Missouri troubles had yet reached the Saints in Kirtland. The contents of this revelation are particularly significant in view of this fact.

1 a. Verily I say unto you, my friends, Fear not, let your hearts be comforted, yea, rejoice evermore, and in everything give thanks, waiting patiently on the Lord;

b. for your prayers have entered into the ears of the Lord of Sabaoth, and are recorded with this seal and testament:

c. the Lord hath sworn and decreed that they shall be granted; therefore, he giveth this promise unto you, with an immutable covenant, that they shall be fulfilled, and all things wherewith you have been afflicted, shall work together for your good, and to my name's glory saith the Lord.

2 a. And now, verily I say unto you, concerning the laws of the land, It is my will that my people should observe to do all things whatsoever I command them, and that law of the land, which is constitutional, supporting that principle of free-

dom, in maintaining rights and privileges belongs to all mankind and is justifiable before me;

b. therefore, I, the Lord, justify you and your brethren of my church in befriending that law which is the constitutional law of the land; and as pertaining to law of man, whatsoever is more or less than these, cometh of evil.

c. I, the Lord God, make you free; therefore, ye are free indeed: and the law also maketh you free; nevertheless when the wicked rule the people mourn;

d. wherefore honest men and wise men should be sought for, diligently, and good men and wise men, ye should observe to uphold; otherwise whatsoever is less than these, cometh of evil.

3 a. And I give unto you a commandment, that ye shall forsake all evil and cleave unto all good, that ye shall live by every word which proceedeth forth out of the mouth of God; for he will give unto the faithful, line upon line, precept upon precept;

b. and I will try you, and prove you herewith; and whoso layeth down his life in my cause, for my name's sake, shall find it again; even life eternal;

c. therefore, be not afraid of your enemies; for I have decreed in my heart, saith the Lord, that I will prove you in all things, whether you will abide in my covenant, even unto death, that you may be found worthy;

d. for if ye will not abide in my covenant, ye are not worthy of me; therefore, renounce war and proclaim peace, and seek diligently to turn the hearts of the children to their fathers, and the hearts of the fathers to the children.

e. And again, the hearts of the Jews unto the prophets; and the prophets unto the Jews, lest I come and smite the whole earth with a curse, and all flesh be consumed before me.

f. Let not your hearts be troubled, for in my Father's house are many mansions, and I have prepared a place for you, and where my Father and I am, there ye shall be also.

4 a. Behold, I, the Lord, am not well pleased with many who are in the church at Kirtland, for they do not forsake their sins, and their wicked ways, the pride of their hearts, and their covetousness, and all their detestable things, and observe the words of wisdom and eternal life which I have given unto them.

b. Verily I say unto you, that I, the Lord, will chasten them and will do whatsoever I list, if they do not repent and observe all things whatsoever I have said unto them.

c. And again, I say unto you, If ye observe to do whatsoever I command you, I, the Lord, will turn away all wrath and indignation from you, and the gates of hell shall not prevail against you.

5 a. Now, I speak unto you, concerning your families; if men will smite you, or your families, once, and ye bear it patiently and revile not against them, neither seek revenge, ye shall be rewarded; but if ye bear it not patiently, it shall be accounted unto you as being meted out a just measure unto you.

b. And again, if your enemy shall smite you the second time, and you revile not against your enemy, and bear it patiently, your reward shall be an hundredfold.

c. And again, if he shall smite you the third time, and ye bear it patiently, your reward shall be doubled unto you fourfold; and these three testimonies shall stand against your enemy, if he repent not, and shall not be blotted out.

d. And now, verily I say unto you, If that enemy shall escape my vengeance that he be not brought into judgment before me, then ye shall see to it, that ye warn him in my name that he come no more upon you, neither upon your family, even your children's children unto the third and fourth generation;

e. and then if he shall come upon you, or your children, or your children's children unto the third and fourth generation, I have delivered thine enemy into thine hands, and then if thou wilt spare him thou shalt be rewarded for thy righteousness; and also thy children and thy children's children unto the third and fourth generation;

f. nevertheless thine enemy is in thine hands, and if thou reward him according to his works, thou art justified, if he has sought thy life, and thy life is endangered by him; thine enemy is in thine hands, and thou art justified.

6 a. Behold, this is the law I gave unto my servant, Nephi; and thy father Joseph, and Jacob, and Isaac, and Abraham, and all mine ancient prophets and apostles.

b. And again, this is the law that I gave unto mine ancients, that they should not go out unto battle against any nation, kindred, tongue, or people, save I, the Lord, commanded them.

c. And if any nation, tongue, or people should proclaim war against them, they should first lift a standard of peace unto that people, nation, or tongue, and if that people did not accept the offering of peace, neither the second nor the third time, they should bring these testimonies before the Lord;

d. then, I, the Lord, would give unto them a commandment, and justify them in going out to battle against that nation, tongue, or people,

e. and I, the Lord, would fight their battles, and their children's battles and their children's children until they had avenged themselves on all their enemies, to the third and fourth generation;

f. behold, this is an ensample unto all people, saith the Lord, your God, for justification before me.

7 a. And again, verily I say unto you, If, after thine enemy has come upon thee the first time, he repent and come unto thee praying thy forgiveness thou shalt forgive him, and shall hold it no more as a testimony against thine enemy,

b. and so on unto the second and the third time, and as oft as thine enemy repenteth of the trespass wherewith he has trespassed against thee, thou shalt forgive him, until seventy times seven;

c. and if he transgress against thee and repent not the first time, nevertheless thou shalt forgive him; and if he trespass against thee the second time, and repent not, nevertheless thou shalt forgive him; and if he trespass against thee the third time and repent not, thou shalt also forgive him;

d. but if he trespass against thee the fourth time, thou shalt not forgive him but shall bring these testimonies before the Lord, and they shall not be blotted out until he repent and reward thee fourfold in all things wherewith he has trespassed against you;

e. and if he do this thou shalt forgive him with all thine heart, and if he do not this, I, the Lord, will avenge thee of thine enemy an hundredfold; and upon his children, and upon his children's children, of all them that hate me, unto the third and fourth generation;

f. but if the children shall repent, or the children's children and turn unto the Lord their God with all their hearts, and with all their might, mind, and strength, and restore fourfold for all their trespasses, wherewith they have trespassed, or wherewith their fathers have trespassed or their father's fathers,

g. then thine indignation shall be turned away and vengeance shall no more come upon them, saith the Lord your God, and their trespasses shall never be brought any more as a testimony before the Lord against them. Amen.

SECTION 96

Revelation given through Joseph Smith, Jr., August 1833, at Kirtland, Ohio. The revelation was addressed to Elder John Murdock. He was the widower whose twin children had been adopted by Joseph and Emma Smith.

1 a. Behold, thus saith the Lord unto my servant John Murdock, Thou art called to go into the eastern countries from house to house, from village to village, and from city to city, to proclaim mine everlasting gospel unto the inhabitants thereof, in the midst of persecution and wickedness;

b. and whoso receiveth you receiveth me, and you shall have power to declare my word in the demonstration of my Holy Spirit;

c. and whoso receiveth you as a little child, receiveth my kingdom, and blessed are they, for they shall obtain mercy; and whoso rejecteth you shall be rejected of my Father and his house: and you shall cleanse your feet in the secret places by the way for a testimony against them.

2 a. And, behold, and lo, I come quickly to judgment, to convince all of their ungodly deeds which they have committed against me, as it is written of me in the volume of the book.

b. And now, verily I say unto thee, that it is not expedient that thou shouldst go until thy children are provided for, and kindly sent up unto the bishop in Zion,

c. and after a few years, if thou desirest of me thou mayest go up also unto the goodly land, to possess thine inheritance; otherwise thou shalt continue proclaiming my gospel until thou be taken. Amen.

SECTION 97

Revelation given through Joseph Smith, Jr., at Perrys-burg, New York, October 12, 1833. Joseph Smith and Sid-ney Rigdon had stopped here at the home of Freeman Nick-erson. They were on a mission to Canada and the East.

1 a. Verily, thus saith the Lord unto you my friends, Sid-ney, and Joseph, your families are well; they are in mine hands, and I will do with them as seemeth me good; for in me there is all power; therefore, follow me, and listen to the counsel which I shall give unto you.

b. Behold, and lo, I have much people in this place, in the regions round about, and an effectual door shall be opened in the regions round about in this eastern land;

c. therefore, I, the Lord, have suffered you to come unto this place; for thus it was expedient in me for the salvation of souls;

d. therefore, verily I say unto you, Lift up your voices unto this people; speak the thoughts that I shall put into your hearts, and ye shall not be confounded before men; for it shall be given you in the very hour, yea, in the very moment, what ye shall say.

2 a. But a commandment I give unto you, that ye shall declare whatsoever things ye declare in my name, in solem-nity of heart, in the spirit of meekness, in all things.

b. And I give unto you this promise, that inasmuch as ye do this, the Holy Ghost shall be shed forth in bearing record unto all things whatsoever ye shall say.

3 a. And it is expedient in me that you, my servant Sid-ney, should be a spokesman unto this people; yea, verily, I will ordain you unto this calling, even to be a spokesman unto my servant Joseph;

b. and I will give unto him power to be mighty in testi-mony; and I will give unto thee power to be mighty in ex-pounding all Scriptures, that thou mayest be a spokesman unto him, and he shall be a revelator unto thee, that thou mayest know the certainty of all things pertaining to the things of my kingdom on the earth.

c. Therefore, continue your journey and let your hearts re-joice; for, behold, and lo, I am with you even unto the end.

4 a. And now I give unto you a word concerning Zion: Zion shall be redeemed, although she is chastened for a little season.

b. Thy brethren, my servants, Orson Hyde and John Gould, are in my hands, and inasmuch as they keep my commandments they shall be saved.

c. Therefore, let your hearts be comforted, for all things shall work together for good to them that walk uprightly, and to the sanctification of the church;

d. for I will raise up unto myself a pure people, that will serve me in righteousness; and all that call on the name of the Lord and keep his commandments, shall be saved. Even so. Amen.

SECTION 98

Revelation given through Joseph Smith, Jr., December 16, 1833, at Kirtland, Ohio. The revelation is addressed to the Saints in Ohio and is concerned with the "brethren who had been afflicted and persecuted and cast from their land of inheritance."

1 a. Verily, I say unto you, concerning your brethren who have been afflicted, and persecuted, and cast out from the land of their inheritance, I, the Lord, have suffered the affliction to come upon them, wherewith they have been afflicted in consequence of their transgressions;

b. yet, I will own them, and they shall be mine in that day when I shall come to make up my jewels.

2 Therefore, they must needs be chastened, and tried, even as Abraham, who was commanded to offer up his only son; for all those who will not endure chastening, but deny me, can not be sanctified.

3 a. Behold, I say unto you, there were jarrings, and contentions, and envyings, and strifes, and lustful and covetous desires among them; therefore by these things they polluted their inheritances.

b. They were slow to hearken unto the voice of the Lord their God; therefore, the Lord their God is slow to hearken unto their prayers, to answer them in the day of their trouble.

c. In the day of their peace they esteemed lightly my counsel; but in the day of their trouble, of necessity they feel after me.

4 a. Verily, I say unto you, Notwithstanding their sins, my bowels are filled with compassion toward them; I will not utterly cast them off; and in the day of wrath I will remember mercy.

b. I have sworn, and the decree hath gone forth by a former commandment which I have given unto you, that I would let fall the sword of mine indignation in the behalf of my people; and even as I have said, it shall come to pass.

c. Mine indignation is soon to be poured out without measure upon all nations, and this will I do when the cup of their iniquity is full.

d. And in that day, all who are found upon the watch-tower, or in other words, all mine Israel shall be saved.

e. And they that have been scattered shall be gathered; and all they who have mourned shall be comforted; and all they who have given their lives for my name shall be crowned.

f. Therefore, let your hearts be comforted concerning Zion, for all flesh is in mine hands: be still, and know that I am God.

g. Zion shall not be moved out of her place, notwithstanding her children are scattered, they that remain and are pure in heart shall return and come to their inheritances; they and their children, with songs of everlasting joy; to build up the waste places of Zion. And all these things, that the prophets might be fulfilled.

h. And, behold, there is none other place appointed than that which I have appointed, neither shall there be any other place appointed than that which I have appointed for the work of the gathering of my Saints, until the day cometh when there is found no more room for them;

i. and then I have other places which I will appoint unto them, and they shall be called stakes, for the curtains, or the strength of Zion.

5 a. Behold, it is my will, that all they who call on my name, and worship me according to mine everlasting gospel, should gather together and stand in holy places, and prepare for the revelation which is to come when the veil of the covering of my temple, in my tabernacle, which hideth the

earth, shall be taken off, and all flesh shall see me together.

b. And every corruptible thing, both of man, or of the beasts of the field, or of the fowls of heaven, or of the fish of the sea, that dwell upon all the face of the earth, shall be consumed; and also, that of element shall melt with fervent heat; and all things shall become new, that my knowledge and glory may dwell upon all the earth.

c. And in that day the enmity of man, and the enmity of beasts; yea, the enmity of all flesh shall cease from before my face.

d. And in that day whatsoever any man shall ask it shall be given unto him.

e. And in that day Satan shall not have power to tempt any man. And there shall be no sorrow because there is no death.

f. In that day an infant shall not die until he is old, and his life shall be as the age of a tree, and when he dies he shall not sleep (that is to say in the earth), but shall be changed in the twinkling of an eye, and shall be caught up, and his rest shall be glorious.

g. Yea, verily I say unto you, In that day when the Lord shall come he shall reveal all things; things which have passed, and hidden things which no man knew; things of the earth by which it was made, and the purpose and the end thereof; things most precious; things that are above, and things that are beneath; things that are in the earth, and upon the earth, and in heaven.

h. And all they who suffer persecution for my name, and endure in faith, though they are called to lay down their lives for my sake, yet shall they partake of all this glory.

i. Wherefore, fear not even unto death; for in this world your joy is not full, but in me your joy is full.

j. Therefore, care not for the body, neither the life of the body; but care for the soul, and for the life of the soul, and seek the face of the Lord always, that in patience ye may possess your souls, and ye shall have eternal life.

k. When men are called unto mine everlasting gospel, and covenant with an everlasting covenant, they are accounted as the salt of the earth, and the savor of men. They are called to be the savor of men.

l. Therefore, if that salt of the earth lose its savor, behold, it is thenceforth good for nothing, only to be cast out and trodden under the feet of men.

m. Behold, here is wisdom concerning the children of Zion; even many, but not all; they were found transgressors, therefore, they must needs be chastened. He that exalteth himself shall be abased, and he that abaseth himself shall be exalted.

6 a. And now, I will show unto you a parable that you may know my will concerning the redemption of Zion.

b. A certain nobleman had a spot of land, very choice; and he said unto his servants, Go ye into my vineyard, even upon this very choice piece of land, and plant twelve olive trees; and set watchmen round about them and build a tower, that one may overlook the land round about, to be a watchman upon the tower;

c. that mine olive trees may not be broken down, when the enemy shall come to spoil and take unto themselves the fruit of my vineyard.

d. Now the servants of the nobleman went and did as their lord commanded them; and planted the olive trees, and built a hedge round about, and set watchmen, and began to build a tower.

e. And while they were yet laying the foundation thereof, they began to say among themselves, And what need hath my lord of this tower? and consulted for a long time, saying among themselves, What need hath my lord of this tower, seeing this is a time of peace?

f. Might not this money be given to the exchangers? for there is no need of these things!

g. And while they were at variance one with another they became very slothful, and they hearkened not unto the commandments of their lord,

h. and the enemy came by night and broke down the hedge, and the servants of the nobleman arose, and were affrighted, and fled; and the enemy destroyed their works and broke down the olive trees.

7 a. Now, behold, the nobleman, the lord of the vineyard, called upon his servants, and said unto them, Why! what is the cause of this great evil? ought ye not to have done even as I commanded you? and after ye had planted the vineyard,

and built the hedge round about, and set watchmen upon the walls thereof,

b. built the tower also, and set a watchman upon the tower, and watched for my vineyard, and not have fallen asleep, lest the enemy should come upon you?

c. and, behold, the watchman upon the tower would have seen the enemy while he was yet afar off, and then you could have made ready and kept the enemy from breaking down the hedge thereof, and saved my vineyard from the hands of the destroyer.

d. And the lord of the vineyard said unto one of his servants, Go, and gather together the residue of my servants; and take all the strength of mine house, which are my warriors, my young men, and they that are of middle age also, among all my servants, who are the strength of mine house, save those only whom I have appointed to tarry;

e. and go ye straightway unto the land of my vineyard, and redeem my vineyard, for it is mine, I have bought it with money.

f. Therefore, get ye straightway unto my land; break down the walls of mine enemies, throw down their tower, and scatter their watchmen;

g. and inasmuch as they gather together against you, avenge me of mine enemies; that by and by I may come with the residue of mine house and possess the land.

8 a. And the servant said unto his lord, When shall these things be?

b. And he said unto his servant, When I will: go ye straightway, and do all things whatsoever I have commanded you; and this shall be my seal and blessing upon you; a faithful and wise steward in the midst of mine house; a ruler in my kingdom.

c. And his servant went straightway, and did all things whatsoever his lord commanded him, and after many days all things were fulfilled.

9 a. Again, verily I say unto you, I will show unto you wisdom in me concerning all the churches, inasmuch as they are willing to be guided in a right and proper way for their salvation, that the work of the gathering together of my Saints may continue, that I may build them up unto my name

upon holy places; for the time of harvest is come, and my word must needs be fulfilled.

b. Therefore, I must gather together my people according to the parable of the wheat and the tares, that the wheat may be secured in the garners to possess eternal life, and be crowned with celestial glory when I shall come in the kingdom of my Father, to reward every man according as his work shall be;

c. while the tares shall be bound in bundles, and their bands made strong, that they may be burned with unquenchable fire.

d. Therefore, a commandment I give unto all the churches, that they shall continue to gather together unto the places which I have appointed;

e. nevertheless, as I have said unto you in a former commandment, let not your gathering be in haste, nor by flight; but let all things be prepared before you;

f. and in order that all things be prepared before you, observe the commandments which I have given concerning these things, which saith, or teacheth, to purchase all the lands by money, which can be purchased for money, in the region round about the land which I have appointed to be the land of Zion, for the beginning of the gathering of my Saints;

g. all the land which can be purchased in Jackson County, and the counties round about, and leave the residue in mine hand.

10 a. Now, verily I say unto you, Let all the churches gather together all their moneys; let these things be done in their time, be not in haste; and observe to have all things prepared before you.

b. And let honorable men be appointed, even wise men, and send them to purchase these lands; and every church in the eastern countries when they are built up, if they will hearken unto this counsel, they may buy lands and gather together upon them, and in this way they may establish Zion.

c. There is even now already in store a sufficient, yea, even abundance to redeem Zion, and establish her waste places, no more to be thrown down, were the churches, who call themselves after my name, willing to hearken to my voice.

d. And again I say unto you, Those who have been scattered by their enemies, it is my will that they should continue to importune for redress, and redemption, by the hands of those who are placed as rulers, and are in authority over you,

e. according to the laws and constitution of the people which I have suffered to be established, and should be maintained for the rights and protection of all flesh, according to just and holy principles, that every man may act in doctrine, and principle pertaining to futurity,

f. according to the moral agency which I have given unto them, that every man may be accountable for his own sins in the day of judgment.

g. Therefore, it is not right that any man should be in bondage one to another.

h. And for this purpose have I established the constitution of this land, by the hands of wise men whom I raised up unto this very purpose, and redeemed the land by the shedding of blood.

11 a. Now, unto what shall I liken the children of Zion?

b. I will liken them unto the parable of the woman and the unjust judge (for men ought always to pray and not faint), which saith, There was in a city a judge which feared not God, neither regarded man.

c. And there was a widow in that city, and she came unto him, saying, Avenge me of mine adversary.

d. And he would not for a while, but afterward he said within himself, Though I fear not God, nor regard man, yet because this widow troubleth me I will avenge her, lest by her continual coming, she weary me. Thus will I liken the children of Zion.

12 a. Let them importune at the feet of the judge; and if he heed them not, let them importune at the feet of the governor; and if the governor heed them not, let them importune at the feet of the president;

b. and if the president heed them not, then will the Lord arise and come forth out of his hiding place, and in his fury vex the nation, and in his hot displeasure, and in his fierce anger, in his time, will cut off these wicked, unfaithful, and unjust stewards, and appoint them their portion among hypocrites and unbelievers; even in outer darkness, where there is weeping, and wailing, and gnashing of teeth.

c. Pray ye, therefore, that their ears may be opened unto your cries, that I may be merciful unto them, that these things may not come upon them.

d. What I have said unto you, must needs be, that all men may be left without excuse; that wise men and rulers may hear and know that which they have never considered;

e. that I may proceed to bring to pass my act, my strange act, and perform my work, my strange work. That men may discern between the righteous and the wicked, saith your God.

13 a. And again, I say unto you, It is contrary to my commandment, and my will, that my servant Sidney Gilbert should sell my storehouse, which I have appointed unto my people, into the hands of mine enemies.

b. Let not that which I have appointed, be polluted by mine enemies, by the consent of those who call themselves after my name; for this is a very sore and grievous sin against me, and against my people, in consequence of those things which I have decreed, and are soon to befall the nations.

c. Therefore, it is my will that my people should claim, and hold claim, upon that which I have appointed unto them, though they should not be permitted to dwell thereon;

d. nevertheless, I do not say they shall not dwell thereon; for inasmuch as they bring forth fruit and works meet for my kingdom, they shall dwell thereon;

e. they shall build, and another shall not inherit it; they shall plant vineyards, and they shall eat the fruit thereof. Even so. Amen.

SECTION 99

This is not a revelation, although it states that the High Council was "appointed by revelation"; it is the minutes of the organization of the Council at Kirtland, February 17, 1834. The day after the Council was organized, President Smith reviewed and corrected the minutes of the initial meeting. On February 19 the Council reassembled, the minutes were read three times, and were then unanimously adopted as a form and constitution of the High Council of the church.

1 a. This day a general council of twenty-four high priests assembled at the house of Joseph Smith, Jr., by revelation, and proceeded to organize the high council of the church of Christ, which was to consist of twelve high priests, and one or three presidents, as the case might require.

b. This high council was appointed by revelation for the purpose of settling important difficulties, which might arise in the church, which could not be settled by the church, or the bishop's council, to the satisfaction of the parties.

2 a. Joseph Smith, Jr., Sidney Rigdon, and Frederick G. Williams, were acknowledged presidents by the voice of the council; and Joseph Smith, Sr., John Smith, Joseph Coe, John Johnson, Martin Harris, John S. Carter, Jared Carter, Oliver Cowdery, Samuel H. Smith, Orson Hyde, Sylvester Smith, and Luke Johnson, high priests, were chosen to be a standing council for the church, by the unanimous voice of the council.

b. The above-named councilors were then asked whether they accepted their appointments, and whether they would act in that office according to the law of heaven;

c. to which they all answered, that they accepted their appointments, and would fill their offices according to the grace of God bestowed upon them.

3 The number composing the council, who voted in the name and for the church in appointing the above-named councilors, were forty-three, as follows: nine high priests, seventeen elders, four priests, and thirteen members.

4 a. Voted: that the high council can not have power to act without seven of the above-named councilors, or their regularly appointed successors, are present.

b. These seven shall have power to appoint other high priests, whom they may consider worthy and capable, to act in the place of absent councilors.

5 a. Voted: that whenever any vacancy shall occur by the death, removal from office for transgression, or removal from the bounds of this church government, of any of the above-named councilors,

b. it shall be filled by the nomination of the president or presidents, and sanctioned by the voice of a general council of high priests, convened for that purpose, to act in the name of the church.

6 a. The president of the church, who is also the president of the council, is appointed by revelation, and acknowledged, in his administration, by the voice of the church;

b. and it is according to the dignity of his office, that he should preside over the high council of the church; and it is his privilege to be assisted by two other presidents, appointed after the same manner that he himself was appointed;

c. and in case of the absence of one or both of those who are appointed to assist him, he has power to preside over the council without an assistant; and in case that he himself is absent, the other presidents have power to preside in his stead, both or either of them.

7 Whenever a high council of the church of Christ is regularly organized, according to the foregoing pattern, it shall be the duty of the twelve councilors to cast lots by numbers, and thereby ascertain who, of the twelve, shall speak first, commencing with number 1; and so in succession to number 12.

8 a. Whenever this council convenes to act upon any case, the twelve councilors shall consider whether it is a difficult one or not; if it is not, two only of the councilors shall speak upon it, according to the form above written.

b. But if it is thought to be difficult, four shall be appointed; and if more difficult, six; but in no case shall more than six be appointed to speak.

c. The accused, in all cases, has a right to one half of the council, to prevent insult or injustice; and the councilors appointed to speak before the council, are to present the case, after the evidence is examined, in its true light, before the council; and every man is to speak according to equity and justice.

d. Those councilors who draw even numbers, that is, 2, 4, 6, 8, 10, and 12, are the individuals who are to stand up in the behalf of the accused, and prevent insult or injustice.

9 a. In all cases the accuser and the accused shall have a privilege of speaking for themselves, before the council, after the evidences are heard, and the councilors who are appointed to speak on the case, have finished their remarks.

b. After the evidences are heard, the councilors, accuser, and accused have spoken, the president shall give a decision according to the understanding which he shall have of the case, and call upon the twelve councilors to sanction the same by their vote.

c. But should the remaining councilors, who have not spoken, or any one of them, after hearing the evidences and pleadings impartially, discover an error in the decision of the president, they can manifest it, and the case shall have a rehearing;

d. and if, after a careful rehearing, any additional light is shown upon the case, the decision shall be altered accordingly; but in case no additional light is given, the first decision shall stand, the majority of the council having power to determine the same.

10 In cases of difficulty respecting doctrine, or principle (if there is not a sufficiency written to make the case clear to the minds of the council), the president may inquire and obtain the mind of the Lord by revelation.

11 a. The high priests, when abroad, have power to call and organize a council after the manner of the foregoing, to settle difficulties when the parties, or either of them, shall request it;

b. and the said council of high priests shall have power to appoint one of their own number, to preside over such council for the time being.

c. It shall be the duty of said council to transmit, immediately, a copy of their proceedings, with a full statement of the testimony accompanying their decision, to the high council of the seat of the first presidency of the church.

d. Should the parties, or either of them, be dissatisfied with the decision of said council, they may appeal to the high council of the seat of the first presidency of the church, and have a rehearing, which case shall there be conducted, according to the former pattern written, as though no such decision had been made.

12 a. This council of high priests abroad, is only to be called on the most difficult cases of church matters; and no common or ordinary case is to be sufficient to call such council.

b. The traveling or located high priests abroad, have power to say whether it is necessary to call such a council or not.

13 a. There is a distinction between the high council of traveling high priests abroad, and the traveling high council composed of the twelve apostles, in their decisions: from the decision of the former there can be an appeal, but from the decision of the latter there can not.

b. The latter can only be called in question by the general authorities of the church in case of transgression.

14 Resolved, that the president, or presidents of the seat of the first presidency of the church, shall have power to determine whether any such case, as may be appealed, is justly entitled to a rehearing, after examining the appeal and the evidences and statements accompanying it.

15 a. The twelve councilors then proceeded to cast lots, or ballot, to ascertain who should speak first, and the following was the result, namely:

b.
OLIVER COWDERY,	No. 1	JOHN JOHNSON,	No. 7
JOSEPH COE,	" 2	ORSON HYDE,	" 8
SAMUEL H. SMITH,	" 3	JARED CARTER,	" 9
LUKE JOHNSON,	" 4	JOSEPH SMITH, SR.,	" 10
JOHN S. CARTER,	" 5	JOHN SMITH,	" 11
SYLVESTER SMITH,	" 6	MARTIN HARRIS,	" 12

c. After prayer the conference adjourned.

OLIVER COWDERY,
ORSON HYDE,
Clerks

SECTION 100

A delegation arrived in Kirtland, February 22, 1834, with information for the First Presidency regarding the condition of the Saints in Missouri. The following revelation was given through Joseph Smith two days later. For "Baurak Ale" read "Joseph Smith." This revelation was first published without conference approval in 1844 and its retention was specifically approved by the 1970 World Conference.

1 a. Verily I say unto you, my friends, Behold, I will give unto you a revelation and commandment, that you may know how to act in the discharge of your duties concerning the salvation and redemption of your brethren, who have been scattered on the land of Zion, being driven and smitten by the hands of mine enemies; on whom I will pour out my wrath without measure in mine own time;

b. for I have suffered them thus far, that they might fill up the measure of their iniquities, that their cup might be full, and that those who call themselves after my name might be chastened for a little season, with a sore and grievous chastisement, because they did not hearken altogether unto the precepts and commandments which I gave unto them.

2 a. But verily I say unto you, that I have decreed a decree which my people shall realize, inasmuch as they hearken from this very hour, unto the counsel which I, the Lord, their God, shall give unto them.

b. Behold, they shall, for I have decreed it, begin to prevail against mine enemies from this very hour, and by hearkening to observe all the words which I, the Lord their God, shall speak unto them, they shall never cease to prevail until the kingdoms of the world are subdued under my feet; and the earth is given unto the saints, to possess it for ever and ever.

c. But inasmuch as they keep not my commandments, and hearken not to observe all my words, the kingdoms of the world shall prevail against them, for they were set to be a light unto the world, and to be the saviors of men;

d. and inasmuch as they are not the saviors of men, they are as salt that has lost its savor, and is thenceforth good for nothing but to be cast out and trodden under foot of men.

3 a. But verily I say unto you, I have decreed that your brethren, which have been scattered, shall return to the land of their inheritances and build up the waste places of Zion; for after much tribulation, as I have said unto you in a former commandment, cometh the blessing.

b. Behold, this is the blessing which I have promised after your tribulations, and the tribulations of your brethren; your redemption, and the redemption of your brethren; even their restoration to the land of Zion, to be established, no more to be thrown down;

c. nevertheless, if they pollute their inheritances, they shall be thrown down; for I will not spare them if they pollute their inheritances.

d. Behold, I say unto you, The redemption of Zion must needs come by power; therefore I will raise up unto my people a man, who shall lead them like as Moses led the children of Israel, for ye are the children of Israel, and of the seed of Abraham;

e. and ye must needs be led out of bondage by power, and with a stretched out arm; and as your fathers were led at the first, even so shall the redemption of Zion be.

f. Therefore, let not your hearts faint, for I say not unto you as I said unto your fathers, Mine angel shall go up before you, but not my presence; but I say unto you, Mine angels shall go before you, and also my presence, and in time ye shall possess the goodly land.

4 Verily, verily I say unto you, that my servant Baurak Ale is the man to whom I likened the servant to whom the Lord of the vineyard spoke in the parable which I have given unto you.

5 a. Therefore, let my servant Baurak Ale say unto the strength of my house, my young men and the middle-aged, Gather yourselves together unto the land of Zion, upon the land which I have bought with moneys that have been consecrated unto me;

b. and let all the churches send up wise men, with their moneys, and purchase lands even as I have commanded them; and inasmuch as mine enemies come against you to drive you from my goodly land, which I have consecrated to be the land of Zion;

c. even from your own lands after these testimonies, which

ye have brought before me, against them, ye shall curse them; and whomsoever ye curse, I will curse; and ye shall avenge me of mine enemies; and my presence shall be with you, even in avenging me of mine enemies, unto the third and fourth generation of them that hate me.

6 a. Let no man be afraid to lay down his life for my sake; for whoso layeth down his life for my sake, shall find it again. And whoso is not willing to lay down his life for my sake, is not my disciple.

b. It is my will that my servant Sidney Rigdon shall lift up his voice in the congregations, in the eastern countries, in preparing the churches to keep the commandments which I have given unto them, concerning the restoration and redemption of Zion.

c. It is my will that my servant Parley P. Pratt, and my servant Lyman Wight should not return to the land of their brethren, until they have obtained companies to go up unto the land of Zion, by tens, or by twenties, or by fifties, or by an hundred, until they have obtained to the number of five hundred of the strength of my house.

d. Behold, this is my will; ask and you shall receive, but men do not always do my will; therefore, if you can not obtain five hundred, seek diligently that peradventure you may obtain three hundred;

e. and if ye can not obtain three hundred, seek diligently that peradventure ye may obtain one hundred.

f. But verily I say unto you, A commandment I give unto you, that ye shall not go up unto the land of Zion, until you have obtained one hundred of the strength of my house, to go up with you unto the land of Zion.

g. Therefore, as I said unto you, Ask and ye shall receive; pray earnestly that peradventure my servant Baurak Ale may go with you and preside in the midst of my people, and organize my kingdom upon the consecrated land; and establish the children of Zion, upon the laws and commandments which have been, and which shall be given, unto you.

7 a. All victory and glory is brought to pass unto you through your diligence, faithfulness, and prayers of faith.

b. Let my servant Parley P. Pratt, journey with my servant Joseph Smith, Jr. Let my servant Lyman Wight, journey with my servant Sidney Rigdon. Let my servant Hyrum Smith, journey with my servant Frederick G. Williams.

c. Let my servant Orson Hyde, journey with my servant Orson Pratt; whithersoever my servant Joseph Smith, Jr., shall counsel them in obtaining the fulfillment of these commandments, which I have given unto you, and leave the residue in my hands. Even so. Amen.

SECTION 101

Revelation given through Joseph Smith, Jr., April 23, 1834, at Kirtland, Ohio. A "United Order of Enoch" had been established to manage the temporal affairs of the church in Kirtland and in Zion. The Order was now in financial difficulties, largely because of losses sustained through mob action. In accordance with this revelation, the Order was now dissolved, its properties being divided among the members of the Order in such fashion as to constitute their individual stewardships.

For an explanation of the unusual names used in this revelation, consult the introduction to Doctrine and Covenants 77. The probable significance of these names is as follows:

The "Order" . . . The United Order of Enoch; "Pelagoram" . . . Sidney Rigdon; "Tahhanes" . . . Tannery; "Mahemson" . . . Martin Harris; "Zombre" . . . John Johnson; "Gazelam" . . . Joseph Smith; "Shederlaomach" . . . Frederick G. Williams; "Olihah" . . . Oliver Cowdery; "Laneshine-house" . . . Printing Office; "Ahashdah" . . . Newel K. Whitney; "Ozondah" . . . Store; "Shinehah" . . . Kirtland; "Shinelah" . . . Print; "Shinelane" . . . Printing; "Cainhannoch" . . . New York; "Shule" . . . Ashery.

1 a. Verily I say unto you, my friends, I give unto you counsel and a commandment, concerning all the properties which belong to the order, which I commanded to be organized and established, to be an united order, and an everlasting order for the benefit of my church, and for the salvation of men until I come,

b. with promise immutable and unchangeable, that inasmuch as those whom I commanded were faithful, they should be blessed with a multiplicity of blessings; but inasmuch as they were not faithful, they were nigh unto cursing.

c. Therefore, inasmuch as some of my servants have not kept the commandment, but have broken the covenant, by covetousness and with feigned words, I have cursed them with a very sore and grievous curse;

d. for I, the Lord, have decreed in my heart, that inasmuch as any man, belonging to the order, shall be found a transgressor; or, in other words, shall break the covenant with which ye are bound, he shall be cursed in his life, and shall be trodden down by whom I will, for I, the Lord, am not to be mocked in these things;

e. and all this that the innocent among you, may not be condemned with the unjust; and that the guilty among you may not escape, because I, the Lord, have promised unto you a crown of glory at my right hand.

f. Therefore, inasmuch as you are found transgressors, ye can not escape my wrath in your lives; inasmuch as ye are cut off by transgression, ye can not escape the buffetings of Satan until the day of redemption.

2 a. And now I give unto you power from this very hour, that if any man among you, of the order, is found a transgressor, and repenteth not of the evil, that ye shall deliver him over unto the buffetings of Satan; and he shall not have power to bring evil upon you.

b. It is wisdom in me; therefore, a commandment I give unto you, that ye shall organize yourselves, and appoint every man his stewardship, that every man may give an account unto me of the stewardship which is appointed unto him;

c. for it is expedient that I, the Lord, should make every man accountable, as stewards over earthly blessings, which I have made and prepared for my creatures.

d. I, the Lord, stretched out the heavens, and builded the earth as a very handy work; and all things therein are mine; and it is my purpose to provide for my saints, for all things are mine; but it must needs be done in mine own way;

e. and, behold, this is the way, that I, the Lord, have decreed to provide for my saints:

f. that the poor shall be exalted, in that the rich are made low; for the earth is full, and there is enough and to spare;

yea, I prepared all things, and have given unto the children of men to be agents unto themselves.

g. Therefore, if any man shall take of the abundance which I have made, and impart not his portion, according to the law of my gospel, unto the poor, and the needy, he shall, with the wicked, lift up his eyes in hell, being in torment.

3 a. And now, verily I say unto you, concerning the properties of the order:

b. Let my servant Pelagoram have appointed unto him the place where he now resides, and the lot of Tahhanes, for his stewardship, for his support while he is laboring in my vineyard, even as I will when I shall command him;

c. and let all things be done according to counsel of the order, and united consent, or voice of the order, which dwell in the land of Shinehah.

d. And this stewardship and blessing, I, the Lord, confer upon my servant Pelagoram, for a blessing upon him, and his seed after him, and I will multiply blessings upon him, inasmuch as he shall be humble before me.

4 a. And again, let my servant Mahemson have appointed unto him, for his stewardship, the lot of land which my servant Zombre obtained in exchange for his former inheritance, for him and his seed after him; and inasmuch as he is faithful, I will multiply blessings upon him and his seed after him.

b. And let my servant Mahemson devote his moneys for the proclaiming of my words, according as my servant Gazelam shall direct.

5 a. And again, let my servant Shederlaomach have the place upon which he now dwells.

b. And let my servant Olihah have the lot which is set off joining the house which is to be for the Lane-shine-house, which is lot number one; and also the lot upon which his father resides.

c. And let my servant Shederlaomach and Olihah have the Lane-shine-house and all things that pertain unto it; and this shall be their stewardship which shall be appointed unto them; and inasmuch as they are faithful, behold, I will bless, and multiply blessings upon them;

d. and this is the beginning of the stewardship which I have appointed them, for them and their seed after them;

and inasmuch as they are faithful, I will multiply blessings upon them and their seed after them; even a multiplicity of blessings.

6 a. And again, let my servant Zombre have the house in which he lives, and the inheritance, all save the ground which has been reserved for the building of my houses, which pertains to that inheritance; and those lots which have been named for my servant Olihah.

b. And inasmuch as he is faithful, I will multiply blessings upon him.

c. And it is my will that he should sell the lots that are laid off for the building up of the city of my saints, inasmuch as it shall be made known to him by the voice of the Spirit, and according to the counsel of the order; and by the voice of the order.

d. And this is the beginning of the stewardship which I have appointed unto him, for a blessing unto him, and his seed after him; and inasmuch as he is faithful, I will multiply a multiplicity of blessings upon him.

7 a. And again, let my servant Ahashdah have appointed unto him, the houses and lot where he now resides, and the lot and building on which the Ozondah stands; and also the lot which is on the corner south of the Ozondah; and also the lot on which the Shule is situated;

b. and all this I have appointed unto my servant Ahashdah, for his stewardship, for a blessing upon him and his seed after him, for the benefit of the Ozondah of my order, which I have established for my stake in the land of Shinehah;

c. yea, verily this is the stewardship which I have appointed unto my servant Ahashdah; even this whole Ozondah establishment, him and his agent, and his seed after him;

d. and inasmuch as he is faithful in keeping my commandments, which I have given unto him, I will multiply blessings upon him, and his seed after him, even a multiplicity of blessings.

8 a. And again, let my servant Gazelam have appointed unto him, the lot which is laid off for the building of my house, which is forty rods long, and twelve wide, and also the inheritance upon which his father now resides;

b. and this is the beginning of the stewardship which I have appointed unto him, for a blessing upon him, and upon his father; for, behold, I have reserved an inheritance for his father, for his support:

c. therefore he shall be reckoned in the house of my servant Gazelam; and I will multiply blessings upon the house of my servant Gazelam, inasmuch as he is faithful, even a multiplicity of blessings.

9 a. And now a commandment I give unto you concerning Zion, that you shall no longer be bound as an united order to your brethren of Zion, only on this wise: after you are organized, you shall be called the united order of the stake of Zion, the city of Shinehah.

b. And your brethren, after they are organized, shall be called the united order of the city of Zion; and they shall be organized in their own names, and in their own name; and they shall do their business in their own name, and in their own names; and you shall do your business in your own name, and in your own names.

c. And this I have commanded to be done for your salvation, and also for their salvation in consequence of their being driven out, and that which is to come.

d. The covenants being broken through transgression, by covetousness and feigned words; therefore, you are dissolved as a united order with your brethren, that you are not bound only up to this hour, unto them, only on this wise, as I said, by loan, as shall be agreed by this order, in council, as your circumstances will admit, and the voice of the council direct.

10 a. And again, a commandment I give unto you concerning your stewardship which I have appointed unto you;

b. behold, all these properties are mine, or else your faith is vain, and ye are found hypocrites, and the covenants which ye have made unto me are broken; and if the properties are mine then ye are stewards, otherwise ye are no stewards.

c. But verily I say unto you, I have appointed unto you to be stewards over mine house, even stewards indeed; and for this purpose I have commanded you to organize yourselves, even to shinelah my words, the fullness of my Scriptures, the revelations which I have given unto you, and which I shall hereafter, from time to time, give unto you,

d. for the purpose of building up my church and kingdom
on the earth, and to prepare my people for the time when
I shall dwell with them, which is nigh at hand.

11 a. And ye shall prepare for yourselves a place for a
treasury, and consecrate it unto my name; and ye shall appoint one among you to keep the treasury, and he shall be
ordained unto this blessing;

b. and there shall be a seal upon the treasury, and all the
sacred things shall be delivered into the treasury, and no man
among you shall call it his own, or any part of it, for it shall
belong to you all with one accord; and I give it unto you
from this very hour;

c. and now see to it, that ye go to and make use of the
stewardship which I have appointed unto you, exclusive of
the sacred things, for the purpose of shinelane these sacred
things, as I have said;

d. and the avails of the sacred things shall be had in the
treasury, and a seal shall be upon it, and it shall not be used
or taken out of the treasury by anyone, neither shall the seal
be loosed which shall be placed upon it, only by the voice
of the order, or by commandment.

e. And thus shall ye preserve all the avails of the sacred
things in the treasury, for sacred and holy purposes; and
this shall be called the sacred treasury of the Lord; and a
seal shall be kept upon it, that it may be holy and consecrated
unto the Lord.

12 a. And again, there shall be another treasury prepared
and a treasurer appointed to keep the treasury, and a seal
shall be placed upon it;

b. and all moneys that you receive in your stewardships,
by improving upon the properties which I have appointed
unto you, in houses or in lands, or in cattle, or in all things
save it be the holy and sacred writings, which I have reserved
unto myself for holy and sacred purposes,

c. shall be cast into the treasury as fast as you receive
moneys, by hundreds or by fifties, or by twenties, or by tens,
or by fives, or in other words, if any man among you obtain
five talents let him cast them into the treasury;

d. or if he obtain ten, or twenty, or fifty, or an hundred,
let him do likewise; and let not any man among you say that
it is his own, for it shall not be called his, nor any part of it;

e. and there shall not any part of it be used, or taken out of the treasury, only by the voice and common consent of the order.

f. And this shall be the voice and common consent of the order: that any man among you, say unto the treasurer, I have need of this to help me in my stewardship;

g. if it be five talents, or if it be ten talents, or twenty, or fifty, or an hundred, the treasurer shall give unto him the sum which he requires, to help him in his stewardship, until he be found a transgressor, and it is manifest before the council of the order plainly, that he is an unfaithful and an unwise steward;

h. but so long as he is in full fellowship, and is faithful, and wise in his stewardship, this shall be his token unto the treasurer that the treasurer shall not withhold.

i. But in case of transgression the treasurer shall be subject unto the counsel and voice of the order.

j. And in case the treasurer is found an unfaithful, and an unwise steward, he shall be subject to the counsel and voice of the order, and shall be removed out of his place, and another shall be appointed in his stead.

13 a. And again, verily I say unto you, concerning your debts,

b. Behold, it is my will that you should pay all your debts; and it is my will that you should humble yourselves before me, and obtain this blessing by your diligence and humility, and the prayer of faith;

c. and inasmuch as you are diligent and humble, and exercise the prayer of faith, behold, I will soften the hearts of those to whom you are in debt, until I shall send means unto you for your deliverance.

d. Therefore write speedily unto Cainhannoch, and write according to that which shall be dictated by my Spirit, and I will soften the hearts of those to whom you are in debt, that it shall be taken away out of their minds to bring affliction upon you.

e. And inasmuch as ye are humble and faithful and call on my name, behold, I will give you the victory.

f. I give unto you a promise, that you shall be delivered this once, out of your bondage; inasmuch as you obtain a chance to loan [borrow] money by hundreds, or thousands, even until you shall loan [borrow] enough to deliver yourselves from bondage, it is your privilege, and pledge the properties which I have put into your hands, this once, by giving your names, by common consent, or otherwise, as it shall seem good unto you.

g. I give unto you this privilege, this once, and, behold, if you proceed to do the things which I have laid before you, according to my commandments, all these things are mine, and ye are my stewards, and the master will not suffer his house to be broken up. Even so. Amen.

SECTION 102

Revelation given through Joseph Smith, Jr., June 22, 1834, at Fishing River, Missouri. The company of Saints known as "Zion's Camp" left Kirtland, Ohio, for Missouri, May 8, 1834 (D. and C. 100:5-6). They reached an elevated piece of land between two branches of the Fishing River June 19 and were obliged to stay there because of a heavy rain and hailstorm. The following revelation was given through Joseph Smith on June 22, 1834. It was first published in 1844 without conference approval and its retention was specifically authorized by the 1970 World Conference.

For "Baurak Ale" read Joseph Smith. "Baneemy" evidently referred to the other leading elders of the church.

1 Verily I say unto you, who have assembled yourselves together that you may learn my will concerning the redemption of mine afflicted people:

2 a. Behold, I say unto you, Were it not for the transgressions of my people, speaking concerning the church and not individuals, they might have been redeemed even now;

b. but, behold, they have not learned to be obedient to the things which I require at their hands, but are full of all manner of evil, and do not impart of their substance, as becometh Saints, to the poor and afflicted among them, and are not united according to the union required by the law of the celestial kingdom;

c. and Zion can not be built up unless it is by the principles of the law of the celestial kingdom, otherwise I can not receive her unto myself;

d. and my people must needs be chastened until they learn obedience, if it must needs be, by the things which they suffer.

3 a. I speak not concerning those who are appointed to lead my people, who are the first elders of my church, for they are not all under this condemnation; but I speak concerning my churches abroad;

b. there are many who will say, Where is their God? Behold, he will deliver in time of trouble; otherwise we will not go up unto Zion, and will keep our moneys.

c. Therefore, in consequence of the transgression of my people, it is expedient in me that mine elders should wait for a little season for the redemption of Zion, that they themselves may be prepared, and that my people may be taught more perfectly, and have experience, and know more perfectly, concerning their duty, and the things which I require at their hands;

d. and this can not be brought to pass until mine elders are endowed with power from on high;

e. for, behold, I have prepared a great endowment and blessing to be poured out upon them, inasmuch as they are faithful, and continue in humility before me;

f. therefore, it is expedient in me that mine elders should wait for a little season, for the redemption of Zion; for, behold, I do not require at their hands to fight the battles of Zion; for, as I said in a former commandment, even so will I fulfill, I will fight your battles.

4 a. Behold, the destroyer I have sent forth to destroy and lay waste mine enemies;

b. and not many years hence, they shall not be left to pollute mine heritage, and to blaspheme my name upon the lands which I have consecrated for the gathering together of my saints.

5 a. Behold, I have commanded my servant Baurak Ale, to say unto the strength of my house, even my warriors, my young men and middle-aged, to gather together for the redemption of my people, and throw down the towers of mine enemies, and scatter their watchmen;

b. but the strength of mine house have not hearkened unto my words; but inasmuch as there are those who have hearkened unto my words, I have prepared a blessing and an endowment for them, if they continue faithful.

c. I have heard their prayers, and will accept their offering; and it is expedient in me, that they should be brought thus far, for a trial of their faith.

6 a. And now, verily I say unto you, A commandment I give unto you, that as many as have come up hither, that can stay in the region round about, let them stay;

b. and those that can not stay, who have families in the east, let them tarry for a little season, inasmuch as my servant Joseph shall appoint unto them, for I will counsel him concerning this matter; and all things whatsoever he shall appoint unto them shall be fulfilled.

7 a. And let all my people who dwell in the regions round about, be very faithful, and prayerful, and humble before me, and reveal not the things which I have revealed unto them, until it is wisdom in me that they should be revealed.

b. Talk not judgment, neither boast of faith, nor of mighty works; but carefully gather together, as much in one region as can be consistently with the feelings of the people;

c. and, behold, I will give unto you favor and grace in their eyes, that you may rest in peace and safety, while you are saying unto the people, Execute judgment and justice for us according to law, and redress us of our wrongs.

8 a. Now, behold, I say unto you, my friends, in this way you may find favor in the eyes of the people, until the army of Israel becomes very great;

b. and I will soften the hearts of the people, as I did the heart of Pharaoh, from time to time, until my servant Baurak Ale, and Baneemy, whom I have appointed, shall have time to gather up the strength of my house, and to have sent wise men, to fulfill that which I have commanded concerning the purchasing of all the lands in Jackson County, that can be purchased, and in the adjoining counties round about; for it is my will that these lands be purchased, and after they are purchased that my saints should possess them according to the laws of consecration which I have given;

c. and after these lands are purchased, I will hold the armies of Israel guiltless in taking possession of their own lands, which they have previously purchased with their moneys, and of throwing down the towers of mine enemies, that may be upon them,

d. and scattering their watchmen, and avenging me of mine enemies, unto the third and fourth generation of them that hate me.

9 a. But firstly, let my army become very great, and let it be sanctified before me, that it may become fair as the sun, and clear as the moon, and that her banners may be terrible unto all nations;

b. that the kingdoms of this world may be constrained to acknowledge that the kingdom of Zion is in very deed the kingdom of our God and his Christ; therefore, let us become subject unto her laws.

10 a. Verily I say unto you, It is expedient in me that the first elders of my church should receive their endowment from on high, in my house, which I have commanded to be built unto my name in the land of Kirtland;

b. and let those commandments which I have given concerning Zion and her law, be executed and fulfilled, after her redemption.

c. There has been a day of calling, but the time has come for a day of choosing; and let those be chosen that are worthy; and it shall be manifest unto my servant, by the voice of the Spirit, those that are chosen, and they shall be sanctified;

d. and inasmuch as they follow the counsel which they receive, they shall have power after many days to accomplish all things pertaining to Zion.

11 a. And again, I say unto you, Sue for peace, not only the people that have smitten you, but also to all people;

b. and lift up an ensign of peace, and make a proclamation for peace unto the ends of the earth;

c. and make proposals for peace, unto those who have smitten you, according to the voice of the Spirit which is in you, and all things shall work together for your good;

d. therefore, be faithful, and, behold, and lo, I am with you even unto the end. Even so. Amen.

SECTION 103

Revelation given through Joseph Smith, Jr., at Kirtland, Ohio, November 25, 1834. It was addressed to Warren A. Cowdery of Freedom, New York.

1 a. It is my will that my servant, Warren A. Cowdery, should be appointed and ordained a presiding high priest over my church in the land of Freedom, and the regions round about, and should preach my everlasting gospel, and lift up his voice and warn the people, not only in his own place, but in the adjoining countries,

b. and devote his whole time in this high and holy calling which I now give unto him, seeking diligently the kingdom of heaven and its righteousness, and all things necessary shall be added thereunto; for the laborer is worthy of his hire.

2 And again, verily I say unto you, The coming of the Lord draweth nigh, and it overtaketh the world as a thief in the night; therefore, gird up your loins that you may be the children of the light, and that day shall not overtake you as a thief.

3 a. And again, verily I say unto you, There was joy in heaven when my servant, Warren, bowed to my scepter, and separated himself from the crafts of men;

b. therefore, blessed is my servant, Warren, for I will have mercy on him, and notwithstanding the vanity of his heart, I will lift him up inasmuch as he will humble himself before me; and I will give him grace and assurance wherewith he may stand;

c. and if he continues to be a faithful witness and a light unto the church, I have prepared a crown for him in the mansions of my Father. Even so. Amen.

SECTION 104

The first members of the Council of Twelve of the Restoration were chosen February 14, 1835. At a meeting held to prepare for their first mission as a quorum of apostles, the brethren asked Joseph Smith to inquire of God and attain a revelation for their comfort and for their enlightenment concerning their duty. In response to this request, the following instruction was received through Joseph at Kirtland, Ohio, March 28, 1835.

1 a. There are, in the church, two priesthoods; namely: the Melchisedec, and the Aaronic, including the Levitical priesthood.

b. Why the first is called the Melchisedec priesthood, is because Melchisedec was such a great high priest: before his day it was called *the holy priesthood, after the order of the Son of God;*

c. but out of respect or reverence to the name of the Supreme Being, to avoid the too frequent repetition of his name, they, the church, in ancient days, called that priesthood after Melchisedec, or the Melchisedec priesthood.

2 All other authorities, or offices in the church are appendages to this priesthood; but there are two divisions, or grand heads—one is the Melchisedec priesthood, and the other is the Aaronic, or Levitical priesthood.

3 a. The office of an elder comes under the priesthood of Melchisedec.

b. The Melchisedec priesthood holds the right of presidency, and has power and authority over all the offices in the church, in all ages of the world, to administer in spiritual things.

4 The presidency of the high priesthood, after the order of Melchisedec, have a right to officiate in all the offices in the church.

5 High priests, after the order of the Melchisedec priesthood, have a right to officiate in their own standing, under the direction of the Presidency, in administering spiritual

things, and also in the office of an elder, priest (of the Levitical order), teacher, deacon, and member.

6 An elder has a right to officiate in his stead when the high priest is not present.

7 The high priest and elder are to administer in spiritual things, agreeably to the covenants and commandments of the church; and they have a right to officiate in all these offices of the church when there are no higher authorities present.

8 a. The second priesthood is called the priesthood of Aaron, because it was conferred upon Aaron and his seed, throughout all their generations.

b. Why it is called the lesser priesthood is, because it is an appendage to the greater, or the Melchisedec priesthood, and has power in administering outward ordinances.

c. The bishopric is the presidency of this priesthood, and holds the keys or authority of the same. No man has a legal right to this office, to hold the keys of this priesthood, except he be a literal descendant of Aaron.

d. But as a high priest of the Melchisedec priesthood has authority to officiate in all the lesser offices, he may officiate in the office of bishop when no literal descendant of Aaron can be found, provided he is called and set apart and ordained unto this power by the hands of the Presidency of the Melchisedec priesthood.

9 a. The power and authority of the higher, or Melchisedec, priesthood, is to hold the keys of all the spiritual blessings of the church; to have the privilege of receiving the mysteries of the kingdom of heaven; to have the heavens opened unto them;

b. to commune with the general assembly and church of the Firstborn; and to enjoy the communion and presence of God the Father, and Jesus the Mediator of the new covenant.

10 The power and authority of the lesser, or Aaronic, priesthood is, to hold the keys of the ministering of angels, and to administer in outward ordinances—the letter of the gospel—the baptism of repentance for the remission of sins, agreeably to the covenants and commandments.

11 a. Of necessity, there are presidents, or presiding offices, growing out of, or appointed of, or from among those who are ordained to the several offices in these two priesthoods.

b. Of the Melchisedec priesthood, three presiding high priests, chosen by the body, appointed and ordained to that office, and upheld by the confidence, faith, and prayer of the church, form a quorum of the Presidency of the church.

c. The twelve traveling councilors are called to be the Twelve Apostles, or special witnesses of the name of Christ, in all the world; thus differing from other officers in the church in the duties of their calling.

d. And they form a quorum equal in authority and power to the three presidents previously mentioned.

e. The seventy are also called to preach the gospel, and to be especial witnesses unto the Gentiles and in all the world —thus differing from other officers in the church in the duties of their calling; and they form a quorum equal in authority to that of the twelve especial witnesses, or apostles, just named.

f. And every decision made by either of these quorums must be by the unanimous voice of the same; that is, every member in each quorum must be agreed to its decisions, in order to make their decisions of the same power or validity one with the other.

g. (A majority may form a quorum, when circumstances render it impossible to be otherwise.)

h. Unless this is the case, their decisions are not entitled to the same blessings which the decisions of a quorum of three presidents were anciently, who were ordained after the order of Melchisedec, and were righteous and holy men.

i. The decisions of these quorums, or either of them, are to be made in all righteousness, in holiness and lowliness of heart, meekness and long-suffering, and in faith and virtue and knowledge; temperance, patience, godliness, brotherly kindness, and charity, because the promise is, if these things abound in them, they shall not be unfruitful in the knowledge of the Lord.

j. And in case that any decision of these quorums is made in unrighteousness, it may be brought before a general assembly of the several quorums which constitute the spiritual authorities of the church, otherwise there can be no appeal from their decision.

12 The Twelve are a traveling, presiding high council, to officiate in the name of the Lord, under the direction of the Presidency of the church, agreeably to the institution of heaven, to build up the church and regulate all the affairs of the same, in all nations; first unto the Gentiles, and secondly unto the Jews.

13 a. The Seventy are to act in the name of the Lord, under the direction of the Twelve, or the traveling high council, in building up the church and regulating all the affairs of the same, in all nations; first unto the Gentiles, and then to the Jews;

b. the Twelve being sent out, holding the keys to open the door by the proclamation of the gospel of Jesus Christ; and first unto the Gentiles, and then unto the Jews.

14 The standing high councils, at the stakes of Zion, form a quorum equal in authority, in the affairs of the church, in all their decisions, to the quorum of the Presidency or to the traveling high council.

15 The high council in Zion forms a quorum equal in authority, in the affairs of the church, in all their decisions, to the councils of the twelve at the stakes of Zion.

16 It is the duty of the traveling high council to call upon the Seventy, when they need assistance, to fill the several calls for preaching and administering the gospel, instead of any others.

17 It is the duty of the Twelve, in all large branches of the church, to ordain evangelical ministers, as they shall be designated unto them by revelation.

18 The order of this priesthood was confirmed to be handed down from father to son, and rightly belongs to the literal descendants of the chosen seed, to whom the promises were made. This order was instituted in the days of Adam, and came down by lineage in the following manner:

19 a. From Adam to Seth, who was ordained by Adam at the age of sixty-nine years, and was blessed by him three years previous to his (Adam's) death, and received the promise of God by his father, that his posterity should be the chosen of the Lord,

b. and that they should be preserved unto the end of the earth, because he (Seth) was a perfect man, and his likeness was the express likeness of his father, insomuch that he seemed to be like unto his father in all things; and could be distinguished from him only by his age.

20 Enos was ordained at the age of one hundred and thirty-four years, and four months, by the hand of Adam.

21 God called upon Cainan in the wilderness, in the fortieth year of his age, and he met Adam in journeying to the place Shedolamak: he was eighty-seven years old when he received his ordination.

22 Mahalaleel was four hundred and ninety-six years and seven days old when he was ordained by the hand of Adam, who also blessed him.

23 Jared was two hundred years old when he was ordained under the hand of Adam, who also blessed him.

24 a. Enoch was twenty-five years old when he was ordained under the hand of Adam, and he was sixty-five and Adam blessed him—and he saw the Lord:
b. and he walked with him, and was before his face continually: and he walked with God three hundred and sixty-five years: making him four hundred and thirty years old when he was translated.

25 Methuselah was one hundred years old when he was ordained under the hand of Adam.

26 Lamech was thirty-two years old when he was ordained under the hand of Seth.

27 Noah was ten years old when he was ordained under the hand of Methuselah.

28 a. Three years previous to the death of Adam, he called Seth, Enos, Cainan, Mahalaleel, Jared, Enoch, and Methuselah, who were all high priests, with the residue of his posterity, who were righteous, into the valley of Adam-ondi-Ahman, and there bestowed upon them his last blessing.
b. And the Lord appeared unto them, and they rose up and

blessed Adam, and called him Michael, the Prince, the Archangel.

c. And the Lord administered comfort unto Adam, and said unto him, I have set thee to be at the head: a multitude of nations shall come of thee; and thou art a prince over them for ever.

29 a. And Adam stood up in the midst of the congregation, and notwithstanding he was bowed down with age, being full of the Holy Ghost, predicted whatsoever should befall his posterity unto the latest generation.

b. These things were all written in the Book of Enoch, and are to be testified of in due time.

30 It is the duty of the Twelve, also, to ordain and set in order all the other officers of the church, agreeably to the revelation which says:

31 a. To the church of Christ in the land of Zion, in addition to the church laws, respecting church business:

b. Verily, I say unto you, saith the Lord of hosts, There must needs be presiding elders, to preside over those who are of the office of an elder; and also priests, to preside over those who are of the office of a priest;

c. and also teachers to preside over those who are of the office of a teacher, in like manner; and also the deacons:

d. wherefore, from deacon to teacher, and from teacher to priest, and from priest to elder, severally as they are appointed, according to the covenants and commandments of the church;

e. then comes the high priesthood, which is the greatest of all; wherefore, it must needs be that one be appointed, of the high priesthood, to preside over the priesthood; and he shall be called President of the high priesthood of the church, or, in other words, the presiding high priest over the high priesthood of the church.

f. From the same comes the administering of ordinances and blessings upon the church, by the laying on of the hands.

32 a. Wherefore the office of a bishop is not equal unto it, for the office of a bishop is in administering all temporal things:

b. nevertheless, a bishop must be chosen from the high priesthood, unless he is a literal descendant of Aaron; for unless he is a literal descendant of Aaron he can not hold the keys of that priesthood.

c. Nevertheless, a high priest, that is after the order of Melchisedec, may be set apart unto the ministering of temporal things, having a knowledge of them by the Spirit of truth, and also to be a judge in Israel, to do the business of the church, to sit in judgment upon transgressors, upon testimony, as it shall be laid before him, according to the laws, by the assistance of his counselors, whom he has chosen, or will choose among the elders of the church.

d. This is the duty of a bishop who is not a literal descendant of Aaron, but has been ordained to the high priesthood after the order of Melchisedec.

33 a. Thus shall he be a judge, even a common judge among the inhabitants of Zion, or in a stake of Zion, or in any branch of the church where he shall be set apart unto this ministry,

b. until the borders of Zion are enlarged, and it becomes necessary to have other bishops, or judges in Zion, or elsewhere:

c. and inasmuch as there are other bishops appointed they shall act in the same office.

34 a. But a literal descendant of Aaron has a legal right to the presidency of this priesthood, to the keys of this ministry, to act in the office of bishop independently, without counselors, except in a case where a President of the high priesthood, after the order of Melchisedec, is tried; to sit as a judge in Israel.

b. And the decision of either of these councils, agreeably to the commandment which says:

35 a. Again, verily I say unto you: The most important business of the church, and the most difficult cases of the church, inasmuch as there is not satisfaction upon the decision of the bishop, or judges, it shall be handed over and carried up unto the council of the church, before the Presidency of the high priesthood;

b. and the Presidency of the council of the high priesthood shall have power to call other high priests, even twelve, to assist as counselors; and thus the Presidency of the high priesthood, and its counselors shall have power to decide upon testimony according to the laws of the church.

c. And after this decision it shall be had in remembrance no more before the Lord; for this is the highest council of the church of God, and a final decision upon controversies, in spiritual matters.

36 There is not any person belonging to the church, who is exempt from this council of the church.

37 a. And inasmuch as a President of the high priesthood shall transgress, he shall be had in remembrance before the common council of the church, who shall be assisted by twelve councilors of the high priesthood; and their decision upon his head shall be an end of controversy concerning him.

b. Thus, none shall be exempted from the justice and laws of God; that all things may be done in order and in solemnity, before him, according to truth and righteousness.

38 And again, verily I say unto you, The duty of a president over the office of a deacon, is to preside over twelve deacons, to sit in council with them, and to teach them their duty—edifying one another, as it is given according to the covenants.

39 And also the duty of the president over the office of the teachers, is to preside over twenty-four of the teachers, and to sit in council with them—teaching them the duties of their office, as given in the covenants.

40 a. Also the duty of the president over the priesthood of Aaron, is to preside over forty-eight priests, and sit in council with them, to teach them the duties of their office, as is given in the covenants.

b. This president is to be a bishop; for this is one of the duties of this priesthood.

41 a. Again, the duty of the president over the office of elders is to preside over ninety-six elders, and to sit in council with them, and to teach them according to the covenants.

b. This presidency is a distinct one from that of the Seventy, and is designed for those who do not travel into all the world.

42 a. And again, the duty of the President of the office of the high priesthood is to preside over the whole church, and to be like unto Moses.

b. Behold, here is wisdom, yea, to be a seer, a revelator, a translator, and a prophet; having all the gifts of God which he bestows upon the head of the church.

43 a. And it is according to the vision, showing the order of the Seventy, that they should have Seven Presidents to preside over them, chosen out of the number of the Seventy, and the seventh president of these presidents is to preside over the six;

b. and these Seven Presidents are to choose other Seventy besides the first Seventy, to whom they belong, and are to preside over them; and also other Seventy until seven times seventy, if the labor in the vineyard of necessity requires it.

c. And these Seventy are to be traveling ministers unto the Gentiles, first, and also unto the Jews, whereas other officers of the church, who belong not unto the Twelve neither to the Seventy, are not under the responsibility to travel among all nations, but are to travel as their circumstances shall allow, notwithstanding they may hold as high and responsible offices in the church.

44 a. Wherefore, now let every man learn his duty, and to act in the office in which he is appointed, in all diligence.

b. He that is slothful shall not be counted worthy to stand, and he that learns not his duty and shows himself not approved, shall not be counted worthy to stand. Even so. Amen.

SECTION 105

Revelation given through Joseph Smith, Jr., July 23, 1837, at Kirtland, Ohio. Having been received subsequent to the publication of the first (1835) edition of the Doctrine and Covenants, it was included in the second (1844) edition as Section 104. This edition was issued after the death of Joseph Smith. Specific approval for the continued publication of this section was given by the 1970 World Conference. This revelation is addressed to Thomas B. Marsh, president of the Council of Twelve, and was apparently prompted by his prayers concerning his brethren of the quorum. Elder Marsh's concern was itself prompted by a rift between Joseph and some of the apostles caused by financial and other difficulties in Kirtland. Note paragraphs 5, 6, 11, and 12 in this connection.

1 Verily, thus saith the Lord unto thee my servant, Thomas, I have heard thy prayers, and thine alms have come up as a memorial before me, in behalf of those thy brethren who were chosen to bear testimony of my name, and to send it abroad among all nations, kindreds, tongues, and people; and ordained through the instrumentality of my servants.

2 a. Verily I say unto thee, There have been some few things in thine heart and with thee, with which I, the Lord, was not well pleased; nevertheless, inasmuch as thou hast abased thyself thou shalt be exalted; therefore, all thy sins are forgiven thee.

b. Let thy heart be of good cheer before my face, and thou shalt bear record of my name, not only unto the Gentiles, but also unto the Jews; and thou shalt send forth my word unto the ends of the earth.

3 Contend thou, therefore, morning by morning, and day after day; let thy warning voice go forth, and when the night cometh, let not the inhabitants of the earth slumber because of thy speech.

4 a. Let thy habitation be known in Zion, and remove not thy house, for I, the Lord, have a great work for thee to do,

in publishing my name among the children of men; therefore, gird up thy loins for the work.

b. Let thy feet be shod also, for thou art chosen and thy path lieth among the mountains, and among many nations; and by thy word many high ones shall be brought low; and by thy word many low ones shall be exalted.

c. Thy voice shall be a rebuke unto the transgressor; and at thy rebuke let the tongue of the slanderer cease its perverseness.

5 a. Be thou humble, and the Lord thy God shall lead thee by the hand, and give thee answer to thy prayers. I know thy heart, and have heard thy prayers concerning thy brethren.

b. Be not partial towards them in love above many others, but let thy love be for them as for thyself; and let thy love abound unto all men, and unto all who love my name.

c. And pray for thy brethren of the Twelve. Admonish them sharply for my name's sake, and let them be admonished for all their sins; and be ye faithful before me unto my name.

d. And after their temptations and much tribulations, behold, I, the Lord, will feel after them, and if they harden not their hearts, and stiffen not their necks against me, they shall be converted, and I will heal them.

6 a. Now, I say unto you,—and what I say unto you I say unto all the Twelve,—Arise and gird up your loins, take up your cross, follow me, and feed my sheep.

b. Exalt not yourselves; rebel not against my servant Joseph, for verily I say unto you, I am with him, and my hand shall be over him, and the keys which I have given unto him, and also to youward, shall not be taken from him till I come.

7 a. Verily I say unto thee, my servant Thomas, Thou art the man whom I have chosen to hold the keys of my kingdom (as pertaining to the Twelve) abroad among all nations, that thou mayest be my servant to unlock the door of the kingdom in all places where my servant Joseph, and my servant Sidney, and my servant Hyrum, can not come;

b. for on them have I laid the burden of all the churches for a little season;

c. wherefore, whithersoever they shall send you, go ye, and I will be with you, and in whatsoever place ye shall proclaim

my name, an effectual door shall be opened unto you, that
they may receive my word;

d. whosoever receiveth my word receiveth me, and whosoever receiveth me, receiveth those (the First Presidency)
whom I have sent, whom I have made counselors for my
name's sake unto you.

8 a. And again I say unto you, that whosoever ye shall
send in my name, by the voice of your brethren, the Twelve,
duly recommended and authorized by you, shall have power
to open the door of my kingdom unto any nation whithersoe-
ever ye shall send them,

b. inasmuch as they shall humble themselves before me,
and abide in my word, and hearken to the voice of my
Spirit.

9 a. Verily, verily, I say unto you, Darkness covereth the
earth, and gross darkness the minds of the people, and all
flesh has become corrupt before my face.

b. Behold, vengeance cometh speedily upon the inhabitants of the earth—a day of wrath, a day of burning, a day
of desolation, of weeping, of mourning, and of lamentation
—and as a whirlwind it shall come upon all the face of the
earth, saith the Lord.

10 a. And upon my house shall it begin, and from my
house shall it go forth, saith the Lord.

b. First among those among you, saith the Lord, who have
professed to know my name and have not known me, and
have blasphemed against me in the midst of my house, saith
the Lord.

11 a. Therefore, see to it that ye trouble not yourselves
concerning the affairs of my church in this place, saith the
Lord;

b. but purify your hearts before me, and then go ye into
all the world, and preach my gospel unto every creature who
has not received it;

c. and he that believeth and is baptized shall be saved,
and he that believeth not, and is not baptized, shall be
damned.

12 a. For unto you (the Twelve), and those (the First

Presidency), who are appointed with you, to be your counselors and your leaders, is the power of this priesthood given, for the last days and for the last time, in the which is the dispensation of the fullness of times,

b. which power you hold in connection with all those who have received a dispensation at any time from the beginning of the creation;

c. for verily I say unto you, The keys of the dispensation which ye have received, have come down from the fathers; and last of all, being sent down from heaven unto you.

13 a. Verily I say unto you, Behold how great is your calling.   Cleanse your hearts and your garments, lest the blood of this generation be required at your hands.

b. Be faithful until I come, for I come quickly, and my reward is with me to recompense every man according as his work shall be.   I am Alpha and Omega.   Amen.

SECTION 106

This revelation was first published in the second (1844) edition of the Doctrine and Covenants as Section 107. By action of the 1970 World Conference its inclusion was confirmed. It was given through Joseph Smith, Jr., at Far West, Missouri, July 8, 1838, in answer to the petition, "O Lord, show unto thy servants how much thou requirest of the properties of thy people for a tithing."

1 a. Verily, thus saith the Lord, I require all their surplus property to be put into the hands of the bishop of my church of Zion, for the building of mine house, and for the laying the foundation of Zion, and for the priesthood, and for the debts of the presidency of my church;

b. and this shall be the beginning of the tithing of my people; and after that, those who have thus been tithed, shall pay one tenth of all their interest annually; and this shall be a standing law unto them for ever, for my holy priesthood, saith the Lord.

2 a. Verily I say unto you, It shall come to pass that all those who gather unto the land of Zion shall be tithed of their

surplus properties, and shall observe this law, or they shall not be found worthy to abide among you.

b. And I say unto you, If my people observe not this law, to keep it holy, and by this law sanctify the land of Zion unto me, that my statutes and my judgments may be kept thereon, that it may be most holy,

c. behold, verily I say unto you, It shall not be a land of Zion unto you; and this shall be an ensample unto all the stakes of Zion. Even so. Amen.

SECTION 107

(See Appendix A, page 383)

SECTION 108

Revelation received through Joseph Smith, Jr., prophet and seer to the church, November 3, 1831, at Hiram, Ohio. The revelation, originally given as the "Preface" to the "Book of Commandments,"* given November 1, 1831, is now Section 1 of the Doctrine and Covenants. The following revelation was to constitute the "close" or "appendix" to the "Book of Commandments." The "Book of Commandments" was never completed; the printing press was destroyed by a mob while the book was in the process of being printed, and the printed material was scattered in the street. This revelation was not included in the incomplete copy. However, it was included in the revelations contained in the 1835 edition as the "appendix." It will be better understood if read in connection with the revelations given prior to November 1831. To follow the precedent of previous editions, it is retained in this place as Section 108.

1 a. Hearken, O ye people of my church, saith the Lord your God, and hear the word of the Lord concerning you;

---

*A number of bound copies of the "Book of Commandments" are in the Historian's Library of the church.

the Lord who shall suddenly come to his temple; the Lord who shall come down upon the world with a curse to judgment; yea, upon all the nations that forget God, and upon all the ungodly among you.

b. For he shall make bare his holy arm in the eyes of all the nations, and all the ends of the earth shall see the salvation of their God.

2 a. Wherefore prepare ye, prepare ye, O my people; sanctify yourselves; gather ye together, O ye people of my church, upon the land of Zion, all you that have not been commanded to tarry.

b. Go ye out from Babylon. Be ye clean that bear the vessels of the Lord. Call your solemn assemblies, and speak often one to another.

c. And let every man call upon the name of the Lord; yea, verily I say unto you again, The time has come when the voice of the Lord is unto you, Go ye out of Babylon; gather ye out from among the nations, from the four winds, from one end of heaven to the other.

3 a. Send forth the elders of my church unto the nations which are afar off; unto the islands of the sea; send forth unto foreign lands; call upon all nations; firstly, upon the Gentiles, and then upon the Jews.

b. And, behold, and lo, this shall be their cry, and the voice of the Lord unto all people:

c. Go ye forth unto the land of Zion, that the borders of my people may be enlarged, and that her stakes may be strengthened, and that Zion may go forth unto the regions round about; yea, let the cry go forth among all people: Awake and arise and go forth to meet the Bridegroom.

d. Behold, and lo, the Bridegroom cometh, go ye out to meet him. Prepare yourselves for the great day of the Lord.

4 a. Watch, therefore, for ye know neither the day nor the hour. Let them, therefore, who are among the Gentiles, flee unto Zion.

b. And let them who be of Judah, flee unto Jerusalem, unto the mountains of the Lord's house. Go ye out from among the nations, even from Babylon, from the midst of wickedness, which is spiritual Babylon.

c. But verily thus saith the Lord, Let not your flight be in haste, but let all things be prepared before you; and he that goeth, let him not look back, lest sudden destruction shall come upon him.

5 a. Hearken and hear O ye inhabitants of the earth.

b. Listen, ye elders of my church together, and hear the voice of the Lord, for he calleth upon all men and he commandeth all men everywhere to repent; for, behold, the Lord God hath sent forth the angel, crying through the midst of heaven, saying:

c. Prepare ye the way of the Lord, and make his paths strait, for the hour of his coming is nigh, when the Lamb shall stand upon Mount Zion, and with him a hundred and forty-four thousand, having his father's name written in their foreheads;

d. wherefore, prepare ye for the coming of the Bridegroom; go ye, go ye out to meet him, for, behold, he shall stand upon the Mount of Olivet, and upon the mighty ocean, even the great deep, and upon the islands of the sea, and upon the land of Zion;

e. and he shall utter his voice out of Zion, and he shall speak from Jerusalem, and his voice shall be heard among all people, and it shall be a voice as the voice of many waters, and as the voice of a great thunder, which shall break down the mountains, and the valleys shall not be found;

f. he shall command the great deep and it shall be driven back into the north countries, and the islands shall become one land, and the land of Jerusalem and the land of Zion shall be turned back into their own place, and the earth shall be like as it was in the days before it was divided.

g. And the Lord even the Savior shall stand in the midst of his people, and shall reign over all flesh.

6 a. And they who are in the north countries shall come in remembrance before the Lord, and their prophets shall hear his voice, and shall no longer stay themselves, and they shall smite the rocks, and the ice shall flow down at their presence.

b. And an highway shall be cast up in the midst of the great deep. Their enemies shall become a prey unto them, and in the barren deserts there shall come forth pools of living water; and the parched ground shall no longer be a thirsty land.

c. And they shall bring forth their rich treasures unto the children of Ephraim my servants. And the boundaries of the everlasting hills shall tremble at their presence.

d. And then shall they fall down and be crowned with glory, even in Zion, by the hands of the servants of the Lord, even the children of Ephraim; and they shall be filled with songs of everlasting joy.

e. Behold, this is the blessing of the everlasting God upon the tribes of Israel, and the richer blessing upon the head of Ephraim and his fellows.

f. And they also of the tribe of Judah, after their pain, shall be sanctified in holiness before the Lord to dwell in his presence day and night for ever and ever.

7 a. And now verily saith the Lord, That these things might be known among you, O inhabitants of the earth, I have sent forth mine angel, flying through the midst of heaven, having the everlasting gospel, who hath appeared unto some, and hath committed it unto man, who shall appear unto many that dwell on the earth;

b. and this gospel shall be preached unto every nation, and kindred, and tongue, and people, and the servants of God shall go forth, saying, with a loud voice:

c. Fear God and give glory to him; for the hour of his judgment is come: and worship him that made heaven, and earth, and sea, and the fountain of waters, calling upon the name of the Lord day and night, saying: O that thou wouldst rend the heavens, that thou wouldst come down, that the mountains might flow down at thy presence.

d. And it shall be answered upon their heads, for the presence of the Lord shall be as the melting fire that burneth, and as the fire which causeth the waters to boil.

8 a. O Lord, thou shalt come down to make thy name known to thine adversaries, and all nations shall tremble at thy presence.

b. When thou doeth terrible things, things they look not for; yea, when thou comest down and the mountains flow down at thy presence, thou shalt meet him who rejoiceth and worketh righteousness, who remembereth thee in thy ways;

c. for since the beginning of the world have not men heard

nor perceived by the ear, neither hath any eye seen, O God, besides thee, how great things thou hast prepared for him that waiteth for thee.

9 a. And it shall be said, Who is this that cometh down from God in heaven with dyed garments; yea, from the regions which are not known, clothed in his glorious apparel, traveling in the greatness of his strength?

b. And he shall say, I am he who spake in righteousness, mighty to save.

c. And the Lord shall be red in his apparel, and his garments like him that treadeth in the wine vat, and so great shall be the glory of his presence, that the sun shall hide his face in shame; and the moon shall withhold its light; and the stars shall be hurled from their places;

d. and his voice shall be heard, I have trodden the winepress alone, and have brought judgment upon all people; and none was with me;

e. and I have trampled them in my fury, and I did tread upon them in mine anger, and their blood have I sprinkled upon my garments, and stained all my raiment; for this was the day of vengeance which was in my heart.

10 a. And now the year of my redeemed is come, and they shall mention the loving kindness of their Lord, and all that he has bestowed upon them, according to his goodness, and according to his loving kindness, for ever and ever.

b. In all their afflictions he was afflicted. And the angel of his presence saved them; and in his love, and in his pity, he redeemed them, and bare them, and carried them all the days of old;

c. yea, and Enoch also, and they who were with him; the prophets who were before him, and Noah also, and they who were before him, and Moses also, and they who were before him, and from Moses to Elijah, and from Elijah to John, who were with Christ in his resurrection, and the holy apostles, with Abraham, Isaac, and Jacob, shall be in the presence of the Lamb.

d. And the graves of the saints shall be opened, and they shall come forth and stand on the right hand of the Lamb, when he shall stand upon Mount Zion, and upon the holy

city, the New Jerusalem, and they shall sing the song of the
Lamb day and night for ever and ever.

11 a. And for this cause, that men might be made partakers of the glories which were to be revealed, the Lord sent
forth the fullness of his gospel, his everlasting covenant, reasoning in plainness and simplicity, to prepare the weak for
those things which are coming on the earth;

b. and for the Lord's errand in the day when the weak
shall confound the wise, and the little one become a strong
nation, and two should put their tens of thousands to flight;
and by the weak things of the earth, the Lord should thresh
the nations by the power of his Spirit.

c. And for this cause these commandments were given;
they were commanded to be kept from the world in the day
that they were given, but now are to go forth unto all flesh.

d. And this according to the mind and will of the Lord,
who ruleth over all flesh; and unto him that repenteth and
sanctifieth himself before the Lord, shall be given eternal
life.

e. And upon them that hearken not to the voice of the
Lord, shall be fulfilled that which was written by the prophet
Moses, that they should be cut off from among the people.

12 a. And also that which was written by the prophet
Malachi:

b. For, behold, the day cometh that shall burn as an oven,
and all the proud, yea, and all that do wickedly, shall be
stubble: and the day that cometh shall burn them up, saith
the Lord of hosts, that it shall leave them neither root nor
branch.

c. Wherefore this shall be the answer of the Lord unto
them:

d. In that day when I came unto my own, no man among
you received me, and you were driven out.

e. When I called again, there was none of you to answer,
yet my arm was not shortened at all, that I could not redeem,
neither my power to deliver.

f. Behold, at my rebuke I dry up the sea. I make the
rivers a wilderness; their fish stinketh, and dieth for thirst.
I clothe the heavens with blackness, and make sackcloth

their covering.   And this shall ye have of my hand, ye shall lie down in sorrow.

13 a. Behold, and lo, there are none to deliver you, for ye obeyed not my voice when I called to you out of the heavens, ye believed not my servants; and when they were sent unto you ye received them not;

b. wherefore, they sealed up the testimony and bound up the law, and ye were delivered over unto darkness; these shall go away into outer darkness, where there is weeping, and wailing, and gnashing of teeth.   Behold, the Lord your God hath spoken it.   Amen.

SECTION 108A
(*See Introduction*)

SECTION 109
(*See Appendix B, page 399*)

SECTION 110
(*See Appendix C, page 402*)

SECTION 111

This section on marriage is not a revelation. It was prepared while the Book of Doctrine and Covenants was being compiled and was read by W. W. Phelps at the general assembly of August 17, 1835. It was adopted unanimously by that assembly as part of the Book of Doctrine and Covenants. It has been retained in every edition of the book published by the Reorganization, and the church knows no other law of marriage than that which is set forth here.

1 a. According to the custom of all civilized nations, marriage is regulated by laws and ceremonies:

b. therefore we believe, that all marriages in this Church of Christ of Latter Day Saints should be solemnized in a public meeting, or feast, prepared for that purpose:

c. and that the solemnization should be performed by a presiding high priest, high priest, bishop, elder, or priest, not even prohibiting those persons who are desirous to get married, of being married by other authority.

d. We believe that it is not right to prohibit members of this church from marrying out of the church, if it be their determination so to do, but such persons will be considered weak in the faith of our Lord and Savior Jesus Christ.

2 a. Marriage should be celebrated with prayer and thanksgiving; and at the solemnization, the persons to be married, standing together, the man on the right, and the woman on the left, shall be addressed, by the person officiating, as he shall be directed by the Holy Spirit; and if there be no legal objections, he shall say, calling each by their names:

b. "You both mutually agree to be each other's companion, husband and wife, observing the legal rights belonging to this condition; that is, keeping yourselves wholly for each other, and from all others, during your lives?"

c. And when they have answered "Yes," he shall pronounce them "husband and wife" in the name of the Lord Jesus Christ, and by virtue of the laws of the country and authority vested in him:

d. "May God add his blessings and keep you to fulfill your covenants from henceforth and for ever. Amen."

3 The clerk of every church should keep a record of all marriages solemnized in his branch.

4 a. All legal contracts of marriage made before a person is baptized into this church, should be held sacred and fulfilled.

b. Inasmuch as this Church of Christ has been reproached with the crime of fornication, and polygamy: we declare that we believe that one man should have one wife; and one woman but one husband, except in case of death, when either is at liberty to marry again.

c. It is not right to persuade a woman to be baptized contrary to the will of her husband, neither is it lawful to influence her to leave her husband.

d. All children are bound by law to obey their parents; and to influence them to embrace any religious faith, or be baptized, or leave their parents without their consent, is unlawful and unjust.

e. We believe that all persons who exercise control over their fellowbeings, and prevent them from embracing the truth, will have to answer for that sin.

SECTION 112

This section, which deals with governments and laws in general, is not a revelation. It was prepared in connection with the publication of the 1835 edition of the Doctrine and Covenants and was read by Oliver Cowdery at the general assembly of August 17, 1835. It was adopted unanimously and ordered to be printed in the first edition of the Doctrine and Covenants (108A:14). It was also published as the political sentiment of the church by authority of the conference of 1863.   This was during the American Civil War.

1 We believe that governments were instituted of God for the benefit of man, and that he holds men accountable for their acts in relation to them, either in making laws or administering them, for the good and safety of society.

2 We believe that no government can exist, in peace, except such laws are framed and held inviolate as will secure

to each individual the free exercise of conscience, the right and control of property, and the protection of life.

3 We believe that all governments necessarily require civil officers and magistrates to enforce the laws of the same, and that such as will administer the law in equity and justice should be sought for and upheld by the voice of the people (if a republic), or the will of the sovereign.

4 a. We believe that religion is instituted of God, and that men are amenable to him and to him only for the exercise of it, unless their religious opinion prompts them to infringe upon the rights and liberties of others;

b. but we do not believe that human law has a right to interfere in prescribing rules of worship to bind the consciences of men, nor dictate forms for public or private devotion;

c. that the civil magistrate should restrain crime, but never control conscience; should punish guilt, but never suppress the freedom of the soul.

5 a. We believe that all men are bound to sustain and uphold the respective governments in which they reside, while protected in their inherent and inalienable rights by the laws of such governments, and that sedition and rebellion are unbecoming every citizen thus protected, and should be punished accordingly;

b. and that all governments have a right to enact such laws as in their own judgments are best calculated to secure the public interest, at the same time, however, holding sacred the freedom of conscience.

6 a. We believe that every man should be honored in his station: rulers and magistrates as such—being placed for the protection of the innocent and the punishment of the guilty;

b. and that to the laws all men owe respect and deference, as without them peace and harmony would be supplanted by anarchy and terror:

c. human laws being instituted for the express purpose of regulating our interests as individuals and nations, between man and man, and divine laws, given of heaven, prescribing rules on spiritual concerns, for faith and worship, both to be answered by man to his Maker.

7 a. We believe that rulers, states, and governments have a right, and are bound to enact laws for the protection of all citizens in the free exercise of their religious belief;

b. but we do not believe that they have a right, in justice, to deprive citizens of this privilege, or proscribe them in their opinions, so long as a regard and reverence is shown to the laws, and such religious opinions do not justify sedition nor conspiracy.

8 a. We believe that the commission of crime should be punished according to the nature of the offense:

b. that murder, treason, robbery, theft, and the breach of the general peace, in all respects, should be punished according to their criminality and their tendency to evil among men, by the laws of that government in which the offense is committed:

c. and for the public peace and tranquillity, all men should step forward and use their ability in bringing offenders, against good laws, to punishment.

9 We do not believe it just to mingle religious influence with civil government, whereby one religious society is fostered and another proscribed in its spiritual privileges, and the individual rights of its members, as citizens, denied.

10 a. We believe that all religious societies have a right to deal with their members for disorderly conduct according to the rules and regulations of such societies, provided that such dealings be for fellowship and good standing;

b. but we do not believe that any religious society has authority to try men on the right of property or life, to take from them this world's goods, or put them in jeopardy of either life or limb, neither to inflict any physical punishment upon them — they can only excommunicate them from their society and withdraw from their fellowship.

11 a. We believe that men should appeal to the civil law for redress of all wrongs and grievances, where personal abuse is inflicted, or the right of property or character infringed, where such laws exist as will protect the same;

b. but we believe that all men are justified in defending themselves, their friends and property, and the government, from the unlawful assaults and encroachments of all persons, in times of exigencies, where immediate appeal can not be made to the laws, and relief afforded.

12 a. We believe it just to preach the gospel to the nations of the earth, and warn the righteous to save themselves from the corruption of the world;

b. but we do not believe it right to interfere with bond servants, neither preach the gospel to, nor baptize them, contrary to the will and wish of their masters,

c. nor to meddle with, or influence them in the least to cause them to be dissatisfied with their situations in this life, thereby jeopardizing the lives of men:

d. such interference we believe to be unlawful and unjust, and dangerous to the peace of every government allowing human beings to be held in servitude.

SECTION 113
(See Appendix D, page 410)

SECTION 114

The first General Epistle of the Twelve under the presidency of Joseph Smith III, son of the Martyr, was addressed: "To all the Saints scattered abroad." To this Epistle an appendix was added by President Smith. The appendix was in the nature of a revelation from God and was so accepted by the church at the semiannual conference of 1871. Its inclusion in the Doctrine and Covenants was authorized by the semiannual conference of 1878.

This is the first revelation given to the church through President Joseph Smith III. It was dated October 7, 1861. The Epistle and appendix were published October 25, 1861.

1 a. In order to place the church in a position to carry on the promulgation of the gospel, and as a means of fulfilling

the law, the Twelve will take measures in connection with the Bishop, to execute the law of tithing;

b. and let them before God see to it, that the temporal means so obtained is truly used for the purposes of the church, and not as a weapon of power in the hands of one man for the oppression of others, or for the purposes of self-aggrandizement by anyone, be he whomsoever he may be.

2 As I live, saith the Lord, in the manner ye execute this matter, so shall ye be judged in the day of judgment.

SECTION 115

Revelation given through Joseph Smith III in March 1863. It is addressed to the elders of the church. The revelation was approved by the 1863 annual conference and inserted in the Doctrine and Covenants by authority of the semi-annual conference of 1878.

1 a. Hearken unto me, O ye elders of my church. Lo! I have seen your efforts in my cause, and they are pleasing unto me.

b. I declare unto you, It is my will that you ordain and set apart my servant William Marks to be a counselor to my servant Joseph, even the president of my church, that the first presidency of my church may be more perfectly filled.

c. And moreover it is expedient in me that my elders in going to declare my gospel to the nations, shall observe the pattern which I have given.

d. Two by two let them be sent, that they may be a help and a support to each other in their ministry.

e. Press onward, ye elders and people of my church, even my little flock, and as I have spoken to you in times past, so will I speak again to you as my friends, inasmuch as you speak in my name; and lo! I am Alpha and Omega, and will be with you unto the end. Amen.

SECTION 116

Revelation given through President Joseph Smith III, May 4, 1865.

A council of the First Presidency and the Quorum of Twelve was in session at the home of Bishop Israel L. Rogers in Kendall County, Illinois, May 1-5, 1865. Among other things the council was concerned about "the ordination of men of the Negro race." President Joseph Smith was asked to seek divine guidance in this connection, and the revelation was received in response to the fasting and prayers of the members of the council. It should be studied against the background of the American Civil War and with the social and educational status of the American Negro of that period in mind.

The revelation was presented to the Quorum of Twelve, who voted unanimously to approve it. The semiannual conference of 1878 authorized its inclusion in the Doctrine and Covenants.

1 a. Hearken! Ye elders of my church, I am he who hath called you friends. Concerning the matter you have asked of me:

b. Lo! It is my will that my gospel shall be preached to all nations in every land, and that men of every tongue shall minister before me:

c. Therefore it is expedient in me that you ordain priests unto me, of every race who receive the teachings of my law, and become heirs according to the promise.

2 a. Be ye very careful, for many elders have been ordained unto me, and are come under my condemnation, by reason of neglecting to lift up their voices in my cause, and for such there is tribulation and anguish:

b. haply they themselves may be saved (if doing no evil) though their glory, which is given for their works, be withheld, or in other words their works are burned, not being profitable unto me.

3 a. Loosen ye one another's hands and uphold one another, that ye who are of the Quorum of Twelve, may all

labor in the vineyard, for upon you rests much responsibility;

b. and if ye labor diligently the time is soon when others shall be added to your number till the quorum be full, even twelve.

4 a. Be not hasty in ordaining men of the Negro race to offices in my church, for verily I say unto you,

b. All are not acceptable unto me as servants, nevertheless I will that all may be saved, but every man in his own order, and there are some who are chosen instruments to be ministers to their own race. Be ye content, I the Lord have spoken it.

SECTION 117

As he approached the annual conference of 1873, President Smith was deeply concerned that he was again the only member of the First Presidency (Counselor William Marks had died in May 1872) and that the death of Apostle Samuel Powers in February 1873 had left the Quorum of Twelve with but five members. This concern was shared by the remaining members of the Twelve, and these were joined by a number of the Seventy in requesting that the prophet seek divine guidance.

In presenting the following revelation to the elders of the church, President Smith stated that it had been received "in answer to long and continued and earnest prayer to God upon the condition of the Quorums of the Church."

The revelation was approved by the available apostles and, on April 10, 1873, was endorsed by the conference. With the ordination of William Wallace Blair and David H. Smith, as provided for in this instruction, the quorum of the First Presidency was now complete for the first time since the reorganization of the church. This was also the first time in the Reorganization that members of the Twelve had been called by revelation through the President of the Church. Prior to this time, and on occasions in the early church, members of the Twelve had been selected by committees.

1 Hearken to the voice of the Spirit, O ye elders of my church; the prayers of my people have prevailed with me.

2 Behold, it is wisdom in me, and expedient in my church that the chief quorums should be more nearly filled, and their organization more nearly completed. Thus saith the Spirit.

3 a. Let my servants, William W. Blair and David H. Smith, be chosen and ordained to be counselors to my servant, the presiding elder of my church.

b. Let them be set apart to this office by the laying on of hands by my servants whose duty it is to ordain and set in order the officers of my church;

c. and let my servants, the president of the high priests' quorum and the president of the lesser priesthood, also lay their hands upon these their brethren who are to be counselors, but let my servants of the Twelve be the spokesmen.

4 a. Let my servants William H. Kelley, Thomas W. Smith, James Caffall, John H. Lake, Alexander H. Smith, Zenas H. Gurley, and Joseph R. Lambert, be chosen as especial witnesses, even of the Quorum of Twelve, for they are called thereunto, that they may take this ministry upon them.

b. Let them be ordained and set apart to this office by the laying on of the hands of my servants Joseph Smith, Jason W. Briggs, and William W. Blair.

5 Verily, I say unto you, If these my servants will henceforth magnify their calling in honor before me, they shall become men of power and excellent wisdom in the assemblies of my people.

6 Let the names of my servants Daniel B. Rasey and Reuben Newkirk be taken from the record of the Quorum of the Twelve and placed with the records of the names of the elders, and let them labor as elders, and their labors will be accepted by me.

7 a. It is my will that my servants, Jason W. Briggs, Josiah Ells, and Edmund C. Briggs, remain and stand in their lot as especial witnesses before me.

b. Let them diligently labor in their ministry, encouraging and directing their brethren in their labors.

c. It is expedient for the good of my cause that my servant Jason take the active oversight of his quorum.

8 a. Let my servants Archibald M. Wilsey, William D. Morton, and George Rarick, be ordained high priests:

b. and let my servants E. C. Brand, Charles W. Wandell, and Duncan Campbell be appointed as special witnesses of the Seventy in their places;

c. and let my servants Joseph Lakeman, Glaud Rodger, John T. Davies, and John S. Patterson be also appointed as witnesses of the Seventy before me.

9 a. Until such time as the quorum of the Twelve shall be filled, the decision of that quorum, a unanimous decision, shall be accounted final, as if such quorum were filled, according to my law as given in the Book of Doctrine and Covenants.

b. And until such time as the quorum of the Seventy shall be filled, their decision, if unanimous and agreeing with that of the quorum of the Twelve, shall be considered the same as if the quorum were filled.

10 a. It is expedient that the Bishop of my church shall choose two counselors, and that they be ordained to their office as my law directs, that there may be henceforth no caviling among my people.

b. The bishop of my church may also choose and appoint Bishop's agents, until it shall be wisdom in me to ordain other bishops, in the districts and large branches of my church.

11 a. It is not expedient in me that there shall be any stakes appointed until I command my people. When it shall be necessary I will command that they be established.

b. Let my commandments to gather into the regions round about, and the counsel of the elders of my church guide in this matter until it shall be otherwise given of me.

12 Behold, if my servants and my handmaidens, of the different organizations for good among my people, shall continue in righteousness, they shall be blessed, even as they bless others of the household of faith.

13 Let contentions and quarrelings among you cease. Sustain each other in peace, and ye shall be blessed with my Spirit, in comforting and strengthening you for my work.

14 It is not expedient that I command you further at this time; but be ye diligent, wise, and faithful, doing all things with an eye single for the glory of your God, and for the good of his people. Thus saith the Lord. Amen.

SECTION 118

Revelation given through President Joseph Smith III, September 28, 1882, at Lamoni, Iowa, in answer to the prayers of the General Conference.

1 a. In asking of me, ye did well. I will hasten my work in its time.

b. Ye can not now prosecute missions in many foreign lands, nor is it expedient that the elders of the first quorums be sent out of the land of America until the work of the reorganization of my church be more fully established, and a greater unity of understanding between them be obtained.

c. Nor is it expedient now to further fill up the quorums, except it be the elders, priests, teachers, and deacons: which ye may do, as ye deem wise, by the direction of conference.

2 Continue the mission in Chicago until the April conference, when if it be found expedient it may be left in the charge of the authorities of the Northern Illinois District.

3 It is my will that ye more fully honor and pay heed to the voice and counsel of the traveling ministry in spiritual things; which if ye do not, the office which they hold is not honored in my service, and the good they should do is made void.

4 a. If they approve themselves as righteous ministers, they shall be blessed; if they be found transgressors, or idle servants, ye shall not uphold them.

b. But be not hasty in withdrawing your support from them, peradventure ye shall injure my work.

c. Even now I am not well pleased with some, but space is granted for repentance and a renewal of diligence. Let no one deceive himself that he shall not account for his stewardship unto me.

JOSEPH SMITH
By command of the Spirit

SECTION 119

Revelation given through Joseph Smith III, April 11, 1887, at Kirtland, Ohio. This inspired instruction was received after the General Conference had observed Saturday, April 9, as a day of fasting and prayer for light concerning "the depleted condition of the Quorum of the Twelve."

To the Elders of the Church:

Thus saith the Spirit:

1 a. It is not yet expedient that the Quorum of the Twelve shall be filled; nevertheless separate my servants, James W. Gillen, Heman C. Smith, Joseph Luff, and Gomer T. Griffiths, unto the office of apostles, that the quorum may be more perfectly prepared to act before me.

b. I have still other men of my church who shall be designated in their time if they still continue faithful unto me and in the work whereunto they are now called.

2 a. There is a great work to be done by mine elders, and that they may be fitted to do this work and the accomplishment thereof be not prevented, it is enjoined upon them that they shall not only be kind of heart and of a lowly spirit, that their wisdom may be the wisdom of the Lord and their strength the strength of the Spirit,

b. but they shall lay aside lightness of speech and lightness of manner when standing to declare the word, and shall study to approve their ministrations to the people by candor in speech and courtesy in demeanor, that as ministers of the gospel they may win souls unto Christ.

3 a. The elders and men of the church should be of cheerful heart and countenance among themselves and in their intercourse with their neighbors and men of the world, yet they must be without blame in word and deed.

b. It is therefore not seemly that they indulge in loud and boisterous speech, or in the relating of coarse and vulgar stories, or those in which the names of their God and their Redeemer are blasphemed.

c. Men of God, who bear the vessels of the Lord, be ye clean in your bodies and in your clothing; let your garments be of a sober character and free from excess of ornamentation.

d. Avoid the use of tobacco and be not addicted to strong drink in any form, that your counsel to be temperate may be made effectual by your example.

4 a. That the work of restoration to which the people of my church are looking forward may be hastened in its time, the elders must cease to be overcareful concerning the return of those who were once of the faith but were overcome in the dark and cloudy day, fearing lest they should bring in hidden heresies to the overthrowing of the work;

b. for verily, there are some who are chosen vessels to do good, who have been estranged by the hindering snares which are in the world and who will in due time return unto the Lord if they be not hindered by the men of the church.

c. The Spirit says "Come"; let not the ministers for Christ prevent their coming.

5 a. And the Spirit saith further: Contention is unseemly; therefore, cease to contend respecting the sacrament and the time of administering it;

b. for whether it be upon the first Lord's day of every month, or upon the Lord's day of every week, if it be administered by the officers of the church with sincerity of heart and in purity of purpose, and be partaken of in remembrance of Jesus Christ and in willingness to take upon them his name by them who partake, it is acceptable to God.

c. To avoid confusion let him who presides in the sacrament meeting, and those who administer it cause that the emblems be duly prepared upon clean vessels for the bread and clean vessels for the wine, or the water, as may be expedient;

d. and the officer may break the bread before it is blessed, and pour the wine before it is blessed; or he may, if he be so led, bless the bread before it be broken and the wine before it be poured;

e. nevertheless both bread and wine should be uncovered when presented for the blessing to be asked upon it.

f. It is expedient that the bread and wine should be administered in the early part of the meeting, before weariness and confusion ensue.

g. Let him that partaketh and him that refraineth cease to contend with his brother that each may be benefited when he eateth at the table of the Lord.

6 a. The service of song in the house of the Lord with humility and unity of Spirit in them that sing and them that hear is blessed, and acceptable with God; but song with grievous sadness in them that sing and bitterness of spirit in them that hear is not pleasing to God.

b. Therefore, in all the congregations of the people of God, let all strife and contention concerning song service cease;

c. and that the worship in the house of the Lord may be complete and wholly acceptable, let them who shall be moved thereto by a desire and the gift to sing take upon them the burden and care of the service, and use therein instruments of music of the reed and of the string, or instruments of brass in congregations that are large, and as wisdom and choice may direct.

d. Let the young men and the maidens cultivate the gifts of music and of song; let not the middle-aged and the old forget the gladsomeness of their youth and let them aid and assist so far as their cares will permit; and remember that Saints should be cheerful in their warfare that they may be joyous in their triumph.

e. Nevertheless, let the organ and the stringed instrument, and the instrument of brass be silent when the Saints assemble for prayer and testimony, that the feelings of the tender and sad may not be intruded upon.

f. To facilitate unity in the song service of the church those to whom the work of providing a book of song has been intrusted may hasten their work in its time.

7 a. And the Spirit saith further: Inasmuch as there has been much discussion in the past concerning the Sabbath of the Lord, the church is admonished that until further revelation is received, or the quorums of the church are assem-

bled to decide concerning the law in the church articles and covenants,

b. the Saints are to observe the first day of the week commonly called the Lord's day, as a day of rest: as a day of worship, as given in the covenants and commandments.

c. And on this day they should refrain from unnecessary work; nevertheless, nothing should be permitted to go to waste on that day, nor should necessary work be neglected.

d. Be not harsh in judgment but merciful in this, as in all other things. Be not hypocrites nor of those who make a man an offender for a word.

8 a. Prosecute the missionary work in this land and abroad so far and so widely as you may.

b. All are called according to the gifts of God unto them; and to the intent that all may labor together, let him that laboreth in the ministry and him that toileth in the affairs of the men of business and of work labor together with God for the accomplishment of the work intrusted to all.

9 a. Be clean, be frugal, cease to complain of pain and sickness and distress of body; take sleep in the hours set apart by God for the rebuilding and strengthening of the body and mind;

b. for even now there are some, even among the elders, who are suffering in mind and body, who have disregarded the advice of the Spirit to retire early and to rise early that vigor of mind and body should be retained.

c. Bear the burdens of body of which the Spirit of healing from the Lord in faith, or the use of that which wisdom directs does not relieve or remove, and in cheerfulness do whatever may be permitted you to perform that the blessing of peace may be upon all. Amen.

KIRTLAND, OHIO, April 11, 1887

SECTION 120

The members of the Quorum of Twelve who were present at the General Conference of 1887 remained in Kirtland and on April 21, 1887, issued an "Epistle" which discussed the duties of branch and district presidents and other matters. The Quorum revised this "Epistle" in 1888 and then asked the General Conference to endorse it. Action was postponed until 1889 and then until 1890. Under these circumstances the Quorum of Twelve asked the President of the Church to seek divine guidance, and in response to their prayers the following revelation was received through President Joseph Smith. It is dated April 8, 1890, at Lamoni, Iowa, and is addressed to "The First Presidency and Traveling High Council" (the Council of Twelve).

Unto my servants, the First Presidency and the traveling High Council of my church; thus saith the Spirit:

1 a. The epistle is to be left without approval, or disapproval by the conference, as the judgment of the Quorum of the Twelve, until further experience shall have tested the matters therein stated.

b. In the meantime, branches and their officers, and districts and their officers are to be considered as provided for by my law to carry on the work of the ministry in caring for the membership of the church, and to relieve the Twelve and Seventy from the vexation and anxiety of looking after local organizations when effected.

c. When branches and districts are organized, they should be so organized by direction of the conferences, or by the personal presence and direction of the Twelve, or some member of that quorum who may be in charge, if practicable;

d. or, if a branch, by the president of the district with the consent, knowledge, and direction of the missionary in charge, when circumstances prevent the missionary in charge being present.

2 a. A branch may be presided over by a high priest, an elder, priest, teacher, or deacon, chosen and sustained by the vote of the branch.

b. Districts may be presided over by a high priest, or an elder, who shall be received and sustained in his office by the vote of the district.

c. If a branch, or district be large, he who is chosen to preside should be an high priest, if there be one possessed of the spirit of wisdom to administer in the office of president;

d. or if an elder be chosen who may by experience be found qualified to preside, as soon as practicable thereafter he should be ordained an high priest by the spirit of wisdom and revelation in the one ordaining, and by direction of a high council, or General Conference, as required in the law.

3 a. There should be no conflict or jealousy of authority between the quorums of the church; all are necessary and equally honorable, each in its place.

b. The Twelve and Seventy are traveling ministers and preachers of the gospel, to persuade men to obey the truth;

c. the high priests and elders holding the same priesthood are the standing ministers of the church, having the watch-care of the membership and nurturing and sustaining them, under the direction and instruction of the Presidency and the Twelve.

d. The Seventy when traveling by the voice of the church, or sent by the Twelve to minister the word where the Twelve can not go, are in the powers of their ministration apostles —those sent—and in meetings where no organization exists should preside, if no member of the Twelve or Presidency be present.

4 a. In both branches and districts the presiding officers should be considered and respected in their offices;

b. nevertheless, the traveling presiding councils of the church being made by the law, their calling and the voice of the church the directing, regulating and advising authorities of the church, and representing it abroad, should when present in either district or branch be regarded and considered as the leading representative authorities of the church, and be respected as such, their counsel and advice be sought and respected when given;

c. and in cases of conflict, or extremity, their decision should be listened to and regarded, subject to the appeal and adjudication provided for in the law.

5 He that heareth him that is sent heareth the Lord who sent him, if he be called of God and be sent by the voice of the church.

6 In these matters there is no conflict in the law.

7 a. In matters of personal importance and conduct arising in branches or districts, the authorities of those branches and districts should be authorized and permitted to settle them;

b. the traveling councils taking cognizance of those only in which the law and usages of the church are involved, and the general interests of the church are concerned.

c. Where cases of difficulty are of long standing, the council may require local authorities to adjust them; and in case of failure to do so, may regulate them as required by their office and duty; and this that the work and church may not be put to shame and the preaching of the word be hindered.

8 That the traveling council of the Twelve may be better prepared to act as a quorum, my servant A. H. Smith may be chosen president of the Twelve, and any one of the council be chosen to act as its secretary, until the quorum be filled, or other instruction be given.

9 a. Those who were presented by the high priests for ordination to their number, if approved by the council of the high priests now present, and the conference, may be ordained;

b. and from their number there may be selected by a committee of conference composed of one of the First Presidency, the president of the Twelve and one other to be chosen by the Council of Twelve, the president of the high priests and one other to be chosen by that council of their number,

c. a sufficient number to fill the vacancies now existing in the high council, that the high council may be properly organized and prepared to hear matters of grave importance when presented to them.

d. And this committee shall make these selections according to the spirit of wisdom and revelation that shall be given unto them, to provide that such council may be convened at any General Conference when emergency may demand, by reason of their residing at or near to places where conferences may be held.

10 a. The presidents of Seventy are instructed to select from the several quorums of elders such as are qualified and in a condition to take upon them the office of Seventy, that they may be ordained unto the filling of the first quorum of Seventy.

b. In making these selections the presidents of Seventy should confer with the several quorums before so selecting, and be guided by wisdom and the spirit of revelation, choosing none but men of good repute.

SECTION 121

A series of inspired instructions were given to the General Conference of 1885 at Independence, Missouri, through President Joseph Smith III. Read paragraph 6 before studying the section as a whole.

1 a. At the April session of conference of 1885, during the consideration of the sustaining of the officers of the church made the special order for the 11th, when David H. Smith, second counselor to the President, was presented, the question was asked whether any communication had been received in regard to it.

b. The President of the church replied: "The voice of the Spirit is that David H. Smith be released. He is in mine hand."

2 a. When the Quorum of the Twelve were presented the question was again asked: Has any information been received concerning said quorum?

b. President Joseph Smith replied: "The voice of the Spirit is that E. C. Briggs be sustained for the present. J. W. Briggs and Z. H. Gurley are in your hands, to approve or disapprove as wisdom may direct. Be merciful, for to him that is merciful shall mercy be shown."

3 On the 14th of the month, the eighth day of the session, when the mission of Elder E. C. Briggs was being considered, the following instruction was presented as the will

of the Lord concerning the Chicago mission, over which some trouble had occurred:

4 a. "It is my will that my servants shall contend no longer one with another in regard to the Chicago Branch. Let the branch be instructed to report to the conference of my Saints of the district where the branch is located, the Northern Illinois District.

b. "My servants, the elders, when passing to and from, should labor in the city when time and opportunity permit, that my people there may be strengthened and encouraged.

c. "And this should be agreeable to the elders in charge of the branch and the district, who should ever be willing to aid such ministration; and this should be without jealousy on either part."

5 a. The following also received in 1885, is added by direction of the conference of 1894:

b. "My servants of the Seventy may select from their number seven; of which number those now being of the seven presidents of Seventy shall be a part; who shall form the presidency of seven presidents of Seventy as provided in my law."

6 a. The foregoing was accepted as proper instruction, and the conference acted upon it as such; but the word received was not presented to the quorums, nor acted upon by them as is the usual custom of the church in regard to revelations received for the guidance of the church.

b. It is given here as having been acquiesced in by all, in answer to prayer and decisive upon the matters referred to.

SECTION 122

During the General Conference of 1894 the First Presidency, the Quorum of Twelve, and the Quorum of High Priests held a joint meeting at which they discussed their respective callings and responsibilities. A report of this Council was submitted to the Conference, but since the Twelve felt that the report did not cover all the issues under consideration they adopted a resolution requesting President

Smith to "ask for further revelation in explanation of the authority and duties of the several quorums and their members, also for instruction providing for filling the vacancies in the leading quorums, including a designation of the Patriarch, if it shall be the pleasure of our heavenly Father to so enlighten us."

The revelation given to President Smith, April 15, 1894, at Lamoni, Iowa, in answer to the petitions of the Saints, was endorsed by the quorums and the Conference, but it was not until the General Conference of 1897 that its inclusion in the Doctrine and Covenants was authorized.

I was, on the fifteenth day of the fourth month, of the year 1894, in fasting and prayer before the Lord, and being commanded of the Spirit I arose from my praying and wrote:

Thus saith the Spirit unto the elders and the church:

1 a. My servants have been harsh one with another; and some have not been sufficiently willing to hear those whose duty it is to teach the revelations which my church has already received.

b. Until my people shall hear and heed those who are set in the church to teach the revelations there will be misunderstanding and confusion among the members.

2 a. The burden of the care of the church is laid on him who is called to preside over the high priesthood of the church, and on those who are called to be his counselors;

b. and they shall teach according to the spirit of wisdom and understanding, and as they shall be directed by revelation, from time to time.

3 a. It is the duty of the Twelve to preach the gospel, and administer in the ordinances thereof, as is directed in the Scriptures which ye have received.

b. They are called and set apart to this duty; and are to travel and preach, under the direction and counsel of the Presidency.

4 a. It is not yet expedient in me that the Quorum of the Presidency, and the Quorum of the Twelve apostles shall be

filled, for reasons which will be seen and known unto you in due time.

b. My servant David H. Smith is yet in my hand and I will do my will in the time for its accomplishment. Be not troubled or fearful in this matter for it shall be well for my work in the end.

5 a. When I said unto mine apostles, "The Twelve will take measures in connection with the bishop, to execute the law of tithing; and let them before God see to it, that the temporal means so obtained is truly used for the purposes of the church, and not as a weapon of power in the hands of one man for the oppression of others, or for purposes of self-aggrandizement by anyone, be he whomsoever he may be";

b. the one whom I had called to preside over the church, had not yet approved himself unto the scattered flock; and I gave this command unto the quorum next in authority in spiritual things that the scattered ones, and those who had been made to suffer might have assurance that I would not suffer that he whom I had called should betray the confidence of the faithful, nor squander the moneys of the treasury for the purposes of self.

c. And for the reason that the law of tithing was but little understood, and would not be observed, unless it should be taught, and enforced by the precepts of the chief missionaries of the church.

d. It was not then intended, nor is it now, to burden them with the duty of looking after the disbursements of the moneys in the treasury, or the management of the properties of the church;

e. except as it may be at times necessary to do so in council with the Presidency, the high council in case of exigency, the Bishopric, bishops, or bishop's agents abroad, or the conferences; and in accordance with the agreement hitherto made.

f. Whatever burden the quorum may have felt rested upon them in this regard, they are now absolved from, the end designed by it having been reached;

g. except that should it become apparent to the quorum that there was abuse in the administration of the temporal affairs of the church, they shall at once make such inquiry and examination through the proper officers of the church as will correct the evil and save the church from injury.

6 a. And further the Spirit saith unto you, that "with the Lord one day is as a thousand years, and a thousand years as a day";

b. therefore, the law given to the church in section forty-two, over the meaning of some parts of which there has been so much controversy, is as if it were given today;

c. and the bishop and his counselors, and the high council, and the bishop and his council, and the storehouse and the temple and the salvation of my people, are the same to me now that they were in that day when I gave the revelation;

d. nevertheless, that portion of that commandment which made it the duty of the high council to assist in looking after the poor and needy of the church, was not intended to put the high council over the bishop in the administration of the affairs of his office and calling,

e. except as they might do so in an advisory manner, and in such way that no one of the poor and the needy should be neglected;

f. nor was it designed that the high council should dictate in the matter of purchasing lands, building houses of worship, building up the New Jerusalem, and the gathering of the people,

g. these last named being within the province of the Presidency, the Twelve as a quorum, the councils or other officers of the branches or stakes where houses of worship are to be built, the conferences and the general assembly of the church, and the direction of the Lord by revelation.

h. The high council could not in justice dictate to the Bishop in direction in any of these matters and then try and condemn and punish him if he did not obey.

7 a. The work now lying before the missionary quorums of the church is of such increased magnitude and importance —the field so white unto the harvest, and the need for laborers so great—that the Twelve and the Seventy under their direction, together with such high priests and elders as can travel and preach as missionaries, shall be free to wait upon their ministry in gospel work,

b. leaving the branches and districts where organization

is effected to the care and administration of the standing ministers, high priests, elders, priests, teachers, and deacons, so far as possible;

c. thus freeing these spiritual authorities and leaving them at liberty to push the preaching of the word into the new fields now widening before them;

d. in which work, if they will but now take counsel, saith the Spirit, they shall feel a peace and vigor of mind surpassing what they have enjoyed in the past.

8 a. That part of the law which says: "It is the duty of the Twelve, also, to ordain and set in order all the other officers of the church," is to be understood by the revelation which went before and in accordance with which it was written; and which follows after it in the book;

b. and when those officers are ordained and set in their order, in the church, they should be left to administer in the things unto which they were ordained, having charge of the affairs over which they are called and set apart to preside;

c. the Twelve and Seventy administering as those prosecuting the work of preaching with the warning voice, baptizing, organizing and setting in order, then pushing their ministry into other fields until the world is warned.

d. It is the will of God that they do this; yea, verily, thus saith the Spirit, If they will now enter upon this work, leaving the burden of care in organized districts, or conferences to the standing ministry, under the Presidency of the church;

e. observing the law already given to ordain and set high priests or elders to preside in large branches and in districts, and also evangelical ministers, then will those officers set in the church be useful and he who gave the law be honored;

f. the differences between the quorums be healed, confidence be restored and good will and peace come to the people as a cherishing fountain.

9 a. The quorums in respect to authority are designed to take precedence in office as follows: The Presidency, the Twelve, the Seventy in all meetings and gatherings of the membership, where no previous organization has been effected.

b. Where organization has been arranged and officers have been ordained and set in order; the standing ministry in their order; high priests, elders, priests, teachers, and deacons;

c. the parallels are: in the Presidency, the President and his counselors; in the second presidency, the Twelve; in the missionary work, first the Twelve, second, the Seventy; in the standing ministry, the Presidency, second, the high priests; third, the elders, then priests, teachers, and deacons in their order.

10 a. Should the church fall into disorder, or any portion of it, it is the duty of the several quorums of the church, or any one of them to take measures to correct such disorder; through the advice and direction of the Presidency, the Twelve, the Seventy, or a council of high priests, in case of emergency;

b. and in case the Presidency is in transgression, the Bishop and his council of high priests, as provided in the law; and the Presidency and high council if the Bishop, or his counselors, if high priests, are in transgression.

c. The Scriptures and the church articles and covenants, with the rules adopted by the church, shall govern in procedure.

11 The Spirit saith further: That it is wisdom that the Presidency and Twelve in council together make such appointments as may be necessary to provide for the fields not named in the appointments made by the Presidency and recommended to the Twelve, as may be agreed by them.

12 a. The Spirit saith further: That Lamoni, Iowa, having been made by the agreement of the church under the law of the land the principal place of business of the church, it is wise and expedient that it should be considered and declared by the conference to be the seat of the Presidency of the church, and in due time be made a stake.

b. In the meantime the district may be left to the care of its district organization subject to the direction of the Presidency, no one of the missionary force being appointed to the charge thereof for the conference year, or longer if it shall be found advisable.

13 a. The Spirit saith further: The Twelve should remain at Lamoni, and continue in council with the Presidency and the Bishop, and his counselors if practicable, a sufficient time after the adjournment of conference to counsel together, and

agree on the things of the law and the general affairs of the church,

b. so that when the traveling council shall separate for their several fields, there may be no longer reason for distrust, suspicion, or dissension;

c. and if these officers will so counsel together in the spirit of moderation and mutual forbearance and concession, my law will be more perfectly understood by them and a unity of sentiment and purpose will be reached by them.

d. It is the will of your Lord and your God that this should be done. It should have been done before, but the adversary hath hindered, desiring to prevent the success of my work in the earth.

14 For the same reasons in me that it is not expedient to fill the quorums of the First Presidency and the Twelve, who are apostles and high priests, it is not expedient that a patriarch for the church should be indicated and appointed.

15 My servant Thomas W. Smith is in my hand; and his bishopric shall be continued for a season; if he fully recover he will enter again into the work; if I take him unto myself, another will be appointed in his stead when the quorum is filled.

16 a. And now I say unto you mine elders, apostles and high priests of my church, Continue ye in the ministry unto which you have been called; and if ye can not fully agree on all the points of the law, be patient and be not contentious; so far as you can agree work together without heat, confusion, or malice.

b. Ye are equal in worth of position and place in the work of the church; and if in honor ye shall prefer one another, ye will not strive for precedence or place in duty or privilege, and shall be blessed of me.

17 a. Yea, verily, thus saith the Lord, unto the elders of the church: Continue in steadfastness and faith.

b. Let nothing separate you from each other and the work whereunto you have been called; and I will be with you by my Spirit and presence of power unto the end. Amen.

JOSEPH SMITH

SECTION 123
(See Appendix E, page 414)

SECTION 124

Revelation given through Joseph Smith III at Lamoni, Iowa, April 1897. The Twelve had renewed their request of 1894 for direction concerning the calling and responsibilities of patriarch-evangelists. They and the church in general were also anxious that the presiding quorums should be more nearly filled. Temporary completion of the First Presidency and more permanent completion of the Quorum of Twelve were authorized in this revelation.

This was the first time that the Twelve had been filled since the Reorganization.

By the grace of God and the Lord Jesus Christ I am permitted to write unto you and the church, in answer to prayer. On the night of the 7th of April in the year of our Lord 1897, and on the morning of the 8th, I was in the Spirit and was commanded to write, and say unto the elders and the church:

1 Thus saith the Spirit of your Lord and Savior Jesus Christ: Your fasting and your prayers are accepted and have prevailed.

2 a. Separate and set apart my servant Alexander Hale Smith to be a counselor to my servant, the President of the church, his brother; and to be patriarch to the church, and an evangelical minister to the whole church.

b. Also, appoint my servant E. L. Kelley, Bishop of the church, to act as counselor to the President of the church, for the conference year, or until one shall be chosen to succeed my servant W. W. Blair, whom I have taken unto myself;

c. he to sit in council with his brethren of the Presidency

and act with and for them and the church; though he shall still be and act in the office of his calling of Bishop of the church with his brethren of the Bishopric.

3 The Quorum of Twelve, my servants, may choose and appoint one of their number to take the place of my servant Alexander H. Smith, and if they shall choose William H. Kelley, from among them for this place it will be pleasing unto me; nevertheless, if directed by the spirit of revelation and wisdom they may choose another.

4 a. And, that the quorum may be filled and be prepared to stand as a unit in the councils of the church, in equality with the Presidency and the Seventy, choose and set apart to act as apostles in the Quorum of Twelve, my servants I. N. White, J. W. Wight, and R. C. Evans, for they are called unto this office and calling.

b. And, if these will accept this appointment and remain humble, faithful, and diligent, they shall with their brethren be greatly blessed in ministering the word and bringing souls unto me. Let the quorum be not doubting but believing and I, the Lord, will bless them.

5 a. My servants, the presidents of the Seventy, may with the consent and approval of their brethren of the Seventy sitting in council together, select from their brethren one to take the place of my servant I. N. White, if he accept the appointment to the Quorum of Twelve, and his choosing be approved by the church;

b. and in like manner they may fill any other vacancy that has occurred or may occur; such selection and appointment to be made in the spirit of prayer and supplication and wisdom, and to be approved by the church.

6 a. It is according to the vision that the seven presidents of the Seventy shall preside over the whole number of the Seventy when assembled in council together;

b. the senior, or chosen president of the seven presidents, shall preside over the six other presidents in their councils as presidents of the Seventy;

c. and when either quorum is sitting in council, as a quorum, then its chosen president shall preside over its sittings.

d. When any quorum of the Seventy may be sitting, any one, or all of the seven presidents, may at their request, or by invitation of such quorum, be present and take part in the deliberations of such council, but the president of such quorum only shall preside, except by consent of the quorum obtained by vote properly taken.

7 a. The sons of my servant the President of the church, the sons of my servant William W. Blair, whom I have taken to myself, the sons of my servant the Bishop of the church, and the sons of my servants of the leading quorums of the church are admonished,

b. that upon their fathers is laid a great and onerous burden, and they are called to engage in a great work, which shall bring them honor and glory, or shame, contempt and final great loss and destruction;

c. as they shall in uprightness, faithfulness and diligence discharge their duties acceptably to God, or shall in carelessness, slothfulness, or wickedness fail in their calling and ministry therein;

d. and to their sons shall come honor, or shame, as they shall approve, or disapprove themselves to God.

e. These sons of my servants are called, and if faithful shall in time be chosen to places whence their fathers shall fall, or fail, or be removed by honorable release before the Lord and the church.

8 a. The Spirit saith further unto the church, Be of good cheer.

b. It has pleased the Father to accept many of the sacrifices of his people; and, notwithstanding some have fallen while engaged in their work; some have been tried, and are still tried; some have been and are afflicted, yet the Lord has seen the affliction and trial and will accept and bless, and no man shall lose his reward.

––––––––––

Brethren of the ministry and members of the church; my soul has been cheered, my spirit and body have been strengthened and my heart made exceeding glad by the blessed and holy influence of the Spirit which was with me, and still is with me as I write; causing me to give praise, honor and glory to God and the Lamb, to whom honor and glory belong, and with whom are might, power, and dominion evermore. Amen.

Your servant for the Christ's sake.

JOSEPH SMITH
President of the Church

LAMONI, IOWA, April 9, 1897

SECTION 125

Revelation given through Joseph Smith III, April 15, 1901, at Independence, Missouri. This revelation was unusual in that—for the first time—the inspired message was presented to the General Conference without prior consideration by the quorums. Joseph explained that he was "bidden" to follow this procedure. The Conference referred the document to the quorums. After the quorums had reported favorably, it was approved by the body. At the same time it was ordered to be included in the Doctrine and Covenants.

STATEMENT AND REVELATION

Before entering further upon the business, I have something to present. I spent a sleepless night. After retiring to my rest, weary, as you must know, I engaged in a season of prayer, quietly, as I had been doing all day; and I suddenly found myself very wide awake; and from that on I was in the Spirit, the spirit of inspiration burning in my breast; and by it I was bidden to come to the house of assembly and tell what was given to me of light and instruction. I trust that it shall be so to you.

VACANCY IN THE PRESIDENCY

1 The successor of my servant W. W. Blair is with the body, but the conditions are not ripe for this addition to the presidency; but it shall be made in due time. In the meantime, let the presidency continue as at present constituted.

VACANCY IN THE TWELVE

2 To fill this vacancy I was instructed to present the name
of "my servant Peter Andersen."

EVANGELICAL MINISTERS

3 a. The patriarch is an evangelical minister. The duties
of this office are to be an evangelical minister; to preach,
teach, expound, exhort, to be a revivalist, and to visit
branches and districts as wisdom may direct, invitation, request, or the Spirit of God determine and require;

b. to comfort the Saints; to be a father to the church; to
give counsel and advice to individuals who may seek for such;
to lay on hands for the conferment of spiritual blessing, and
if so led, to point out the lineage of the one who is blessed.

4 a. He is to be free from responsibility—ministerial—as a
traveling minister, and from the care of the local branch or
church and district affairs.

b. When traveling and preaching, holding revival meetings,
he is to labor in connection with the branch and district officers, not subject to the ministerial control of the missionary
in charge, except he should transcend his bounds and teach
false doctrine or be found in transgression.

c. He is not to meddle with branch affairs or district
affairs.

d. He is not to listen to complaints made by individuals
to him, but if persons insist upon presenting their troubles,
he is to request them and require them to make them in
writing, signing the name, giving time, place, and character
of the trouble, with the witnesses, which it will be his duty
to present to the branch or district officers, as the case may
require.

e. He is not to be put in charge of either branch or district.
These are the privileges which attach to the office of patriarch
and evangelical minister.

5 a. The Presiding Patriarch is to be considered the first,
and when patriarchs meet in council, is to preside.

b. Besides these duties, the patriarch may meet with
quorums in their quorum meetings, where he may be asked
for counsel, but will not have either voice or vote, except by
courtesy, having no direct control of quorums.

6 a. Other evangelical ministers beside the Presiding Patriarch have similar duties in the districts where they are appointed.

b. Revelations have been given, as my people know, that these men should receive ordination, but hitherto those upon whom this burden has lain have neglected, for the reason that they did not understand the duties and prerogatives that attach to the office. Let my servants take heed and hesitate no longer.

RULES OF REPRESENTATION

7 a. My servant was directed to present to the church rules of representation, and he so stated to the body at different times that he was so led; but the conferences of my people saw proper to change these articles and rules of representation, and propositions are pending that they be still further changed.

b. The direction of the Spirit is that they be left as they now are until such time as the increased numbers of the members of the church shall require either an enlargement of the number entitled to delegate, or that there may be a closer line drawn as to the number of delegates which the church shall require to meet.

8 The word *elders* used in the law signifies those holding the Melchisedec priesthood only; all classes and orders of this priesthood are characterized by the word *elder*.

9 The only qualification for delegates chosen by the branches or districts should be membership and good standing, it being given by the Spirit that those other than the eldership should be represented in this way.

STAKES

10 a. My people are directed to establish two stakes; one at Independence, one at Lamoni, Iowa, organizing them after the pattern which is found in the law; a presiding high priest with counselors, a high council, and a bishop and his counselors.

b. These stakes shall be made to comprise the boundaries

of the districts as they now stand, the center at the towns and places named;

c. and the majority of the councils that should be chosen should be residents of the places named, in order that there may ever be a sufficient body to transact the business required.

TRACTS

11 a. It is the duty of the church to provide tracts in the Scandinavian, German, Chinese, Japanese, and Portuguese languages, and others, as the missions may require;

b. these tracts to be written by those in the ministry and those of the brothers who are not of the ministry who have a talent for writing, and to be submitted to the Presidency before being published.

c. They should be short, clearly stated, and a sufficient number should be printed to furnish the traveling ministry with the quantities desirable for them to distribute.

FOREIGN MISSIONS

12 a. The missions abroad other than those in the land of Joseph which were opened officially during the lifetime of the martyrs shall be considered as having been opened unto us, whether they were at once undertaken and prosecuted during the lifetime of the martyrs, or whether subsequent to their death they were prosecuted in righteousness—wherever they were sent.

b. Other missions not thus opened, it will be requisite that the Twelve shall either go, or in the exercise of their missionary authority send, as provided in the law, of the Seventy.

13 a. For prosecuting the work in two of these missions, this is offered and directed:

b. Send the Bishop to England with my servant Gomer T. Griffiths, to aid in arranging the affairs of the church there, organizing the ministry locally and determining what help in the missionary field may be required from America.

c. Authorize the selection and the ordination of a high priest to officiate in the office of bishop in England, that it may be accomplished as soon as practicable and without fail, in answer to the request made by my servants in that land.

d. Authorize the patriarch as one of the Presidency to visit Australia and the islands of the sea, the Society Islands, authorizing him to assist the authorities there in arranging their missionary labor by his advice,

e. and also selecting and ordaining a high priest to act in the office of bishop, carrying with him the authority of the conference.

14 a. Branches and districts are to be conducted according to the rules given in the law as directed in a former revelation: They shall take the things which have been given unto them as my law to the church to be my law to govern my church.

b. And these affairs are not to be conducted by manifestations of the Spirit unless these directions and manifestations come through the regularly authorized officers of branch or district.

c. If my people will respect the officers whom I have called and set in the church, I will respect these officers; and if they do not, they can not expect the riches of gifts and the blessings of direction.

15 a. Prophesying over them that are sick in administering to them has been a fruitful source of trouble among my people.

b. They must observe that this they are not required to do except there be a direct manifestation of the Spirit which may direct it.

c. Pray over the sick, anoint them with oil, as commanded in the law, and leave them in my hands, that the Spirit may deal with them according to my wisdom.

d. Many spiritual manifestations have been had. Some of these have been false, and under the operation of the law which I gave many, many years ago, those who make these false presentations are not to be feared among my people.

e. They are not justified in permitting their human sympathies to overcome that which has been written in my Scriptures. The spirit of the prophets is subject to the prophets.

16 a. The college debt should be paid, the ministers going out from the conferences held by the elders of my church are not expected or authorized to throw obstacles in the way of the accomplishment of that which has been intrusted to the Bishopric to pay this great debt.

b. Their right to free speech, their right to liberty of conscience, does not permit them as individuals to frustrate the commands of the body in conference assembly.

c. They are sent out as ministers to preach the gospel, and their voices if opposed to what may be presented to the conference should be heard in the conferences, and not in the mission fields, to prevent the accomplishment of the object with which the officers of the church have been intrusted.

SECTION 126

This section is an account of an open vision received by President Joseph Smith at Lamoni, April 16, 1902. It was accepted by the quorums and the General Conference as inspired guidance to meet the existing needs of the church.

To the Officers and Members of the Conference:

1 On the night of April 16 I made the condition of the church a subject of prayer, intensely desirous of receiving light and information in relation thereto and my duty. I awoke at the hour of three and had in presentation the following vision:

2 a. I saw the assembly of the Saints and the general authorities, the latter being arranged upon a platform with the seats arranged in lines, each line from the front of the platform slightly raised to the rear.

b. On that platform I saw the quorum of the Presidency, the Bishopric, the Twelve, and a line above the Twelve on the seat behind them, a number of the brethren, including four of the present members of the Twelve and the patriarchs now ordained and recognized in the church.

c. The Quorum of the Twelve was filled, and the places of the four whom I saw on the upper tier of seats were occupied by others known to the church.

3 I asked the question who these men occupying the upper row of seats were, and I was told that they were evangelical ministers, called to minister in spiritual blessings to the church and to preach the gospel undeterred by the burden of the care and anxiety of presiding over missions and districts.

4 I saw in the Presidency two known to the church, but who have not hitherto been connected with the Presidency.

5 a. I saw the Bishopric as at present constituted, with the attendant bishops upon either side. I asked what was the meaning of this.

b. I was told that the Bishop should not be burdened with the spiritual care of the church except as such might be brought before him in pursuance of the law which provided for the bishop's court.

6 I then asked what was meant by the choosing of members for the presidency so young in years. I was informed that it was for the purpose that before the Presidency should be invaded by death these younger men should be prepared by association to be of assistance to whosoever should be chosen as the President upon the emergency which should occur.

7 a. The names of those of the present Quorum of Twelve whom I saw upon the upper tier of seats were James Caffall, John H. Lake, Edmund C. Briggs, and Joseph R. Lambert. These were sitting with the other evangelical ministers.

b. Those whom I saw sitting with the Quorum of the Twelve were Frederick A. Smith, Francis M. Sheehy, Ulysses W. Greene, Cornelius A. Butterworth, and John W. Rushton.

8 Sitting with the Presidency were Frederick M. Smith and Richard C. Evans.

9 The assembly seemed to be large and orderly, with the different officers of the church in their quorums assembled in much the same order as observed at our annual conferences, but did not seem to be so large as at other times I had seen them.

10 a. In regard to the gathering and the work of the Bishopric in regard to the law of tithing and consecration, I made inquiry what should be the attitude of the church in regard thereto.

b. To this question I was answered, that the Book of Doctrine and Covenants as accepted by the church was to guide the advice and action of the Bishopric, taken as a whole, each revelation contained therein having its appropriate bearing upon each of the others and their relation thereto;

c. and unless the liberties of the people of the church should be in jeopardy, the application of the law as stated by the bishopric should be acceded to.

d. In case there should be a flagrant disregard of the rights of the people, the quorums of the church in joint council should be appealed to, and their action and determination should govern.

e. I inquired what quorums of the church were meant, and I was answered, the three quorums the decisions of which are provided for in the law—the Presidency, the Twelve, and the Seventy.

11 In case of transgression in his office the Bishop should be called in question before the council which is provided for in the law, to which court all the general officers of the church are to be subject.

12 After much thought and pondering upon what I had seen as related above, together with the information contained in the answers to my inquiries, I did not see my way clear to present the matters therein contained in yesterday's session until the church had by its votes sustained the officers of the quorums referred to.

13 It will be seen that there is an apparent invasion of the rule which has been supposed to govern the selection of evangelical ministers, but for this I am not responsible; and the whole matter is hereby submitted for the approval or disapproval of the church.

                                                JOSEPH SMITH

LAMONI, IOWA, April 18, 1902

SECTION 127

In the first decade of the twentieth century, the establishment of the Independence and Lamoni stakes (1901) and the kingdom concern of President Frederick M. Smith combined with other favorable factors to quicken church-wide interest in the Gathering. The building of Zionic institutions is vital to any significant gathering. By 1906 Graceland College had weathered her first ten difficult years, the Saints' Home was giving good ministry, and leading women were showing interest in a children's home.

At the pre-Conference sessions of April 1906, the First Presidency recommended to the Quorum of Twelve that a sanitarium be established with Dr. Joseph Luff of that quorum as its presiding officer. The Twelve favored the basic proposal, but expressed concern regarding the assignment of an apostle to the responsibilities proposed for Dr. Luff. The Quorum stated that they would "gladly engage in an effort to learn the Master's will" in this matter. The prayerful inquiries resulting from this action prepared the way for the following revelation given through President Joseph Smith. It was presented to the General Conference, April 14, 1906, at Independence, Missouri, and accepted by unanimous vote.

Thus saith the Spirit unto the Church:

1 a. It is the will of the Lord that a sanitarium, a place of refuge and help for the sick and afflicted, be established by the church, at Independence, Missouri, as my servant Joseph Smith has already stated to you.

b. This should be done as soon as it is found to be practicable, and without unnecessary delay.

c. The Presiding Bishop and his counselors and the Bishopric of the Independence Stake should take counsel together in locating and establishing this sanitarium.

2 a. It is also expedient that these should be assisted by the advice and counsel of one of my servants who is acquainted with the laws of health and the practice of medicine, and who may have charge when the institution is established.

b. It is in accordance with the instruction given to my servant Joseph Smith that my servant Joseph Luff, who has been giving his attention to the study of medicine and has been preparing himself for usefulness in this direction, be associated with this sanitarium as a medical director and physician to the church and be put in charge,

c. that he may be an assistant to those who seek the aid of this institution of the church, in his spiritual office and his calling as a physician,

d. with those who from time to time may be called to administer in laying hands upon the afflicted and sick, where they may be removed from the influences and environments unfavorable to the exercise of proper faith unto the healing of the sick.

e. And this my servant Joseph Luff may do and retain and exercise his apostleship.

3 There should also be a home for children established, and the efforts of the Daughters of Zion should be approved and carried unto completion as soon as is consistent with the necessary demands of the work of the church in other directions.

4 a. In the establishment of the sanitarium and the home for children, debt should not be contracted nor too large nor expensive buildings be built at the outset.

b. Those to whom this work is assigned should exercise the necessary degree of wisdom that the work be effectual for the intent and purposes designed.

5 a. It is necessary that some one or more be sent to the South Sea Islands. The heaving of the sea beyond its bounds has been trying to the faith of many of the Saints in that far-off region.

b. They should be visited and comforted and encouraged.

c. Some one of experience and knowledge of the situation should be sent, accompanied by another, who should be prepared to make a stay of years, if necessary, in the mission to those islands.

d. My servant Joseph F. Burton, though aged, will be an efficient officer and representative of the faith, and, choosing some one to go with him, may be intrusted with this difficult mission.

6 It is the will of the Lord that the mission to Utah and the west should be continued, and suitable representatives of the church be sent and maintained there under the conditions prevailing at the present time. It is essential that the church have proper representatives there.

7 a. As the Saints have heretofore been instructed in reference to the gathering, they are now again admonished that the gathering must not be in haste, nor without due preparation,

b. and must be done in accordance with the revelation given to the church upon Fishing River and in accordance with the counsel and advice of the elders of the church whose duty it has been made to counsel and advise the Saints.

c. The spirit of speculation, the exhibition of greed for gain is unseemly in the Saints and officers of the church, and should be avoided. It has the appearance of evil.

d. Heed should be paid to the admonitions of those who from time to time preach and write upon the gathering to remove the principle of selfishness from the hearts of the Saints and especially from those upon whom rests the burden of the church and its ministrations abroad.

8 a. Inasmuch as misunderstanding has occurred in regard to the meaning of a revelation hitherto given through my servant Joseph Smith in regard to who should be called to preside in case my servant should be taken away or fall by transgression,

b. it is now declared that in case of the removal of my servant now presiding over the church by death or transgression, my servant Frederick M. Smith, if he remain faithful and steadfast, should be chosen, in accordance with the revelations which have been hitherto given to the church concerning the priesthood.

c. Should my servant Frederick M. Smith prove unstable and unfaithful, another may be chosen, according to the law already given.

INDEPENDENCE, MISSOURI, April 14, 1906

SECTION 128

At the annual Conference of 1909, Presiding Bishop E. L. Kelley requested that a meeting of the eldership be called to consider organizations and procedures in connection with the Gathering and the care of the poor. At the meeting called in this connection the elders asked the First Presidency for instruction. At a subsequent meeting President Smith asked for the support and prayers of the ministry as he

*sought divine guidance, and accordingly April 18 was ob-
served by the eldership as a day of fasting and prayer for
such guidance.*

*The following revelation through President Joseph Smith
was presented to the elders April 19, 1909, and by them
referred to the quorums. After receiving their approval, the
elders adopted a resolution "that the document be accepted
as a whole," and their action was reported to the Conference. The revelation is dated April 18, 1909, at Lamoni,
Iowa. It was accepted by the Conference and ordered included in the Doctrine and Covenants.*

To the Eldership; Brethren: So far as the burden of the
conference and its peculiar conditions have enabled me to do
I have steadfastly presented the matter stated by the Bishop
for our consideration to the Lord for instruction. Whether
that which has come to me will bring relief to the situation,
I know not; but such as it is, I hereby present it.

1 a. The conditions surrounding the work, the increase of
the membership of the church, the increasing desire for
gathering together, and the necessity existing for the obtaining places for settlement in the regions round about,

b. under the existing laws of the United States, and especially the state of Missouri, require that the Bishopric be
authorized to take such measures as will bring to pass the
organization of those who are desirous and willing to form
parts in colonization under terms of association in different
localities

c. where settlements may be made and may lawfully secure
and hold property for the benefit of themselves and their
fellow church members and the whole body of the church
when organized.

2 a. The work to be done belongs to those who are by
command of God made the custodians of the properties of
the church;

b. and these by their appointment are empowered to prosecute the work of caring for and using such properties as are
confided to their care to accomplish the end designed.

3 a. The Bishop and his counselors, together with the other bishops of the church, and such other officers as the Bishop may call together, with whom he may confer in council, are authorized to devise the methods of procedure;

b. and they will be guided by the spirit of wisdom and revelation to do the work intrusted to their care.

4 a. Counsel has already been given to those gathering into the regions round about to consult with the elders and the bishops before removing into those regions,

b. that such removal may be accomplished through the having of all things prepared before them who seek to remove and become resident in the regions round about.

5 It is well to understand that the term *regions round about* must mean more than a small area of country round about the central spot, and that the necessity of the great majority of the church in gathering together can only be provided for by settling carefully together as many in one region as may be practicable and profitable and in accordance with the feelings of the people under the laws existing in the places where such settlements are to be made.

6 a. The great variety of callings, avocations, and professions will present difficulties precluding the practicability of all settling and living in near proximity to each other.

b. It is therefore within the province of those upon whom the burden of organization may rest to provide for other organizations or associations than those simply pastoral or agricultural.

c. Under this head there may be placed industrial associations of such sorts as the varied qualifications existing among workmen may demand.

7 a. It has been prophesied that the Gentiles shall assist in rebuilding the waste places of Zion.

b. This can not refer to the inhabitants of Zion who are the pure in heart, but must refer to the places which have been occupied or which it may be contemplated to occupy in the regions round about.

c. The Saints can not occupy in any place on the land of Zion which is not under the domination of civil law, and as citizens of the state, holding their liberties under the law, there must be a proper recognition and observance of these laws.

d. The Lord has said that this condition of obedience to law must continue until he comes whose right it is to come and assumes to reign over his people.

e. Under the provisions of the laws these organizations or associations must be instituted and carried to completion if they shall be of benefit to those who shall be engaged in them.

8 a. The Spirit saith further: That these organizations contemplated in the law may be effected and the benefits to be derived therefrom be enjoyed by the Saints, in such enjoyment they can not withdraw themselves so completely from a qualified dependence upon their Gentile neighbors surrounding them as to be entirely free from intercommunication with them;

b. yet it is incumbent upon the Saints while reaping the benefits of these organizations to so conduct themselves in the carrying into operation the details of their organizations as to be in the world but not of it,

c. living and acting honestly and honorably before God and in the sight of all men, using the things of this world in the manner designed of God, that the places where they occupy may shine as Zion, the redeemed of the Lord.

9 The Bishop should be directed and authorized to proceed as soon as it shall be found practicable by consultation with the general authorities of the church who are made the proper counselors in spiritual and temporal things to carry out the provisions of the law of organization which are by the law made the duty of the Bishop.

JOSEPH SMITH

LAMONI, IOWA, April 18, 1909

SECTION 129

The General Conference of 1909 observed Thursday, April 15, as a day of fasting and prayer for divine direction. The following revelation was given through the prophet Joseph Smith III at Lamoni, Iowa, and dated April 18, 1909. It was endorsed by the Conference, and provision was made for its inclusion in the Doctrine and Covenants.

To the Church: After constant meditation and prayer, both before and after coming to conference and during the sessions, so far as the peculiar conditions obtaining in our sittings had permitted, I was in the Spirit during the nights of the 15th and 16th of the month and the day passing between at such times during the calm that occasionally ensued and the quiet of the night when the burden of my care forbade sleep. My dreams also have been enlightening and encouraging.

1 a. The voice of the Spirit to me is: Under conditions which have occurred it is no longer wise that my servant R. C. Evans be continued as counselor in the Presidency;

b. therefore it is expedient that he be released from this responsibility and another be chosen to the office. He has been earnest and faithful in service and his reward is sure.

2 a. My servant Joseph Luff can not fulfill the duties of a member of the Quorum of Twelve in actively looking after and caring for the missionary work in the field and discharge the duties of his calling as a physician ministering to the many seeking his advice and aid with safety to himself and others.

b. It is wise therefore that the church release him from the responsibilities of the active apostleship as a member of the quorum, that he may act unreservedly in his calling.

c. Another may be chosen to the office in the quorum. He has been faithful, and his record and reward are in my hand.

3 a. That the historian of the church, my servant Heman C. Smith, may more freely and efficiently pursue his duties and privileges as historian, the church may release him from the burden attendant upon him as an apostle in the quorum and choose another to occupy therein.

b. He has been long in the service, has done his duties well in the spirit of self-sacrifice, and his reward is with me. He will be blessed in diligent service in his calling as historian when relieved of the double responsibility.

4 These my servants who are relieved from their responsibilities of the quorum work have wrought well in their service with their fellow-servants, and must retain their right to labor in the ministry, holding the high priesthood and entitled to all that appertains to that calling when need requires or wisdom directs.

5 The Spirit saith further to me: To fill the vacancy caused by the releasing of Counselor R. C. Evans, present the name of my servant Elbert A. Smith, the son of my servant David H. Smith, who was taken and who awaits his reward, to be chosen, appointed, and ordained as counselor to my servant Joseph Smith and to be one of the Presidency.

6 a. The Spirit saith further: In order that the places of those taken from the Twelve may be supplied and the quorum filled that it may act as a whole, my servants J. F. Curtis and Robert C. Russell may be chosen and set apart to the office of apostles and be enrolled and sustained in the quorum.

b. Other servants there are who will be called and appointed ere long, but not now.

7 a. Those who are holding the office of patriarchs are to be enrolled with the high priests, the same as the bishops, who are acting in their office by virtue of their being high priests.

b. These men in their office are an order in the priesthood, the same as the high councils of the church and the stakes and as the bishops who hold as high priests, as the quorum of the twelve, and as the presidency are but orders in the priesthood, there being but two priesthoods; and these are orders in the Melchisedec priesthood.

c. There is no difference in the priesthood, though there may be and is in the office in which the several orders may occupy and act.

8 a. The Spirit saith further: The attention of the church is called to the consideration of the revelation, given in an-

swer to earnest supplication, with regard to temporal things.

b. The word has been already given in agreement with revelations long since delivered to the church, that the temporalities of the church were to be under the charge and care of the Bishopric, men holding the office of bishop under a presiding head acting for the church in the gathering, caring for, and disbursing the contributions gathered from the Saints of moneys and properties under the terms of tithing, surplus, free-will offerings, and consecrations.

c. The word which has been given at a late period should not have been so soon forgotten and disregarded by the church or any of its members.

d. "I am God; I change not"; has been known to the church and the eldership since the coming of the angel with the message of restoration.

e. Under it the church has sought the Lord and received from time to time that which was deemed sufficient for the time to govern the church and its ministers, both of the spiritual and the temporal divisions of the work.

f. The church has been directed to accede to the rendition of the Bishopric with respect to the temporal law;

g. and until such heed is paid to the word which has been given, and which is in accordance with other revelations given to the church, which had been before given, the church can not receive and enjoy the blessings which have been looked for when Zion should be fully redeemed.

h. Therefore, hearken once again unto the voice of inspiration, in warning and instruction, and conform to that which is given and receive what is awaiting the upright and the pure in heart.

9 a. The Spirit saith further unto the church: The Lord is well pleased with the advancement which has been made in approaching unity during the conference year;

b. and though there may have been differences of opinion, these differences have been held in unity of purpose and desire for the good of my people, and will result in helping to bring to pass a unity of understanding.

c. So be ye encouraged and press on to the consummation designed of God for his people—unity, honor, sanctification, and glory. Amen.   JOSEPH SMITH

LAMONI, IOWA, April 18, 1909

SECTION 130

*Instruction given through President Joseph Smith III,
April 14, 1913, at Lamoni, Iowa. It was endorsed by the
quorums and the assembly as a revelation from God, and
the Conference authorized its inclusion in the Doctrine and
Covenants.*

*Elder Joseph R. Lambert had been acting as Presiding
Evangelist since the death of Elder Alexander H. Smith in
1909. There was widespread concern that a more permanent
successor should be selected. Bishop E. L. Kelley and Apostles W. H. Kelley, I. N. White, and J. W. Wight were also
finding the burdens of their several responsibilities arduous.
These, and other needs of the church, undoubtedly found
a prominent place in the petitions of the prophet and of the
Saints in general prior to the convening of the Conference
and while it was yet in session.*

1 In obedience to the spirit and design of the day of
fasting and prayer, I observed the day with the church. I
have hitherto made supplication to the God whom we serve
and renewed my supplication in the spirit of the desire of
the church, for instruction and light, and I am now prepared to lay before the church what has come to me as the
presiding officer, through whom the Master may speak to his
people.

2 a. Thus saith the voice of the Spirit: In order that the
Quorum of Twelve may be placed in better condition to carry
on the work of the ministry in various fields of occupation,
   b. it is expedient that Elders W. H. Kelley, I. N. White,
and J. W. Wight be released from the active duties of the
apostolic quorum, on account of increasing infirmities of age
and incapacity, caused by illness of body,
   c. and stand with their associates among the high priests
and patriarchs of the church for such special service as may
be open to them, according to wisdom and the call of the
Spirit.

3 a. It is also expedient that Elder Frederick A. Smith be
released from the quorum activities, that he may take the

place of his father, Elder Alexander H. Smith, as the Presiding Patriarch of the church.

b. According to the tradition of the elders he should be chosen and ordained to this office, thus releasing elder Joseph R. Lambert from the onerous duties in which he has faithfully served since the death of the Presiding Patriarch.

4 a. To fill the vacancies caused by the release of these elders from the apostolic quorum, Elders James E. Kelley, William M. Aylor, Paul M. Hanson, and James A. Gillen may be chosen and ordained as apostles to take with others of the quorum active oversight of the labors in the ministerial field.

b. These servants, so called and chosen, if faithful, will receive the blessings which those have enjoyed who have preceded them in the apostolic quorum,

c. and will be entitled to receive such ministration of the Spirit as will continue to qualify them for the discharge of the duties of the position whereunto they are called.

d. The Twelve in its reorganization for its work may choose its own officers (president and secretary) by nomination and vote.

5 a. The Spirit saith further: Elder E. A. Blakeslee is hereby called into the more active participation of the duties of the Bishopric than he has hitherto engaged in,

b. in order that he may give such assistance to the Bishop, E. L. Kelley, as is essential unto the success of the work intrusted to the Bishopric.

c. It is also expedient that he be ordained unto the office of Bishop, that he may serve as did his father, George A. Blakeslee, who has preceded him.

6 a. The Spirit saith further: That the Bishopric may be still further put in condition to perform the duties of the office of caring for the temporalities of the church, the imminent necessity of which appears clear to all,

b. the church should authorize the Presiding Bishop to make choice of some one who may be qualified to take active participation in the work of the Bishopric and become in due time a part thereof;

c. and this one so chosen should receive the support and sanction of the church until he shall have approved or disapproved himself as a servant of the Master, in the office whereunto he shall be called.

7 a. The Spirit saith further unto the church assembled and at large:

b. In order that the temporal affairs of the church may be successfully carried on and the accumulated debt of the church in its respective departments where debts have accumulated may be properly met and in due time discharged,

c. the church is instructed, both as members and as the body at large, to avoid the unnecessary building of houses of worship or places of entertainment or otherwise expending the tithes and offerings of the church in that which may not be essential unto the continued onward progress of the general work;

d. and both in private and in public expenditure carry into active exercise the principle of sacrifice and repression of unnecessary wants;

e. and thus permit the accumulation of tithes and offerings in such amounts as may be needful to properly discharge the existing indebtedness of the church as a body. And the Spirit counseleth the church in this regard.

8 a. The Spirit saith further: That the elders and delegates assembled in business capacity are counseled to cease permitting the spirit of recrimination and accusation to find place in their discourse, either public or private,

b. as it tends to destroy confidence and create distrust not only in those present at councils where they occur, but to those to whom the knowledge of such a course of procedure comes by the voice of those who are present and witness what is said and done.

c. There should be harmony, and the Spirit enjoins it upon all, that the Master may be remembered as in meekness and due sobriety he carried on the great work to which he was called.

9 a. The Spirit saith further: That the church has been warned heretofore that the sons of the leading officers of the church are called and may be chosen to the respective offices to which the Spirit may direct,

b. and the church should be prepared when necessity arises to properly choose such officers as may be pointed out as those who should fill the positions to which they are respectively called.

c. There are others still in reserve who are fitted through the testimony that Jesus is the Christ and the doctrine is true to serve as those who are sent as apostles of peace, life, and salvation to those who are laboring in the valleys of humiliation and distress of spirit.

LAMONI, IOWA, April 14, 1913

SECTION 131

Revelation given through Joseph Smith III, prophet and seer to the church, April 14, 1914, at Independence, Missouri. It was addressed to the officers, delegates, and members of the church. It was first presented to the various quorums of the church and endorsed by them. Later it was placed before the assembly of delegates to the Conference and endorsed by standing vote. Provision was made for its incorporation in the Doctrine and Covenants. It was the last revelation given to the church through Joseph Smith III, who died December 10, 1914. He had served the church as President of the High Priesthood for more than fifty-four years.

1 a. In agreement with the notice for the general fast of the church to be observed on the first Sunday, being the fifth day of April, 1914, I, Joseph Smith, President of the church, in common with the custom of the brotherhood, observed the rule requiring the fast, and spent that day in meditation and prayer upon the work of God and our present duty in the affairs intrusted to our care.

b. Before the hour of breaking the fast came, I was blessed by the presence of the Holy Spirit resting upon me in quiet assurance and in power.

c. In the still small voice which giveth light and understanding to the intelligence of man, exalting the soul and sanctifying the spirit, there came unto me the directing voice of Him whose work we are engaged in.

2 a. Thus saith the Spirit unto the church: The time has now come when the necessities of the work require that the servants of the church, Bishops Edwin A. Blakeslee and Edmund L. Kelley, should be more closely associated in the carrying on of the financial affairs of the church and caring for the various organizations requiring the expenditure of moneys collected from the membership of the church and the care of the properties belonging to the church as an organization under the laws of the church and of the land.

b. To accomplish this object the servant of the church, Edwin A. Blakeslee, should make himself more thoroughly acquainted with the affairs in the office of the Bishopric, that he may be better prepared to advise, strengthen, and aid in controlling the affairs of the Bishopric to the successful accomplishment of the object in view when he was called and ordained to the Bishopric.

3 a. The Spirit saith further, that it is expedient that additional aid be given to the Bishopric in charge of the general affairs of the finances,

b. and to do this Richard C. Kelley, son of my servant Bishop Edmund L. Kelley, should be called and ordained to the office of an elder, that he may act with the Bishopric in case of necessities and to work in the office of the Bishop in looking after and caring for the affairs appertaining to that office;

c. and in due time, if he approve himself in this work, he should receive an ordination to the high priesthood which would authorize him to act fully as a part of the Bishopric.

4 a. The Spirit saith further, that the spirit of distrust and want of confidence in those who are called and ordained to act in the various responsible positions in the priesthood and in authority in the church is unbecoming those professing faith in God, Jesus Christ his Son, and the Holy Spirit of truth, and evinces a serious lack of that charity which Paul, an apostle of Christ, declared to be the quality of Christian virtue which thinketh no evil.

b. Those who go out from the assemblies and solemn conclaves of the church should exercise great care in their ministration abroad both to the branches where they may officiate and in their preaching the gospel to those outside, to avoid sowing seeds of distrust and suspicion either in public ministration or in private conversation.

c. The church has been admonished heretofore in this respect and the Spirit saith again, It is unbecoming to the character and calling of those who administer in the name of Jesus Christ the Lord.

5 In witness whereof I, Joseph Smith, president and servant of the church, hereto set my hand this fourteenth day of April, in the year of our Lord, 1914.

(Signed)   JOSEPH SMITH

SECTION 132

President Joseph Smith died at Independence, Missouri, December 10, 1914. His oldest living son, Frederick Madison Smith, had been designated as his successor and was accepted by the church in this capacity. He was set apart as President of the Church and the High Priesthood at the Stone Church in Independence on May 5, 1915.

The Conference of 1915 had given consideration to the honorable release of Presiding Bishop E. L. Kelley, but referred any necessary action to the Presidency and Council of Twelve. President F. M. Smith reported the situation to a council of the Presidency, Council of Twelve, and Presiding Bishopric. By action of this council the text of the revelation was taken from the body of President F. M. Smith's report and presented to the General Conference, where it was endorsed and approved for inclusion in the Doctrine and Covenants.

The matter of selecting one to succeed Bishop E. L. Kelley in the office of Presiding Bishop has received by me careful and prayerful consideration.

1 I am therefore now prepared to say that the voice of the Spirit to me is, that Bishop E. L. Kelley should be released from the responsibilities of Presiding Bishop, though he may act as traveling bishop, counseling and advising on the law

of temporalities in harmony with his successor and the Presidency.

2 Let Benjamin R. McGuire be set apart and ordained Presiding Bishop of the church, and two of the brethren be set apart as counselors to him, one to be selected by him and supported by the conference, the other to be Bishop James F. Keir.

3 a. I admonish the church, and particularly those of the priesthood, that the hastening time being upon us there is great necessity for confidence in the men of the church chosen for positions of great responsibility,

b. and all should consecrate of their talents, abilities, and substance for the prosecution of the great work intrusted to us.

4 Everywhere the demand for great activity exists, and for the accomplishment of our work the great essential is fraternal co-operation in service to man and devoted consecration to God and his work.

Your servant,

FREDERICK M. SMITH

INDEPENDENCE, MISSOURI, April 5, 1916

SECTION 133

Revelation given through President Frederick Madison Smith at Independence, Missouri, April 7, 1920. This message was submitted first to the General Conference and then presented to the various quorums. After it was approved by the quorums and the Conference, provision was made for its inclusion in the Doctrine and Covenants.

To the Church: Having given to the general missionary needs of the church and the condition of the Quorum of Twelve much thought and prayer, I am permitted to say to the church by way of instruction, through inspiration received:

1 Let Francis M. Sheehy and Peter Andersen be released from the Quorum of Twelve; and to fill the vacancies created by these releases let Myron A. McConley and Thomas W. Williams be ordained apostles.

2 a. Let the Quorum of Twelve be admonished that to discharge the responsibilities of the burden of the missionary work upon them, they should in humility before God and in sincerity of purpose apply themselves to this great task with unreserved devotion. The work in this line must be hastened.

b. Let them not be unduly concerned with the work of the standing ministry, only as they shall be directed by the Presidency therein; and let contention cease concerning the prerogatives of the leading quorums.

c. The work awaiting the efforts of the missionary forces is great and there is no time for contentions.

d. Let the apostles move out, as they have in the past been directed, in the task of taking to the peoples of the world the message of peace, and they shall find comfort and satisfaction in their labors.

FREDERICK M. SMITH
President of the Church
INDEPENDENCE, MISSOURI, April 7, 1920

SECTION 134

Revelation given through President Frederick M. Smith at Independence, Missouri, October 2, 1922.

This message was presented to the General Conference, and by them referred to the various quorums. The Council of Twelve and Presiding Bishopric joined in recommending that action on it be "deferred pending the settlement of important matters pending before the Joint Council of Presidency, Twelve, and Presiding Bishopric, in which the . . . personnel of the Twelve are vitally interested." Debate on this procedural matter broadened into a review of the entire administration of President Smith. The document was approved by a divided vote on October 12.

To the Church: To the matter of filling the leading quorums of the church in which vacancies now exist I have given prayerful and careful consideration and meditation, and the voice of inspiration to me is:

1 Let Floyd M. McDowell be ordained counselor to the

president as a member of the First Presidency to fill the vacancy now existing.

2 Let Gomer T. Griffiths, Ulysses W. Greene, Cornelius A. Butterworth, and Robert C. Russell be released from further responsibility as apostles, to devote their activities as their strength and opportunity might permit, to local work or as evangelical ministers as might be determined by subsequent procedure.

3 To fill the vacancies in the Quorum of Twelve let the following be ordained apostles: Clyde F. Ellis, John F. Garver, Daniel T. Williams, F. Henry Edwards, Edmund J. Gleazer, Roy S. Budd.

4 Let James A. Gillen be ordained president of the Quorum of Twelve.

5 a. The field is large and the time opportune.
b. Let the missionary work be prosecuted with great vigor, and if the Twelve will devote themselves wholeheartedly to this work the church will be greatly blessed through their ministration.

6 a. And let the Quorum of Twelve be further admonished that upon them rests the onerous burden of the missionary work of the church,
b. and be not concerned with local administrative work except in emergencies or as sent by the Presidency, leaving the care of the local work to those officers previously indicated in the law.

7 Let contention cease.

FREDERICK M. SMITH

INDEPENDENCE, MISSOURI, October 2, 1922

SECTION 135

In the years prior to 1925 the Reorganization was passing through a period which brought to the fore problems of administrative prerogatives. These involved the leading quorums of the church. A climax was reached in the General Conference of 1925. A conflict of views between the First Presidency and the Presiding Bishopric occurred. The Order of Bishops presented a motion to the Conference recommending the honorable release from their positions of members of the Presiding Bishopric. The General Conference by motion deferred action and approved an appeal to the Lord through the prophet, in fasting and prayer. In response to the plea of the church the following revelation was received through President Frederick M. Smith, prophet and seer to the church, April 18, 1925.

To the Church: Before and since the decision of the conference to have a season of prayer for divine direction in the matter before the conference I have presented to the Lord the needs of the people; and through the voice of inspiration I am directed to say to the church:

1 It is wisdom that the brethren of the present Presiding Bishopric be released from further responsibility in that office, and that Albert Carmichael be ordained to act in the office of Presiding Bishop for a time, he to choose from among the bishops two to act as counselors.

2 a. It is well that the documents from the joint council of April, 1924, have been approved; and the church is admonished once again that the great task laid upon it can not be accomplished if contention continues.

b. The hastening time is here and greater unity than ever before is necessary if the forces of opposition are to be met;

c. and such unity will prevail if those holding the priesthood will remember their commission to preach the gospel, and each officer will strive to discharge his own duty and magnify his calling.

3 a. The promise has been given that no power shall stay

the hand of God in the accomplishment of his purposes among his people;

b. and as the church shall move forward in its great work, the fulfillment of prophecy may cause the Saints to tremble at the exhibition of divine power, yet they shall rejoice in the protection of his grace.

4 The authorities of the church whose duty it is to appoint men to missionary tasks should remember the previously given instructions to send out by twos; and so far as practicable let the missionaries be so sent. There is wisdom and safety in this.

Your servant,
FREDERICK M. SMITH
KANSAS CITY, MISSOURI, April 18, 1925

SECTION 136

The widespread financial and economic depression which began near the close of 1929 put the church into serious financial difficulties. Early in 1930 the counselors in the Presiding Bishopric resigned; and by agreement between the Presidency, Twelve, and Presiding Bishop, Bishops L. F. P. Curry and G. Leslie DeLapp were chosen to serve as counselors to Bishop Albert Carmichael subject to the action of the next General Conference. The following revelation was approved by the quorums and the Conference.

To the Church: To the condition of the church and the personnel of the Quorum of Twelve and Presiding Bishopric I have in official capacity as well as in personal meditation and prayer given much thought, and have earnestly sought divine wisdom and guidance. Believing that such wisdom and inspiration have been given me, I present the following as the word of the Lord to us now:

1a. Under conditions existing it is well that Bishop Albert Carmichael should be released from further responsibility as Presiding Bishop, he being commended for the faithful devotion to the onerous tasks which have been his to perform.

b. In his stead let Bishop L. F. P. Curry be chosen to give such time and energy to this office as opportunity and the conditions surrounding him will permit, working toward the time when he can give his full time and attention to the work of the office to which he is thus called.

c. In the work of the office Bishop G. Leslie DeLapp should be associated as counselor, and one other be named by Bishop Curry, as wisdom and the voice of inspiration may indicate, the selection to be ratified by the conference.

2 To fill a vacancy existing in the number of the Twelve, let George G. Lewis be set apart and ordained as an apostle, and take his place with that quorum, and enter with his brethren upon the active work of the apostolic quorum and as representatives of the church.

3 a. The movements toward better understanding of ministerial responsibilities, duties, and goals, and toward unity of endeavor in teaching, preaching, evangelizing, and the perfecting of the Saints, are pleasing to the Lord.

b. Contentions, bickerings, and strife are unseemly, hinder the work of the church, and should not find place among the Saints.

c. Only in the peace of fraternity and the unity of those caught up in the spirit of Zionic redemption can the work of the Lord be accomplished. To this task let the church devote its energies.

FREDERICK M. SMITH
President of the Church
INDEPENDENCE, MISSOURI, April 14, 1932

SECTION 137

Revelation given through President Frederick M. Smith at Independence, Missouri, April 7, 1938. The Conference adopted this "communication with its provisions as the voice of divine inspiration to the church."

To the Church: Since the creation of two vacancies in the Quorum of Twelve I have been quite concerned about the condition of that quorum, as well as other bodies in the church, and after due meditation and prayer for divine light, I am permitted to present the following for the consideration and action of the conference members:

1 Let J. Frank Curtis, of the Twelve, who has long and faithfully served in that quorum, be honorably released from further responsibility as an apostle, and take place in the ranks of the order of evangelists.

2 To fill the vacancies in the Quorum of Twelve, let the following named brethren be ordained and set apart as apostles: C. George Mesley, Arthur A. Oakman, and Charles R. Hield.

3 It is wise that Frederick A. Smith, who has become aged in long years of faithful service to the church in various offices, be released from further responsibility as active president of the order of evangelists, though he may be given the honor of being president emeritus of that order.

4 a. To maintain the working condition of the order of evangelists, let Elbert A. Smith be released from further responsibility as counselor to the president of the church, to take up the work of presiding over the order of evangelists.

b. And let the church be admonished that the functioning and work of this order is of great importance in the work of perfecting the Saints, and the appointing authorities be reminded that the members of the order so far as possible are to be relieved of administrative work and keep themselves in condition for better functioning as evangelists whose task is to build up faith in the gospel and the church and its work.

c. And let those whose duty it is to select from the members of the priesthood those for setting apart as evangelists be admonished that the work of this class of ministers requires vigor, deep faith, and unreserved consecration, and men should be selected accordingly.

5 Until such time as the vacancy in the First Presidency shall be duly filled, let the work of the presidency be carried on with the aid of such assistants as may be arranged without undue interference with other departments.

6 a. Let the church be admonished that the times are portentous and demand faithful adherence to the faith and work

of the church, that mankind may be blessed by and find peace in those religiously social reforms and relationships which have been divinely imposed as a great task of achievement.

b. Remember and keep the commandments, be alert to keep out of the church and from its members those forces which make for disunity, and in harmony and saintly accord be about the task of freeing Zion from her bondage.

Frederick M. Smith

President of the Church

Independence, Missouri, April 7, 1938

SECTION 138

After Elder Elbert A. Smith was ordained Presiding Evangelist at the Conference of 1938, the First Presidency continued with Elder F. M. McDowell as the sole remaining counselor to President Frederick M. Smith. President McDowell resigned in October 1938. With the approval of the Council of Twelve, acting under the inspiration given to him at the time, President Frederick M. Smith associated Elders Israel A. Smith and L. F. P. Curry with himself in the Presidency. In the following revelation this arrangement is confirmed. The revelation was received by unanimous action of the Conference and was ordered included in the Doctrine and Covenants.

To the Saints in General Conference Assembled:

1 a. As a result of the conditions existing when the Joint Council of First Presidency, Quorum of the Twelve and Presiding Bishopric, met in October, 1938, Brother Floyd M. McDowell, Second Counselor, presented his resignation to me to take effect immediately.

b. This left the President without Counselors; and to meet the situation, acting under such inspirational impulses as were given me at the moment, I presented the names of Brethren Israel A. Smith and Lemuel F. P. Curry to fill the vacancies in the First Presidency, these selections being unanimously approved by the Quorum of Twelve.

c. I suggested to the brethren named the wisdom of at once entering upon their tasks in the Presidency.

d. This was done, and there was thrown upon Brother Curry a double responsibility, for it was thought best for him to continue his work as Presiding Bishop until further instructions were given.

e. Acting further under the impulsion referred to I now present the names of Israel A. Smith and Lemuel F. P. Curry for ratification as Counselors in the First Presidency, Brother Curry to be released from further responsibility as Presiding Bishop.

2 To effect necessary reorganization of the Presiding Bishopric let G. Leslie DeLapp be selected and ordained as Presiding Bishop, he being left free to nominate his counselors in due time.

3 a. Let the church again be admonished that the task of establishing Zion presses heavily upon us.

b. Barriers and hindrances to the achievement of this goal should be removed as speedily as possible and practicable.

c. To lay securely the foundations for Zion and her buildings the work should be accomplished in peace and harmony. Unity should prevail.

d. To this end all the Saints should work together in the rich fraternity which can and will prevail among them when they keep faithfully the commandments.

e. Great blessings are in store for the church if it will in faith and saintly devotion go forward in its tasks.

FREDERICK M. SMITH
President of the Church

INDEPENDENCE, MISSOURI, April 10, 1940

SECTION 139

President Frederick Madison Smith died March 20, 1946, and was succeeded as prophet, seer, and revelator by his brother, Elder Israel A. Smith. The need to fill the quorum of the First Presidency was urgent, and the newly ordained president gave this his immediate and prayerful attention. The following revelation was presented to the quorums and

*to the Conference by President Israel A. Smith early in the
Conference sessions. After it had been approved in the
usual manner, and those named had been ordained to their
respective offices, the work of the Conference proceeded
under the direction of the newly constituted Presidency.*

To the Quorums and to the General Conference;
Beloved Brethren:

Realizing our urgent need to receive light and instruction
in order that the quorums might be filled, I have wrestled in
prayer to God in my weakness, on behalf and in the interest
of the church, sensing deeply that it has been but a few hours
ago when the burden of the church was laid upon me, yet in
confidence and faith that God will not fail the church when
called upon.

In the early hours of yesterday and today I was blessed by
the Spirit in power and assurance such as I have never before
experienced. The mind of the Lord was manifested to me,
and in the order named my brethren have been presented
to me, as follows, and accordingly I have written:

1 a. "It is my will, saith the Spirit, that my servants of the
Quorum of Twelve, John F. Garver and F. Henry Edwards,
be ordained and set apart to be counselors to my servant,
the president of the church, and to be presidents in the
Quorum of the First Presidency.

b. "They are my chosen vessels and are qualified by experience. Their apostleship is extended in presidency and if
they will go forward in loving service, their ministry will be
very effective.

2 a. "To fill one of the vacancies in the Quorum of Twelve
Apostles, I have presented to my servant the name of D.
Blair Jensen of the High Priests Quorum, who is called and
chosen to this office, and should be ordained and set apart
as a special witness in the Quorum of Twelve."

My heart has been made to rejoice, as I feared that through
my weakness and inexperience, the work of the church might
suffer loss. I present this word to you soon after its reception, and, as I write, it is confirmed again unto me.

May God bless you in your deliberations; and if the quorums and the body shall have this message confirmed unto them, I shall rejoice, and I have faith that the church thereby will be blessed.

Your servant in Christ,

ISRAEL A. SMITH

President of the Church

INDEPENDENCE, MISSOURI, April 9, 1946

SECTION 140

Revelation given through President Israel A. Smith, April 7, 1947, at Independence, Missouri. It was approved by the various councils and quorums of the church and then endorsed by the Conference as an expression of the divine will and ordered to be published in the Doctrine and Covenants.

To the Quorums and Councils of the Church and to the General Conference:

For some time I have given prayerful consideration to the church and its present needs, in harmony with the call for prayer, and I am directed to present the following as the will of the Lord:

1 a. The unity among my people and in the councils of the church is commendable.

b. If those of the priesthood will perform their responsibilities in good fellowship, and sustain each other, they will be supported by the faith and prayers of the church and the work will go forward with increasing power.

2 To fill vacancies already existing, let Roscoe E. Davey and Maurice L. Draper, now serving as Seventies, be ordained Apostles and occupy with their brethren in the Quorum of Twelve.

3 My servant John W. Rushton has served his generation and the church long and faithfully, and he is honorably released from further responsibility as a member of the Quorum

of Twelve, continuing to minister in his priesthood as he can and may desire, without specific assignment. His works are with me and his reward is sure.

4 a. W. Wallace Smith is called and should be ordained an Apostle and take his place in the councils of the church.

b. This call was made known before, but my servant withheld it from the body for reasons that he believed were sufficient.

5 a. The church is admonished again that all movements toward Zion and the gathering and temporalities connected therewith are within my law, and all things should be done in order,

b. the advice and counsel of the elders and of the Bishop and his council be sought and honored when received, as before enjoined, though of necessity their counsel when given is not intended to dictate or to deny any man his agency.

c. The work of preparation and the perfection of my Saints go forward slowly, and Zionic conditions are no further away nor any closer than the spiritual condition of my people justifies;

d. but my word shall not fail, neither will my promises, for the foundation of the Lord standeth sure.

Respectfully submitted,

ISRAEL A. SMITH

INDEPENDENCE, MISSOURI, April 7, 1947

SECTION 141

Revelation given through President Israel A. Smith during the World Conference of 1948 held at Independence, Missouri. There was a vacancy in the ranks of the Twelve because of the death of Elder G. G. Lewis. Also, Elder M. A. McConley had become incapacitated by illness. The instruction given was endorsed by the various quorums and by the Conference, and provision was made for its inclusion in the Doctrine and Covenants.

To the Quorums, Councils and Orders of the Church and the General Conference:

Since the day set for a fast and especially since the loss by death of Apostle Lewis, I have been led to seek the divine mind respecting the needs of the body. Light and intelligence have been manifested as a result, and I am permitted to present the following by way of encouragement and direction:

To the Church:

1 My servant George G. Lewis has been taken for mine own purposes. He has been faithful, and his labors have been acceptable to me.

2 My servant Myron A. McConley is honorably released from further duty as an Apostle, and he should be ordained to the office of evangelist and labor as a member of that order.

3 In order that the Council of Twelve may be filled and the work of that Quorum be carried forward, it is my will that my servants Percy E. Farrow and Reed M. Holmes be ordained and set apart unto the apostolic office and appointed to mission responsibility.

4 a. There are others of the leading councils who have likewise served faithfully, whose ministry in my wisdom is continued for a season, but who may be taken to myself, or because of age or infirmity released in mine own due time.

b. There are those with the body of my priesthood who are called and who will be chosen to succeed them, if faithful; therefore, all are admonished to qualify themselves in spirit by ministry and by witnessing for Christ.

5 The hastening time is upon us; the period until the next General Conference, as already provided, must be one of unusual preparation for my church as an organization, for my people, and especially for my priesthood if there shall be those who will be qualified to assume and to carry the responsibilities of those who fall or fail or who are released.

6 a. Let the Seventies under appointment as far as practicable relieve my servants of the Quorum of Twelve from labor in outlying or undeveloped areas, and let the Twelve seek to perfect the work in regions closer to the Center, opening up the work in new places.

b. In these labors, the standing ministers, and especially district and stake authorities, are called to assist.

c. Many of the elders not under appointment have a desire and will labor in new places if requested and given responsibility.

7 a. The unity and spirit of tolerance evidenced by my servants in the councils of the church are commended of me.

b. Each should strive prayerfully for sustained and greater devotion to the work whereunto he is called.

c. My servants should not become weary of well-doing. The adversary is quick to discourage and thus destroy their effectiveness.

8 a. The church is admonished again that joint responsibility is laid on all.

b. Properly and equally borne, this responsibility will insure success, the consummation will be glorious, and all will share in that glory.

ISRAEL A. SMITH,
Servant of the Church

INDEPENDENCE, MISSOURI, October 2, 1948

SECTION 142

Revelation presented by President Israel A. Smith to the General Conference on April 2, 1950. It was considered and approved by the quorums and the Conference and accepted as the word of God to the church. Provision was made for its inclusion in future editions of the Doctrine and Covenants. In an introductory paragraph, the prophet said:

"We approach the general Conference with a vacancy in our official circle. The death of President Garver left the Quorum of the First Presidency incomplete. This and other conditions have given me grave concern for the church.

"I have earnestly sought divine guidance, and it is with gratitude that I am able to transmit through the

*appointed channels that which the voice of inspiration
directs me to say:"*

To the Elders and to the Church:

1 a. It is wisdom that the leading quorums should be filled.
Therefore, to take the place of my servant John F. Garver,
whose sacrifices and labor were acceptable to me,

b. it is my will that William Wallace Smith be ordained
and set apart to take his place as counselor to the president
of the high priesthood and as a member of the Quorum of
the First Presidency, to which office he is now called.

2 To fill the vacancy thus created in the Quorum of
Twelve, Donald O. Chesworth is called. He should be ordained to the office of an apostle, and be relieved of his
present bishopric, and assume the duties of a special witness
in that council.

3 My servants of the Joint Council are commended for the
spirit of moderation which they have shown in their deliberations. I have accordingly blessed their efforts, and the Cause
has been measurably enriched.

4 a. The church as a whole is commended for the spiritual
growth and the preparation of the priesthood during the conference period, and this necessary work should proceed.

b. It will be profitable for my servants of the eldership
to meet often for study, under the direction of those having
responsibility to teach, at such times and places as may be
practicable, in preparation for the greater endowment of
spiritual power which has been promised and which awaits
the time when they can receive it.

5 a. The hopes of my people and the goals of my church,
while not yet fully realized, and at times and to many seem-
ingly distant, are closer to realization than many recognize.

b. It is yet day when all can work. The night will come
when for many of my people opportunity to assist will have
passed.

Your Servant,

ISRAEL A. SMITH

INDEPENDENCE, MISSOURI, April 2, 1950

SECTION 143

Revelation given through President Israel A. Smith during the World Conference of 1954.

A vacancy in the Quorum of Twelve and the need for more seventies to meet the opportunities for missionary expansion had occupied the thought and prayers of the prophet. After some debate the revelation was approved in the usual manner.

To the Councils, Quorums, and Orders of the Church and to the General Conference:

1 a. When I was in England in 1952 I was given the assurance that Donald V. Lents, a high priest, was called to be an apostle.

b. Now that there is a vacancy in the Council of Twelve, and realizing the great need for apostolic ministry and direction, I have made it a subject of prayer, and I am directed to submit this name to you, the voice of inspiration to me being:

2. My servant Donald V. Lents is called and he is now chosen to the holy office of an apostle and should be ordained to that office as soon as practicable. Pending that time he should be placed in charge of the English and European Missions.

3 a. The voice of inspiration to me also is as follows:

It is wisdom for the church to accept the direction of the Council of Presidents of Seventy and complete their organization. My servants of this council should not be overcareful in selecting elders, under the law, to occupy as Seventies.

b. The field of opportunity in new places is great in all areas, and there are many who earnestly desire to do missionary work who are called to be Seventies, and when they are ordained to that office the church should devise ways and means, as far as practicable, for them to be given missionary assignment.

4. The growing desire for missionary work will be amply rewarded, and the church will be blessed even more than in the past.

ISRAEL A. SMITH
Servant of the Church

INDEPENDENCE, MISSOURI, April 7, 1954

SECTION 144

On May 28, 1952, President Israel A. Smith prepared and signed the following statement and placed it in the hands of his counselor, Elder F. Henry Edwards. After the death of President Smith on June 14, 1958, this document was brought to the attention of the Council of Twelve and other general church officers, and at the World Conference of 1958 it was unanimously approved by the quorums and orders of the priesthood and by the Conference assembly. The Conference ordered its insertion in the Doctrine and Covenants.

Elder William Wallace Smith was ordained as President of the High Priesthood and prophet, seer, and revelator to the church at the Auditorium at Independence, Missouri, on October 6, 1958.

To the church and to the Council of Twelve Apostles:

1 As I am about to go overseas and realize the usual hazards of travel, and being ever conscious of the uncertainties of life and the certainty of death, and in order that my demise, whether soon or longer postponed, may not cause confusion, I hereby declare that in the event of my death, whenever it shall occur, my brother, William Wallace Smith, should be selected to succeed me as president of the high priesthood of the church, this having been manifested to me by the Lord at the time he was chosen and set apart as an apostle and again when he was called to be a counselor and

member of the Quorum of the First Presidency, at the General Conference of 1950.

2 I feel at liberty to make this appointment at this time because he has become better acquainted with the members since he was called in 1947 and has proved himself to the body.

3 This action is taken by me pursuant to the authority vested in me by the terms of Section 43 of the book of Doctrine and Covenants, in connection with other references in the law, notably paragraph 8 of Section 127, all as interpreted by my father, the late President Joseph Smith, in the *Saints' Herald* of March 12, 1912, and all of which I believe is in complete harmony with precedents established by the church in General Conferences of 1860, 1915, and 1946.

(Signed) ISRAEL A. SMITH

Witnessed this 28th day of May, 1952
F. Henry Edwards
G. Leslie DeLapp

SECTION 145

President W. Wallace Smith introduced the following revelation to the World Conference of 1958 with an explanatory document which said, in part:

"Since it became apparent that the burden of its prophetic leadership would be mine, I have given additional prayerful consideration to the needs of the church, and have sought earnestly for light with such powers of mind and body as are at my command. As a result of this, and other experiences which I deem inspirational, I bring this word to the Saints as being the mind and will of God unto his people.

"It is now almost seven weeks since the initial experience took place. As I write, these things are confirmed unto me."

After consideration by the councils, quorums, and orders of the priesthood, the revelation was presented to the Conference and there endorsed as an expression of the mind and will of God and ordered to be published in the Doctrine and Covenants.

To the Elders of the Church and the General Conference:

1 I have taken unto myself my own. It was wisdom that my servant Israel A. Smith be released from his onerous duties. He has found his reward with the faithful.

2 It is my will that F. Henry Edwards be sustained as a counselor to the President of the High Priesthood and the Church, and as a member of the quorum of the First Presidency. He is called to this office by reason of his preparation through long years of faithful service and should be ordained for the strength and support he can give to his associates and in the councils of my church.

3 To fill the other vacancy in the quorum of the First Presidency Maurice L. Draper is called from among his brethren. His apostleship is extended in presidency as he takes his place as a counselor to the President of the Church and a member of the quorum of the First Presidency.

4 a. Due to the infirmities of the flesh, my beloved and faithful servant Elbert A. Smith has responded to the direction of the Spirit in resigning his office as Presiding Patriarch of the church.

b. To fill this position in my church Roy A. Cheville is called and should be chosen and set apart to this high and holy office, and be given the responsibility of presiding over the brethren of the patriarchal order as Presiding Patriarch. This is in harmony with my instructions to the Saints at an early date.

5 a. The wisdom of changes in the Council of Twelve was a continuing question in the mind of my servant who has gone to his reward. It is a continuing grave concern of the one whom I have designated to lead you as his successor

and, while I am not yet ready to reveal all that shall be, the following changes should be made.

b. Few in my church have served as long and as faithfully as my servant, Paul M. Hanson. He is honorably released from his responsibilities as a member of the Council of Twelve, but is free to labor as a member of the high priesthood wherever and whenever the opportunity is present and his strength will permit.

c. Likewise my servants, Daniel T. Williams and Edmund J. Gleazer, who have also served in the councils of the church over a long period and with evident distinction, are honorably released from their responsibilities in the Council of Twelve.

6 a. While there is but one office in the patriarchal order, there are multiple functions. All my servants who have been called to this office will not be equally proficient in each of the separate functions.

b. My servant Daniel T. Williams has ability to counsel, advise, and give blessings. If faithful, my servant Edmund J. Gleazer will be especially blessed in the ministry of the preached word while he maintains his health and vigor.

c. These, my sons, are now called to be patriarchs and should be ordained pursuant to and in harmony with my will revealed through the spirit of wisdom. This should be done as soon as practicable in order that not one jot or tittle of their ministerial effectiveness be lost to me.

7 In harmony with my will now revealed to you, Charles D. Neff and Clifford A. Cole should be ordained apostles and take their places in the Council of Twelve along with their brethren whose duty it is to spread the gospel into all the world as especial witnesses.

8 It is my will that the day shall soon come when the provisions within the law may be sufficiently understood to enable the bonds of indecision to be loosed and the fulfillment of my purposes to be accomplished.

9 There are others of my priesthood who are called to the apostleship who, if faithful, will find their places in due

course. Though it is desirable for the quorums to be filled it is not expedient that it shall be done at this time. As I have made known to my servant, the time is yet a little while until all shall be made clear. Amen.

Your servant in Christ,

W. WALLACE SMITH

INDEPENDENCE, MISSOURI
October 8, 1958

SECTION 146

At the opening of the first business session of the Amboy Centennial Conference of 1960, President W. Wallace Smith presented a revelation received by him, introducing it as follows:

"Having made the needs of the church a matter of almost constant thought every waking hour for many months I engaged in prayer, as is my custom before retiring. On the night of March 27 the burden of my prayer had to do with the filling of the vacancies in the Council of the Twelve Apostles, and other matters which had claimed my attention.

"As a result of this concern, and in answer to my prayers, I am prompted by the Spirit of Almighty God to bring his word to the church."

To the Elders of the Church and the General Conference:

1 a. My servants Cecil R. Ettinger and Duane E. Couey have discharged their duties and responsibilities in humility and faithfulness before me, and are now called to serve as apostles in my church.

b. Accordingly they should be set apart and take their places with their brethren in the labors of the apostolic office as members of the Council of Twelve.

2 a. My servants of the leading councils and quorums of my church are commended for the unity of purpose which they have demonstrated.

b. They are now counseled to take full advantage of the willingness of my people to follow the leadership which I have provided and to which my people have given their consent.

c. This principle is at the heart of the gospel which I restored through my servant Joseph and which is preserved in the reorganization of my people.

3. Let any remaining contention over minutiae cease in order that my purpose, already revealed in my word to the church, may be fulfilled and my work continue to prosper in love.   Amen.

Your humble servant in Christ,

W. WALLACE SMITH
President of the Church

INDEPENDENCE, MISSOURI, April 2, 1960

SECTION 147

President W. Wallace Smith received a revelation for the church March 11, 1964, and presented it to the World Conference with the following introductory statement:

"With the needs of the church constantly before me I have made these matters the burden of my prayers. In seeking the will of my heavenly Father as a guide to the church I was awakened early on the morning of March 11 and was directed by the Spirit to write the following as instruction to you who are assembled in Conference and to the church at large:"

To the Councils, Quorums, and Orders of the Church and to the General Conference:

1. My servant, Charles R. Hield, who has served in the Council of Twelve with devotion and in the spirit of sacrifice,

is relieved of his duties as a member of the quorum, but his apostolic witness is to be extended to the church through continued research and translation. He will also continue to make his ministry felt among my people by bearing his testimony of the restored gospel through preaching and writing ministries as a high priest in my service.

2. My servant, Roscoe E. Davey, has served faithfully in the councils of the church for many years. His contribution made in these positions is acceptable and will be rewarded accordingly. He has been blessed by the presence of my spirit in ways and at times of great need known to him and will continue, if faithful, to receive direction as he continues his witnessing ministry in the Order of Evangelists to which office he is now called and should be ordained.

3. Arthur A. Oakman has magnified the gift of communicating the beauties of the gospel through the spoken word as he has served in the councils of my church. In order that he may have more freedom to advance my work through his special talents in ministry he is relieved of his duties as a member of the leading missionary quorum and should be given an assignment within the patriarchal order, as an evangelist, to which order he is called, to carry on revival witnessing in key centers of church establishment and expansion.

4. To fill two of the vacancies thus created my servants Russell F. Ralston and William E. Timms are called from their present positions to become apostles in the Council of Twelve of my church. They should be ordained and take their place with the others of the council as soon as practicable.

5 a. Stewardship is the response of my people to the ministry of my Son and is required alike of all those who seek to build the kingdom. The spiritual authorities are urged to so teach with renewed vigor in recognition of the great need, and let nothing separate them from those who have more specific responsibilities in the temporal affairs of the church.

b. In this regard you are reminded of the instructions given to you through one of my servants at an earlier time. Repression of unnecessary wants is in harmony with the law of stewardship and becomes my people.

6 a. As your leader I have sought diligently for light on the question of representation in the General Conferences of the church. As a result of the prompting of the Spirit I bring the following as guidance to the church in this important matter:

b. Nothing which has been given hitherto by way of instruction should be so interpreted as to restrict the right of the General Conference to determine its own membership or to exercise its best judgment on legislative matters. It is required only that the body shall act according to the basic principles already made known: leadership by the general presiding authorities of the church, and common consent according to the covenants of the church and the prayer of faith.

7. I am further permitted to say by the Spirit: Instruction which has been given in former years is applicable in principle to the needs of today and should be so regarded by those who are seeking ways to accomplish the will of their heavenly Father. But the demands of a growing church require that these principles shall be evaluated and subjected to further interpretation. This requisite has always been present. In meeting it under the guidance of my spirit, my servants have learned the intent of these principles more truly.

W. WALLACE SMITH
President of the Church

Presented this sixth day of April in the year of our Lord, 1964.

SECTION 148

The revelation given through President W. Wallace Smith at Independence, Missouri, April 18, 1966, was accompanied by this preparatory statement:

"During the last inter-Conference period I have given continuing consideration to the condition of the councils and quorums and orders of the church. This has been done hoping that I would receive light on matters of grave importance to the future of the church. In this I have sought earnestly for divine guidance and also that I might have wisdom to rightly conduct the affairs entrusted into my care. This has been done through personal meditation and prayer.

"On one of these occasions after retiring I was awakened and made aware that I would again have the responsibility of communicating the will of the Lord to his people.

"Believing that such inspiration and direction have been given me, I present the following as the word of the Lord to us and ask the consideration and action of the members of the Conference upon the matters thus presented."

The revelation was considered by the various quorums and councils of the church, and by the General Conference, and was endorsed by them and ordered to be published in the Doctrine and Covenants.

To the Councils and Quorums and Orders of the Church and to the General Conference:

1. My servant F. Henry Edwards has served my church long and well in the capacity of a missionary elder, an apostle and, with his apostleship being extended in presidency, as a counselor to the President of the High Priesthood and the church. He is now honorably released from the Presidency and from the heavy responsibilities which he has borne nobly and well. Thus relieved of presiding he should

find satisfaction in pursuing his talents of writing and teaching without the heavy administrative requirements which have been placed upon him in recent years. As a high priest he is free to minister through his apostolic witness to the church as his health and circumstances permit and opportunities develop.

2. To fill the vacancy thus created Duane E. Couey is called from the ranks of the Council of Twelve to become a member of the Quorum of the First Presidency and a counselor to the President of the High Priesthood and the church. In this capacity his apostolic witness is extended in presidency and his ordination should take place as soon as practicable.

The following changes in the personnel of the Council of Twelve are presented after careful and prayerful consideration and with the confirmation of the spirit of inspiration:

3. My servants D. Blair Jensen and Percy E. Farrow have each made a significant contribution to my work through their ministry in many fields of labor. The last twenty years of Apostle Jensen's ministry have been given as a member of the Council of Twelve. Apostle Farrow has served as a seventy, President of Seventy, and for the past eighteen years as a member of the Council of Twelve. The time has come when they should be honorably released from the council and be left free to serve as high priests in those fields of ministry which later may be designated for them by the appropriate councils and quorums involved.

4. To fill the places thus left vacant by the brethren relieved of their responsibility in the Council of Twelve, Earl T. Higdon, Alan D. Tyree, and Aleah G. Koury are called to be apostles in my church. They should be ordained as special witnesses as soon as practicable and be given assignments commensurate with their abilities and devotion.

I have also given the matter of the reorganization of the Presiding Bishopric a great deal of careful and prayerful consideration.

5. My servant G. Leslie DeLapp, having given service to the church over a long period of time in the capacity of Presiding Bishop, should be honorably released from the onerous responsibilities he has been carrying, though he may act as a traveling bishop and in other capacities, counseling and advising on the law of temporalities in relation to spiritual purposes in harmony with his successor and the First Presidency. He has served the church and his fellowmen with a high degree of skill, evident devotion, great distinction, and at times with a great deal of personal sacrifice on the part of himself and family. He is commended for his good work.

6. Henry L. Livingston should be relieved of his responsibilities as a counselor to the Presiding Bishop. My servant has given many years of service to my Cause through the church in a variety of capacities and places, in all of which he has performed nobly. I commend him for the kindness and goodness which he displays in so many ways. He is called and, if willing, should be ordained to the office of patriarch to act as a spiritual father to the Saints.

7. Walter N. Johnson should be chosen and ordained as Presiding Bishop to serve in this capacity for a time.

8. To assist him as counselors and to serve as members of the Presiding Bishopric my servants Francis E. Hansen and Harold W. Cackler are called and should be ordained and set apart in their places.

The spirit of the Lord prompts me to say further:

9 a. The hastening time is at hand when the principles of stewardship accounting and Zionic procedures must be applied more fully than hitherto. This should be done with care to avoid the appearance of a desire by the Saints to take what does not rightly belong to them. But if they will move with assurance under the direction of those who are knowledgeable, capable, and dedicated, my purposes can be achieved more fully even now.

b. In this the Presidency, Twelve, and Bishopric each has a part to play according to their several callings. But others of my priesthood who are prepared are also to be enlisted so that their skills may be applied to the work which is entrusted to all.

10 a. To more fully effect the unity of my church, the Presidency and Council of Twelve should be associated more closely in their mutual endeavors. The members of the Council of Twelve are commended for their desire to work diligently to accomplish my purposes.

b. They should continue to exercise their calling as the "second presidency" in harmony with their primary responsibility in new fields. As such second presidency, the council should share with the First Presidency in reviewing and determining policies of church administration, but at the same time should recognize that the burden of the care of the church is laid upon him who is called to preside over the high priesthood of the church and on those who are called to be his counselors.

c. As the members of the Council of Twelve withdraw from detailed administration in organized areas, responsibility to carry on the work in stakes and regions will fall more heavily upon those who have been chosen for this purpose. Their work is necessary and they should be honored in their places, each working with each to perfect my kingdom.

d. Thus freed from detailed administrative duties, the Council of Twelve can give more attention to their primary work of pushing the work into new fields at home and abroad. To this the Council should give major attention even though some apostles may be assigned to general supervision of the work in organized areas and to church-wide functions.

e. In this manner the power of the testimonies of those who are called as special witnesses in my church will add spiritual depth and meaning to my work, both in reviewing and determining principles and procedures in spiritual and temporal realms and in redemptive evangelism at home and abroad.

> Your servant in Christ,
> W. WALLACE SMITH
> *President of the Church*

Independence, Missouri
April 18, 1966

SECTION 149

Revelation given through W. Wallace Smith, prophet and seer to the church, April 1, 1968. A vacancy had existed in the Council of Twelve since 1964, and the honorable release of two members of the Council in 1966 resulted in three vacancies in that body, two of which were filled at that time.

The need for clarifying relationships between ministerial programs and direction of the use of temporalities was recognized, and guidance was given accordingly.

In the search for effective interpretations of the gospel in a rapidly changing society the presiding quorums had been engaged in studies in which resources were tapped both from within and without the church. The quorums were commended for their pursuit of understanding by such means.

In reference to the dedication of the temple site in 1831, instruction was given to begin the active development of plans for use of the temple and the gathering of resources for its construction.

The document was considered by the quorums, councils, and orders and adopted by the Conference on April 4, 1968.

The prophet stated in his introduction to the document that he had "come to know that such direction is not neces-

sarily limited to a once-per-biennium expression of the will of our heavenly Father. However, since the church must give its approval to any document which I may present purporting to contain the will of God, I have limited the presentation of any prophetic utterance for the guidance of the church as a whole to a time when such a message could have almost immediate consideration. Thus having given prayerful consideration to the pressing needs of the church for enlightenment on various subjects and having received what I consider the confirmation of the Spirit of God, I am prepared to bring the following message to you for your consideration and action."

To the Councils, Quorums, and the Church:

1. In order to fill the existing vacancy in the Council of Twelve, Howard S. Sheehy, Jr., is called to be an apostle of Jesus Christ. While the knowledge of the call came to my servant at a previous time, it was withheld to permit the confirmation of the Spirit so necessary in such matters. He should be set apart without undue delay and take his place among his brethren in the Council of Twelve, so that the church shall have the benefit of his contribution as soon as possible.

My servant is further directed to say:

2. My word to the leaders in stakes and other jurisdictions is to be diligent in seeking ways to implement the program called for in the principles of spiritual leadership so necessary to the effective carrying out of my purpose.

3. Instructions given formerly are to be observed, and since the office of bishop is a "necessary appendage" to the high priesthood and members of the Order of Bishops are charged with the ministry of temporalities, they will act in support of leadership given by the spiritual authorities for the achievement of the purposes of my church. Temporal officers are to be supported in their rightful place, but must

be guided by the needs of the field in their work of helping to furnish the means to finance my program.

4. Some of you have sought security in the words and phrases by which the faithful of earlier days have expressed their knowledge of me. My ways are still the ways of my Son. My servants of the holy priesthood will need to be alert as never before to see that my work is not vitiated by the designs of the adversary. They must also bring to their searching for truth and their service to my people all the treasures of understanding I have opened for them elsewhere. It is necessary for all to promote unity so that my blessings can be yours as you willingly bend your strength to kingdom-building enterprises.

5. My servants of the leading quorums are commended for their diligence in seeking more light and truth from all available sources. For have I not told you that my glory is intelligence and he that seeketh learning by study and by faith will be rewarded in this life and the life to come? Your efforts to find ways to more successfully implement the goals of my church must be continued.

6 a. The time has come for a start to be made toward building my temple in the Center Place. It shall stand on a portion of the plot of ground set apart for this purpose many years ago by my servant Joseph Smith, Jr. The shape and character of the building is to conform to ministries which will be carried out within its walls. These functions I will reveal through my servant the prophet and his counselors from time to time, as need for more specific direction arises.

b. Money for this purpose should come from the consecration of surplus by my people inasmuch as the building of houses of worship is one of the purposes of the Storehouse.

c. As you are diligent in moving to effect this project I will pour out the blessings of my Spirit and you will know that I am God.

7. I have not forsaken you, my people, even though you have at times and in diverse ways failed to live up to your potential under the direction you have received from me through my servants. I change not; neither are my purposes to fail by the evil designs of men.

Your servant in Christ,

W. WALLACE SMITH

President of the Church

Independence, Missouri
April 1, 1968

SECTION 149A

Revelation given through W. Wallace Smith, prophet and seer, on April 5, 1968. During the consideration of Section 149 by the quorums, councils, and orders, certain questions of interpretation arose regarding the role of the bishop and the nature of the financial support to be given to the construction of the temple.

An explanatory statement offered by the prophet carried evidences of inspiration which led to a request for him to give the Conference further instructions concerning it. President Smith then presented the following instruction to the quorums, councils, and orders, and it was approved by them and the Conference. In a covering letter President Smith requested that it be numbered 149A and recognized as being closely related to the matter contained in Section 149.

The prophet wrote further: "Having made the needs of the church a matter of earnest prayer during the time that the document which is now Section 149 was being considered by the councils, quorums, and orders, I became acutely aware that there was need for additional instruction as guidance for the church. As a consequence, I was awakened at a very early hour on the morning of April 4 and, being motivated by the Spirit of the Lord, prepared the following document as further guidance in relation to matters already under consideration pertaining to the work of the bishop and the building of the temple."

To the Councils, Quorums, Orders, and the Church:

1. Nothing contained in the April 1 document is in derogation of the work of the bishop. On the contrary it recognizes him as a "necessary appendage belonging unto the high priesthood" (Doctrine and Covenants 83:5). The emphasis in this case is on "necessary." The instructions given in Doctrine and Covenants 128:2, 3 and 129:8 are still valid for the guidance of the church, but the work alluded to must necessarily be carried out under the general guidance of those who are rightfully in charge of the work as the presidency in any jurisdictional division of the church.

2. This further means that the bishop, when assigned, will be recognized in his rightful place as a bishop in his own right to initiate in consultation with the local authorities those programs which under the law are recognized as necessary in his ministry, being responsible in such matters to the local, stake, regional, or district conference having jurisdiction.

3. In further interpretation of the role of the bishop, it is necessary to understand that his support of programs will be sought by administrative officers in consultation at time of formulation and when agreed will be administered in accordance with that agreement and budgets applicable thereto; it being understood that those in the administrative line will give general direction and be kept fully informed as to the progress being made.

4. It should be further understood that in cases of difference, the rightful line of appeal is to the proper administrative officer in that jurisdiction with final appeal to the First Presidency.

5. In explanation of the use of the word "surplus" in reference to building the temple so that no one shall be denied an opportunity to participate as fully as possible, surplus shall be construed in its wider meaning to include that amount available for special appropriation from the tithes and offerings of the Saints after the budgetary needs of the church have been met, as well as those funds which are consecrated as surplus under the more restrictive use of the term.

6. It is also to be noted that the full and complete use of the temple is yet to be revealed but that there is no provision for secret ordinances now or ever, although there will be provision for instructional opportunities which will of necessity be restricted to the particular category concerned, *viz*, high priests, patriarchs, bishops, seventies, elders, Aaronic priesthood, and so forth.

Beyond these more specific instructions I am extremely happy to be able to express my deep appreciation for the devotion evidenced in the support you have given to the work entrusted to all. Be faithful and diligent and the blessings of God will be yours in abundance.

Your servant in Christ,

W. WALLACE SMITH
President of the Church

Independence, Missouri
April 5, 1968

SECTION 150

On April 14, 1972, the World Conference adopted this message given through W. Wallace Smith "as embodying the word of God to the church at this time, authorizing the ordinations called for and directing its inclusion in the Doctrine and Covenants in its appropriate place." It provides for one change in the Council of Twelve and the reorganization of the Presiding Bishopric.

Other inspired instruction is related to the church's response to opportunities for evangelism in several national and cultural situations developed during the decade of the 1960's. Continued studies of Temple functions are commanded and funding is seen in expanded dimensions. The stewardship of conservation in the use of natural resources is emphasized. The role of prophetic leadership by church officers is noted.

The Saints are admonished to bear the burdens of those whose pre-Christian way of life is expressed in unfamiliar social structures while the work of redemptive grace goes on among them.

The prophet introduced his message with this preamble:

"After seeking diligently for light regarding the welfare and needs of the church, I present the following as the will of the Lord for his church, interpreted and brought to you through the spirit of inspiration and wisdom. In explanation and for clarity, I awoke extremely early on the morning of February 16, 1972, and wrote as the Spirit directed me.

"Now by virtue of my position I am permitted to bring this inspired message to you as guidance to the church in these latter days. Your prayerful consideration and acceptance are sought in the spirit of humility and goodwill."

1 a. To my servant, Donald O. Chesworth: Your services as an apostle have been acceptable unto me. You are now to be relieved of your duties as a member of the Council of Twelve.

b. You are called to continue to minister to the Saints in the capacity of an evangelist-patriarch with the emphasis on revival preaching. If willing, you should be set apart in this office as soon as practicable and take up your ministry with your brethren in the Order of Evangelists.

2 a. To fill the vacancy thus created, my servant, John C. Stuart, is called to be an apostle and should be set apart as a member of the Council of Twelve so that his ministry as a high priest can be extended into apostleship.

b. As a special witness he will take his place with his brethren of the council as soon as ordination can be provided for in order that there shall be no interruption of the work of spreading the gospel in this and other lands where my name must be known.

3 a. In times of stress and under trying circumstances my servant, Walter N. Johnson, has served to capacity in discharging his duties as a bishop. As Presiding Bishop for the past six years he has done much to promote the work of the church and to advance the cause of the kingdom.

b. He is now to be relieved of his onerous task and is to take his place among the high priests as a bishop. He will serve in this capacity in various geographic locations as time and circumstances permit but without specific assignment.

4 a. To fill a need thus created and in harmony with my will now revealed through my servant, the prophet, Francis E. Hansen is called and should be set apart as Presiding Bishop of my church in these latter days.

b. As such he will be charged with the responsibility to act as president of the Aaronic priesthood in matters of teaching and training in harmony with provisions in the law of the church.

5 a. Further in harmony with my will and in order to give continuity in office, Harold W. Cackler is called to remain in the Presiding Bishopric as a counselor.

b. To complete the organization in the Presiding Bishopric my servant, Gene M. Hummel, is called as a counselor to the Presiding Bishop and should be set apart to this office.

The Spirit prompts me to reveal further words of advice and direction.

6. Collectively and individually you, my people, are commended for your excellent response to the needs of my church, both in sharing the gospel and bringing new members into the body of Christ, and also for making your accounting and paying your tithing. By compliance you have furnished the funds necessary to finance projects which have brought ministry to many in need of spiritual and physical assistance.

7. These are portentous times. The lives of many are being sacrificed unnecessarily to the gods of war, greed, and avarice. The land is being desecrated by the thoughtless waste of vital resources. You must obey my commandments and be in the forefront of those who would mediate this needless destruction while there is yet day.

8. Continue your study toward defining the purpose and selecting a place for erecting a temple in my name for the teaching of my priesthood. If you will be faithful in this, continuing to raise funds, even if for a time it may seem a sacrifice, you will be blessed with enough and to spare.

9. You are admonished to support your officers whom I have chosen to be set apart that I may honor them by my Spirit also. In this manner instructions given to you regarding membership participation and priesthood training may go forward at an accelerated rate and according to instruction given in previous commandments.

10 a. Monogamy is the basic principle on which Christian married life is built. Yet, as I have said before, there are also those who are not of this fold to whom the saving grace of the gospel must go.

b. When this is done the church must be willing to bear the burden of their sin, nurturing them in the faith, accepting that degree of repentance which it is possible for them to achieve, looking forward to the day when through patience and love they can be free as a people from the sins of the years of their ignorance.

11 a. To this end and for this purpose, continue your ministry to those nations of people yet unaware of the joy

freedom from sin can bring into their lives. In this way they will be brought to a knowledge of the teachings of my gospel and be made ready and willing to help spread the message of reconciliation and restoration to other worthy souls.

b. In this ministry the apostolic council, as the chief witnesses of the gospel, are directed to interpret and administer the doctrines and ordinances of the gospel in a manner appropriate to the circumstances in which they find such persons.

12 a. The spirit of unity must prevail if my church is to survive these perilous times and continue as a viable force in the world, fulfilling its destiny. You, my people, have been called apart to assist in this great work in these last days.

b. Put aside petty differences and join together as never before that all may labor together according to the gifts with which I have endowed you, and my Spirit will be with you now and forever more. Amen.

Your servant in Christ,
W. Wallace Smith
President of the Church

Independence, Missouri
April 11, 1972

Section 151

This revelation addressed the need for changes in the presiding leadership of the church. Apostles Holmes, Ettinger, and Higdon were released from the Council of Twelve. Roy A. Cheville was succeeded by Reed M. Holmes as Presiding Patriarch.

Vacancies were filled by William T. Higdon, serving as President of Graceland College at the time of his call, Lloyd B. Hurshman and Paul W. Booth, both of whom had served in

*field assignments and in church-wide functions as Director of
Administrative Services and Director of Program Planning.*

*The church was admonished to explore differences over
procedure and program materials in the spirit of reconciliation.*

*The Conference approved the revelation on April 3, 1974,
after supporting action was reported by quorums, councils,
and orders.*

*To the Councils and Quorums and Orders of the Church and
to the World Conference:*

*After serious and prayerful consideration and in the spirit
of inspiration and wisdom I bring the following word regarding
changes in the general leadership of the church as well as
counsel and advice to the membership as a whole.*

1a. Roy A. Cheville, who has served as Presiding Patriarch
for the past sixteen years, is relieved of this responsibility and
should be given the honor of superannuation and the title of
Presiding Patriarch Emeritus to the church.

b. Thus in retirement he can make his contribution but in a
less demanding way and without the stress of presiding
authority in the order or assignment to the field.

2. Reed M. Holmes, having served acceptably as an
apostle—an especial witness—for many years, is called and, if
willing, will become the Presiding Patriarch, assuming the
duties and responsibilities of that office as soon as arrangement for his ordination can be made and consummated.

3a. Cecil R. Ettinger, having prepared himself educationally
and spiritually, has served as an apostle and has contributed
much to the progress of the church in this capacity.

b. His apostolic witness is to be extended as a high priest in
the Order of Melchisedec with specific responsibilities assigned
and adjusted from time to time by the presidency of the high
priesthood.

4a. Earl T. Higdon responded to the call to become an apostle and serve with his brethren in the Council of Twelve knowing that his contribution in that capacity would be limited in time.

b. The time has come for him to be relieved of the arduous tasks imposed on him by the demands of travel and administrative detail. He will be given the honor of retirement in due time without further specific assignment.

To fill the vacancies thus created I am—under what I interpret as the direction of the Holy Spirit—calling upon the following brethren to accept positions in the Council of Twelve as apostles and especial witnesses of their Lord Jesus Christ, under whose leadership and guidance we all have our commission and derive our authority.

5a. Elder William T. Higdon has the demonstrated capacity to be an especial witness to peoples throughout the world regardless of color, race, or creed. For this and other significant reasons he is called to become an apostle and is to be ordained and set apart to that office.

b. The call was made known at a previous time but, because of circumstances having such far-reaching importance to the youth of the church in his capacity as president of Graceland College, it was withheld from consideration. His ordination is now timely and should be consummated and arrangements made to relieve him of his duties at the college as expeditiously as possible.

6. Elder Lloyd B. Hurshman is called to be an apostle. He will extend his outreach to a wider circle of influence as he makes his contribution, continuing in various ways now assigned to him but with the added authority bestowed upon him by ordination and setting apart as an apostle in these latter days.

7. Elder Paul W. Booth has demonstrated his ability to serve the church in various capacities. He is now called to be an

apostle. He will be ordained and set apart to that office that he may make his contribution in concert with his brethren as a member of the Council of Twelve.

I have strong feelings regarding the future of the work which according to the word of God "has been entrusted to all." Those feelings can be articulated under the influence of my heavenly Father as direction to the church.

8a. Do not let pride of personal accomplishment turn you away from my purposes in you as brothers and sisters in Christ and objects of my creation. You are called apart to do the will of your heavenly Father in whose name you serve.

b. Seek to be reconciled one with another. Let not your differences over procedures and program materials separate you and thus vitiate my influence for good in the world which is torn asunder by the devastating powers of evil.

9. You who are my disciples must be found continuing in the forefront of those organizations and movements which are recognizing the worth of persons and are committed to bringing the ministry of my Son to bear on their lives.

10. Working together to this end will promote unity, resolve conflicts, relieve tensions between individuals, and heal the wounds which have been sapping the strength of the church, spiritually and materially. This you must do in the spirit of love and compassion as revealed in my Son during his journey in your midst.

In the spirit of humility but with the authority of my office and the confirmation of the power of God motivating my action I submit this document to the church through its councils, quorums, orders, and delegates for consideration and final action.

> Your servant in Christ,
> W. Wallace Smith
> *President of the Church*

Independence, Missouri
April 1, 1974

SECTION 152

Provisions in the document submitted to the 1976 World Conference set a new precedent in the procedures for presidential succession in the church. In respect to this matter President W. Wallace Smith wrote in his transmittal letter as follows:

"*In spite of the precedent which up to now has seen the president of the church remain in office until his death, the time has come for me to name my successor and also to designate the time for him to succeed me as the presiding officer of the church, to serve as Prophet, Seer, and Revelator and President of the High Priesthood and the church, subject to the will of the Conference (Doctrine and Covenants 43:2a).*"

The document names Wallace Bunnell Smith as prophet and president designate and provides for the retirement of W. Wallace Smith after approximately two years of "spiritual preparation and study" by his successor.

Apostle Russell F. Ralston is honorably released from the apostolic council and commended for faithful service. The vacancy is filled by the designation of C. Eugene Austin, Sr.

The grace of God is recognized in that he loves us even when we turn from him, and the call to repentance and reconciliation is accompanied by the renewed assurance of divine blessing.

I have given serious and sustained consideration over a long period of time to the question of "who shall be my successor in office." Consequently, I have taken this matter to God in prayer repeatedly, petitioning for light so I might know the will of my heavenly Father, and knowing it have the wisdom and strength to do it.

Thus having sought the mind and will of God in matters

pertaining to conduct and growth of the kingdom I am prepared to bring the following message.

To the Councils and Quorums and Orders of the Church and to the General Conference:

1a. In order that my church shall continue to be led by my spirit through the heritage of its founder, my servant Elder Wallace Bunnell Smith is called into the service of the church as an assistant to his father and to the Quorum of the Presidency, with the title, *prophet and president designate.*

b. He will serve in this capacity during a period of spiritual preparation and study approximating two years, after which time, if he remain faithful, through the process of common consent of the body of my church, he is to be chosen as president to succeed his father.

c. At that time, if his life is extended, W. Wallace Smith, my servant who will have served as the leader of my church for a period of twenty years, shall retire and be given the title of president emeritus.

2a. My servant, Elder Russell F. Ralston, having served in numerous capacities during the period of his appointment as a full-time minister in my church, the last twelve years of which as a member of the Council of Twelve, is to be honorably released from his responsibility as a member of that council.

b. As a faithful servant in my kingdom his reward is sure if he shall continue to uphold those tenets of the gospel which he knows to be true. His apostolic witness is to be extended through his high priestly ordination and the spirit of testimony which has motivated his ministry for so many years.

c. As a special representative under the direction of the president of the Council of Twelve he will be given opportunities to expound the gospel through preaching and teaching assignments as time and strength are available and circumstances permit, but without the burden of administrative responsibility or extensive travel in a specific geographic jurisdiction. If he continues in faith I the Lord will bless him and his family with a degree of health and strength and peace of mind equal to their needs.

3a. To fill the vacancy thus created, Elder C. Eugene Austin, Sr., is called to be an apostle in my church. The consummation of this call by ordination as a member of the Council of Twelve should be accomplished as expeditiously as possible to ensure continuity of leadership in the various jurisdictions where members of the Council of Twelve serve as directed by the Presidency of the High Priesthood.

4a. The Spirit saith further: I, God, have not forsaken you nor have I changed in regard to the great and important work of the Restoration which I have called you to do. Neither have I turned from you my people. This is true in spite of the fact that some of you have turned away from me and my purposes.

b. Some have been led to inactivity, yea and even lulled to sleep by the spirit of carelessness and indifference. Some have been overcome by the grosser sins of the world—the spirit of revelry, wanton living, use of drugs, drinking, and fornication—and have fallen away. And still others have turned away for personal aggrandizement, rejecting my leadership because of trivial offenses.

c. All who have done any of these things are counseled to repent with a contrite heart and heaviness of spirit while there is yet time. You are further admonished to covenant with me anew that you may again be clean men and women, and find peace.

d. My promises are sure; my yoke is easy and my burden is light for those who love me and walk in the light of my Spirit.

W. WALLACE SMITH
President of the Church

Independence, Missouri
March 29, 1976

APPENDIX A

SECTION 107

This statement was removed from the main body of the book by the action of the 1970 World Conference. Its subject is primarily concerned with arrangements for the construction of a boardinghouse in Nauvoo and with the practice of the ordinance of baptism for the dead. It will be noted that several paragraphs are devoted to references to such practices as "washings," "anointings," and "memorials for your sacrifices" and matters which "have been kept hid from before the foundation of the world" (paragraphs 10, 11, 12, 13).

Concerning such esoteric practices the Reorganized Church of Jesus Christ of Latter Day Saints declared as early as April 9, 1886, that "we know of no temple building, except as edifices wherein to worship God, and no endowment except the endowment of the Holy Spirit of the kind experienced by the early saints on Pentecost Day." And also, "that 'baptism for the dead' belongs to those local questions of which the body has said by resolution: 'That the commandments of a local character, given to the first organization of the church, are binding on the Reorganization only so far as they are either reiterated or referred to as binding by commandments to this church.' And that principle has neither been reiterated nor referred to as a commandment" (Conference Resolution 308, paragraphs 2, 3).

Instruction to the church bearing on this matter is contained in a revelation through W. Wallace Smith on April 5, 1968, referring to temple building in which the church is told that "there is no provision for secret ordinances now or ever" and that one temple function is priesthood education (Doctrine and Covenants 149A:6).

This section is retained in the Appendix for its historical value in relation to the development of ordinances for the dead and other ordinances for which the Reorganized

Church of Jesus Christ of Latter Day Saints finds no justification either in the historical scriptures or in the documents approved by the church as latter-day revelation.

1 a. Verily, thus saith the Lord unto you, my servant Joseph Smith, I am well pleased with your offering and acknowledgments, which you have made, for unto this end have I raised you up, that I might show forth my wisdom through the weak things of the earth.

b. Your prayers are acceptable before me, and in answer to them I say unto you that you are now called immediately to make a solemn proclamation of my gospel, and of this stake which I have planted to be a corner stone of Zion, which shall be polished with that refinement which is after the similitude of a palace.

c. This proclamation shall be made to all the kings of the world, to the four corners thereof—to the honorable president elect, and the high-minded governors of the nation in which you live, and to all the nations of the earth, scattered abroad.

d. Let it be written in the spirit of meekness, and by the power of the Holy Ghost, which shall be in you at the time of the writing of the same; for it shall be given you by the Holy Ghost to know my will concerning those kings and authorities, even what shall befall them in a time to come.

e. For, behold, I am about to call upon them to give heed to the light and glory of Zion, for the set time has come to favor her.

2 a. Call ye, therefore, upon them with loud proclamation, and with your testimony, fearing them not, for they are as grass, and all their glory as the flower thereof, which soon falleth, that they may be left also without excuse,

b. and that I may visit them in the day of visitation, when I shall unveil the face of my covering, to appoint the portion of the oppressor among hypocrites, where there is gnashing of teeth, if they reject my servants and my testimony which I have revealed unto them.

c. And again, I will visit and soften their hearts, many of them, for your good, that ye may find grace in their eyes, that they may come to the light of truth, and the Gentiles to the exaltation or lifting up of Zion.

d. For the day of my visitation cometh speedily, in an hour when ye think not, and where shall be the safety of my people, and refuge for those who shall be left of them?

3 Awake! O kings of the earth! Come ye, O come ye, with your gold and your silver, to the help of my people, to the house of the daughters of Zion!

4 a. And again, verily I say unto you, Let my servant Robert B. Thompson help you to write this proclamation; for I am well pleased with him, and that he should be with you;

b. let him, therefore, hearken to your counsel, and I will bless him with a multiplicity of blessings; let him be faithful and true in all things from henceforth, and he shall be great in mine eyes; but let him remember that his stewardship will I require at his hands.

5 And again, verily I say unto you, Blessed is my servant Hyrum Smith, for I, the Lord, love him, because of the integrity of his heart, and because he loveth that which is right before me, saith the Lord.

6 a. Again, let my servant John C. Bennett, help you in your labor in sending my word to the kings of the people of the earth, and stand by you, even you my servant Joseph Smith, in the hour of affliction, and his reward shall not fail, if he receive counsel; and for his love he shall be great; for he shall be mine if he do this, saith the Lord.

b. I have seen the work which he hath done, which I accept, if he continue, and will crown him with blessings and great glory.

7 a. And again, I say unto you, that it is my will that my servant Lyman Wight should continue in preaching for Zion, in the spirit of meekness, confessing me before the world,

b. and I will bear him up as on eagle's wings, and he shall beget glory and honor to himself, and unto my name, that when he shall finish his work, that I may receive him unto myself, even as I did my servant David Patten, who is with me at this time,

c. and also my servant Edward Partridge, and also my aged

servant Joseph Smith, Sr., who sitteth with Abraham, at his right hand, and blessed and holy is he, for he is mine.

8 a. And again, verily I say unto you, My servant George Miller is without guile; he may be trusted because of the integrity of his heart; and for the love which he has to my testimony, I, the Lord, love him:

b. I, therefore, say unto you, I seal upon his head the office of a bishop, like unto my servant Edward Partridge, that he may receive the consecrations of mine house, that he may administer blessings upon the heads of the poor of my people, saith the Lord.

c. Let no man despise my servant George, for he shall honor me.

9 a. Let my servant George, and my servant Lyman, and my servant John Snider, and others, build a house unto my name, such a one as my servant Joseph shall show unto them; upon the place which he shall show unto them also.

b. And it shall be for a house for boarding, a house that strangers may come from afar to lodge therein; therefore, let it be a good house, worthy of all acceptation, that the weary traveler may find health and safety while he shall contemplate the word of the Lord, and the corner stone I have appointed for Zion.

c. This house shall be a healthful habitation, if it be built unto my name, and if the governor, which shall be appointed unto it shall not suffer any pollution to come upon it. It shall be holy, or the Lord your God will not dwell therein.

10 a. And again, verily I say unto you, Let all my Saints come from afar; and send ye swift messengers, yea, chosen messengers, and say unto them,

b. Come ye, with all your gold, and your silver, and your precious stones, and with all your antiquities; and with all who have knowledge of antiquities, that will come may come, and bring the box tree, and the fir tree, and the pine tree, together with all the precious trees of the earth;

c. and with iron, with copper, and with brass, and with zinc, and with all your precious things of the earth, and build a house to my name, for the Most High to dwell therein;

d. for there is not a place found on earth that he may

come and restore again that which was lost unto you, or, which he hath taken away, even the fullness of the priesthood;

e. for a baptismal font there is not upon the earth; that they, my saints, may be baptized for those who are dead; for this ordinance belongeth to my house, and can not be acceptable to me, only in the days of your poverty, wherein ye are not able to build a house unto me.

f. But I command you, all ye my Saints, to build a house unto me; and I grant unto you a sufficient time to build a house unto me, and during this time your baptisms shall be acceptable unto me.

11 a. But, behold, at the end of this appointment, your baptisms for your dead shall not be acceptable unto me; and if you do not these things at the end of the appointment, ye shall be rejected as a church with your dead, saith the Lord your God.

b. For, verily I say unto you, that after you have had sufficient time to build a house to me, wherein the ordinance of baptizing for the dead belongeth, and for which the same was instituted from before the foundation of the world, your baptisms for your dead can not be acceptable unto me; for therein are the keys of the holy priesthood ordained, that you may receive honor and glory.

c. And after this time, your baptisms for the dead, by those who are scattered abroad, are not acceptable unto me, saith the Lord; for it is ordained that in Zion, and in her stakes, and in Jerusalem, those places which I have appointed for refuge, shall be the places for your baptisms for your dead.

12 a. And again, verily I say unto you, How shall your washings be acceptable unto me, except ye perform them in a house which you have built to my name?

b. For, for this cause I commanded Moses that he should build a tabernacle, that they should bear it with them in the wilderness, and to build a house in the land of promise, that those ordinances might be revealed which had been hid from before the world was;

c. therefore, verily I say unto you, that your anointings, and your washings, and your baptisms for the dead, and your solemn assemblies, and your memorials for your sacrifices, by the sons of Levi, and for your oracles in your most holy places, wherein you receive conversations, and your statutes and judgments, for the beginning of the revelations and foundation of Zion, and for the glory, honor, and endowment of all her municipals, are ordained by the ordinance of my holy house, which my people are always commanded to build unto my holy name.

13 a. And verily I say unto you, Let this house be built unto my name, that I may reveal mine ordinances therein, unto my people;

b. for I deign to reveal unto my church things which have been kept hid from before the foundation of the world; things that pertain to the dispensation of the fullness of times;

c. and I will show unto my servant Joseph all things pertaining to this house, and the priesthood thereof; and the place whereon it shall be built;

d. and ye shall build it on the place where you have contemplated building it; for that is the spot which I have chosen for you to build it.

e. If ye labor with all your might, I will consecrate that spot, that it shall be made holy; and if my people will hearken unto my voice, and unto the voice of my servants whom I have appointed to lead my people, behold, verily I say unto you, They shall not be moved out of their place.

f. But if they will not hearken to my voice, nor unto the voice of these men whom I have appointed, they shall not be blessed, because they pollute mine holy grounds, and mine holy ordinances and charters, and my holy words, which I give unto them.

14 a. And it shall come to pass, that if you build a house unto my name, and do not the things that I say, I will not perform the oath which I make unto you, neither fulfill the promises which ye expect at my hands, saith the Lord;

b. for instead of blessings, ye, by your own works, bring cursings, wrath, indignation, and judgments, upon your own heads, by your follies, and by all your abominations, which you practice before me, saith the Lord.

15 a. Verily, verily I say unto you, that when I give a commandment to any of the sons of men, to do a work unto my name, and those sons of men go with all their might, and with all they have, to perform that work, and cease not

their diligence, and their enemies come upon them, and hinder them performing that work;

b. behold, it behooveth me to require that work no more at the hands of those sons of men, but to accept of their offerings; and the iniquity and transgression of my holy laws and commandments, I will visit upon the heads of those who hindered my work, unto the third and fourth generation, so long as they repent not, and hate me, saith the Lord God.

c. Therefore, for this cause have I accepted the offerings of those whom I commanded to build up a city and a house unto my name, in Jackson County, Missouri, and were hindered by their enemies, saith the Lord your God;

d. and I will answer judgment, wrath and indignation, wailing and anguish, and gnashing of teeth, upon their heads, unto the third and fourth generation, so long as they repent not, and hate me, saith the Lord your God.

16 a. And this I make an example unto you, for your consolation, concerning all those who have been commanded to do a work, and have been hindered by the hands of their enemies, and by oppression, saith the Lord your God;

b. for I am the Lord your God, and will save all those of your brethren who have been pure in heart, and have been slain in the land of Missouri, saith the Lord.

17 And again, verily I say unto you, I command you again to build a house to my name, even in this place, that you may prove yourselves unto me that ye are faithful in all things whatsoever I command you, that I may bless you, and crown you with honor, immortality, and eternal life.

18 a. And now I say unto you, as pertaining to my boarding house, which I have commanded you to build, for the boarding of strangers,

b. Let it be built unto my name, and let my name be named upon it, and let my servant Joseph and his house have place therein, from generation to generation; for this anointing have I put upon his head, that his blessing shall also be put upon the head of his posterity after him;

c. and as I said unto Abraham, concerning the kindreds of the earth, even so I say unto my servant Joseph, In thee, and in thy seed, shall the kindred of the earth be blessed.

d. Therefore, let my servant Joseph, and his seed after

him, have place in that house, from generation to generation, for ever and ever, saith the Lord, and let the name
of that house be called the Nauvoo House; and let it be a
delightful habitation for man, and a resting place for the
weary traveler,

e. that he may contemplate the glory of Zion, and the
glory of this the corner stone thereof; that he may receive
also the counsel from those whom I have set to be as plants
of renown, and as watchmen upon her walls.

19 a. Behold, verily I say unto you, Let my servant George
Miller, and my servant Lyman Wight, and my servant John
Snider, and my servant Peter Haws, organize themselves, and
appoint one of them to be a president over their quorum for
the purpose of building that house.

b. And they shall form a constitution whereby they may
receive stock for the building of that house.

c. And they shall not receive less than fifty dollars for a
share of stock in that house, and they shall be permitted to
receive fifteen thousand dollars from any one man for stock
in that house; but they shall not be permitted to receive over
fifteen thousand dollars stock from any one man;

d. and they shall not be permitted to receive under fifty
dollars for a share of stock from any one man, in that house;
and they shall not be permitted to receive any man as a
stockholder in this house, except the same shall pay his stock
into their hands at the time he receives stock;

e. and in proportion to the amount of stock he pays into
their hands, he shall receive stock in that house; but if he pay
nothing into their hands, he shall not receive any stock in
that house.

f. And if any pay stock into their hands, it shall be for
stock in that house, for himself, and for his generation after
him, from generation to generation, so long as he and his
heirs shall hold that stock, and do not sell or convey the
stock away out of their hands by their own free will and act,
if you will do my will, saith the Lord your God.

20 a. And again, verily I say unto you, If my servant
George Miller, and my servant Lyman Wight, and my servant
John Snider, and my servant Peter Haws, receive any stock
into their hands, in moneys or in properties, wherein they
receive the real value of moneys, they shall not appropriate

any portion of that stock to any other purpose, only in that house;

b. and if they do appropriate any portion of that stock anywhere else, only in that house, without the consent of the stockholder, and do not repay fourfold for the stock which they appropriate anywhere else, only in that house,

c. they shall be accursed, and shall be moved out of their place, saith the Lord God; for I, the Lord, am God, and can not be mocked in any of these things.

21 a. Verily I say unto you, Let my servant Joseph pay stock into their hands for the building of that house, as seemeth him good;

b. but my servant Joseph can not pay over fifteen thousand dollars stock in that house, nor under fifty dollars; neither can any other man, saith the Lord.

22 a. And there are others also, who wish to know my will concerning them; for they have asked it at my hands;

b. therefore, I say unto you, concerning my servant Vinson Knight, If he will do my will, let him put stock into that house for himself and for his generation after him, from generation to generation, and let him lift up his voice, long and loud, in the midst of the people, to plead the cause of the poor and the needy, and let him not fail, neither let his heart faint, and I will accept of his offerings;

c. for they shall not be unto me as the offerings of Cain, for he shall be mine, saith the Lord.

d. Let his family rejoice, and turn away their hearts from affliction, for I have chosen him and anointed him, and he shall be honored in the midst of his house, for I will forgive all his sins, saith the Lord. Amen.

23 Verily I say unto you, Let my servant Hyrum put stock into that house, as seemeth him good, for himself and his generation after him, from generation to generation.

24 a. Let my servant Isaac Galland put stock into that house, for I, the Lord, love him for the work he hath done, and will forgive all his sins; therefore, let him be remembered for an interest in that house from generation to generation.

b. Let my servant Isaac Galland be appointed among you, and be ordained by my servant William Marks, and be blessed of him, to go with my servant Hyrum, to accomplish the work that my servant Joseph shall point out to them, and they shall be greatly blessed.

25 Let my servant William Marks pay stock into that house, as it seemeth him good, for himself and his generation, from generation to generation.

26 Let my servant Henry G. Sherwood pay stock into that house, as seemeth him good, for himself and his seed after him, from generation to generation.

27 a. Let my servant William Law pay stock into that house, for himself and his seed after him, from generation to generation.

b. If he will do my will, let him not take his family unto the eastern lands, even unto Kirtland; nevertheless, I, the Lord, will build up Kirtland, but I, the Lord, have a scourge prepared for the inhabitants thereof.

c. And with my servant Almon Babbitt there are many things with which I am not well pleased; behold, he aspireth to establish his council instead of the council which I have ordained, even the presidency of my church, and he setteth up a golden calf for the worship of my people.

d. Let no man go from this place who has come here essaying to keep my commandments.

e. If they live here let them live unto me; and if they die let them die unto me; for they shall rest from all their labors here, and shall continue their works.

f. Therefore let my servant William put his trust in me, and cease to fear concerning his family, because of the sickness of the land.

g. If ye love me, keep my commandments, and the sickness of the land shall redound to your glory.

28 a. Let my servant William go and proclaim my everlasting gospel with a loud voice, and with great joy, as he shall be moved upon by my Spirit, unto the inhabitants of Warsaw, and also unto the inhabitants of Carthage, and also unto the inhabitants of Burlington, and also unto the inhabitants of Madison, and await patiently and diligently for further instructions at my General Conference, saith the Lord.

b. If he will do my will, let him from henceforth hearken to the counsel of my servant Joseph, and with his interest support the cause of the poor, and publish the new translation of my holy word unto the inhabitants of the earth; and if he will do this, I will bless him with a multiplicity of blessings, that he shall not be forsaken, nor his seed be found begging bread.

29 a. And again, verily I say unto you, Let my servant William be appointed, ordained, and anointed, as a counselor unto my servant Joseph, in the room of my servant Hyrum;

b. that my servant Hyrum may take the office of priesthood and patriarch, which was appointed unto him by his father, by blessing and also by right, that from henceforth he shall hold the keys of the patriarchal blessings upon the heads of all my people, that whoever he blesses shall be blessed, and whoever he curseth shall be cursed;

c. that whatsoever he shall bind on earth shall be bound in heaven; and whatsoever he shall loose on earth shall be loosed in heaven;

d. and from this time forth, I appoint unto him that he may be a prophet, and a seer, and a revelator unto my church, as well as my servant Joseph, that he may act in concert also with my servant Joseph, and that he shall receive counsel from my servant Joseph,

e. who shall show unto him the keys whereby he may ask and receive, and be crowned with the same blessing, and glory, and honor, and priesthood, and gifts of the priesthood, that once were put upon him that was my servant Oliver Cowdery;

f. that my servant Hyrum may bear record of the things which I shall show unto him, that his name may be had in honorable remembrance from generation to generation, for ever and ever.

30 a. Let my servant William Law also receive the keys by which he may ask and receive blessings; let him be humble before me, and be without guile, and he shall receive of my Spirit, even the Comforter, which shall manifest unto him the truth of all things, and shall give him, in the very hour, what he shall say, and these signs shall follow him:

b. He shall heal the sick, he shall cast out devils, and shall be delivered from those who would administer unto him deadly poison, and he shall be led in paths where the poisonous serpent can not lay hold upon his heel, and he shall mount up in the imagination of his thoughts as upon eagle's wings; and what if I will that he should raise the dead, let him not withhold his voice.

c. Therefore let my servant William cry aloud and spare not, with joy and rejoicing, and with hosannas to him that sitteth upon the throne for ever and ever, saith the Lord your God.

31 Behold, I say unto you, I have a mission in store for my servant William, and my servant Hyrum, and for them alone; and let my servant Joseph tarry at home, for he is needed. The remainder I will show unto you hereafter. Even so. Amen.

32 a. And again, verily I say unto you, If my servant Sidney will serve me, and be counselor unto my servant Joseph, let him arise and come up and stand in the office of his calling and humble himself before me;

b. and if he will offer unto me an acceptable offering, and acknowledgements, and remain with my people, behold, I, the Lord, your God, will heal him that he shall be healed; and he shall lift up his voice again on the mountains, and be a spokesman before my face.

c. Let him come and locate his family in the neighborhood in which my servant Joseph resides, and, in all his journeyings let him lift up his voice as with the sound of a trump, and warn the inhabitants of the earth to flee the wrath to come;

d. let him assist my servant Joseph; and also let my servant William Law assist my servant Joseph in making a solemn proclamation unto the kings of the earth, even as I have before said unto you.

e. If my servant Sidney will do my will, let him not remove his family unto the eastern lands, but let him change their habitation, even as I have said.

f. Behold, it is not my will that he shall seek to find safety and refuge out of the city which I have appointed unto you, even the city of Nauvoo. Verily I say unto you, Even now, if he will hearken to my voice, it shall be well with him. Even so. Amen.

33 a. And again, verily I say unto you, Let my servant Amos Davis pay stock into the hands of those whom I have

appointed to build a house for boarding, even the Nauvoo House;

b. this let him do if he will have an interest, and let him hearken unto the counsel of my servant Joseph, and labor with his own hands, that he may obtain the confidence of men;

c. and when he shall prove himself faithful in all things that shall be intrusted unto his care—yea, even a few things —he shall be made ruler over many; let him, therefore, abase himself that he may be exalted. Even so. Amen.

34 a. And again, verily I say unto you, If my servant Robert D. Foster will obey my voice, let him build a house for my servant Joseph, according to the contract which he has made with him, as the door shall be open to him from time to time;

b. and let him repent of all his folly, and clothe himself with charity, and cease to do evil, and lay aside all his hard speeches, and pay stock also into the hands of the quorum of the Nauvoo House, for himself and for his generation after him, from generation to generation,

c. and hearken unto the counsel of my servants Joseph and Hyrum and William Law, and unto the authorities which I have called to lay the foundation of Zion, and it shall be well with him for ever and ever. Even so. Amen.

35 a. And again, verily I say unto you, Let no man pay stock to the quorum of the Nauvoo House unless he shall be a believer in the Book of Mormon and the revelations I have given unto you, saith the Lord your God;

b. for that which is more or less than this cometh of evil, and shall be attended with cursings, and not blessings, saith the Lord your God. Even so. Amen.

36 a. And again, verily I say unto you, Let the quorum of the Nauvoo House have a just recompense of wages for all their labors which they do in building the Nauvoo House, and let their wages be as shall be agreed among themselves, as pertaining to the price thereof;

b. and let every man who pays stock bear his proportion of their wages, if it must needs be, for their support, saith the Lord, otherwise their labors shall be accounted unto them for stock in that house. Even so. Amen.

37 Verily I say unto you, I now give unto you the officers belonging to my priesthood, that ye may hold the keys thereof, even the priesthood which is after the order of Melchisedec, which is after the order of my only begotten Son.

38 First, I give unto you Hyrum Smith to be a patriarch unto you, to hold the sealing blessings of my church, even the Holy Spirit of promise, whereby ye are sealed up unto the day of redemption, that ye may not fall, notwithstanding the hour of temptation that may come upon you.

39 a. I give unto you my servant Joseph, to be a presiding elder over all my church, to be a translator, a revelator, a seer, and prophet.

b. I give unto him for counselors my servant Sidney Rigdon and my servant William Law, that these may constitute a quorum and First Presidency, to receive the oracles for the whole church.

40 a. I give unto you my servant Brigham Young, to be a president over the twelve traveling council, which Twelve hold the keys to open up the authority of my kingdom upon the four corners of the earth, and after that to send my word to every creature;

b. they are: Heber C. Kimball, Parley P. Pratt, Orson Pratt, Orson Hyde, William Smith, John Taylor, John E. Page, Wilford Woodruff, Willard Richards, George A. Smith.

c. David Patten I have taken unto myself; behold, his priesthood no man taketh from him; but verily I say unto you, Another may be appointed unto the same calling.

41 a. And again I say unto you, I give unto you a high council, for the corner stone of Zion; namely: Samuel Bent, H. G. Sherwood, George W. Harris, Charles C. Rich, Thomas Grover, Newel Knight, David Dort, Dunbar Wilson.

b. Seymour Brunson I have taken unto myself; no man taketh his priesthood, but another may be appointed unto the same priesthood in his stead (and verily I say unto you, let my servant Aaron Johnson be ordained unto this calling in his stead), David Fulmer, Alpheus Cutler, William Huntington.

42 a. And again, I give unto you Don C. Smith to be a president over a quorum of high priests, which ordinance is instituted for the purpose of qualifying those who shall

be appointed standing presidents or servants over different stakes scattered abroad, and they may travel, also, if they choose, but rather be ordained for standing presidents; this is the office of their calling, saith the Lord your God.

b. I give unto him Amasa Lyman and Noah Packard for counselors, that they may preside over the quorum of high priests of my church, saith the Lord.

43 And again I say unto you, I give unto you John A. Hicks, Samuel Williams, and Jesse Baker, which priesthood is to preside over the quorum of elders, which quorum is instituted for standing ministers; nevertheless they may travel, yet they are ordained to be standing ministers to my church, saith the Lord.

44 a. And again, I give unto you Joseph Young, Josiah Butterfield, Daniel Miles, Henry Herriman, Zera Pulsipher, Levi Hancock, James Foster, to preside over the quorum of seventies, which quorum is instituted for traveling elders to bear record of my name in all the world, wherever the traveling high council, my apostles, shall send them to prepare a way before my face.

b. The difference between this quorum and the quorum of elders is, that one is to travel continually, and the other is to preside over the churches from time to time;

c. the one has the responsibility of presiding from time to time, and the other has no responsibility of presiding, saith the Lord your God.

45 And again, I say unto you, I give unto you Vinson Knight, Samuel H. Smith, and Shadrach Roundy, if he will receive it, to preside over the bishopric; a knowledge of said bishopric is given unto you in the Book of Doctrine and Covenants.

46 a. And, again I say unto you, Samuel Rolfe and his counselors for priests, and the president of the teachers and his counselors, and also the president of the deacons and his counselors, and also the president of the stake and his counselors:

b. The above offices I have given unto you, and the keys thereof, for helps and for governments, for the work of the ministry, and the perfecting of my saints,

c. and a commandment I give unto you that you should fill all these offices and approve of those names which I have mentioned, or else disapprove of them, at my General Conference, and that ye should prepare rooms for all these offices in my house when you build it unto my name, saith the Lord your God. Even so. Amen.

APPENDIX B

SECTION 109

The following letter from Joseph Smith, Jr., addressed to the Saints of Nauvoo, Illinois, September 1, 1842, was published first in "Times and Seasons," 3:919. It was included in the second (1844) edition of the Doctrine and Covenants and has been continued in all subsequent editions. The Conference of 1970 ordered its removal to the Appendix. Concerning "baptism for the dead" see the introduction to Section 107 (Appendix A).

NAUVOO, September 1, 1842

1 a. Forasmuch as the Lord has revealed unto me that my enemies, both in Missouri and this state, were again on the pursuit of me; and inasmuch as they pursue me without a cause, and have not the least shadow or coloring of justice or right on their side in the getting up of their prosecutions against me;

b. and inasmuch as their pretensions are all founded in falsehood of the blackest dye, I have thought it expedient and wisdom in me to leave the place for a short season, for my own safety and the safety of this people.

c. I would say to all those with whom I have business, that I have left my affairs with agents and clerks, who will transact all business in a prompt and proper manner; and will see that all my debts are canceled in due time, by turning out property, or otherwise as the case may require, or as the circumstances may admit of.

d. When I learn that the storm is fully blown over, then I will return to you again.

2 a. And as for the perils which I am called to pass through, they seem but a small thing to me, as the envy and wrath of man have been my common lot all the days of my life;

b. and for what cause it seems mysterious, unless I was ordained from before the foundation of the world, for some good end, or bad, as you may choose to call it. Judge ye for yourselves. God knoweth all these things, whether it be good or bad.

c. But nevertheless, deep water is what I am wont to swim in; it all has become a second nature to me.

d. And I feel like Paul to glory in tribulation, for to this day has the God of my fathers delivered me out of them all, and will deliver me from henceforth; for, behold, and lo, I shall triumph over all my enemies, for the Lord God hath spoken it.

3 Let all the Saints rejoice, therefore, and be exceeding glad, for Israel's God is their God; and he will mete out a just recompense of reward upon the heads of all your oppressors.

4 a. And again, verily thus saith the Lord, Let the work of my temple, and all the works which I have appointed unto you, be continued on and not cease; and let your diligence and your perseverance, and patience, and your works be redoubled; and you shall in nowise lose your reward, saith the Lord of hosts.

b. And if they persecute you, so persecuted they the prophets and righteous men that were before you. For all this there is a reward in heaven.

5 a. And again, I give unto you a word in relation to the baptism for your dead. Verily, thus saith the Lord unto you concerning your dead:

b. When any of you are baptized for your dead, let there be a recorder; and let him be eyewitness of your baptisms; let him hear with his ears, that he may testify of a truth, saith the Lord;

c. that in all your recordings, it may be recorded in heaven, that whatsoever you bind on earth, may be bound in heaven; whatsoever you loose on earth may be loosed in heaven; for I am about to restore many things to the earth pertaining to the priesthood, saith the Lord of hosts.

6 And again, let all the records be had in order, that they may be put in the archives of my Holy Temple, to be held in remembrance from generation to generation, saith the Lord of hosts.

7 a. I will say to all the Saints, that I desired, with exceeding great desire, to have addressed them from the stand,
on the subject of baptism for the dead, on the following
Sabbath.

b. But inasmuch as it is out of my power to do so, I will
write the word of the Lord from time to time, on that subject, and send it to you by mail, as well as many other
things.

8 I now close my letter for the present, for the want of
more time; for the enemy is on the alert, and, as the Savior
said, The prince of this world cometh, but he hath nothing
in me.

9 Behold, my prayer to God is, that you all may be saved.
And I subscribe myself your servant in the Lord, prophet
and seer of the Church of Jesus Christ of Latter Day Saints.

JOSEPH SMITH

APPENDIX C

SECTION 110

This section is a continuation of the letter of Joseph Smith, Jr., addressed to the Saints of Nauvoo, Illinois (Doctrine and Covenants 109). It was written September 6, 1842, while Joseph was hiding from his persecutors and was first published in the "Times and Seasons" for October 1, 1842 (3:934). It was included in the second (1844) edition of the Doctrine and Covenants and has been retained in all subsequent editions. The Conference of 1970 ordered its removal to the Appendix. Concerning "baptism for the dead" see the Introduction to Section 107 (Appendix A).

NAUVOO, September 6, 1842

1 a. As I stated to you in my letter before I left my place, that I would write to you from time to time, and give you information in relation to many subjects, I now resume the subject of the baptism for the dead;

b. as that subject seems to occupy my mind, and press itself upon my feelings the strongest, since I have been pursued by my enemies.

2 a. I wrote a few words of revelation to you concerning a recorder. I have had a few additional views in relation to this matter, which I now certify.

b. That is, it was declared in my former letter that there should be a recorder, who should be eyewitness, and also to hear with his ears, that he might make a record of a truth before the Lord.

3 a. Now, in relation to this matter, it would be very difficult for one recorder to be present at all times, and to do all the business.

b. To obviate this difficulty, there can be a recorder appointed in each ward of the city, who is well qualified for taking accurate minutes; and let him be very particular and precise in taking the whole proceedings, certifying in his record that he saw with his eyes and heard with his ears, giving the date and names, etc., and the history of the whole transaction;

c. naming, also, some three individuals that are present, if there be any present, who can, at any time when called upon, certify to the same, that in the mouth of two or three witnesses every word may be established.

4 a. Then let there be a general recorder, to whom these other records can be handed, being attended with certificates over their own signatures, certifying that the record which they have made is true.

b. Then the general church recorder can enter the record on the general church book, with the certificates and all the attending witnesses, with his own statement that he verily believes the above statement and records to be true, from his knowledge of the general character and appointment of those men by the church.

c. And when this is done on the general church book, the record shall be just as holy, and shall answer the ordinance just the same as if he had seen with his eyes and heard with his ears, and made a record of the same on the general church book.

5 You may think this order of things to be very particular, but let me tell you that they are only to answer the will of God, by conforming to the ordinance and preparation that the Lord ordained and prepared before the foundation of the world, for the salvation of the dead who should die without a knowledge of the gospel.

6 a. And further, I want you to remember that John the Revelator was contemplating this very subject in relation to the dead, when he declared, as you will find recorded in Revelation 20: 12,

b. "And I saw the dead, small and great, stand before God; and the books were opened: and another book was opened, which is the book of life: and the dead were judged out of those things which were written in the books, according to their works."

7 a. You will discover in this quotation that the books were opened, and another book was opened, which was the book of life; but the dead were judged out of those things which were written in the books, according to their works;

b. consequently, the books spoken of must be the books which contained the record of their works, and refer to the records which are kept on the earth.

c. And the book which was the book of life, is the record which is kept in heaven; the principle agreeing precisely with the doctrine which is commanded you in the revelation contained in the letter which I wrote to you, previous to my leaving my place, "that in all your recordings it may be recorded in heaven."

8 a. Now the nature of this ordinance consists in the power of the priesthood, by the revelation of Jesus Christ, wherein it is granted that whatsoever you bind on earth should be bound in heaven, and whatsoever you loose on earth shall be loosed in heaven;

b. or, in other words, taking a different view of the translation, whatsoever you record on earth shall be recorded in heaven, and whatsoever you do not record on earth shall not be recorded in heaven;

c. for out of the books shall your dead be judged, according to their own works, whether they themselves have attended to the ordinances in their own *propria personae* or by the means of their own agents, according to the ordinance which God has prepared for their salvation from before the foundation of the world, according to the records which they have kept concerning their dead.

9 a. It may seem to some to be a very bold doctrine that we talk of—a power which records or binds on earth and binds in heaven; nevertheless, in all ages of the world, whenever the Lord has given a dispensation of the priesthood to any man by actual revelation, or any set of men, this power has always been given.

b. Hence, whatsoever those men did in authority, in the name of the Lord, and did it truly and faithfully, and kept a proper and faithful record of the same, it became a law on earth and in heaven, and could not be annulled, according to the decrees of the great Jehovah. This is a faithful saying. Who can hear it?

10 And again, for a precedent, Matthew 16: 18, 19. "And I say also unto thee, That thou art Peter, and upon this rock I will build my church; and the gates of hell shall

not prevail against it. And I will give unto thee the keys of the kingdom of heaven: and whatsoever thou shalt bind on earth shall be bound in heaven; and whatsoever thou shalt loose on earth shall be loosed in heaven."

11 a. Now the great and grand secret of the whole matter, and the *summum bonum* of the whole subject that is lying before us, consists in obtaining the powers of the holy priesthood.

b. For him to whom these keys are given there is no difficulty in obtaining a knowledge of facts in relation to the salvation of the children of men, both as well for the dead as for the living.

12 a. Herein is glory and honor, and immortality and eternal life. The ordinance of baptism by water, to be immersed therein in order to answer the likeness of the dead, that one principle might accord with the other.

b. To be immersed in the water, and come forth out of the water, is in the likeness of the resurrection of the dead in coming forth out of their graves; hence this ordinance was instituted to form a relationship with the ordinance of baptism for the dead, being in likeness of the dead.

13 a. Consequently the baptismal font was instituted as a simile of the grave, and was commanded to be in a place underneath where the living are wont to assemble, to show forth the living and the dead;

b. and that all things may have their likeness, and that they may accord one with another; that which is earthly conforming to that which is heavenly, as Paul hath declared. (I Corinthians 15: 46-48.)

14 a. "Howbeit that was not first which is spiritual, but that which is natural; and afterward that which is spiritual. The first man is of the earth, earthy: the second man is the Lord from heaven. As is the earthy, such are they also that are earthy: and as is the heavenly, such are they also that are heavenly."

b. And as are the records on the earth in relation to your dead, which are truly made out, so also are the records in heaven. This, therefore, is the sealing and binding power, and in one sense of the word, the keys of the kingdom, which consists in the key of knowledge.

15 a. And now my dearly beloved brethren and sisters, let me assure you that these are principles in relation to the dead and the living that can not be lightly passed over, as pertaining to our salvation.

b. For their salvation is necessary and essential to our salvation, as Paul says concerning the fathers, "that they without us can not be made perfect"; neither can we without our dead be made perfect.

16 And now in relation to the baptism for the dead, I will give you another quotation of Paul. 1 Corinthians 15: 29. "Else what shall they do which are baptized for the dead, if the dead rise not at all? why are they then baptized for the dead?"

17 a. And again, in connection with this quotation, I will give you a quotation from one of the prophets, who had his eye fixed on the restoration of the priesthood, the glories to be revealed in the last days, and in an especial manner this most glorious of all subjects belonging to the everlasting gospel; namely: the baptism for the dead:

b. for Malachi says, last chapter, verses 5 and 6, "Behold, I will send you Elijah the prophet before the coming of the great and dreadful day of the Lord: and he shall turn the heart of the fathers to the children, and the heart of the children to their fathers, lest I come and smite the earth with a curse."

18 a. I might have rendered a plainer translation to this, but it is sufficiently plain to suit my purpose as it stands.

b. It is sufficient to know in this case that the earth will be smitten with a curse, unless there is a welding link of some kind or other, between the fathers and the children, upon some subject or other, and, behold, what is that subject?

c. It is the baptism for the dead. For we without them can not be made perfect; neither can they without us be made perfect.

d. Neither can they or we be made perfect without those who have died in the gospel also; for it is necessary in the ushering in of the dispensation of the fullness of times; which dispensation is now beginning to usher in, that a whole, and complete, and perfect union, and welding together of dispensations, and keys, and powers, and glories should take place, and be revealed, from the days of Adam even to the present time;

e. and not only this, but those things which never have been revealed from the foundation of the world, but have been kept hid from the wise and prudent, shall be revealed unto babes and sucklings in this the dispensation of the fullness of times.

19 a. Now, what do we hear in the gospel which we have received?

b. "A voice of gladness! A voice of mercy from heaven; and a voice of truth out of the earth, glad tidings for the dead: a voice of gladness for the living and the dead; glad tidings of great joy; how beautiful upon the mountains are the feet of those that bring glad tidings of good things; and that say unto Zion, Behold, thy God reigneth! As the dews of Carmel, so shall the knowledge of God descend upon them."

20 a. And again, what do we hear? Glad tidings from Cumorah! Moroni, an angel from heaven, declaring the fulfillment of the prophets—the book to be revealed.

b. A voice of the Lord in the wilderness of Fayette, Seneca County, declaring the three witnesses to bear record of the book.

c. The voice of Michael on the banks of the Susquehanna, detecting the Devil when he appeared as an angel of light.

d. The voice of Peter, James, and John, in the wilderness between Harmony, Susquehanna County, and Colesville, Broome County, on the Susquehanna River, declaring themselves as possessing the keys of the kingdom, and of the dispensation of the fullness of times.

21 a. And again, the voice of God in the chamber of old Father Whitmer, in Fayette, Seneca County, and at sundry times, and in divers places, through all the travels and tribulations of this Church of Jesus Christ of Latter Day Saints.

b. And the voice of Michael, the archangel; the voice of Gabriel, and of Raphael, and of divers angels, from Michael or Adam, down to the present time,

c. all declaring each one their dispensation, their rights, their keys, their honors, their majesty and glory, and the power of their priesthood;

d. giving line upon line, precept upon precept; here a little and there a little—giving us consolation by holding forth that which is to come, confirming our hope.

22 a. Brethren, shall we not go on in so great a cause? Go forward and not backward. Courage, brethren; and on, on to the victory!

b. Let your hearts rejoice, and be exceeding glad. Let the earth break forth into singing.

c. Let the dead speak forth anthems of eternal praise to the King Immanuel, who hath ordained before the world was that which would enable us to redeem them out of their prisons; for the prisoners shall go free.

23 a. Let the mountains shout for joy, and all ye valleys cry aloud; and all ye seas and dry lands tell the wonders of your eternal King.

b. And ye rivers, and brooks, and rills, flow down with gladness. Let the woods and all the trees of the field praise the Lord; and ye solid rocks weep for joy.

c. And let the sun, moon, and the morning stars sing together, and let all the sons of God shout for joy. And let the eternal creations declare his name for ever and ever.

d. And again I say, How glorious is the voice we hear from heaven, proclaiming in our ears, glory, and salvation, and honor, and immortality, and eternal life; kingdoms, principalities, and powers.

24 a. Behold, the great day of the Lord is at hand, and who can abide the day of his coming, and who can stand when he appeareth, for he is like a refiner's fire and like fuller's soap;

b. and he shall sit as a refiner and purifier of silver, and he shall purify the sons of Levi, and purge them as gold and silver, that they may offer unto the Lord an offering in righteousness.

c. Let us, therefore, as a church and a people, and as Latter Day Saints, offer unto the Lord an offering in righteousness, and let us present in his holy temple, when it is finished, a book containing the records of our dead, which shall be worthy of all acceptation.

25 a. Brethren, I have many things to say to you on the subject; but shall now close for the present, and continue the subject another time.

b. I am, as ever, your humble servant and never deviating friend,   JOSEPH SMITH

APPENDIX D

SECTION 113

This section is not a revelation. It was published in the 1844 edition of the Doctrine and Covenants and has been retained in all subsequent editions. The Reorganized Church has deemed it better to leave it as it is rather than to omit or revise it. As far as the facts are stated, they are a part of the history of the event discussed. The Conference of 1970 ordered its removal to the Appendix.

1 a. To seal the testimony of this book and the Book of Mormon, we close with the martyrdom of Joseph Smith the prophet and Hyrum Smith the patriarch.

b. They were shot in Carthage jail on the 27th of June, 1844, about five o'clock p.m., by an armed mob, painted black—of from one hundred and fifty to two hundred persons.

c. Hyrum was shot first, and fell, calmly exclaiming, "I am a dead man!" Joseph leaped from the window, and was shot dead in the attempt, exclaiming, "O Lord my God!"

d. They were both shot after they were dead, in a brutal manner, and each received four balls.

2 John Taylor and Willard Richards, two of the Twelve, were the only persons in the room at the time; the former was wounded in a savage manner with four balls, but has since recovered; the latter, through the promises of God, escaped "without even a hole in his robe."

3 a. Joseph Smith, the prophet and seer of the Lord, has done more (save Jesus only) for the salvation of men in this world, than any other man that ever lived in it.

b. In the short space of twenty years he has brought forth the Book of Mormon, which he translated by the gift and power of God, and has been the means of publishing it on two continents:

c. has sent the fullness of the everlasting gospel which it contained, to the four quarters of the earth;

d. has brought forth the revelations and commandments, which compose this Book of Doctrine and Covenants, and many other wise documents and instructions for the benefit of the children of men;

e. gathered many thousands of the Latter Day Saints; founded a great city, and left a fame and name that can not be slain.

f. He lived great, and he died great in the eyes of God and his people, and like most of the Lord's anointed in ancient times, has sealed his mission and works with his own blood; and so has his brother Hyrum.

g. In life they were not divided, and in death they were not separated!

4 a. When Joseph went to Carthage to deliver himself up to the pretended requirements of the law, two or three days previous to his assassination, he said:

b. "I am going like a lamb to the slaughter; but I am calm as the summer's morning; I have a conscience void of offense, toward God, and toward all men—I SHALL DIE INNOCENT, AND IT SHALL YET BE SAID OF ME, HE WAS MURDERED IN COLD BLOOD."

c. The same morning, after Hyrum had made ready to go —shall it be said to the slaughter? Yes, for so it was—he read the following paragraph near the close of the fifth chapter of Ether, in the Book of Mormon, and turned down the leaf upon it:

5 a. "And it came to pass that I prayed unto the Lord that he would give unto the Gentiles grace, that they might have charity. And it came to pass that the Lord said unto me, If they have not charity, it mattereth not unto thee, thou hast been faithful; wherefore thy garments shall be made clean.

b. "And because thou hast seen thy weakness, thou shalt be made strong, even unto the sitting down in the place which I have prepared in the mansions of my Father.

c. "And now I, Moroni, bid farewell unto the Gentiles, yea, and also unto my brethren whom I love, until we shall meet before the judgment seat of Christ, where all men shall know that my garments are not spotted with your blood."

d. The testators are now dead and their testament is in force.

6 a. Hyrum Smith was 44 years old February, 1844, and Joseph Smith was 38 in December, 1843, and henceforward their names will be classed among the martyrs of religion;

b. and the reader in every nation, will be reminded that the "Book of Mormon" and this Book of Doctrine and Covenants of the church, cost the best blood of the nineteenth century, to bring it forth for the salvation of a ruined world.

c. And that if the fire can scathe a *green tree* for the glory of God, how easy it will burn up the "dry trees" to purify the vineyard of corruption.

d. They lived for glory, they died for glory, and glory is their eternal reward. From age to age shall their names go down to posterity as gems for the sanctified.

7 a. They were innocent of any crimes, as they had often been proved before, and were only confined in jail by the conspiracy of traitors and wicked men; and their *innocent blood* on the floor of Carthage jail, is a broad seal affixed to Mormonism, that can not be rejected by any court on earth;

b. and their *innocent blood* on the escutcheon of the State of Illinois, with the broken faith of the state as pledged by the governor, is a witness to the truth of the everlasting gospel, that all the world can not impeach;

c. and their *innocent blood* on the banner of liberty, and on the *magna charta* of the United States, is an ambassador for the religion of Jesus Christ, that will touch the hearts of honest men among all nations;

d. and their *innocent blood,* with the innocent blood of all the martyrs under the altar that John saw, will cry unto the Lord of hosts, till he avenges that blood on the earth. Amen.

APPENDIX E

SECTION 123

This section is a report of the Joint Council held in compliance with the instructions of Doctrine and Covenants 122:13. It was included in the Doctrine and Covenants at the request of the Council of Twelve and concurred in by the General Conference of 1895. It is not a revelation. The Conference of 1970 ordered its removal to the Appendix.

JOINT COUNCIL

1 a. In compliance with the requirement of paragraph thirteen of the revelation received during conference and by agreement between the quorums affected, the First Presidency, the Twelve, and the Bishopric met in joint council in the editor's room of the Herald Office at nine a.m., Friday, April 20, 1894.

b. There were present: Joseph Smith and W. W. Blair, of the First Presidency; Alexander H. Smith, E. C. Briggs, James Caffall, W. H. Kelley, J. H. Lake, J. R. Lambert, Heman C. Smith, Joseph Luff, and Gomer T. Griffiths, of the Twelve; E. L. Kelley, G. H. Hilliard, and E. A. Blakeslee, of the Bishopric.

2 a. President Joseph Smith was chosen to preside, and E. A. Blakeslee to act as secretary.

b. A. H. Smith offered prayer, after which the President made a few remarks bearing upon the object of the council, and advising forbearance and toleration in speech and feeling, regardless of the distance between those present in their judgment upon the matters under discussion.

3 A number of questions were named and noted for discussion, and considerable informal talk was indulged in, after which resolutions were presented, discussed, and adopted in the following order, all decisions being finally made unanimous, with the sole exception noted:

LAMONI COLLEGE

4 Resolved that we look with favor upon the effort to build a college at Lamoni, to be controlled by the church.

5 Resolved, further, that we believe it should be a purely educational institution and free from sectarian influences or bias.

6 Resolved, further, that we give our hearty support to the present movement looking in the above direction.

CHURCH HISTORY

7 Resolved that it is the opinion of this council that there is nothing in the resolution of April, 1893, on church history, that should in any way interfere with the preparation and publication of an authentic church history by the church.

8 Resolved, further, that it is the opinion of this council that church history, both ancient and modern, may be freely used as a means of information, for what the same may be worth.

DISCUSSIONS IN HERALD

9 Whereas there seems to be a demand for a publication that may be a medium for more progressive and controversial articles for the good of the body than can be supplied by the *Herald*, therefore be it,

10 Resolved that the board of publication be requested to provide for such want as soon as practicable and without injury or interference with the circulation of the *Herald*.

UTAH CHURCH

11 a. The present attitude of the Utah Church was discussed and the council informally expressed itself as of the opinion that the ministry should boldly stand as aggressors or defensors everywhere where the questions at issue between the two churches were introduced.

b. The Presidency received unmistakable assurance of support in their efforts to direct such controversy as might be invited by contingencies arising.

LOCATING IN REGIONS ROUND ABOUT

12 Resolved that all parties wishing to change their location be recommended to correspond with the Bishopric for information.

PRESIDING COUNCILS

13 a. Resolved that it is the opinion of this joint council, that the words "presiding councils" in the fourth and seventh paragraphs of section 120 (of the Book of Doctrine and Covenants) refer to the traveling ministry—the Twelve and Seventy.

b. From this decision President W. W. Blair dissented.

DOCTRINAL TRACTS

14 a. Resolved that the members of the Quorum of Twelve and the Presidency be requested to write tracts on such gospel topics as each may select, all of which shall be placed in the hands of the Presidency for examination;

b. said tracts, when approved, to be placed in the hands of the board of publication to be issued as soon as possible.

DIRECTING LABOR OF HIGH PRIESTS

15 Resolved that it is the opinion of this council that high priests, when needed for missionary service abroad, may be appointed by the First Presidency or the Twelve or both jointly, and should labor after such appointment under the direction of the Twelve, the same as Seventies.

16 Resolved, further, that when high priests are acting in their own standing as local presidents, they are subject to the direction and counsel of members of both the First Presidency and the Twelve, whose duty it is to regulate.

17 Resolved, further, that when a necessity occurs for changing men or placing new men in the field, between conferences, to meet special exigencies, those making the appointment should notify the ministers in charge of the fields affected, if practicable, so as to avoid irregularity or possible conflict.

GOSPEL BOAT

18 Resolved as the opinion of this joint council, that Brother E. L. Kelley should proceed to San Francisco at the earliest possible time and secure the proposed boat for the Society Islands.

DETROIT BRANCH

19 Resolved that we advise that the colored members in Detroit, Michigan, be organized in a separate branch as soon as practicable.

BISHOP'S COUNCIL

20 After some deliberation the consensus of opinion of the council was secured to the effect that the words "the Bishop and his council" found in paragraph 6 of the revelation of 1894, mean the Bishop and his two counselors, and a vote obtained in support of such understanding.

PRESIDENTS OF HIGH COUNCIL

21 a. The following was adopted by regular vote:

b. It is our opinion that the counselors referred to in paragraph 6, section 99, are the counselors of the President in the Presidency of the church, but whether or not under certain circumstances the President would not be privileged to call others to assist him, is a query.

COUNSEL TO BE HONORED

22 a. Resolved that it is the opinion of this council that the statements found in paragraphs 1, 2, and 3 of the revelation of 1894 should be understood in the same sense as paragraph 3 of the revelation of 1882 and paragraph 4 of the revelation of 1890,

b. and that it is the duty of the Saints to honor more fully the counsel and advice of the First Presidency, the Twelve, and the Seventy in spiritual things.

PRESIDENCY OF THE TWELVE, AND MEANING OF THE WORD "ABROAD"

23 a. The following opinion of the First Presidency, as

communicated to the Quorum of the Twelve, in 1890, was adopted as the opinion of this joint council:

b. "As a traveling, presiding council, your quorum has the active supervision and presidency, under the First Presidency, over the entire field of ministerial labor, and control over districts, branches, and the ministry as a whole and as church organizations, and not as local presiding officers in these several organizations;

c. "holding special local presidency where no organization has been perfected; in a similar way as the First Presidency presides over the whole church, differing in this, that the First Presidency is necessarily local, while your province is not localized;

d. "nor do we mean by this that the word 'abroad' is to be construed to mean foreign lands, but in the field of itinerant gospel labor everywhere, as contradistinguished from branch, district, or other local organizations."

REVELATION OF 1861

24 a. Resolved that paragraph 5 of the revelation of April 15, 1894, relating to the duty of the Twelve under the authority of the revelation of 1861 (Doctrine and Covenants, section 114), teaches that said revelation is still in force;

b. but that whatever duty the Twelve might have felt rested upon them in "looking after the disbursements of the moneys in the treasury, or the management of the properties of the church," more than what is set forth in the agreement between the Twelve and the Bishopric, as effected in April, 1878, and reaffirmed in April, 1888, or indicated in the revelation of April, 1894, "they are now absolved from, the end designed by it having been reached."

REQUEST FOR ARTICLES FOR PUBLICATION

25 The *Herald* editors were, by vote, advised to call for articles from any who might be disposed to write upon leading gospel topics, said articles to be subjected to the inspection of the committee as heretofore named, and to be accepted or rejected at its discretion.

26 It was then ordered that the president and secretary of the council prepare the minutes of proceedings for publication in the *Herald*.

27 The special business of the council having ended, Brother James Caffall expressed a desire that the usual custom of setting foreign missionaries apart by laying on of hands and blessing be observed in his behalf, as he had been appointed to labor in Europe.

28 a. The council then knelt and was led in prayer by President Joseph Smith, who earnestly invoked the divine blessing upon Brother Caffall and his labors, after which Brethren Joseph Smith, W. W. Blair, A. H. Smith, and E. L. Kelley laid their hands upon him and set him apart, President W. W. Blair being mouth in supplication.

b. The Spirit of the Master fell upon those present and the service and season was one of joyful solemnity and peace. "Redeemer of Israel" was then sung and the benediction pronounced by President Joseph Smith.

29 a. Thus ended the work of the council convened in accordance with the requirement of the revelation which had been formerly accepted by the church.

b. All present were convinced that the appointment had been wisely made and that the results were and would be such as would fully attest the divinity of the call.

30 a. The sessions continued until the afternoon of the 25th, adjournment being had about four o'clock.

b. Brother Gomer T. Griffiths was excused and left for home on the 23d, and Brother E. A. Blakeslee at noon on the 25th. Brother Joseph Luff was then chosen secretary for the closing session.

31 a. To God whose hand has led us and whose patience has borne with our infirmities, the generous praise of his church is due.

b. May our renewed consecration under the better conditions his mercy has brought about, bring to him added glory and to his church prosperity and peace.

JOSEPH SMITH, *President*
JOSEPH LUFF, *Secretary*

TOPICAL INDEX
TO THE BOOK OF
DOCTRINE AND COVENANTS

NOTE: To provide the maximum amount of reference material in the space allowed, it has been necessary to reduce multiple references to a minimum. Where there are multiple references to the same section, those in parentheses relate to the main topic, and not to the preceding subtopic. Those who wish a more complete set of references should consult *A Concordance to the Doctrine and Covenants*, by Arthur E. Starks.

Aaronic priesthood, 26: 2; 83: 3, 4, 5, 6; keys of, 68: 2; 104: 10, 32; presidency of, 68: 2; 104: 8, 40; right to bishopric in, 68: 2; confirmed on Aaron, 83: 3, 5; continueth, 83: 4; appendages to, 83: 5; called lesser, 104: 8; duties of, 104: 40.

Account, in day of judgment, 70: 1; render an, 72: 1, 3, 4; may give an, 101: 2.

Accountability, years of, 16: 6; 17: 20; 68: 4.

Accountable, children, 28: 13; 68: 4; may be, 98: 10; every man, 101: 2.

Adam-ondi-Ahman, foundations of, 77: 3; valley of, 104: 28.

Administration, differences of, 46: 6; through, 87: 3; abuse in, 122: 5.

Administrative work, with local, 134: 6; relieved of, 137: 4.

Adultery, commit not, 59: 2; 66: 5; 42: 7, 20, 22; in their hearts, 63: 5.

Adulterers, 42: 7, 20, 22; 63: 4.

Agency, of man, 36: 7; 90: 5; given to Adam, 28: 9-14; to man, 36: 7; 37: 2; 58: 6; the moral, 98: 10.

Agents, men are, 28: 10; 58: 6; 60: 3; of bishop, 51: 2; 53: 2; 58: 10; unto themselves, 101: 2; my affairs with, 109: 1; by means of,

110: 8; appoint bishop's, 117: 10; bishop's, 122: 5.

Anderson, Peter, to fill vacancy, 125: 2; be released, 133: 1.

Angel, ministered unto first elder, 17: 2; shall sound trump, 45: 7; 49: 4; in authority rebelled, 76: 3; ordained by, 83: 4; sounding of the seven trumps, 85: 26-35; the destroying, 86: 3; go before you, 100: 3; Moroni an, 110: 20.

Angels, ministering of, 17: 2, 6; 36: 6; 43: 6; 67: 3; 83: 4; 104: 10; gospel confirmed by, 26: 2, 3; 76: 3; Devil and his, 28: 7-10; 76: 3, 4; declare repentance, 28: 12; of Satan rejoiced, 36: 5, 6; innumerable company of, 76: 5; charge given, 83: 6; round about you, 83: 15; shall fly, 85: 25.

Anoint, with oil, 125: 15.

Anointed, chosen and, 107: 22; of the Lord's, 113: 3.

Anointing, may claim their, 68: 2.

Anointings, are ordained, 107: 12.

Anxiously engaged in a good cause, 58: 6.

Apocrypha, 88: 1.

Apostle, an, 16: 3; 19: 3; an elder, 17: 8; duties of, 17: 8.

Apostles, calling, duties, qualifications, work of, 16: 5, 6; 17: 8; are elders, 17: 8; you are mine, 83;

10; school of, 92: 3; special witnesses, 104: 11; those sent, 120: 3; and high priests, 122: 14; move out as directed, 133: 1, 2; others to be called in due course, 145: 9.

Archangel, Michael the, 85: 35; Adam called the, 104: 28.

Arm, of flesh, not trust in, 1: 4; not shortened, 34: 3; of Lord to fall, 45: 7; of Lord be revealed, 87: 3.

Ask, shall receive, 66: 5; and ye shall receive, 85: 16; 100: 6.

Assemble, commanded to, 41: 1; together, 45: 12; upon land of Zion, 62: 2; not in haste, 63: 8; together, 85: 20; living wont to, 110: 13.

Assemblies, your solemn, 107: 12; who go out from, 131: 4.

Assembly, call a solemn, 85: 19, 36; 92: 1; 104: 11.

Atonement, sanctified through, 74: 3; through shedding of blood, 76: 5.

Austin, C. Eugene, apostle, 152: 3.

Authority, of Lord and servants, 1: 2; person who has, 17: 21; ordained by one who has, 42: 4; given to act, 68: 1; over all offices, 104: 3; of higher priesthood, 104: 9; of lesser priesthood, 104: 10; quorum equal in, 104: 11, 14.

Baptism, 16: 4, 6; 39: 2; 55: 1; administering, commandment, 17: 7, 21; of fire and Holy Ghost, 18: 4; 32: 2; 39: 2; 55: 1; gospel of, 83: 4; of repentance, 104: 10; for dead, 107: 10-12; 109: 5, 7; 110: 1, 12, 16, 17, 18; by water, 110: 12.

Baptismal font, is not, 107: 10; a simile, 110: 13.

Baptize, twelve to, 16: 5; apostle, elder, to, 17: 8; in name of Christ, 16: 6; 49: 2; priest's duty to, 17: 10; in name of Father, Son, and Holy Spirit, 17: 21; 36: 1; by water, 34: 2.

Baptized, in his holy name, 17: 5; 49: 2; under old covenant availeth nothing, 20: 1; he that is, saved, 68: 1; children be, 68: 4; in water, 76: 5; in childhood, 83: 4; by water, 83: 10; and are not, 83: 12; believeth and is, 105: 11; for the dead, 107: 10; 110: 16; for your dead, 109: 5; before a person is, 111: 4.

Baptizing, by water, 39: 5, 6; 42: 2; 52: 3; in name of, 68: 1; for the dead, 107: 11; and setting in order, 122: 8.

Bible, law to govern church, 42: 5, 15, 16; items taken from, 108A:1.

Bishop, ordination of, 17: 17; counselors to, 42: 8; 58: 6; lay things before, 42: 10; 58: 7; 72: 3; decides stewardships, 42: 19; present at trials, 42: 22; discern gifts, 46: 7; Presidency and, direct gathering, 48: 2; keep money and food, 51: 4; wants supplied, 51: 4; appoints agent, 53: 2; make preparations for gathering, 57: 6; a judge, 58: 4; 64: 8; receive consecrations, 58: 7; purchase lands, 58: 11; state privileges of lands, 58: 12; unfaithful condemned, 64: 8; others set apart, 68: 2; literal descendants of Aaron, 68: 2; appointed, 68: 2; 72: 1; high priests, appointed by Presidency, 68: 2; trial of, before Presidency, 68: 3; not exempt from law, 70: 3; duty of, 72: 3; account unto, 72: 4; office of, 83: 5; send moneys to, 83: 18; high priest officiate as, 104: 8; temporal office of, 104: 32; duty of, 104: 32; be a judge, 104: 33; over Aaronic priesthood, 104: 40; surplus in hands of, 106: 1; concerning tithing law, 114: 1; as counselor to president, 124: 2; stakes to have, 125: 10; subject to court, 126: 11; concerned with Sanitarium, 127: 1; confer in council, 128: 3; carry out law of organization, 128: 9; role of, 149: 3; 149A: 1-3.

Bishopric, to look after poor, govern property, etc., 38: 8; 42: 8-11; location of, 58: 6; moneys sent to, 63: 10-12; manage all things of, 81: 4; presidency of Aaronic priesthood, 104: 8; agreement between twelve and, 123: 24; concerning work of, 126: 10; to effect organization, 128: 1; temporalities under, 129: 8 (130: 6); role of, interpreted, 149: 3; 149A.

Bishop's Agents, appoint, 117: 10.

Bishop's Council, 42: 8, 10; not be settled by, 99: 1; meaning of, 123: 20.

Bishops, authority to ordain, 17: 17; 68: 2; counselors to, 42: 8, 19; 58: 6; council, 42: 10; remunerated, 42: 19; privileges of lands stated by, 58: 12; descendants of Aaron, 68: 2; appointed by Presidency, 68: 2, 3; duties of, by commandment and conference, 72: 1-5; others act according to first, 72:1; records of, to bishop in Zion, 72: 1, 3, 4; judges or bishops in Zion, 72: 4; in districts and branches, 117: 10; hold as high priests, 129: 7; counsel to be sought in regard to gathering, 140: 5.

Blair, W. W., chosen counselor, 117: 3; dissented, 123: 13.

Blakeslee, E. A., called to be bishop, 130: 5; be more closely associated, 131: 2.

Blakeslee, G. A., who has preceded, 130: 5.

Blessings, promised, 41: 1; partaker of, 93: 2; multiplicity of, 94: 2 (101: 2); 101: 7; keys of spiritual, 104: 9 (31); keys of patriarchal, 107: 29.

Bodies, spirits absent from, 45: 2; celestial, 76: 5, 6; 85: 4; sanctified, 83: 6 (85: 6); filled with light, 85: 18 (85: 38); washing, 86: 1; clean, 119: 3.

Body, not weary, 83: 13; spirit and soul, 85: 6; care not for, 98: 5.

Bondage, release from, 18: 5; of sin, 83: 7; not be in, 98: 10; led out of, 100: 3; delivered of, 101: 13; free Zion from, 137: 6.

Book of Mormon, translate, 1: 5; purpose, 2: 6 (15: 1); translation, 3: 1; 5: 1; 9: 1-5; printing, 18: 3; witnesses, view of, 15: 1; Joseph Smith chosen to write, 23: 1; fullness of gospel, 26: 2; 42: 5; given for instruction, 32: 3; teach principles of, 42: 5; new covenant, 83: 8; believe in, 107: 35; items taken from, 108A: 1; testimony of, 113: 1-6.

Books for children, 55: 2; best, 85: 36; all good, 87: 5; were opened, 110: 6 (110: 7, 8).

Booth, Paul W., apostle, 151:7.

Branch, a judge in any, 104: 33; how organized, 120: 1, 2; to report, 121: 4; care of local, 125: 4; manifestations in, 125: 14.

Branches, large, pattern for, 72: 4; in large, 104: 17; bishops in large, 117: 10; how organized, 120: 1; care of, 122: 3; visit, 125: 3; delegates of, 125: 9; how conducted, 125: 14; exercise care in, 131: 4.

Bread, administering of, 17: 22; idle not eat, 42: 12; after partaking, 85: 46; vessels for, 119: 5; breaking of, 119: 5; blessing of, 119: 5; be uncovered, 119: 5.

Breastplate, view, 15: 1; of righteousness, 26: 3.

Briggs, E. C., special witness, 117: 7; sustained, 121: 2; mission of, 121: 3; in council, 123: 1; seen in vision, 126: 7.

Briggs, J. W., ordain twelve, 117: 4; witness, 117: 7; oversight, 117: 7; in your hands, 121: 2.

Brotherly, kindness, 4: 2.

Budd, R. S., apostle, 134: 3.

Burton, J. F., to islands, 127: 5.

Butterworth, C. A., with twelve, 126: 7; released, 134: 2.

Cackler, Harold W., to Presiding Bishopric, 148: 8; continued, 150: 5.

Caffal, J., to twelve, 117: 4; council, 123: 1; set apart, 123: 28; upper seat, 126: 7.

Called, many, 92: 1; all are, 119: 8; to great work, 124: 7.

Calling, to exhortation, 21: 2-4; attend to, 23: 4; magnifying, 83: 6; 85: 21; duties of, 104: 11.

Callings, and gifts, 16: 5; of your several, 83: 24; and offices, 94: 3; variety of, 128: 6.

Campbell, D., appointed, 117: 8.

Carmichael, A., ordained, 135: 1; released, 136: 1.

Celestial, bodies, 76: 5-7; kingdom, 85: 2; glory, 85: 4; bodies of, 85: 4; abide law of, 85: 5.

Charity, qualifies, 4: 1, 2; have, 6: 8; cannot assist without, 11: 4; can do nothing without, 16: 4.

Chastened, 42: 23; not part until, 61: 2; for murmurings, 75: 2.

Chastening, 98: 2.

Chastisement, 92:1; grievous, 100:1.

Cheerful, saints, 119: 6.

Cheerfulness, enjoined, 59: 4.

Chesworth, D. O., apostle, 142: 2; released, 150: 1.

Cheville, Roy A., presiding evangelist, 145:4; released, 151:1.

Children, blessed by elders, 17: 19; of men tempted, 28: 10; Satan cannot tempt little, 28: 13; parents responsible for, 28: 13; 68: 4; cannot bear all things, 50: 8; education of, 55: 2; of God, inheritance for, 58: 11; 70: 4; grow old, 63: 13; baptized, 68: 4; holy, 74: 1; sanctified, 74: 3; have not understood, 77: 4; claim for maintenance, 82: 2; of men, 90: 6; provided for, 96: 2; bound by law, 111: 4; home for, 127: 3, 4.

Chinese, tracts in, 125: 11.

Choosing, a day of, 102: 10.

Christ, coming of, 1: 6; 28: 3; 33: 1; 34: 6; 35: 3; 36: 12, 14; 38: 5; 39: 6; 41: 2; 43: 7; 45: 2, 4, 6, 10, 15; 49: 2, 4; 51: 5; 61: 6; 63: 13; 64: 5; 65: 1; 68: 4; 76: 5; all things in name of, 46: 9; the light of, 85: 2; the law of, 85: 5.

Christ's the firstfruits, 85: 27; at his coming, 85: 28.

Church, foundation of, 1: 5; 16: 1; 19: 1; established, 3: 13; 32: 2; 3: 16; described, 3: 17; gates of hell not prevail, 15: 3; 16: 1; 19: 2; out of wilderness, 5: 3; 32: 2; build up, 42: 3, 4; 45: 12; of devil, 16: 4; abominable, cast down, 28: 5; upon rock, 32: 3; properties not taken from, 42: 9; law to govern, 42: 16; 48: 2; 58: 5; organized, 44: 2; gifts given to, 46: 1-8; instructions to, 48: 1, 2; house of prayer, 59: 2; common property of, 81: 5; that great, 85: 26; oracles to, 87: 2; covenants of, 104: 7; blessings of, 104: 9; presidency of, 104: 11; of Zion, 106: 1; rejected as a, 107: 11; government, 108A: 1; Reorganized, 113, preface; history, 123: 7; duty of, 125: 11; law to, 125: 14; institution of, 127: 2; representatives of, 127: 6; revelations to, 127: 8.

Churches, strengthen, 50: 8; watch over, 52: 9; return to, 60: 3; gather together, 98: 9.

Cole, Clifford A., apostle, 145: 7.

College, to build a, 123: 4; debt be paid, 125: 16.

Colored members, 123: 19.

Comforter, manifestations of, 19: 3; knoweth all things, 34: 5; 42: 5; teach things of kingdom, 35: 1; to teach by, 50: 5; teach all things expedient, 75: 2; to teach truth, 78: 1.

Commandment, great, 59: 2; great and last, 18: 5; I give a new, 81: 3; till I give, 91: 4; have not considered, 92: 1; contrary to my, 98: 13; have not kept, 101: 1.

Commandments, preface, to, 1: 2; of Lord, 1: 5; 2: 4; faithful; decrees, promises, prophecies fulfilled; true, to be searched, 1: 7; according to, 6: 4; 10: 4; keep, 6: 4; 10: 4, 10; 11: 3; to be kept in all things, 16: 7; 17: 3-6; 42: 8, 21; none to receive but J. Smith, Jr., 27: 2; not carnal nor sensual, spiritual, 28: 9; bound by, 34: 6; receive not unauthorized, 43: 2; of men or devils, 46: 3; blessed in keeping, 58: 1; 63: 7; stewards over, 70: 1, 2; priesthood by, 83: 2; law of carnal, 83: 4; not kept, 90: 7, 8; fulfillment of, 100: 7; covenants and, 104: 7; holy laws and, 107: 15; kept from world, 108: 11; book of Lord's, 108A: 5; given by inspiration, 108A: 5.

Common consent, all done by, 25: 1; 27: 4; of conferences, 27: 4; voice of church, 38: 8; ordinations by, 42: 4; only by voice and, 101: 11, 12; this shall be the, 101: 12; giving names by, 101: 13.

Communion, and presence of God, and Jesus, 104: 9.

Companions, put away for cause, 42: 20.

Condemnation, rich and poor, 56: 5; are under, 63: 15; receive greater, 81: 1; church under, 83: 8; shall turn unto, 85: 16; not all under, 102: 3; elders under my, 116: 2.

Condemned, 64: 2; innocent not be, 101: 1.

Conference, elders meet, preside by voice of, 27: 4; common consent of, 27: 4; 58: 12, 13, 15; carrying authority of, 125: 13; commands of body in, 125: 16; what may be presented to, 125: 16.

Conferences, counsel of, 58: 12, 13; in Zion, 58: 15; voice of, 72: 1; 73: 1; organized by direction of, 120: 1; in council with, 122: 5; within the province of, 122: 6.

Confess, not, delivered, 42: 23; every tongue, 85: 31.

Confirm, those baptized, 17: 8, 18.

Confirmation meetings, 46: 3, 4.

Confirmed, priesthood, 83: 3.

Conscience, exercise of, 112: 2; void of offense, 113: 4; liberty of, 125: 16.

Consecrate, properties, 42: 8-11, 19; 51: 1; riches of Gentiles, 42: 11; for poor, 42: 19; land, 51: 4; 52: 1; 58: 13; and dedicate, 58: 13; treasury, 101: 11; spot for Lord's house, 107: 13; talents, etc., 132: 3.

Consecrated, not to receive again, 42: 11; unto bishop, 51: 1; unto inhabitants of Zion, 70: 2; moneys, 83: 18; residue of money, 87: 7; for building, 91: 1; land of Zion, 100: 5; land, 100: 6; treasury, 101: 11; for the gathering, 102: 4.

Consecration, after first, 42: 10; according to laws of, 102: 8; law of, 126: 10; to God, 132: 3; unreserved, 137: 4.

Consecrations, storehouse kept by, 82: 2; to receive, 107: 8; gathered from saints, 129: 8.

Consent, all done by common, 25: 1; 27: 4; prayer with one, 90: 10; of the order, 101: 3; voice and common, 101: 12; names by common, 101: 13.

Constitution, be maintained, 98: 10; they shall form, 107: 19.

Constitutional law of land, 95: 2.

Contention, is unseemly, 119: 5; concerning song service, 119: 6; concerning prerogatives, 133: 2; cease, 134: 7; warning concerning, 135: 2; let, cease over minutiae, 146: 3.

Contentious, be not, 122: 16.

Contrite, humble and, 54: 1; 56: 2;

spirit, 59:2; 94: 2.

Co-operation, is essential, 132: 3.

Couey, Duane E., apostle, 146: 1; to presidency, 148: 2.

Council, to preside in, 87: 5; a general, 99: 1; a standing, 99: 2; voice of general, 99: 5; president of, 99: 6; privilege before, 99: 9; abroad, 99: 11-13; in Zion, 104: 15; of the church, 104: 35-37; for cornerstone, 107: 41; to confer in, 128: 3.

Counsel, according to, 58: 5; not wrongfully, 64: 4; listen to, 97: 1; esteemed lightly, 98: 3; of the order, 101: 3; as they follow, 102: 10; let him hearken to, 107: 4; if he receive, 107: 6; of my servant, 107: 28, 33, 34; if they will take, 122: 7; may be asked for, 125: 5; and advice of elders, 127: 7; has been given, 128: 4; to be sought on gathering and temporalities, 140: 5.

Court, of church, 42: 22, 23; findings of, to be affirmed, 42: 22; of Kirtland house, 91: 2, 3; 92: 3; the bishop's, 126: 5; officers subject to, 126: 11.

Covenant, be established, 1: 3, 4; been broken, 1: 3; 54: 1; old, new, everlasting, 20: 1; 45: 2; 49: 2; gospel, the, 39: 3; light, standard, Gentiles to seek, 45: 2; 49: 2; cannot be broken, 42: 8; 77: 2; nations to bow to, 49: 2; heirs according to, 52: 1; Jesus mediator of, 76: 5; be bound by, bind yourselves by, 81: 4; priesthood oath and, 83: 6; remember the new, 83: 8; faith and, 83: 17; remembrance of the everlasting, 85: 40, 41; remember the, 87: 6; with an immutable, 95: 1; with an everlasting, 98: 5; Mediator of the new, 104: 9; gospel, his everlasting, 108: 11.

Covenants, old done away, 20: 1; nothing contrary to, 27: 4; remember the church, 32: 3; bound by, 34: 6; shall observe, 42: 5, 18, 21; 68: 2, 3; church shall receive, 42: 18; items in addition, 68: 2; being broken, 101: 9, 10; agreeably to the, 104: 7, 10; as the doctrine and, 108A: 4; keep you to fulfill, 111: 2; church articles and, 122: 10.

Cowdery, Oliver, revelations to, sections 6; 7; 8; 9; 15; 16; 21; 23; 25; 27; build church among Lamanites, 27: 3, 5; 31: 1; literary labors, 55: 1, 2; 57: 5; not intrusted alone with documents, 69: 1.

Creation, mourned, 36: 11; answer end of, 49: 3; measure of its, 85: 4, 6.

Cross, Son of Man lifted on, 36: 11; take up, and follow, 56: 1; take up your, 105: 6.

Crown, shall receive, 17: 3; of righteousness, 24: 4; of immortality, 80: 1; promised you, 101: 1; prepared, 103: 3.

Crucified, Jesus, by sinful men, 19: 3; for sins of world, 19: 3; 45: 9; 46: 5; crucified Christ unto themselves, 76: 4.

Curry, L. F. P., chosen presiding bishop, 136: 1; placed in First Presidency, 138: 1; released as presiding bishop, 138: 1.

Curtains, of Zion, 98: 4.

Curtis, J. F., apostle, 129: 6; evangelist, 137: 1.

Damned, 42: 16; 49: 1; 68: 1; 83: 12; 105: 11; 58: 6.

Davey, Roscoe E., apostle, 140: 2; to Order of Evangelists, 147: 2.

Days, last, 61: 3; without beginning of, 83: 2; in the last, 83: 24; for the last, 105: 12; 110: 17.

Deacon, ordained, 17: 8, 12; office of, 104: 5; to teacher, 104: 31; over office of, 104: 38; may preside, 120: 2.

Deacons, duties, 17: 11, 15, 26; offices of teachers and, 83: 5; standing ministers, 83: 22; school for, 85: 39; preside over, 104: 31; over twelve, 104: 38; president of, 107: 46.

Dead, come forth, 28: 3; rest from labors, 59: 1; blessed in Lord, 63: 13; rest of the, 85: 29; baptisms for, 107: 11, 12; 109: 5, 7; salvation of, 110: 5 (6, 8, 12, 16-19,

22, 24); after they were, 113: 1; testators are, 113: 5.

Death, power over, 7: 1; first, last, 28: 11, 12; sweet to righteous, bitter to unrighteous, 42: 12; overtake, 45: 1; shadow of, 57: 4; in life or, 58: 1; 61: 6; second, 63: 5; 76: 4; not any more see, 85: 35; covenant unto, 95: 3; no, 98: 5.

Debt, bondage, pay, 18: 5; 72: 3; to enemies forbidden, 64: 6; discharge, 87: 6; you are in, 101: 13; college, pay this great, 125: 16; not to contract, 127: 4; of the church, 130: 7.

Debts, pay all your, 101: 13; surplus for, 106: 1; be canceled, 109: 1; be properly met, 130: 7.

DeLapp, G. L., chosen, 136: 1; as Presiding Bishop, 138: 2; released, 148: 5.

Delegates, number of required, 125: 7; qualification for, 125: 9; are counseled, 130: 8.

Desires, to serve God, 4: 1; 7: 3; your, 10: 8; who have, 11: 4; lustful, 85: 37; offering holy, 92: 1; covetous, 98: 3.

Devil (see Satan), power over own dominion, 1: 6; nature, power, section 3; church of, 16: 4; general statements, 28: 7-10; 76: 3, 4; 85: 35; 110: 20.

Devils, cast out, 23: 6; 34: 3; in everlasting fire, 28: 7; doctrines of, 46: 3; reign with, 76: 4; and angels in eternity, 76: 4; power of, 76: 4; redeemed from, 76: 7; cast out, 83: 11; 107: 30.

Discerning, of spirits, 46: 7.

Disciples, to declare word, 1: 1; desired, 3: 10; twelve called, 16: 5; plan of redemption, 45: 2 (4, 5); inheritances, 57: 4; shall open hearts, 58: 1.

Dispensation, of gospel, 26: 3; of fullness of times, 105: 12; 107: 13; of priesthood, 110: 9; now beginning, 110: 18; of fullness of times, 110: 18.

Dispensations, 110: 18.

Districts, bishops in, 117: 10; provided for, 120: 1; presiding over, 120: 2, 4; authorities of, 120: 7;

advocate with, 28: 2; 45: 1; record borne of, 36: 1; 42: 5; from, to son, 68: 2; receiveth my, 83: 6; teacheth, 83: 7.

Fathers, testimony, 2: 6; promises remain in, 26: 2; lost their, 82: 1; lineage of, 83: 2; 84: 3; tradition of, 90: 6; turn hearts to, hearts of, 95: 3; keys come from, 105: 12; burden upon, fall or fail, 124: 7.

Fellowship, not have, 82: 1; receive to, 85: 41; so long as in, 101: 12; dealing for, withdraw from, 112: 10.

Field, ready to harvest, 4: 1; 6: 2; 10: 2; 12: 2; white, 30: 2; 32: 1, 2; reap in, 30: 2; was the world, 84: 1; to be burned, 84: 2; 130: 4; is large, 134: 5.

Fields, be secured, 23: 2; into new, 122: 7; provide for, 122: 11; their several, 122: 13.

Fig tree, parable of, 34: 4; off a, 85: 24.

Fire, baptism of, 18: 4; 32: 2; 39: 2; everlasting, 28: 7; out of, 35: 2; wicked into, 43: 7; 45: 8, 10; lake of, second death, 63: 5; 76: 4; consume wicked, 63: 9; not quenched, 76: 4; cast into, 94: 2; scathe green tree, 113: 6.

First fruits, the, 85: 27.

First presidency, bishop appointed by, 68: 2; tried before, 68: 3; receiveth, 105: 7; counselors, 105: 12; not fill, 122: 14; subject to, 123.

Fishing River, revelation, 102; given upon, 127: 7.

Flesh, not trust arm of, 1: 4; all, 1: 6; death in the, 16: 3; in the, 17: 1, 5; fall from bones, 28: 5; eaten by flies, 28: 5; as Christ stood in, 45: 2; they twain, one, 49: 3; of beasts, for man, 86: 2; my tabernacle, 90: 1; reign over all, 108: 5; Lord over all, 108: 11.

Flight, not haste, 58: 12; by, 63: 9; not haste, 108: 4.

Fold, not of this, 3: 14.

Forbearance, mutual, 122: 13.

Forgive, doeth it no more, 42: 7; sins, 61: 1; one another, Lord forgives, 64: 2; I the Lord, 81: 1; thou shalt, 95: 7.

Forgiven, repents, 1: 5; 50: 8; 58: 9; 64: 3; 68: 3; sins are, 30: 2; 50: 7; not be, 42: 7; as you have, 81: 1.

Forgiveness, none for murderer, 42: 6, 21; none for second offense in adultery, 42: 7; for those who confess, 64: 2; none for sons of perdition, 76: 4; not have, 83: 6.

Fornication, wine of wrath, 34: 3; guilty cast out, 42: 20; wrath of, 85: 26, 32; crime of, 111: 4.

Fraternity, peace of, 136: 3.

Free, bond and, to repent, 43: 5; ye are, 95: 2; prisoners, 110: 22.

Freedom, supporting, 95: 2; in land of, 103: 1; not suppress, 112: 4; of conscience, 112: 5.

Friends, among your, 21: 5; wounds in house of, 45: 9; make, 81: 6; ye are my, 83: 10; call you, 83: 13; you, my, 85: 16; will call you, 90: 8; unto you my, 97: 1; 102: 8; defending their, 112:11.

Fruit, with much, 52: 7; bring forth, 83: 8; in season, 86: 2; for man, 86: 3; precious, 94: 2; shall eat, 98: 13.

Frustrated, cannot be, 2: 1.

Garments, plain, work of own hands, 42: 12; idle not wear those of laborer, 42: 12; beautiful, 81: 4; cleanse hearts and, 105: 13; be made clean, 113: 5; be sober, 119: 3.

Garver, J. F., be ordained, 134: 3; counselor to President, 139: 1.

Gather, his people, 28: 1; 43: 6; from east, 45: 12; 49: 5; should, 98: 5; my people to places appointed, 98: 9; command to, 100: 5; carefully, 102: 7; to Zion, 106: 2; 108: 2; unto regions, 117: 11.

Gathering, of the people, 3: 15; 57: 1-6; promised, 28: 2; preparations for, 57: 6; all to observe temporal law, 57: 6; not in haste, 58: 10-12; 63: 8, 9; beginning of, 98:

9; carefully together, 128: 5; counsel regarding, 140: 5.

General Assembly, church of First-born, just men made perfect, 76: 5; commune with, 104: 9.

General Conference, 17: 13; 17: 17; names to, 107: 46; authority of, 113: 7; direction of, 120: 2.

Generation, this, 3: 6, 13; 5: 2, 3, 5; 6: 4; 10: 4, 10; crooked, pre-verse, 32: 1; 33: 1; untoward, 35: 2; from, to, 56: 6; 69: 2; temple in this, not all pass, 83: 2; built in this, 83: 6.

Gentiles, gospel from, to Israel, 12: 5; and house of Israel, 16: 2; fullness of gospel to, 17: 2; great work among, 34: 3; consecration of 42: 11; standard for, 45: 2; time of, fulfilled, 45: 3, 4; witnesses unto, 104: 11, 12, 13; record unto, 105: 2.

Gift, no more, 2: 4; lost your, 3: 1, 2; to translate, 5: 1; thou hast, 6: 5 (6: 11-13; 8: 2, 3; 10: 5); of eternal life, 12: 3 (15: 3); of Holy Ghost, 39: 5, 6; 68: 4; none else appointed, 43: 1, 2 (51: 1; 83: 18; 85: 7).

Gifts, and callings, 16: 5; 17: 5, 12; seek best, 46: 4; retain in mind, 46: 5; purpose, use, 46: 5-8; discerned by bishop and others, 46: 7; come from God, 46: 7; having all, 104: 42.

Gillen, J. A., be chosen, 130: 4; be ordained, 134: 4.

Gillen, J. W., chosen, 119: 1.

Gleazer, E. J., apostle, 134: 3; released, 145: 5.

Glories, if desired, 43: 3; partakers of the, 66: 1; celestial, terrestrial, telestial, 76; were revealed, 108: 11; to be revealed, 110: 17.

Glory, come in, 6: 14; 7: 1; 45: 2, 10; not look upon, 22: 6-20; 23: 5; my work and my, 22: 23 (24: 4); single to my, 26: 1; 59: 1; 63: 4; come in power and, 33: 1; 36: 1; 45: 6; crowns of, 36: 11; crowned with, 58: 2; eternal, 63: 16; brightness of, 65: 1; the three glories, celestial, terrestrial, telestial, section 76; of your Father, 77: 1 (77: 2; 83: 2, 6,

14, 17); prepared for celestial, 85: 4-6; single to my, 85: 18; fullness of, 90: 1, 2; dwell upon earth, 98: 5.

Goals, understanding of, 136: 3.

God, designs not frustrated, 2: 1; power of, 15: 2; unchangeable, 17: 2, 4; attributes, commandments, works, 17: 4; 76: 1; workmanship of, 22: 3, 6, 19-24 (36: 7) (28: 6, 8, 9; 32: 1; 33: 1; 34: 1; 45: 2; 76: 5); nature of, 36: 6, 7; no respecter of persons, 38: 4, 5; law of, 42: 22, 23; whether it be of, 46: 6; gifts from, 46: 5-9; characteristics of, 50: 6-8; coming in power, 56: 6 (58: 2, 4, 5; 63: 3; 64: 2); kingdom of, 65: 1; carnal eye has not seen, 67: 3; no one has seen, except quickened, 67: 3; no Savior beside, 76: 1 (76: 2-5) (81: 1; 83: 3, 4, 15; 85: 2, 3); judgments of, 85: 25; mighty works, 85: 34, 35; house of, 85: 35, 44; glory of, intelligence, 90: 6; not mocked, 107: 22 (32); see salvation of, 108: 1.

Godliness, remember, 4: 1, 2; mystery of, 18: 2; power of, 83: 3.

Good, do, 6: 16; for their, 51: 4; as seemeth him, 64: 6; none doeth, 81: 1; work together for, 87: 6; cleave unto, 95: 3; work for, 97: 4; 102: 11.

Gospel, proclaimed, 1: 4; 42: 2, 4; 57: 4; 58: 9, 15; 66: 2; 68: 1; 71: 1; 73: 1; 75: 3; to Lamanites, 3: 10, 12; rock, 10: 11; foundation of, 16: 1; declared by Holy Ghost, 16: 5; twelve to declare, 16: 4, 5; to Jews and Gentiles, 12: 5; 16: 5; 17: 2; 18: 3; 42: 11; unchangeable, 17: 2; given by inspiration, confirmed by angels, 17: 2; 26: 2, 3; 65: 1; 76: 3; principles of, 32: 1-3; 42: 5; fullness of, 34: 3; 45: 4; 66: 1; to poor and meek, 34: 4 (39: 2, 3); three books contain, 42: 5 (58: 15; 68: 1; 79: 1); to ends of earth, 65: 1; everlasting, 68: 1; preparatory, 83: 4; of salvation, 87: 3; fullness of, 87: 4.

Governments, and laws, read, 108A: 14; section on, 112.

Grace, sufficient, 15: 3; 16: 5; full of, and truth, 22: 4; 36: 1; protection of his, 135: 3.

Greene, U. W., seen in vision, 126: 7; be released, 134: 2.

Griffiths, G. T., apostle, 119: 1; in council, 123: 1; to England, 125: 13; released, 134: 2.

Gurley, Z. H., be chosen, 117: 4; in your hands, 121: 2.

Hansen, Francis E., to Presiding Bishopric, 148: 8; Presiding Bishop, 150: 4.

Hanson, P. M., chosen apostle, 130: 4; released, 145: 5.

Harris, Martin, manuscript lost by, 2: 5; witness to Book of Mormon, 5: 1, 5; 15: 1; revelation to, 15: 18; chosen councilor, 99: 2.

Harvest, is white, 4: 1; 6: 2; 10: 2; 11: 2; 12: 2; all ready to, 32: 1, 2.

Haste, gathering not in, 58: 12; 63: 8; preach word not in, 60: 3; upon errand and mission, 61: 2, 3; servants make, 90: 10, 11; be not in, 98: 9.

Hastening time, is here, 135: 2; is upon us, 141: 5.

Healed, not faith to be, 42: 12, 13; 46: 7.

Healing, sick, 23: 6; 46: 7; spirit of, 119: 9; faith unto, 127: 2.

Heart, penetrated, 1: 1; all of required, 4: 1; 17: 7; 59: 2; 64: 7; only God knows, 6: 7; right, 39: 3; love wife with all, 42: 7; not proud in, 42: 12; pure in, 56: 6; love Lord with all, 59: 2.

Heaven, sword of Lord bathed in, 1: 3; kingdom of, 3: 13; 39: 5; 42: 2; 65: 1; creator of, 17: 4; God in, 17: 4; one third of hosts of, turned away, 28: 10; kingdom of, at hand, 32: 2; come in glory in clouds of, 45: 2, 6; 76: 5; reward in, 58: 1; names written in, 76: 5; curtain of, pillar of, 85: 27; reward in, 109: 4, 5; record kept in, recorded in, 110: 7 (110: 7-23).

Heavens, created by Christ, 12: 5; not be numbered, 22: 23; Son of

man reigneth in, 49: 2; Lord ruleth in, 60: 2.

Heirs, of salvation, 7: 2; 76: 7; according to covenant, 52: 1.

Hell, down to, 3: 3; gates of, not prevail, 3: 17; 15: 3; 16: 1; 19: 2; 32: 3; bitterness of, 22: 13; place prepared, 28: 10; able to cast soul to, 63: 1; thrust down to, 76: 7; gather hosts of, 85: 35.

Herald, discussion in, 123: 9 (10, 25, 26).

Hield, Charles R., be apostle, 137: 2; released, 147: 1.

Higdon, Earl T., apostle, 148: 4; released, 151: 4.

Higdon, William T., apostle, 151: 5.

High Council, ordinations by direction, 17: 17; and bishopric look after poor, 42: 10; composition of, 99: 1; organization of, 99: 1; seven to act for, 99: 4; president of, 99: 6; procedure of, 99: 7-10; in Zion, 104: 15 (of the church, 104: 35); for cornerstone, 107: 41; at Kirtland, in Missouri, 108A: 3, 4.

High Councilors, 17: 16, 17; stewardships, 42: 19; cast lots, 99: 7, 15.

High Councils, 42: 10; form a quorum, 104: 14; are an order, of church and stakes, 129: 7.

High Priest, ordained by direction, 17: 17; appointed bishop, 68: 2; act in lesser offices, 68: 2; of Melchisedec priesthood, 68: 2; tried before presidency, 68: 3; instructions concerning trial of, 68: 3; ordained a presiding, 103: 1; Melchisedec, 104; act as bishop, 125: 13.

High Priesthood, ordained unto, 17: 17; 77: 1; keys to presidency, 80: 1; appendage to, 83: 5; presidency of, 104; to preside over, 122: 2; holding the, 129: 4; ordination to, 131: 3.

High priests, counselors to bishop, 42: 8; families supported, 42: 19; of my church, 72: 1; ye are God's, 83: 10; to travel, 83: 22; beginning at, 85: 39; council of, 99: 1; standing council of, 99: 2; vote of, 99: 3; traveling, 99: 13 (104: 5-35); president over, 107: 42; ordained, 117: 8; standing ministers, 120: 3; as missionaries, 122:

7; to preside, 122: 8; presidency and twelve are, 122: 14; exhorted, 122: 16; local presidents, 123: 16.

Hilliard, G. H., in council, 123: 1.

History, John Whitmer, to write, 47: 1, 2; 69: 1; obtain knowledge of, 90: 12; to be recorded, 110: 3; comment on church, 123: 7, 8; of recent development, 132:1.

Holmes, Reed M., apostle, 141:3; presiding patriarch, 151:2.

Holy Ghost, promised, 12: 4; 16: 4; manifests all things expedient, 16: 4; gift of, 17: 5; 32: 3; 39: 6; 68: 4; to lead elders, 17: 8, 9; baptism of, 17: 8; 18: 4; 32: 2; power of, 33: 2; receive the, 34: 2; 35: 1; 39: 6; knoweth all things, 34: 5; speak as moved by, 68: 1; filled with, 83: 4; shall receive, 83: 10.

Holy One, counsel, direction of, 77: 3; of Zion, foundation, 77: 3; without beginning of days or end, 77: 3.

Holy Scriptures, 17: 2, 6; for instruction, 32: 3; Inspired Version, 34: 5; principles of, Inspired Version to be taught, 42: 5, 15; law to govern, 42: 15, 16.

Holy Spirit, not always strive, 1: 5; beareth record, true, 1: 8; leadeth to do good, 10: 6; enlighten mind, 10: 7; of revelation, prophecy, 10: 11; baptism of, 32: 2; bears record, 36: 1; elders endowed by, 38: 7; 43: 4; 44: 2; 46: 7; not teach without, 42: 5; taken for guide, 45: 10; to preach by, 50: 4-7; discern by, 63: 11; taught by, 63: 16; indicate who shall gather, 72: 5; lightens, qualifies, 76: 2; received by laying on of hands, 76: 5; ministration of, 76: 7; understood by power of, 76: 8; of promise, 85: 1; tabernacle of, 85: 44; demonstration of, 96: 1; blessed with, 131: 1.

Hope, qualifies, 4: 1; commanded, 6: 8; cannot assist without, 11: 4; 16: 4; of resurrection, 42: 12.

Hot drinks, 86: 1.

Hour, nigh, 28: 2; 45: 5; Eleventh, 32: 1; and day unknown, 49: 2; you think not, 51: 5; is not yet, 58: 2; separation at that, 63: 13; this very, 83:12, 14, 15; first, second, 85: 13; every man in his, 85: 14; ye know not, 108: 4; of coming nigh, 108: 5.

House, leave, 18: 5; of Israel, 28: 3; govern in meekness, 30: 3; Joseph Smith, Jr., should have, 41: 3; shall never fall, 45: 3; of printing, 58: 7; leave blessings upon, 75: 3; of my Father, 80: 1; be built, 83: 2, 6; woe unto that, 83: 16; left desolate, 83: 23; of prayer, of learning, of order, 85: 36, 39; of God, 85: 42, 44; set in order, 90: 6, 7; of Lord to be built, sections 91-94, 98, 99, 101, 102, 105, 107.

House of the Lord, sacrifice in, 83: 6.

Houses, building of, 42: 10; set in order, 87: 5; of worship, 122: 6.

Humble, cannot assist except, 11: 4; themselves, 17: 7; become truly, 54: 1; yourselves, 67: 3.

Hummel, Gene M., Presiding Bishopric, 150: 5.

Hurshman, Lloyd B., apostle, 151:6.

Husband, shall support, 24: 2; soul delight in, 24: 4; unbelieving, 74: 1, 2; and wife, 111: 2; but one, will of, to leave her, 111: 4.

Husbands, lost their, claim on, 82: 1.

Hyde, O., commission, revelation to, 68: 1; in my hands, 97: 4; chosen councilor, 99: 2; journey of, 100: 7; one of twelve, 107: 40; clerk, 108A: 2.

Hymns, selected by Emma Smith, 24: 3.

Hypocrites, among you, 50: 3; woe unto, 50: 2; portion with, 98: 12; ye are found, 101: 10; be not, 119: 7.

Hyrum (Smith), stock in house, 107: 23; accomplish work, 107: 24; patriarch, bear record, 107: 29; mission for, 107: 31; hearken to, 107: 34; smot, 113: 1.

12; in council at, 122: 13; college at, 123: 4; stake at, 125: 10.

Land, possess this, 3: 11; labors on, 25: 1; from depths of sea, 36: 2; of promise, 38: 4; laws of, 42: 21, 22; let no man break, 58: 5; sickness, 45: 4; consecrate, 51: 4; 52: 1; 58: 13; of inheritance, 52: 2, 9; 55: 2; flee from, 54: 2; of promise, 57: 1 (2, 6); learn concerning, 58: 1 (3-15); blessed for use, 61: 3; rejoice in, 62: 2; of Zion, Lord holdeth in own hands, 63: 8 (9, 10, 12, 13); obedient eat good of, 64: 7 (68: 4; 69: 2); have consecrated, 81: 4 (82: 1); not pollute, 83: 8; judgments on, 85: 21 (35); of Zion, 94: 1, 2, 3; law of, 95: 2; the goodly, 96: 2; may possess, 98: 7 (9, 10); of Zion, 100: 1 (3, 5, 6); sanctify, of Zion, 106: 2; sickness of, 107: 27; gather on, of Zion, 108: 2 (3, 5; 108: 6; 119: 8; 122: 12; 128: 7; 131: 2).

Lands, impart of, 18: 5; purchase of, 42: 10; war in own, 45: 11 (12); for inheritance, 48: 1, 2; 52: 9; 57: 1; improvement, settlement, 58: 7-12; to be sold, 63: 10; purchase, 98: 9, 10; may buy, 98: 10; to purchase, 100: 5; properties in, 101: 12; in Jackson County, be purchased, possession of, 102: 8; sent to foreign, 108: 3; seas and dry, 110: 23; purchasing, 122: 6; foreign, 123: 23.

Latter Day Saints, book of, 108A:4; seer of, 109: 9; to church of, 110, salutation; travels of, 110: 21; gathered, 113: 3.

Laughter, not much, 59: 4; excess, 85: 19; cease, 85: 37.

Law, cursed by, 23: 7; not temporal, 28: 9; receive at Ohio, 38: 7; to govern church, 41: 1 (2); hear, obey, 42: 1 (16, 18, 21, 22); successorship, 43:1-3; of man, 44: 2; those without to be tolerated, 45: 10; of land, no man to break, 58: 4, 5; 63: 8; of temporalities, 58: 7; of Moses fulfilled, 74: 2, 3; they who died without, 76: 6; penalty unto, 81: 1; sanctified

through, 85: 5 (6, 8, 9, 11, 21, 23); of land, maketh free, 95: 2 (6); of gospel, 101: 2 (7) (10); be a standing, 106: 1 (2); not be annulled, 110: 9; bound by, 111: 4 (112: 3, 4, 11); fulfilling, of tithing, 114: 1; no conflict in, 120: 6; and usages, 120: 7; in section 42; 122: 6; be honored, 122:8 (12, 13, 16); to govern church, 125: 14; for bishop's court, 126: 5 (10, 11); chosen according to, 127: 7, 8, 9; temporalities, 132: 2.

Law, Wm., 107: 27-32, 34, 39.

Laws, holy, 17: 4; none but mine, 38: 5; given at Ohio, 38: 7; given in Scriptures, 42: 7; 58: 4; break not, 42: 13; 58: 5; shall observe, 42: 18; 58: 4; of land, 42: 21; enable to keep, 44: 2; organize according to, 51: 4; in revelations, 58: 5; of land, 82: 1; knowledge of, 90: 12; of land, 95: 2; and constitution, 98: 10; possess according to, of consecration, 102: 8 (9); of church business, 104: 31 (32); marriage regulated by, 111: 1; making or administering, 112: 1-8, 11; of health, 127: 2; of United States, of Missouri, 128: 1; observance of, organizations under, 128: 7; an organization under, 131: 2.

Laying on of hands, 17: 8, 18; 32: 3; 34: 2; 39: 6; 42: 12; 49: 2; 52: 3; 53: 2; 55: 1; 66: 5; 68: 4; 76: 5; blessings by, 104; 31; set apart by, 117: 3, 4; and blessing, 123: 27; for blessing, 125: 3; upon the sick, 127: 2.

Learned, firstly, 58: 3.

Learning, house of, 85: 36.

Lents, Donald V., apostle, 143: 1.

Lesser offices, officiate in, 104: 8.

Lehi, directors given to, 15: 1.

Letter, of membership, 17: 26; called by, 44: 1; of gospel, 104: 10.

Levi, purify sons of, 110: 24.

Levitical order, priest of, 104: 5.

Levitical priesthood, including, 104: 1; Aaronic or, 104: 2.

Lewis, G. G., be apostle, 136: 2; death, 141: 1.

License, elders, priests, teachers, deacons, 17: 13-15.

Life, not seek neighbor's, 18: 3; will preserve thy, 24: 1; eternal, 28: 7, 12; 45: 2; of world, 33: 1; peaceable things bringeth, 42: 17; riches of, 43: 6; everlasting, 45: 1; 63: 7; power to seal unto, 68: 1; words of eternal, 83: 7; treasure words of, 83: 14; the staff of, 86: 2; lay down his, 95: 3 (4, 5); all days of, 109: 2; the book of, 110: 7; protection of, 112: 2; not divided in, 113: 3; and salvation, 130: 9.

Light, taken from disobedient, 1: 5; rather than, 3: 3; shineth in darkness, 3: 14; 6: 10; bring to, 3: 15; of world, 3: 18; 33: 1; 45: 2; bringing to, 6: 12; 10: 9; keys of, 6: 13; Christ a, 12: 5; break forth, 45: 4, 5; continuing in, receiveth more, 50: 6; truth is, Spirit giveth, 83: 7; of truth, of Christ, 85: 2 (3, 10, 11, 12, 14, 18, 37); the true, 90: 1 (4, 5, 6); set to be, 100: 2; children of, 103: 2 (3); as angel of, 110: 20; voice which giveth, 131: 1.

Literary labors, O. Cowdery, W. W. Phelps in, 55: 1, 2.

Livingston, H. L., released from Presiding Bishopric, 148: 6.

Lord, voice of, to all, 1: 1-3; called upon Joseph Smith, 1: 4; no respecter of persons, 1: 6; 38: 4; tempt the, 3: 5; talk face to face, 15: 1; 36: 1; way prepared, 32: 2; second coming, 33: 1; dwelt with his people, 36: 2 (7, 10, 12); be ruler, 41: 2; day of, nigh at hand, 43: 5-7; 45: 6 (7, 8, 12, 15); Jesus, believe, 49: 2; reason with you, 50: 4; crucified for sins, 53: 2; anger of, 56: 1; commandeth, revoketh, 56: 2, 6; rules, 60: 2; blessed, cursed waters, 61: 3; faithful, cannot lie, 62:2; angry with wicked, 63: 1, 2, 9 (4, 8, 14, 15); forgives, 64: 2 (3, 4, 6); keys of, man, 65: 1; testimony, 67: 2; merciful and gracious, 76: 2 (3); forgive you, 81: 1 (2, 3, 4); priesthood confirmed by, 83: (2), 3 (4, 7, 16, 17, 18, 24); angels crying unto, 84: 2; of

Sabaoth, 85: 1 (27, 36, 39, 41, 44); house dedicated to, 91: 3; maketh you free, 95: 2 (4, 6, 7); reveal all things, 98: 5 (12); of vineyard, 100: 4; not be mocked, 101: 1 (2, 11); coming of, 103: 2; officiate in name of, 104: 12 (13, 19, 24); come to temple, 108: 1 (3, 5, 7, 9, 11, 12); write word of, 109: 7; great day of, 110: 24; worship in house of, 119: 6 (7, 9); heareth the, 120: 5; to direct, 122: 6; movements pleasing to, 136: 3.

Lord's day, observance of, 59: 2; sacrament on, 119: 5; be observed, 119: 7.

Lord's house, size, 92: 3.

Lot, at the Temple, 83: 1; for presidency, 91: 1; for house unto me, 91: 3 (4); for stewardship, 101: 4.

Lots, divided into, 93: 1; to cast, 99: 7; laid off for city, 101: 6.

Love, qualifies for work, 4: 1; arms of my, 6: 9; cannot assist unless full of, 11: 4; wife with all thy heart, 42: 7; keeping commandments, 42: 8; live together in, 42: 12; shall wax cold, 45: 4; God with heart, mind, might, strength; neighbor as self, 59: 2; one another, 85: 38 (41); whom I, 92: 1; 113: 5; unto all men, 105: 5; redeemed them in, 108: 10.

Luff, J., an apostle, 119: 1; in council, 123: 1 (30); medical director and physician, 127: 2; released from quorum, 129: 2.

Majority, determine decision, 99: 9; be residents, 125: 10; necessities of, 128: 5.

Mammon, make friends with, 81: 6.

Man, walketh in own way, 1: 3; not trust in arm of flesh, 1: 4; work frustrated, 2: 2 (3); wicked, 2: 5; 3: 1; qualifications named, 4: 1, 2; creation, 17: 4; may fall, 17: 6; must repent or suffer, 18: 1; 49:2; natural and spiritual, 22: 7; immortality, eternal life, 22: 23; probation, 28: 12; agency, 36:

7; 58: 6; to choose, 37: 2; keep all commandments, 42: 7; steward, accountable, 42: 8-10; delivered to law of land, 42: 22; equality of, 49: 3; be true, 50: 3; purified, 50: 6; portion appointed, 51: 1; reward every, 56: 6; be anxiously engaged, 58: 6 (7, 9); all things made for, 59: 4; Christ knoweth weakness of, 62: 1; to take righteousness, faithfulness, 63: 9; old to die, not sleep, changed, 63: 13; keys committed to, 65: 1; natural, cannot abide presence of God, 67: 3; strong take the weak, 83: 19; stand in own office, 83: 21; receive not gift, 85: 7; warn neighbor, 85: 22; herbs, flesh, grain, animals for 86: 2 (3); who has riches, 87: 6; is spirit; tabernacle of God, 90: 5 (6, 12); enmity of, cease, 98: 5; accountable, 101: 2; gospel committed to, 108: 7; one wife, 111: 4; governments for benefit of, 112: 1; in hands of one, 114: 1; 122: 5; in his own order, 116: 4; to intelligence of, 131: 1; service to, 132: 3.

Marks, Wm., ordained by, 107: 24; pay stock, 107: 25; be counselor, 115: 1.

Marriage, one wife, transgressors against, 42: 7, 20, 22; ordained of God, 49: 3; of Lamb, 58: 3; article on, 108A: 13; section on, 111; solemnization of, 111: 1, 2; contracts, 111: 4.

Marvelous work, 4: 1; 16: 7; great and, 6: 1; among Gentiles, 34: 3.

Matthew, quotation, 110: 10.

McConley, M. A., be ordained, 133: 1; release from Twelve, 141: 2.

McDowell, F. M., be ordained, 134: 1; resigned, 138: 1.

McGuire, B. R., 132: 2.

Meats, uses; whoso forbiddeth not of God, 49: 3.

Mediator, new covenant, 104: 9.

Meeting, elders take lead of all, conduct, as led by Holy Ghost, 17:9; 46: 1; take lead of, 17: 10, 11; not before world, 42: 23; members and nonmembers not be cast from,

46: 1; solemnized in public, 111: 1.

Melchisedec, priesthood, 68: 2; 80; order of, 76: 5; priestly lineage of, 83: 2; section 104; classes and orders of, 125: 8; orders in, 129: 7.

Member, visit house of each, 17:10; commandment to every, 38: 9; body need of, 83: 21; be a lively, 89: 2; of the order, 93: 2; officiate as, 104: 5; must be agreed, 104: 11.

Members, duty, 17: 18 (24, 25, 26); stewardships, 42: 19 (23); right to deal with, 112: 10; colored, 123: 19; fellow church, 128: 1; word forgotten by, 129: 8; of the order, 137: 4; disunity, 137: 6.

Men, persuasions of, 2: 3; obey commandment, 17: 6; judgments, 28:8; wickedness, 38:6; duties, 38: 8; to all nations, 39: 4; hearts shall fail, 45: 4; commandments of, 46: 3; all given gifts, 46: 4-8; 60: 3; repent, 49: 2; agents to themselves; should be anxiously engaged, 58:6; honorable, blinded, 76: 6; spirits, judged, 85: 29; secret acts, 85: 34; interpolations by, 88: 1; good and wise, uphold, 95: 2; honorable, appointed, 98: 10; be saviors of, 100: 2; let churches send, 100: 5; crafts of, 103: 3; be partakers of glories, 108: 11; accountable, 112: 1 (4, 5, 6, 8, 11, 12); every tongue, 116: 1; of Negro race, 116:4; of power, 117: 5; of God, be clean, 119; 3 (4, 6, 8).

Mesley, C. G., apostle, 137: 2.

Messenger, to prepare way, 45: 2; of salvation, 90: 1.

Messengers, swift, 107: 10.

Messiah, look not for another, 18: 3; king of Zion, 36: 10; shall come, 36: 10.

Millennium, 28: 2, 6; 36: 14; 43: 7.

Mind, darkened, 3: 1; serve with, 4: 1; inspired, 8: 1; understand, 9: 3; 10: 7; 17: 6; love with, 59: 2; willing, 64: 7; spiritual, 67: 3; not weary, 83: 13; strengthening of, 119: 9; peace of, 122: 7 (9, 14) (38).

Ministering, angel, 7: 2; of angels, 104: 10; blessed in, 124: 4; to the many, 129: 2.

Ministers, standing, 83:22; traveling, 104:43; 120: 3; to their own race, 116: 4; as righteous, 118: 4; standing, 120:3; evangelical, 104: 17; 122: 8; 125: 6; 126: 3, 7, 13; 134: 2; should notify, 123: 17; going out; sent out as, 125: 16; sufficient to govern, 129: 8; this class of, 137: 4.

Ministration, of terrestrial, 76: 7; care in; in public, 131: 4; blessed through, 134: 5.

Ministrations, to approve, 110: 2; of church, 127: 7.

Ministry, gospel and, 6: 13, 14; keys of, 7: 2; 26: 3; 104: 34; called to, 23: 1; pattern for, 23: 7; general instructions, 28:1, 2; power of, 34: 4; called unto, 83: 15; perfected in, 85: 23; 87: 3; those called to, 85: 39; understanding of, 94: 3; support in, 115: 1; labor in, 117: 7; heed traveling, 118: 3; laboreth in, 119: 8; work of, 120:1; standing, 122: (7) 8 (9, 16); boldly stand, 123: 11; twelve over, 123: 23; organizing, 125: 13; right to labor in, 129: 4; work of standing, 133: 2; all to qualify, 141: 4.

Miracles, required not unless commanded; exceptions, 23: 6; to be shown, 34: 3; received by faith, 42: 13; power to do, 45: 2; working of, 46: 7.

Missionaries, by precepts of, 122:5 (7); by twos, 135: 4.

Missionary, work, prosecute, 119:8; in charge, 120: 1; 125: 4; quorums, 122: 7 (9, 12); authority, 125: 12; labor, arranging, 125:13; caring for, 129: 2; burden of, 133: 2; 134: 6; be prosecuted, 134: 5; tasks, 135: 4.

Missions, hour, 30: 2; by voice of conference, 73: 1; foreign lands,

118: 1; tracts, 125: 11; abroad, 125: 12; work, 125: 13; presiding, 126: 3.

Money, church shall give, 23: 7; agent for, 48: 12; 51: 2; kept by bishop, 51: 4; to buy lands, 57: 4; give you, 83: 16; receive, residue, 87: 7; to exchangers, 98: 6; bought with, 98: 7; purchase by, 98: 9; to loan, 101: 13.

Moneys, to pay, 54: 2; lay before bishop, 58: 7; to purchase land, 58: 10; bishops to impart, 60: 3; to repay, 60: 3; sent unto Zion, 63: 10, 12; not alone be intrusted with, 69: 1; be consecrated, 83: 18; churches gather, 98: 10; land bought with, 100: 5; for proclaiming words, 101: 4; in stewardships, 101: 12; keep our, 102: 3 (8); value of, 107: 20; disbursements, 122: 5; in the treasury, 123: 24; contributions of, 129: 8; collected, 131: 2.

Monogamy, a basic principle, 150: 10.

Moroni, to reveal Book of Mormon, 26: 2; an angel, 110: 20; bid farewell, 113: 5.

Moses, led children of Israel, 8: 2; law of, 20: 1; 74: 2; saw God face to face, 22: 1-25; received revelations as, 27: 2; law done away, 74: 2, 3; priesthood, 83: 2 (6); lead them as, 100: 3; be like unto, 104: 42; tabernacle of, 107: 12; written by, 108: 11.

Mountains, glad tidings upon, 18: 4; fled, 36: 2; made low, 49: 4; path among, 105: 4; break down, 108: 5; flow down, 108: 7, 8; beautiful upon, 110: 19; shout for joy, 110: 23.

Music, gifts of, 119: 6.

Mysteries, of God unfolded, 6: 3; 8: 3; 10: 3; great, 6: 5; keys of, 27: 2; 64: 2; mayest know, 42: 17 (18); of kingdom, 43: 3; to him who keepeth commandments, 63: 7; expounding the, 71: 1; revealed to, 76: 2; key of, 83: 3; to unfold, 87: 5; expounding, 94: 2; receiving, 104: 9.

Only Begotten, similitude of, 22:4, 9, 10; full of grace and truth, 22:4 (12, 14, 21); created through him, 76:3 (4); glory of, 90:1.

Oracles, given to church, 87:2; for the church, 107:39.

Ordain, call and, 5:3; priest's, elder's duty to, 17:8-10; those who desire to warn sinners, 63:15; to be spokesman, 97:3; twelve to, 104:17, 30; of every race, 116:1.

Ordained, of me, 16:5; twelve to be, 16:5; by power of Holy Ghost, 17:12 (16, 17; 77:1); all whom thou hast, 23:7; even as Aaron, 26:2; by one who has authority, 42:4; shall come in at the gate, 43:2; unto what were ye? 50:4; especial instructions to ministers, 50:4-7; John, by angel, 83:4; who are, 83:20; herbs God hath, 86:2; unto this power, 87:4; to keep treasury, 101:11; appointed and, 104:11; by ordinance, 107:12; for good end or bad, 109:2; elders been, 116:2; officers, 122:9.

Ordaining, privilege of, 17:16; not hasty in, 116:4.

Ordinance, unto you, 19:3; received by, 85:45; conforming to, 110:5; nature of, 110:8.

Ordinances, strayed from, 1:3; to be obeyed, 52:4, 5; 64:2; take upon you mine, 53:2; power of God in, 83:3; in outward, 104:8, 10.

Ordination, elders, priests, teachers, deacons, 17:12, 15-17; presented for, 120:9; of high priest, 125:13.

Ordinations, 17:14-17; provided for, 35:1, 2; rules governing, 42:4; purpose, methods of ministry, 50:4-7.

Organ, be silent, 119:6.

Organization, where no, exists, 120:3; where no previous, 122:9; been arranged, 122:9; burden of, 128:6; benefits of, 128:8; law of, 128:9; church as an, 131:2.

Organizations, of the different, 117:12; to colonize, 128:1; provide for other, 128:6; must be instituted, 128:7; contemplated, 128:8; caring for, 131:2; emphasizing worth of persons, 151:9.

Organize, church according to law, 17:1; obtain power to, 44:2; receive directions to, 51:1, 4; yourselves, 77:2; 85:20, 36; 101:2; on consecrated land, 100:6; command to, 101:2; commanded to, 101:10; 107:19.

Organized, and established, 17:1; school be, 87:3; united order, 89:1; order to be, 101:1 (9); benefit church when, 128:1.

Organizing, and setting in order, 122:8; after pattern, 125:10; ministry locally, 125:13.

Page, J. E., one of twelve, 107:40.

Parable, fig tree, 34:4; given, 38:6; second coming, 45:5; ten virgins, 45:10; wheat and tares, 84:1; 98:9; likened unto, 85:15; will show you, 98:6; unjust judge, 98:11; lord spoke in, 100:4.

Parents, teach children to understand, obey, 68:4; children claim upon, 82:2; children to obey, 111:4.

Partridge, Edward, ordained by Presidency, 35:1; called to preach, 35:1; ordained bishop, 41:3; leave merchandise, 41:3; preside over conference in Zion, 58:15; Satan sought to destroy, 64:3; is with me, 107:7.

Patriarch, martyrdom of, 113:1; duties of, 125:3, 4; not meddle; not listen, 125:4; the presiding, 125:5, 6; mission of, 125:13.

Patriarchs, enrollment of, 129:7; high priests and, 130:2.

Paul, Apostle, 16:3; quoted, 110:16; teaching of, 131:4.

Peace, taken from earth, 1:6; proclaim, 95:3; lift standard of, 95:6; sue for; ensign of, 102:11.

People, all to hear, 1:1, 3; my, 2:6; 3:12; unto this, 3:10; deliver from bondage, 22:18; John, to prophesy before many, 7:1; de-

clare repentance unto, 14: 3;
hearts open, 30: 3; free, 38: 5;
assemble to Ohio, 39: 4, 5; Lord
delights to bless, 41: 1; may be
my, 42: 3; reserve a pure, 43: 3;
preach repentance to, 44:2; heark-
en, 45: 1, 2; 46: 1; 56: 1; this,
51: 1-4; have many things to do,
56: 4; send goods unto, 57: 4;
push together, 58: 9; restoration
of, 83: 1; before face of, 83: 4;
redeemed; in midst of, 83: 17;
warn the, 83: 23; 85: 22; reign
with, 83: 24; shall fear, 85: 25;
saying to all, 85: 31; acquainted
with, 87: 5; mourn, 95: 2; not
battle against, 95: 6; in this place,
97: 1; raise up a pure, 97: 4; prepare my, 101: 10; may be taught;
transgression, 102: 3 (7, 8, 11);
warn the, 103: 1; testimony to,
105: 1; safety of my, 107:2 (13);
Savior in midst of, 108: 5 (11);
voice of, 112: 3; gathering of,
122: 6; liberties of, 126: 10;
feelings of, 128: 5; reign over his,
128: 7; good of my, 129: 9; may
speak to his, 130: 1; among his,
135: 3.

Perfected, by law, 85: 8; they may
be, 94: 3.

Persons, no respecter of, 1: 6; who
exercise control, 111: 4.

Peter, desire of, 7: 2; to minister for
John and James, 7: 1-3; hold keys
of kingdom, 26: 3; apostle, 49: 2;
thou art, 110: 10.

Peterson, Ziba, labor among Lamanites, 31: 1; taken from him, 58:
14.

Phelps, W. W., printing, writing for
schools, 55:1, 2; 57: 5; admonished,
58: 9; 61: 3; chastened, 61: 2;
one of stewards over revelations,
70: 1; organized Missouri council,
108A: 3; read testimony, 108A:5;
read marriage article, 108A 13.

Physician, T. B. Marsh a, 30: 4;
J. Luff, to church, 127: 2; his
calling as, 129: 2.

Pillar, of heaven, 85: 27.

Place, return to own, 85: 6; tarry
in this, 85: 19; standing in his,
85: 39; continue upon, 87: 6 (8);

remove out of, 90: 8, 9; divided
into lots, 93: 1; for you, 95: 3;
people in this, 97: 1; appointed,
98: 4; in house have, 107: 18;
wisdom to leave, 109: 1.

Plates, preserved, 2: 6; of Nephi,
record upon, 3: 8-10; have got, 5:
1; gift to translate, 5: 1; witness
of, 5: 1; view of, promised, 15: 1.

Polygamy (provided against, 42: 7;
49: 3); reproached with, 111: 4.

Poor, gospel preached to, 34: 4; none
among them, 36: 2; complain,
provision for, 38: 4, 8; consecrate
properties for, 42: 8, 11, 19; visit,
relieve, 44: 3; be remembered,
52: 9; men, woe unto, 56: 5;
pure, blessed, 56: 6; come to marriage of Lamb, 58: 3; come to
supper, 58: 3; storehouse for, 77:
1; manage affairs of, 81: 4; be
provided for, 82: 2; bishop search
after, 83: 23; shall inherit earth,
85: 4; be exalted; impart not unto, 101: 2; support cause of, 107:
28; not be neglected, 122: 6.

Power, to seal, 1: 2; lay foundation
of church, 1: 5; to translate, 3:
2; 17: 2; give them, 5: 3; of God,
5: 5; over death, 7: 1; give this,
7: 2; no other, save of God, 8: 3;
of Christ, 10: 5; 15: 2; 16: 5;
created by word of, 28: 8; to organize yourselves, 44: 2; of godliness, 83: 3; sun, moon, and
stars, 85:2 (12); Devil not have,
85: 35; Christ received all, 90:2;
wicked one hath, 90: 6, 8; give
unto you, 101: 2; of priesthood,
110: 8; sealing and binding, 110:
14; become men of, 117: 5; in assurance and, 131: 1; no, stay hand
of God, 135: 3.

Powers, of darkness, 38: 3.

Pratt, Orson, called to preach, 33:1;
one of twelve, 107: 40.

Pratt, P. P., preached to Lamanites,
31: 49; strengthen churches, 50:
8; preside over school, 94: 2;
journey of, 100: 7; one of twelve,
107: 40.

Pray, in faith, 8: 1; vocally and in
secret, 18: 4; lest enter into temp-

tation, 30: 4; teach children to, 68: 4; over the sick, 125: 15.

Prayer, in mighty, 5: 5; kneel in solemn, 17: 22; public and private, 18: 4; song of righteous a, 24: 3; united in, 28: 2; lift heart in, 29: 2; fasting and, 59: 3; taught through, 63: 16; house of, 85: 36; and covenant, 85: 43 (44, 46); with one consent, 90: 10 (11); marriage solemnized by, 111: 2; fasting and, 130: 1; meditation and, 131: 1.

Prayerful, be very, 102: 7.

Prayers, their, 3: 10-12; leave blessings upon land, 3: 11; things told because of, 38: 6; in season, neglect judged, 68: 4; alms of, recorded, 85: 1; of brethren, 87: 1; be granted, 95: 1; slow to hear, 98: 3; I have heard, 102: 5; give answers to, 105: 5; have prevailed, 117: 1; accepted, 124: 1.

Preach, not until called, 10: 8, 10; when called, 10: 8; unto world, 16: 6; naught but repentance, 18: 2; the truth, 21: 1; gospel to Lamanites, 27: 3; principles of gospel, 42: 5; repentance and remission of sins, 53: 2; 55: 1; in congregations of wicked, 60: 3; in regions round about, 73: 2; gospel of kingdom, 83: 13; everlasting gospel, 103: 1.

Preaching, teaching, by power of Spirit, 16: 5-7; 50: 5-7; time devoted to, 25: 1; character of, 38: 9; 42: 5; not teach without spirit, 42: 5; according to Spirit and power, 71: 1.

Prepared, earth be, 85: 4; all things be, 98: 9; be, before you, 108: 4; younger men be, 126: 6; all things, 128: 4.

Preside, Joseph to, 27: 4; either president may, 99: 6; duty to, 104: 38-43; high priest to, 120: 2.

Presidency, and Bishopric direct gathering, 48: 2; keys belongeth unto, 80: 1; of school, 85: 39; continue in the, 87: 5; ministry of, 91: 1; council of, seat of, 99: 11; hold right of, section 104; the first, 105: 7, 12; debts of, 106: 1;

to receive oracles, 107: 39; assembly blessed by, 108A: 15; under direction of; be present, 120: 3; one of first, 120: 9; of seven, 121: 5; sections 122, 123; in council with, 124: 2; in equality with, 124: 4; not ripe for, 125: 1 (11, 13); saw quorum of, 126:2 (4, 6, 8, 10); are but orders, 129: 7; in harmony with, 132: 2; directed by, 133: 2; as sent by, 134: 6; work of, 137: 5; second, 148: 10 b.

President, of high priesthood, how ordained, 17: 17; appointed to be, 85: 39 (46); importune, 98: 12; nomination of, 99: 5; of church; of council, 99: 6; appointed by revelation, 99: 6; give decision, 99: 9; may inquire of Lord, 99: 10; determine appeals, 99: 14; section 104; proclamation to, 107: 1, 4; one to be, 107: 19; of twelve, 107: 40; of high priests, 107: 42; revelations by, 113: 7; of lesser priesthood, 117: 3; branch or district, 120: 2; made remarks, 123: 2; counselors of, 123: 21; counselor to, 124: 2; senior or chosen, 124:6; sons of, 124: 7; be chosen as, 126: 6; of evangelists; emeritus, 137: 3; counselor to, released, 137: 4.

Presidents, section 99; twelve equal to three, 104: 11; of seventy, 104: 43; stake, 107: 42; of seventy, 107: 44; of the day, 108A: 3; of seventy, 120: 10; 121: 5; high priests as local, 123: 16; of seventy select, 124: 5; of seventy preside; one or all, 124: 6.

Presiding, elder, how ordained, 17: 17; 85: 46; elders; priests; teachers; high priest, 104:31; elder over church, 107:39; responsibility of, 107: 44; elder of church, 117: 3; branch and district, officers traveling, councils, 120:4; councils defined, 123:13; patriarch, duties of, 125:5, 6; anxiety of, 126:3; bishop take counsel, 127: 1; choose worker, 130: 6.

Priest, duties of, 17: 8, 10-12, 15, 22, 26; commandment to, 38: 9; presiding high, 103: 1; of Leviti-

Purified, from sin, 50: 6.
Purify, your hearts, 85: 20.
Purse, and scrip not take, 23: 7; not to have, 83: 13; let no man take, 83: 15.

Qualifications, essential, 4: 1, 2; 11: 4; among workmen demand, 128: 6.
Quarrelings, cease, 117: 13.
Quickened, glory by which, 85: 6; in and by him, 85: 12; saints alive be, 85: 27.
Quorum, majority form, 104: 11; stake councils, 104: 14; house, 107: 19 (36); high priests', 117: 3; decision of, 117: 9; of twelve, judgment, 120: 1; presidency and twelve, 122: 4 (5, 6, 15); communicated to; of twelve as presiding council, 123: 23; of seventy, 124: 6; patriarch in, meetings, 125: 5; of twelve admonished, 133: 2; be admonished, 134: 6.
Quorums, decision by, 104: 11; equally honorable, 120: 3; missionary, 122: 2; agreement, 123: 1; sons of leading, 124: 7; patriarch meet with, 125: 5; officers in their, 126: 9; three, appealed to, 126: 10; prerogatives of leading, 133: 2.

Race, ordain of every, 116: 1; ministers to their own, 116: 4.
Ralston, Russell F., apostle, 147: 4; released, 152: 2.
Rebel, not against Joseph, 105: 6.
Rebellion, of brethren, 83: 12; unbecoming, 112: 5.
Rebellious, be pierced, 1: 1 (2); anger against, 56: 1, 2; 63: 1 (2); cut off, 64: 7.
Reconciliation, required, 46:1; encouraged, 151:8.
Record, of Nephites, 1:5; 3:9; Spirit beareth, 1: 8; 36: 1; 42: 5; 59: 5; kept by John Whitmer, 47: 2; receive, 90: 3.
Recorder, 17: 25; John Whitmer, 47: 1; let there be a, 109: 5; revelation concerning, 110:2; be eyewitness, 110: 2; in each ward, 110: 3; be a general, 110: 4.
Records, on plates, 2: 6; kept back, contain gospel, 6: 12; sacred, ancient, 8: 1, 3; other, 9: 1; of

membership, 17: 25, 26; 47: 1; be in order, 109: 6; to be true, 110: 4 (7, 8, 9, 14, 24).
Redeem, abundance to, 98: 10; out of their prisons, 110: 22.
Redeemed, from spiritual fall, 28: 12; people, 43: 7; heathen, 45: 10; after sufferings of wrath, 76: 4; his people, 83: 17; from the fall, 90: 6; Zion shall be, 97: 4; by shedding blood, 98: 10; might have been, 102: 2; year of, is come, 108: 10; when Zion should be, 129: 8.
Redeemer, God and, 8: 1; 13: 1; 14: 1; suffered death, risen again, 16: 3; of world, 18: 1; word quick and powerful, 26: 1; of Israel sung, 123: 28.
Redemption, through faith, 28: 12; hour of, 36:14; be perfected, 45: 7; day of, 77: 3; buffetings till day of, 81:5; resurrection through, 85:4 (28); of Zion, 86 (10); duties of brethren, 100: 1; of Zion by power, 100: 3; till day of, 101: 1; learn concerning, 102: 1, 3, 5, 10; sealed unto day of, 107: 38; spirit of zionic, 136: 3.
Regions, round about; purchase lands in, 48: 1; people in, round about, 97: 1; who dwell in, round about, 102: 7; Zion unto, round about, 108: 3, 9; gather into, round about, 117: 11; section 128.
Remnant, Lamanites remnant of Jews, 18: 3; scattered among nations, 45: 3; gathered, 45: 6; of Jacob, 52: 1.
Reorganization, work of, 118: 1; the twelve in its, 130: 4.
Reorganized Church, revelations to, mention, 113: 7.
Repent, that might, 1: 5; and walk uprightly, 5: 4; men stirred to, 16: 2 (3, 4, 6); 18: 2; 49: 2; all men must, or suffer, 17: 6, 21; 18: 1, 2; and prepare way of Lord, 32: 2; for kingdom of heaven at hand, 42: 2; not, be cast out, 42: 7; old and young, 43: 5; inhabitants to, 45: 12; let him, 50: 8; of many things, 56: 4;

speedily lest judgment come, 63:
4; of things not pleasing, 66: 2;
condemnation until they, 83: 8;
that they shall, 83: 12; brethren
begin to, 87: 8; family must
needs, 90: 8; if enemy does not,
95: 5; and come unto thee, 95:
7; all men everywhere to, 108:
5; counseled to, 152:4.
Repentance, obedience brings, 1: 5;
through their, 2: 6; say nothing
but, 6: 4; 10: 4; shalt declare, 12:
4; 13: 3; 18: 4; Gentiles and
Jews stirred to, 16: 2 (3, 4); capa-
bility of required, 17: 20; preach
naught but, 18: 2; declared by
angels, 28: 12; cry unto perverse generation, 33: 1; baptize
unto, 34: 2; is gospel, 39: 2;
preach unto people, 44: 2; 53: 2;
55: 1; how known, 58: 9; warn
sinners to, 63: 15; gospel of, 83:
4; baptism of, 104: 10; space
granted for, 118: 4.
Repenteth, and cometh unto me, 3:
16; not, be cast out, 42: 11.
Representation, rules of 125: 7, 9;
to be determined by conference,
147: 6.
Representative, authorities of church,
120: 4.
Responsibilities, 129: 4; be released
from, 132: 2; of missionary work,
133: 2; ministerial, 136: 3.
Responsibility, of presiding, 107: 44;
patriarch free from, 125: 4; positions of great, 132: 3; laid on
all, 141: 8.
Restoration, of all things, 26: 2;
84: 3; of Israel, 45: 2; of his
people, 83: 1; to land of Zion,
100: 3; of priesthood, 110: 17;
work of, be hastened, 119: 4;
angel with message of. 129: 8.
Resurrection, 28: 3, 6, 7; 36: 12;
hope of glorious, 42: 12; first,
second, just, unjust, 43: 5; 45: 2,
7, 10; 76: 3, 5; heathen in first,
45: 10; 76: 6; first, unclean no
part in, 63: 5; preached by apostles, 63: 13; through triumph of
Lamb, 76: 3-5; speaking of, 76: 3;
of dead, 76: 4; last, 76: 7;
through redemption, 85: 4; im-
mersion likeness of, 110: 12.

Retire, to thy bed early, 85: 38;
advice of Spirit to, 119: 9.
Revelation, spirit of, 8: 2; 10: 6-11;
church only through Joseph
Smith, 27: 2; nothing to be received contrary to, 27: 4; to
church in presence of six elders,
28: 1; shalt receive, 42: 17, 18;
promised, 59: 1; of Jesus Christ,
87: 4; prepare for the, 98: 5.
Revelations, may have many, 2: 2;
shall come hereafter, 17: 6; appointed to receive, 27: 2; 43: 1;
receive not, 43: 2; labor and
fruits according to, 52: 4, 5; in
their time, 59: 1; stewards over,
70: 1; prepare a way for, 71: 2;
ye call for, 81: 1; for bringing
forth, 83: 18; shall receive, 87: 5;
work, in obtaining, 91: 1; I shall
give, 101: 10; be a believer in,
107: 35; custom concerning, 121:
6; duty to teach, 122: 1; concerning ordination, 125: 6; given
to church, 129: 8.
Revelator, he shall be a, 97: 3; to
be a, 104: 42; Hyrum Smith be a,
107: 29; Joseph to be a, 107: 39;
John the, 110: 6.
Reward, reap good for, 6: 15; great,
12: 5; lurketh beneath, 58: 6; according to deeds, 64: 2; in no
wise lose, 83: 16; be doubled, 95:
5; according to works, 95: 5; I
shall come to, 98: 9; in nowise
lose, 109: 4; 124: 8; his, is sure,
129: 1; who awaits his, 129: 5.
Rich, that hath eternal life is, 6:
3; 10: 3; accountable, earth rich,
38: 4, 9; not give, condemned,
56: 5; rich, learned, wise, noble,
first in preparation of Zion, 58: 3
(9); by humbling the, 83: 23; be
made low, 101: 2.
Richards, W., one of twelve, 107:
40; in room at time, 113: 2.
Riches, seek not, 6: 3; of earth, 38:
4; of eternity, 38: 9; consecrate
of, 42: 11; canker your souls, 56:
5; of eternity, mine, 67: 1; of
eternity, yours, 77: 4; agent who
has, 87: 6.
Rigdon, Sidney, instructions to Smith
and Rigdon, section 34; consecrate

land for temple, 58: 11-13; come not again upon waters, 61: 4; not open mouth in congregation of wicked, 61: 5; as president, 99: 2; counselor to Joseph, 107: 32; for counselor, 107: 39; on committee, 108A: 2; organized council, 108A: 3; explained voting, 108A: 4; return thanks, 108A:15.

Righteous, cannot always judge from wicked, 3: 7; gathered on right hand, 28: 7; death sweet to, 42: 12; be changed, 43: 7; to Zion, 45: 14; that from above, 67: 2; know, from wicked, 83: 7; shall inherit earth; rise a spiritual body, 85: 6; warn the, 112: 12.

Righteousness, pertaining unto, 10: 7; who work, receive eternal life, 17: 3; crown of, 24: 4; 28: 3; to come out of heaven, 36: 12; day of, 45: 2; beware lest ye do that not in, 50: 3; who doeth receive reward, 59: 5; mysteries revealed, wisdom, understanding, 76: 2; cut short in, 83: 16; reproving in, 83: 24; rewarded for, 95: 5; seek diligently, 103: 1; decisions must be in, 104: 11; meet him who worketh, 108: 8; who spake in, 108: 9; an offering in, 110: 24; continue in, 117: 12.

Rock, build upon, 3: 17; 6: 16; 10: 8, 11; 50: 8; is gospel, 10: 11; 16: 1, 4; 32: 3; foundation of, 10: 8; 16: 1; build church upon, 32: 3; of heaven, 36: 10; that buildeth upon, 50: 8; build church upon, 110: 10.

Rulers, gospel proclaimed to kings and, 1: 4; over many kingdoms, 77: 3; importune by hands of, 98: 10; may hear, 98: 12; be honored, 112: 6; enact laws for protection, 112: 7.

Rules, adopted by church, 122: 10; of representation, 125: 7-9; given in the law, 125: 14.

Rushton, J. W., sitting with the twelve, 126: 7; released from Twelve, 140: 3.

Russell, R. C., to be apostle, 129: 6; released, 134: 2.

Sabaoth, ears of Lord of, 85: 1; 95: 1.

Sabbath, holy day, 59: 2; keep holy, 68: 4; on the following, 109: 7; discussion concerning, 119: 7.

Sacrament, 17: 8, 10, 11, 18, 22, 23; preparation for, 26: 1, 2; nonmembers not cast from meetings, 46: 1, 2; offer a, unto the Most High, 62: 2; dedicated for, 92: 3; time of administering, 119: 5.

Sacraments, offer upon holy day, 59: 2; wine only for, 86: 1.

Sacrifice, shalt offer, 59: 2; a day of, 64: 5; acceptable offering and, 83: 6; observe covenants by, 94: 2; to accept many, 124: 8; exercise principle of, 130: 7.

Saints, Lord have power over, 1: 6; arose, 36: 11; shall come forth, 45: 7; place of safety for, 45: 12; land purchased by, 57: 1 (3, 4); way for journeying of, 61: 4; assemble, 63: 8, 9; inheritances in Zion; 64: 6; devil maketh war with, 76: 3; gathering of, 83: 1, 2; 98: 4, 9; 102: 4; prepare for judgment, 85: 23 (26, 27, 33, 35); salvation of, 86, preface; who keep sayings, 86: 3; earth given unto, 100: 2; to provide for, 101: 2 (6); cheerful in warfare, 119: 6; observe first day, 119: 7; duty of, 123: 22; remove selfishness from, 127: 7; benefits enjoyed by, 128: 8; perfecting of, 136: 3; 137: 4.

Salutations, in name of Lord, 85: 36.

Salvation, in kingdom of God, 6: 2 (5); heirs of, 7: 2; everlasting, 10: 2; 43: 6; commandment given for, 38: 4; of people, 42: 10; children grow up unto, 45: 10; signs not unto, 63: 2; keys of, 77: 3; turn to you for, 81: 3; your profit and, 83: 11; the temporal, 86, preface; gospel of, 87: 3; messenger of, 90: 1; 94: 3; duties concerning, 100: 1; order established for, 101: 1; be done for, 101: 9; ends of earth see, 108: 1; of dead, 110: 5 (8, 11, 15, 23); of world,

113: 6; of my people, 122: 6; apostles of, 130: 9.

Sanctification, just and true, 17:6; of the church, 97: 4; consummation of, 129: 9.

Sanctified, by that received, 43: 3; unbelieving husband and wife, 74: 1; by the Spirit, 83: 6; earth must be; for this intent, 85: 4; who are not, 85: 5 (6, 8, 35); can not be, 98: 2; let army be, 102: 9 (10); tribe of Judah be, 108: 6; gems for, 113: 6.

Sanctify, yourselves, 43: 4; Moses sought to, 83: 4; yourselves, 85: 18, 20.

Sanitarium, 127: 1, 2, 4.

Satan (see Devil), power, methods, works of, 3: 1-6; 36: 5; seeks to destroy souls, 64: 3; and works to be destroyed, 18: 1; tempted Moses, 22: 8-14; claimed to be the Only Begotten, 22: 12 (14, 15, 17); can not tempt little children, 28: 13; shall tremble, 34: 6; great chain in hand, 36: 5 (7); bound, loosed, 43: 7; have no place in hearts, 45: 10; sought to deceive, 50: 1; abroad, deceiving nations, 52: 4; tempteth to anger and shedding of blood, 63: 8; maketh war with Saints, 76: 3, 4, 7; rebellion of, 76: 3, 4; seeketh to turn from truth, 77: 2, 3; 81: 5; 101: 1; is bound, 83: 17; sitteth to reign, 84: 1; shall be bound, 85: 35; not tempt man, 98: 5; delivered over unto, 101: 2.

Saved, endure to the end, 16: 4, 7; 17: 5; Israel shall be, 38: 7; mine Israel be, 98: 4; that you may be, 109: 9; all may be, 116: 4.

Savior, knowledge of, 2: 6; faith on, 18: 4, 6; full of grace and truth, 22: 4; of world, 43: 8; in midst of people, 108: 5; quotation of, 109: 8.

School, of prophets, 85: 39 (44, 45); keys of, of prophets, 87: 3 (5); for, of apostles, 92: 2, 3; should be, in Zion, 94: 2.

Scribe, O. Cowdery to Joseph Smith, 9: 2; Emma Smith to Joseph, 24: 2; F. G. Williams, 87: 6.

Scrip, take no purse or, 23: 7; not take purse or, 83: 13, 15.

Scripture, parts of my, 8: 1; shall be, 68: 1.

Scriptures, people wrest, 3: 15; parts of hidden, brought to light, 6: 12; given of him, 17: 5 (8, 24); expounding of, 23: 3; 24: 2; 68: 1; 71: 1; might be fulfilled, 23: 6; time devoted to studying, 25: 1; shall be given, 34: 5; be preserved, 42:15 (16); do with as saith, 64:2; that spoken by Holy Spirit, 68: 1; hasten to translate, 90: 12; in expounding all, 94: 2; mighty in expounding, 97: 3; fullness of my, 101: 10; as directed in, 122: 3 (10); written in, 125: 15.

Seal, power given to, 1: 2; to eternal life, 68: 1; up the testimony, 85: 23; recorded with this, 95: 1; this shall be my, 98: 8; upon the treasury, 101: 11, 12.

Secret, acts revealed, 1: 1; pray in, 18: 4; 21: 5; chambers, 38: 4 (6); combinations coming on earth, 42:18; dust from feet in, 60: 4; reveal the, acts, 85: 34, 35; cleanse feet in, 96: 1; of whole matter, 110: 11.

Seer, Joseph Smith called a, 19: 1; president to be, 104: 42; Hyrum a, to church, 107: 29; Joseph Smith a, 107: 39; I subscribe myself, 109: 9; Joseph Smith the, 113: 3.

Self-sacrifice, 129: 3.

Servant, slothful, if compelled, 58: 6; manifest unto, 102: 10; in the Lord, 109: 9; removal of; if unstable, 127: 8; approved or disapproved, 130: 6.

Servants, chosen, commanded; none to stay them, 1: 1 (2, 3, 5, 8); sent east, west, north, south, 42: 18; word of Lord to, 44: 1; report accounts to Zion, 69: 2; blessings to faithful, 70: 4; that receiveth my, 83: 6; I called you; ye are their, 90: 8; sinned, 92:

107: 31; patriarch, 107: 38; second nomination, 108A: 2; martyrdom, 113: 1; age, 113: 6.

Smith, Israel A., placed in First Presidency, 138: 1; released from duties by death, 145:1.

Smith, Joseph, to ordain twelve, 117: 4; present in council, 123: 1, 2, 28; instruction to, 127: 1, 2, 8; counselor to, 129: 5; observed rule to fast, 131: 1.

Smith, Joseph, Jr., translated record of Nephites, 1: 5; revelations to, sections 2, 3, 6, 7, 16, 19, 22, 23, 25, 34, 37, 40, 44, 47, 71, 73, 76; strict commands, 2: 3-5; 3: 1-18; as witness; gift to translate, 5: 1; firm in keeping commandments; granted eternal life if slain, 5: 4; instructions concerning translating, 5: 6; given keys, 6: 13; 26: 2, 3; 27: 2; 34: 4; 64: 2; directed, 15: 2; eternal life, 16: 2; baptized Cowdery, 16: 2; ordained apostle, first elder, 17: 1; 19: 3; seer, translator, prophet, 19: 1 (2, 3); to write Book of Mormon; attend to calling, 23: 1-4; hold conferences, 25; study Scriptures, preach, ordained, 26: 3; receive revelations as Moses, 27: 2; fullness of gospel by hand of, 34:4 (5); strengthen church, 37: 1; to translate, 41: 3; travel for a season, 42: 2; to receive commandments, none other so appointed, no other appointed except through him, 43: 1, 2; journey and preach, 52: 2, 6; directions given through, 60: 4-6; not preach in congregations of wicked, 61: 5; discern who go to Zion, 63: 11; keys not taken from, 64: 2; imperfections of, 67: 2; confound enemies, 71: 1, 2; 73: 1, 2; vision in the Spirit, 76: 3; dedicated by, 83: 1; rebuked, 90: 8; make haste, 90: 11; acknowledged president, 99: 2; journey of, 100: 7; Lord pleased with, 107: 1, 6, 21, 31; on doctrinal committee, 108A: 2; letters of, 109, 110; martyrdom of, 113: 1.

Smith, Joseph, Sr., marvelous work, great commandment, 4; calling of, 21: 4; continue with family, 87: 6; high councilor, 99: 2; is with me, 107: 7.

Smith, Samuel H., revelation to, 21: 3; journey and labor, 52: 6; 61: 6; 66: 4; 75: 3; high councilor, 99: 2; over bishopric, 107: 45; nominated committee, 108A: 2.

Smith, T. W., one of twelve, 117: 4; in my hand, 122: 15.

Smith, Wm., one of twelve, 107: 40.

Smith, Wallace B., called to assist father (prophet-president designate), 152: 1.

Smith, W. Wallace, apostle, 140: 4; to presidency, 142: 1; chosen as president, 144: 1; to retire, 152: 1.

Society Islands, boat for, 123: 18; patriarch to visit, 125: 13.

Solemnities, of eternity upon minds, 43: 8; of eternity, 108A: 3.

Son, in name of, 17: 21-23; ascended, 17:5; record borne of, 36: 1, 14; comforter beareth record of, 42: 5; of Man, signs of coming of, 45: 6; 49: 4; 64: 5; 65: 1; of God, crucified for sins of world, 46: 5; power of, on right hand of glory, 49: 2; not in form of a woman, 49: 4; in an hour ye think not, 61: 6; come down in heaven, 65: 1; no Savior besides, section 76; Ahman, prepared all things, 77: 4; was called, of God, 90: 2; after order of, 104: 1; 107: 37; from father to, 104: 18.

Songs, of everlasting joy, 45: 14; 98: 4; of Israel, 108: 6.

Sons, power to become, 10: 12; 39: 1; receive gospel, 24: 1; of God, 33: 1; 34: 1; of perdition, 76: 4; of Moses, 83: 6; shout for joy, 110: 23; admonished; are called, 124: 7; of officers called, 130: 9.

Soul, salvation, 4: 1; bring to destruction, 8: 2; fill with joy, 10: 7; 16: 3, 4; treasure up for salvation, 11: 2; if bring but one, 16: 3; Moses beheld every, 22: 19; not saved, 56: 5; able to cast down, 63: 1; Satan seeketh to destroy, 64: 3; spirit and body the, 85: 4; who forsaketh sin, 90: 1; care for, 98: 5; freedom of, 112: 4; has been cheered, 124: 9; exalting the, 131: 1.

Souls, lead to destruction, 3: 3; bring unto me, 7: 1, 2; 13: 3; worth of,

der account, 72: 1-4; not a wise, 72: 5; inherit all things, 77: 4.

Stewards, over revelations, etc., 70: 1, 2; render account, 71: 2; wise, faithful, 72: 4; 77: 4; have claim for assistance, 72: 4; cut off unfaithful, 98: 12; every man accountable as, 101: 2 (10, 13).

Stewardship, stand in place of, 42: 14 (19); unfaithful; be condemned, 64: 8; account required, 70: 1, 3; 72: 1; give account of, 72: 4; every man his; give account of, 101: 2-12; his, will I require, 107: 4; shall account for, 118: 4; repression of unnecessary wants in harmony with law of, 147: 5.

Stewardships, priests, teachers, 42: 19; accounts sent to Zion, 69: 2; managing concerns of, 81: 4; moneys you receive in, 101: 12.

Storehouse, law governing, 42: 10 (14); management of, 51: 2-5; place for, 58: 7; more than is needful given unto, 70: 2; not exempt from law, 70: 3; kept by bishop, 72: 3; regulating and establishing affairs of, 77: 1; be cast into, 81: 4; children claim upon; kept by consecrations, 82: 2; discharge debt of, 87: 6; should not sell, 98: 13; same to me now, 122: 6.

Strength, not labor beyond, 3: 1; sufficient, 9:4; Moses received, 22: 7, 12, 13; not have, 23: 4; in weakness or in, 23: 5; love Lord with, 59: 2; earth brought forth, 83: 17; of house, 102: 8.

Strengthen, the church, 21: 2, 3; be prepared to, 131: 2.

Strengthen, stakes, be, 81: 4.

Stringed instrument, be silent, 119: 6.

Strong, he may become, 83: 19; bands are made, 85: 26; shalt be made, 113: 5.

Strong drink, condemned, 26: 1; is not good, 86: 1; be not addicted to, 119: 3.

Strong ones, Lord plead with, 87: 8.

Stuart, John C., apostle, 150: 2.

Study, it out in your mind, 9: 3; my word, 10: 10; seek learning by, 85: 36; and learn, 87: 5; to approve ministrations, 119: 2.

Suffer, must repent or, 18: 1.

Suffered, death; pain of all, 16: 3; I, God, have, 18: 2.

Sufferings, Christ, 18: 2; be sore, 18: 2.

Support, they shall, 23: 2; husband shall, 24: 2; withdrawing, 118: 4; to present movement, 123: 6; bishopric worker receive, 130: 6; your officers, 150: 9.

Surplus, consecrated, 42: 10; 70: 2; I require all, 106: 1; be tithed of their, 106: 2; under terms of, 129: 8; temple building and, 149A: 5.

Suspicion, no reason for, 122: 13; distrust and, 131: 4.

Susquehanna, banks of, 110: 20.

Swear, in name of him, 85: 35.

Talent, may improve, 81: 4; tracts by those with, 125: 11.

Talents, may gain other, 81: 4; cast into treasury, 101: 12; consecrate of their, 132: 3.

Tares, burned, 38: 3; choke the wheat, 84:1, 2; she is the, 85:26; parable of, 98: 9.

Tarry, until I come, 7: 1, 2; with him, 34: 5; disciples who shall, 63: 11, 12; in this place, 85: 19; and labor, 85:23; commanded you to, 92: 2; appointed to, 98: 7.

Taught, not sent to be, 43: 4; not, light and truth, 90: 6; more perfectly, 102: 3.

Taylor, J., one of twelve, 107: 40; was wounded, 113: 2.

Teacher, ordained, 17: 12, 15; appendage to priesthood, 83: 5; appoint a, 85: 37 (39, 40, 41, 43); officiate in office of, 104: 5; over office of, 104: 31; may preside, 120: 2.

Teachers, duty of, 17: 11 (12, 25, 26); teach principles of gospel, 42: 5; have stewardships, 42: 19; and deacons, 83: 5; watch over church, 83: 22; presiding, 104: 31; duty of president of, 104: 39; the president of, 107: 46; order of ministry, 122: 9.

Temple, shall come to, 42: 10; in Jerusalem, 45: 3; spot for, 57: 1; spot of, dedicate, 58: 13; city beginning at, 83:1 (2); whatsoever, is defiled, 90: 5; veil of covering

(8, 9); Spirit concerning the, 121: 2; sections 122, 123; may choose president, 124: 3 (4, 5); to open missions, 125:12; decisions of, 126: 10; may be supplied, 129: 6; order in priesthood, 129: 7; may choose officers, 130: 4; exhorted, 133: 2; president of, 134: 4, 5; admonished, 134: 6.

Twos, to send out by, 135: 4.

Tyree, Alan D., apostle, 148: 4.

Unbelievers, hypocrites and, 98: 12.

Unbelieving, to seal up, 1: 2; hold their lips, 63: 2; husband and wife, 74: 1.

Unchangeable, God, 2: 1; 17: 4.

Unclean, else were your children, 74: 1; cease to be, 85: 38; no, thing to come in, 91: 2; 94: 4.

Uncleanliness, keep far from you, 87: 5.

Understanding, necessary, 1: 5; 50: 4-7; 71: 2; reach to heaven, 76: 2; of ministry, 94: 3; greater unity of, 118: 1; light and, 131: 1; towards better, 136: 3.

Understandings, quickeneth your, 85: 3.

Unfaithful, stewards, 98: 12; and unwise steward, 101: 12; prove unstable and, 127: 8.

Unite, duty to, 21: 5.

United order, revelation, 89: 1; established, 101: 1 (9).

Unity, all to labor in, 38: 6, 9; a greater, 118: 1; of sentiment reached, 122: 13; differences held in, pass, 129:9; greater, necessary, 135: 2; of endeavor, 136: 3; commended, 140: 1; 141: 7; leading councils and quorums commended for, 146: 2; promoted, 150: 12, 151: 10.

Unjust, not condemned with, 101: 1; unlawful and, 112: 12.

Unlawful, assaults, 112: 11 (12).

Unrighteousness, have pleasure in, 56: 4; forsake all, 66: 5; no, in revelations, 67: 2; cleanse from, 76: 4; the mammon of, 81: 6; decision made in, 104: 11.

Unspotted, keep thyself, 59: 2; 76: 5, 8.

Uprightly, walk more, 5: 4; 16: 5; if ye walk, 87: 6.

Urim and Thummim, means of

translating, 3: 1; 17: 2; view of promised, 15: 1.

Valleys, exalted, 49: 4; not found, 108: 5; cry, 110: 23.

Vengeance, of just God, 2: 2; upon wicked, 28: 4; visit Zion with, 94: 5; if enemy escape, 95: 5, 7; upon inhabitants, 105: 9; was day of, 108: 9.

Vessels, be clean that bear, 38: 9; 108: 2; of wrath doomed to suffer, 76: 4; some are chosen, 119: 4; for sacrament, 119: 5.

Victory, through diligence, 100: 7; I will give you, 101: 13; on to the, 110: 22.

Vineyard, laborers in blessed, 19: 3; called to prune, 23: 7; 39: 5; call laborers into, 32: 1; 39: 4; 43:7; 50: 8; labor in, 43: 7; 71: 2; bishop appointed in, 72: 1; continue in, 85: 23; apostles to prune, 92: 1; go ye into, 98: 6, 7; lord of, spoke, 100: 4; while laboring in, 101: 3; to purify, 113: 6; twelve labor in, 116: 3.

Virgins, parable of, 45: 10; foolish among wise, 63: 13.

Virtue, to be remembered, 4: 2; walk paths of, 24: 1; practice before me, 38: 5; 46: 9; loveth virtue, 85: 10; quality of Christian, 131: 4.

Visit, house of each member, 17: 10; poor and needy, 44: 3; in second hour, 85: 13.

Visited, they should be, 127: 5.

Vote, necessary to ordain, 17: 16; sanction by, 99: 9; by assembly councils, 108A: 4-14; obtained on meanings, 123: 20, 21; consent obtained by, 124: 6; no voice or, 125: 5; nomination and, 130: 4.

Votes, sustained officers, 126: 12.

Wages, receive from whom they obey, 28: 12; recompense of, as agreed, 107: 36.

Walk, humbly, 10: 6; godly walk and conversation, 17: 18; and not faint, 86: 3; in darkness, 92: 3.

Walked with God, 36: 14.

Wants, according to his, 42: 9; 81: 4; and needs, 51: 1; repress unnecessary, 130: 7.

Warn, teacher's duty to, 17: 11; sent to testify and, 85: 22; him in my name, 95: 5.

Warned, whom they have, 85: 19; you, and forewarn, 86: 1; till world is, 122: 8; church has been, 130: 9.

Warning, voice of, 1: 1; day of, 63: 15; and ponder the, 85: 19; and instruction, 129: 8.

Warning voice, 38: 9; 63: 9.

Wars, in far countries, 38: 6; rumors of, 45: 4, 11; your own lands, 45: 11; decreed upon earth, 63: 9; and perplexities of nations, 85: 21.

Washing, of your bodies, 86: 1.

Washing of feet, ordinance of, 85: 45, 46.

Washings, be acceptable; are ordained, 107: 12.

Waste, places, 98: 10; places of Zion, 100: 3; nothing go to, 119: 7.

Water, witnesses born of, 5: 3; go down into the, 17: 21; baptize by, 34: 2; baptizing by, 52: 3; living, 63: 7; baptized by, 83: 10; not baptized in, 83: 12; cleanse feet with, 83: 16; pools of living, 108: 6; baptism by; immersed in, 110: 12; for sacrament, 119: 5.

Waters, of life, 3: 15; stronger than many, 22: 17; many destructions upon, 61: 1; not needful to move swiftly upon, 61: 1; blessed by John; cursed in last days, 61: 3; sitteth upon many, 85: 26; sea and fountain of; causeth, to boil, 108: 7.

Way, make straight the, 83: 4; unveil face in own, 85: 18.

Weak, confound mighty, 1: 4, 5; 16: 7; he that is, 83: 19; your faith is, 84: 2; adapted to, 86, preface; confound the wise, 108: 11.

Weapon, none against, to prosper, 71: 2; not as a, of power, 114: 1; 122: 5.

Weary, shall not be, 83: 13; ye may not be, 85: 38; run and not be, 86: 3.

Wept, God of heaven, 36: 6; Enoch, 36: 8, 10, 11.

Wheat, parable of, 84: 1, 2; for man, 86: 3; secured in garners, 98: 9.

White, geld is, 4: 1; 6: 2; 10: 2; 11: 2; 12: 2; garments pure and, 17: 2.

White, I. N., to act as apostle, 124: 4; take place of, 124: 5; be released, 130: 2.

Whitmer, David, revelation to, sections 13, 25, 29, 47; labor in 3; 12: 4; 15: 1; same calling as Paul, 16: 3; admonished, rebuked, intrusted, 29: 1; home at father's, 29: 1; journey and preach, 52: 6.

Whitmer, John, revelation to, sections, 13, 25, 29, 47; labor in Zion, 29: 3; proclaim gospel, 29: 3; write, keep regular history, 47: 1; assist Joseph Smith in transcribing, 47: 1; keep church record and history, 47: 2; organized Missouri council, 108A: 3; testimony of, 108A: 4.

Whitmer, Peter, Jr., revelation to, sections 14, 29; declare gospel, 29: 2; labor among Lamanites, 31: 1.

Whitney, N. K., impart money, 63: 12; to retain store, 64: 5; appointed bishop, 72: 2; to travel about, 83: 23; need be chastened, 90: 9; organized counselors, 108A: 3; bore record, 108A: 6.

Wicked, wrath without measure upon, 1: 2; judgments upon, 3: 13; 34: 3; 36: 12, 14; 43: 5, 7; 56: 1; 61: 1-5; fiery darts of, 26: 3; desolation upon, 28: 2; ashamed to own, 28: 7; tribulations among, 33: 1, 2; will not hear, 38: 1; found among, 43: 5; scourges upon, curse God, 45: 4 (13); proclaim word in congregations of, 60: 3, 4; 61: 6; 62: 2; anger of Lord kindled against, 63: 1 (2, 9, 13); be burned, 64: 5; know righteous from, 83: 7; desolation awaiting, 85: 23 (37); spirit of, one, 90: 4 (6); shall mourn, 94: 5; rule, people mourn, 95: 2; will cut off these, 98: 12;

lift up eyes with, 101: 2; conspiracy of, 113: 7.

Wickedness, full of, 3: 3; records kept back because of, 6: 12; not had because of, 22: 16; be destroyed, 28: 2-6; and misery, 36: 8; not practiced, 52: 9; children growing up in, 68: 4; scourge them for, 83: 16.

Widows, be provided for, 82: 2.

Wife, not covet, 18: 3; love, faithful to, 42: 7; should have but one, 49: 3; unbelieving, 74: 1; should have one, 111: 4.

Wight, J. W., to act as apostle, 124: 4; be released, 130: 2.

Wight, Lyman, beware of Satan, 52: 3; take journey, 52: 3; obtain companies, 100: 6; journey of, 100: 7; to preach for Zion, 107: 7; organize to build house, 107: 19; not appropriate stock, 107: 20.

Wilderness, church come out of, 5: 3; directors to Lehi in, 15: 1; church called out, 32: 2; Jacob shall flourish in, 49: 5; Moses taught in, 83: 4; drive church into, 84: 1; voice crying in, 85:17; commanded Moses to build in, 107: 12; make rivers a, 108: 12; of Fayette, 110: 20.

Williams, D. T., to twelve, 134: 3; released, 145: 5.

Williams, F. G., not sell his farm, 64: 4; high priest, counselor to Joseph Smith, 80: 1; equal in holding keys, 87: 3 (6); make haste also, 90: 11; a president, 99: 2; on committee, 108A: 2.

Williams, T. W., to Twelve, 133: 1.

Wine, to administer bread and, 17: 8, 10, 22, 23; partake of only new, not purchase of enemies, 26: 1; of wrath, all nations drink, 34: 3; nations drink of, 85: 32; partaking of, 85 :46; should be pure, 86: 1; treadeth in, vat, 108: 9; for sacrament, 119: 5.

Wisdom, those who seek, 1: 5; is greater, 3: 9; to be sought, 6: 3; seek not riches, but, 10: 3; write by, 27:2; of righteous great, of wise perish, 76: 2; for your good, 81: 4; and this is, 81: 6;

receiveth wisdom, 85: 10 (36); Word of, 86; whereby ye may know, 93: 1; seeking to learn, 94: 1 (4); concerning churches, 98: 9; reveal not until, 102: 7; men of excellent, 117: 5; to administer office, 120: 2; spirit of, 120: 9; 122: 2.

Wise, to be, 46: 7; first the, 58: 3; wisdom of, perish, 76: 2; be ye, and faithful, 117: 14.

Wise men, be sought for; ye should uphold, 95: 2; be appointed, 98: 10; to purchase land, 100: 5.

Witness, Joseph Smith to stand as, 5: 1; 12: 4; commanded to testify, 5: 5; further, 6: 11.

Witnesses, testimony of three, 5: 3; 15: 1-3; word established by two or three, 6: 13, 15; 42: 22; world be judged by, 17: 3; especial of my name, 26: 3; in adultery cases, 42: 22; apostles, or special, 104: 11; two or three, 110: 3, 4, 20; chosen special, 117: 4; time, place, with, 125: 4.

Witnessing, for Christ, 141: 4.

Women, must repent and be baptized, 16: 6; not lust after, 63: 5; but one as wife, 42: 7; 49: 3; rob; be delivered to law of land, 42: 22; Son of Man cometh not in form of, 49: 4; that lust after, 63: 5; parable of, 98: 11; on the left, 111: 2; one husband for; not right to persuade, 111: 4.

Women, laws; claim on husbands, 82: 1.

Woodruff, W., one of twelve, 107: 40.

Word, verified, 5: 3; quick and powerful, 6: 1; 10: 1; 11: 1; 12: 1; 26: 1; beginning to bring forth, 84: 2; of wisdom, 86: 1 may receive the, 87: 3; in beginning, was; he was the, 90: 1; bringing forth my, 93: 1, 2; live by every, 95: 3; power to declare, 96: 1; must be fulfilled, 98: 9; been already given, 129: 8.

Word of Lord, not pass away, 1:8; 36: 2; 63: 1; give heed to, 6: 1; 10: 1; 11: 1; 12: 1; power, qualities of, 6:1; 10:1, 8; 32:1; treasure up, 6: 9; establish by witnesses, 6: 13; build according to, 10: 11; 16: 5; to be studied, 10: 10; to rely upon, 15: 1; 16: 1; to be revealed, 26: 3; to be received, 34: 5; to be held sacred, 41: 3; of truth, receive by the Spirit, 50: 5; preaching by the way, 52: 3.

Work, of God not frustrated, 2: 1; cunning plan to destroy my, 3:1-10; marvelous, to come forth, 4: 1; 6: 1; 10: 1; 16: 7; perform with soberness, 6: 16; stand fast in the, 9: 5; assist to bring forth my, 10: 4; establish this, 11: 4; knowledge of this, 17: 3; this is my, 22: 23; great, among the Gentiles, 34: 3; great, laid up in store, 38: 7; laying foundation of great, 64: 6; cut short, 83: 16; will hasten my, 85: 20; perform my strange, 98: 12; command to do a, 107: 15; of temple, 109:4; will hasten; of reorganization, 118: 1; refrain from unnecessary, 119: 7; entrusted to all, 119: 8; be well for my, 122: 4 (7, 8, 13, 16); to engage in, 124: 7; while engaged in, 124: 8; of presidency, 137: 5.

Workmanship, of my hands, 22: 3.

Works, designs and purposes of God, 2: 1; marvelous; of other sheep, 3: 15; do marvelous, 8: 3; manifest by, 17: 7, 18; judged according to, 18: 1; blessings upon his, 19: 2; dead, 20: 1; no end to my, 22: 23; shall follow, 59: 1; mighty, by faith, 63: 3; men judged by, 76: 7; of Lord great, marvelous, 76: 8; many wonderful, 83: 11; destroyed their, 98: 6; not boast of, 102: 7; according to, 110: 6 (7, 8); are burned, 116: 2.

World, likeness of, 1: 3; judgment upon, 1: 6; get glory of, 3: 2; show not to, 3: 7; life and light of, 10: 12; 11: 5; ripening in iniquity, 16: 2; must preach unto, 16: 6; be judged, 17: 3; end of, 18: 1; beheld by Moses, 22: 6; lay aside things of, 24: 3; given me out of, 26: 3; light and life

of, 33: 1; 39: 1; 45: 2; things from foundation of, 34: 4; weak things of, called upon, 34: 4; for space of many generations, 36: 1; Christ light and life of, 39: 1; not forgiveness in, 42: 6; meetings not held before, 42: 23; Savior of, 43: 8; everlasting covenant sent into, 45: 2; 49: 2; end of, 45: 3; keep things from going unto, 45: 15; Jesus Christ crucified for sins of, 46: 5; 76: 4; lieth in sin, 49: 3; overcome of, 50: 3; you shall forsake, 53: 2; seeketh praise of, 58: 8; keep unspotted from, 59: 2; faithful to overcome, 63: 13; 64: 1; sanctify the, 76: 4; no forgiveness in, 83: 6 (7, 9, 10-15, 24); the field was, 84:1; then hid from; prophets since, began, 84: 3; them of celestial, 85: 1; while thou art in; neither in, to come, 87: 2; that cometh into, 90: 1 (11); light unto, 100: 2; kingdoms of this, 102: 9; overtaketh, 103: 2; go ye into, 105: 11; proclamation to kings of, 107: 1; hid from foundation of, 107: 13; commandments kept from, 108: 11; prince of, cometh, 109: 8; before foundation of, 110: 5, 8; salvation of ruined, 113: 6; until, is warned, 122:8; to be in the, 128: 8; message to peoples of, 133: 2.

Worlds, without number, 22: 21, 23; created by Christ, 76: 3, 4; made by him, 90: 1.

Worship, the Father, 16: 6; 17: 4, 6; houses of, 42: 10; God, 76: 3; may know how to, 90: 3; prescribing rules of, 112: 4; may be complete, 119: 6; day of, 119: 7; houses of, 122: 6; building houses of, 130: 7.

Worth, of most, 13: 1; 14: 1.

Worthy, to see and know, 67: 4; to those not, 87: 6; be chosen that are, 102: 10; not be counted, 104: 44.

Writings, into hands of wicked, 3: 1, 8; sacred, 101: 12.

Written, things are true, 16: 1, 5; 23: 6.

Wrongs, redress us of, 102: 7.